In the Tracks of the Ten Thousand

IN THE TRACKS OF THE TEN THOUSAND

A journey on foot through Turkey, Syria and Iraq

Shane Brennan

ROBERT HALE · LONDON

© Shane Brennan 2005
First published in Great Britain 2005

ISBN 0 7090 7885 4

Robert Hale Limited
Clerkenwell House
Clerkenwell Green
London EC1R 0HT

A catalogue record for this book is available from the British Library

2 4 6 8 10 9 7 5 3 1

Typeset by e-type, Liverpool
Printed in Great Britain by
St Edmundsbury Press Limited
and bound by
Woolnough Bookbinding Limited

For my mother

Contents

Acknowledgements

This project could not have been undertaken without the generous support of Mrs Anna Lambrakis (*Archaeology and Arts* magazine, Athens). Sincere thanks also to Xenophon and Annie Voudouroglu, Mike Tsoukias (Trekking Hellas), and Richard Donovan.

A number of people helped with the research and preparation for the journey. I would like to thank all of them, especially Maria Nikolopoulou, Konstantina Tzovara, Nikos Heliopolis, Andriette Stathi-Schoorel (RIP), Rebecca Ross and Maria Gegomimaki. For sorting paperwork and other problems: Selçuk Ünal at the Turkish Foreign Ministry; Younus Sahar and Bakr al-Qaysi, formerly of the Embassy of Iraq, Athens; and Sean O'Regan at the Irish Embassy in Ankara. I would also like to record my gratitude to Nursun Emren, Cem Yatman (Izmir), Yigit Yavuz (Trabzon), Ali and Neslihan Işım (Istanbul), Caroline Knox, and Nancy Hannon (London).

I would not have been able to return to Iraq prior to the war in 2003 without the support of my agent, Carolyn Whitaker; moreover, this book would never have come to light without her patience and encouragement. Nor would it have been realized without the support of my father and sister, and my aunts, Brid and Nano Brennan.

Foreword

Travel, the lexicographers say, derives from travail and, ultimately, from the *trepalium*, a three-pronged instrument of torture. *Safar*, the Arabic equivalent, shares its root with *sifr*: the unrolling of a scroll, of miles beneath feet; and the unveiling of eyes. To follow Cyrus and his Ten Thousand – alone, on foot, via Xenophon's *Anabasis*, across Turkey and Syria and into Saddam Hussein's Iraq on the approach of war – looks like travel of the first sort, in all its etymological horror.

But what Shane Brennan has written about his journey is more than a catalogue of trials, more than an antiquarian ramble heading for darkness. As the miles unscroll, so does Shane's personal anabasis – from a distant, all but unvisitable past, into a present haunted by memories of recent slaughter and forebodings of yet more to come. He begins by peering through the time-veiled eyes of Cyrus and Xenophon, and comes to see clearly with his own.

He travels light, but packs solid rations of history and copious supplies of pluck. Courage sees him through the nightmarish calm of Iraq, before the American invasion shattered the calm and made the nightmare still more terrifying. He endures suspicion, even physical assault, with extraordinary forbearance. At times the gritty stoicism of Doughty's *Arabia Deserta* comes to mind; so too its spaciousness – Shane, like Doughty, is 'guest of the Night, and of the vast Wilderness' – and its claustrophobia.

Shane carries all the mental equipment a traveller could need. As a writer, honesty is one of his biggest assets. The two paths – his and Cyrus' – touch and cross from time to time but do not intertwine. He can add little to Xenophon's nineteenth-century commentators. All this he admits. It doesn't matter. What does is that he saw his journey through in an age when journeys are often at best excursions or, at worst, invasions; and that he did it slowly. Walking, he says, brings out the meaning of places. He might have added that the spaces in between the walking – the pausing and talking, looking and listening – bring out the meaning of people: the dignity of ordinary lives lived patiently in the clamp of tyranny and sanctions; the tragedy of other lives vaporized by a Cruise missile.

Cyrus' Ten Thousand are now Bush's Three Hundred Thousand. The speed of invasion has accelerated by the same degree, or more. Xenophon's report took years to see the light; history is served up now in seconds, in pixels. The whole round world is caught in a web spun by all-seeing satellites. But to see with real clarity, we still need walks and books like this one.

Tim Mackintosh-Smith
Bayt al-Sayrafi, San'a
May 2005

Maps and Illustrations

Note: *Anabasis*, 'March Upcountry', is abbreviated to *A* on the maps, and in the text when referring to the route stages. The stages are detailed in Appendix II.

Illustrations

Between pages 100 and 101

1 The Temple of Artemis, Sardis. Starting point of the journey
2 The Maeander River beyond Yenicekent (Tripolis)
3 Sunset on the Maeander Valley
4 Cave of Marsyas, Dinar
5 Fountain of Midas, Ulupınar
6 Wheat field on Konya Plain
7 Turkish girl, Alaşehir
8 Making bread in the Taurus Mountains
9 Yayla, summer meadow
10 Mountain valley, east side of the Taurus
11 Antakya Gate, Aleppo
12 View of Aleppo from citadel

Credits

All maps by Dominik Lorentzen.
Photographs by author.

Note on Spelling and Dates

Spelling

In most cases Greek words have been transliterated, the exceptions being where a particular word has currency in its Latin or anglicized form (e.g. Byzantium not Byzantion).

Turkish words, except where there is a received English form, are given in their true form. The modern language uses the Latin alphabet, expanded to allow a separate letter for each main sound. Consonants have roughly the same sound as they do in English, with the following exceptions:

c is pronounced *j* as in 'job'
ç is *ch* as in 'church'
ğ is silent, acting to lengthen the preceding vowel
j is pronounced as the French, as in '*jour*'
ş is *sh* as in 'shed'

Vowels have the following values:

a as in *u* in 'luck'
e as in 'tell'
ı similar to the *e* in 'carpet', or the *u* in 'album'
i as in *ee* in 'bee' (capital also has a dot, *İ*)
o as in 'pot'
ö as French *oeu* in 'oeuvre', or German ö in 'Wörter'
u as in 'room'
ü like French *u*

For Arabic words I have tried to use the most common Latin transcriptions.

XIII

Any confusion about place names or people arising from the above is entirely my own fault.

Dates

All dates cited in the text are BC unless otherwise indicated.

A man should strive to be rich not in possessions, but in courage and merit.

Saying of the Spartans

An Introduction to Persia and Background to the Expedition of Cyrus

The Persian Empire was founded by Cyrus the Great in the mid-sixth century. His tribe, the Achaemenids, displaced the Medes, the ruling power of Persia, and under his charge went on to conquer the kingdoms of Lydia (546) and Babylonia (539). At its height, during the reign of Darius I, the empire stretched from the Hellespont in the west to the Indus River in the east; from the Black Sea to the Persian Gulf; and from Central Asia to Egypt. No people in history had ever controlled anything like such a swathe of the world.

In spite of what the Greeks say of them, the Persians were one of the great civilizing forces of history. The hallmarks of their rule were competent estate management, civil justice, and a tolerance of subject peoples. They developed a highly effective system of imperial administration, and were pioneering road and bridge builders. Their courier system was famed in the ancient world – and would quite possibly be competitive today. Herodotus said of it: 'No mortal thing travels faster than the Persian courier. They have horses and men posted at intervals along the route ... whatever the conditions – snow, rain, blazing heat, darkness – they never fail to complete their assigned journey in the fastest possible time.'

Unlike their western neighbours, the Persians did not seek to embody their power in building. They were an earthly people: they loved to travel, to cultivate and drink fine wines, and to stroll in parks of their own creation. The word 'paradise' comes from the Persian for an enclosed garden. Diodoros says that the famous Hanging Gardens at Babylon were created at the behest of a Persian woman who pined for the luscious meadows of her native land; less well known are the stunning parks of the Persian governors abroad, 'artistically laid out at great expense with plants and all other things which contribute to luxury and the enjoyment in peace of the good things in life' (Diodorus).

The Greek view of the Persians as 'barbarians' persists in part because the material legacy of the Achaemenids is comparatively slight, and in part because it was the Greeks who wrote history. The accounts of Persia that come down to us are nearly all written by Greeks, and they are invariably biased in their portrayal of events. Xerxes' destruction of Athens in 480 appears almost insignificant as against the earlier defence of a pass by a band of Spartans. 'Here once was three million of the foe, opposed by four thousand from the Peloponnese' (Herodotus citing an inscription set up by the Greeks at Thermopylae). The art of obfuscation has a long history in the Western tradition.

Notwithstanding the Hellenic literature, the greatest threat to the integrity of the Persian Empire always lay within. Cyrus the Great had warned his countrymen that 'soft lands tend to breed soft men'. As time passed, and wealth unimaginable accumulated in the treasury of Persepolis, his words were forgotten. When Darius III went to seek out Alexander of Macedon in 333, he had with him a hundred pages, a corps of valets to see to his wardrobe, perfume makers, chaplet weavers and specialist shoemakers. For his culinary needs he had a legion of royal cooks, among them 277 confectioners, 13 makers of 'milk dishes', 17 drink mixers and 70 wine strainers. A train of mule carts carried boiled water from a *paradeisos* at Susa in silver urns. To the hardy Macedonians who cornered this pampered procession in the narrow plain at Issos, the Persians were an easy prey.

That the huge empire had held together for so long was remarkable. Softness had set in early, and virtually every changeover of power since the great Cyrus had been attended by unrest. The monarchs were also subject to the influence of powerful court figures, whose interests frequently did not coincide with the state's. One of the most notorious of these was Parysatis, the wife and half-sister of Darius II, who reigned from 424 to 404. Parysatis was instrumental in her husband taking power, and was at the centre of political life for more than thirty years thereafter. Her position was strengthened by the fact that she was of the royal bloodline and owned a number of wealthy estates, but it was her forceful personality that gained her decisive sway. She was regarded by those who knew her as fiercely intelligent, and possessed of 'a lofty spirit'. There were few things she wanted that she did not get, and any who crossed her were liable to pay a heavy price. Many years after an offence her boiling vengeance could explode in some part of the empire, and if she felt a punishment at the court was unduly lenient, she was quick to step in to redress the matter. Plutarch, in his biography of her eldest son, gives several instances of her ruthlessness.

> 'O King, do not let this accursed Karian off so easily, but leave him to me, and he shall receive the fitting reward for his daring words.' So the King consigned the man to Parysatis, who ordered the executioners to take him and rack him on the wheel for ten days, then to gouge out his eyes, and finally to drop molten brass into his ears until he died.

The queen bore her husband thirteen children, four of them sons: Artaxerxes, Cyrus, Ostanes, and Oxathres. As the eldest, Artaxerxes was heir to the throne, but Parysatis' favourite was Cyrus, and she formed ambitions to make him king. Named after Cyrus the Great, from an early age he showed himself to be cut from the same purple as his namesake. He took at once to horse riding, and excelled at archery and javelin throwing. His tutors reported that he had a keenness for learning, and listened with the same attention to farmers as he did to scientists and philosophers. When he came of age to hunt, Cyrus showed a royal indifference to risk and danger. On one occasion, a she-bear charged at him, and rather than pull away he engaged the animal. The bear dragged him off his horse, tearing at his body, but he succeeded in drawing his dagger and dispatching the animal.

Artaxerxes, in contrast, was docile and withdrawn. He was poor at activities and unremarkable in the classroom. Dice was his favourite pastime, yet he was not lucky, and relied on his position to avoid heavy debt. He married a noblewoman, Stateira, in accordance with his parents' wishes. Like her mother-in-law she had a strong personality, and Artaxerxes became deeply dependent upon her. When the King suspected her of involvement in an intrigue, he went to his mother and threw himself at her feet, begging her in tears not to have the girl taken away from him. She eventually agreed to inter-vene, but his display must have convinced her that he had not the qualities to be king.

Darius, however, was opposed to her wish to have Cyrus named as his heir. He had seized power himself from his brother, and did not wish to have a civil war as the legacy of his long rule. Persevering, Parysatis came up with the argument that, as Cyrus had been born after Darius had assumed the throne, he was the rightful successor, but the King continued to resist. Seeing his intransigence, and thinking perhaps that if Cyrus proved himself in command, the King might be more easily persuaded, she sought to have him made satrap of Lydia. Outside of the Persian heartland, this was the wealthiest and most powerful province (satrapy) in the empire. In the event she secured for the young prince an unprecedented amount of power in the west: Satrap of Lydia, Greater Phrygia, and Kappadokia, and commander-in-chief of all the forces who mustered in the Plain of Kastolos.

*

The younger Cyrus' appointment to Asia Minor was not without risk for the King. The primary aim of Persian policy in the west was to keep the hands of the mainland Greeks off Asia Minor, an objective that was being successfully pursued by one Tissaphernes, arguably the most able statesman in the Mediterranean in the fifth century. He had been sent to Lydia by Darius in 416 to quell a rebellion by the then Satrap, Pissuthnes. Pissuthnes had been supported in his uprising by Athens, then embroiled in a bitter and costly war with Sparta. The decision to become involved with the rebel brought Persia directly into the conflict, and through Tissaphernes, the Persians took control of it. A policy of stop-start financing to the Spartans ensured that they and their allies were never able to consolidate victories. In the words of Thucydides, the strategy of Tissaphernes was to 'allow the Hellenes to wear each other out'.

In sidelining Tissaphernes – transferred to Miletos to govern the coastal strip of Ionia – the King was aware that the balance could be upset, and that he could end up with a single strong adversary on the western boundary. Accordingly he furnished Cyrus with instructions on what he was to do, and gave him sufficient gold to keep the Spartans afloat.

In the summer of 407, not long after he had arrived in Sardis, Cyrus was visited by a delegation of Spartans. They were led by one Lysander, who was himself a newly appointed commander (of the

Spartan fleet), and like Cyrus was young and ambitious. In the forth-right manner of his countrymen, Lysander reported how Tissaphernes had reneged on monies promised, and had intrigued with their enemy.

Cyrus, whose education had imbued in him an appreciation for Greek culture, was impressed by the Spartan, and at the same time he was angry that Persia's ally had been treated so poorly. Keen to make amends, he went against his father's instructions: he settled all arrears, and raised the pay of the Peloponnesian sailors from 3 to 4 obols a day. As a further gesture of goodwill, from his own pocket he contributed a month's wages in advance. He was by nature a generous man, and his friends, or any who did him a good turn or whom he admired, were never left wanting.

Following this, Cyrus himself went to war. The Pisidians and Mysians, indigenous tribes of the interior, had been giving trouble to satraps for years, and he set out with a force to pacify them. This also gave him and Aspasia, his Greek mistress, the opportunity to tour the provinces. At the Phrygian capital, Kelainai, Cyrus built a lodge over the source of the Maeander River, and he designed a park into which he had wild animals introduced for hunting. He laid out another *paradeisos* at Sardis, a magnificent one that was said to evoke like no other the verdant pastures of his homeland. On one occasion, after a meeting in the capital, he showed Lysander special favour by inviting him to see the garden. The Spartan was struck by what he saw:

'Truly Cyrus, though I admire all these things for their beauty, yet I marvel much more at the man who measured out and arranged each of [the trees] for you.'

And when Cyrus heard this he was pleased and said:

'Well Lysander, I both measured out and arranged all of them; and there are some of them,' he added, 'which I also planted myself.'

And Lysander related how he looked at him and beheld both the beauty of his garments, and of the chains and armlets he was wearing, and said:

'What do you mean Cyrus? Are you saying you planted these with your own hands?'

And Cyrus in reply said: 'Are you so surprised at this Lysander? I swear to you by Mithras that whenever in good health, I have never dined before exerting myself on some military or horticultural matter, or in pursuing some object of my ambition.'

Xenophon, *Oeconomicus*

Cyrus' support for Sparta in the Peloponnesian War was decisive. In 404 the Athenians unconditionally surrendered and their Long Walls were torn down. Lysander discontinued the democracy and installed an oligarchy loyal to his own government.

That same year King Darius became ill, and sensing that his end was near, he asked for his sons to be at his side. Cyrus, taking with him Tissaphernes and his Greek bodyguard, set off immediately for Susa. But the party arrived too late: by the time they had reached the royal capital, Darius had passed away.

By tradition the Persian kings were invested in Pasargadai, a city in Persis inland from the gulf. Here, in a beautiful park where lay the tomb of Cyrus the Great, an initiation ceremony was performed by the priests, the Magi. The monarch-in-waiting was led into a sanctuary, where he laid aside his own robe, and put on that of Cyrus. Then he had to eat a cake of figs, chew some turpentine wood, and drink a cup of sour milk. Other rites were performed but these were known only to the participants.

Now as he was readying himself to be received by the *magi*, Artaxerxes was approached by Tissaphernes, who had with him an elderly man, a former tutor of Cyrus'. Tissaphernes said the tutor had come to him claiming that Cyrus was plotting to swoop on his brother inside the holy sanctuary and put on the robe himself. He supported his charge by pointing to the prince's bodyguard of 300 Greeks. Frightened, Artaxerxes had his own guard seize Cyrus and disarm the Greeks. An execution order was imminent when Parysatis rushed forward and clasped her arms around Cyrus and pressed her neck against his. As Artaxerxes had done for his wife, she now begged with tears for the life of her younger son.

Realizing that he would have to kill both of them, Artaxerxes dithered, and relented. Cyrus was bundled away and the ceremony went ahead without further disruption.

After the royal procession had made its way back to Susa, Parysatis went to the King, and persuaded him to have Cyrus released. She further managed to have him given back his position in the west, arguing that he would be far away from the centre of power, and had a better relationship with the mainland Greeks than Tissaphernes. This was not the outcome Tissaphernes had expected, for he must have thought he would once again govern in Asia Minor. Instead he had to make do with the Greek coastal enclave granted him by the late Darius.

Cyrus left for Sardis at once. On the long ride downcountry, his near escape from death to the fore of his mind, he resolved that he would never again allow himself to come under the power of his brother. If he could, he would raise a force sufficient to march on Susa, and contest the Persian throne.

*

Cyrus was limited in the number of troops that he could raise from his own provinces. Indeed, had he twice the number, it would still only be a fraction of what the King could summon. In addition to his standing army of 10,000 *Immortals*,* the monarch could call up troops from all his subject peoples. Herodotus lists forty-five peoples brought by Xerxes to Greece in 480, estimating their numbers at (an almost certainly exaggerated) 1,800,000.

However, the fact was that raising levies took time, and Cyrus knew that if he could assemble his force without the King suspecting his motive, he could catch him when he was vulnerable. His other trump card was to be the deployment of Greek *hoplites*, the shock troops of the ancient world.

Hoplites were heavily armed infantrymen, and in the Classic Age they made up the cutting edge of Greek armies. Their name derived from the enormous circular shield, the *hoplon*, which they carried. Depending on materials, this could weigh up to 10 kilograms, and typically extended from the shoulder to the knee. Embossed on its surface was a letter that identified the city-state for whom the *hoplite* fought. The most feared was the lambda, Λ, of Sparta. For a *hoplite* to lose his shield in battle was the ultimate disgrace.

---

* The Immortals were the elite of the Persian army. They were so-called by the Greeks because their number never varied: a slain or injured man was immediately replaced by another from a reserve unit. The Persian army itself was not especially large. Contrary to the impression given by the Greeks, the Persians were not a numberless horde. In fact, as J.M. Cook comments, there were far more Greeks in the world than Persians.

The *hoplites*' main offensive weapon was a 2-metre long spear, used for thrusting at close quarters. They also carried, slung over the right shoulder, a single-sided slashing sword. Helmets were worn, as were body armour and greaves (metal shin-guards). Though the soldiers were highly skilled in the use of their arms, it was when fighting as a unit that they acquired their greatest potency. In formation the *hoplite* phalanx was formidable. Fifty men across and eight deep, they moved as one body across a battlefield to meet their opponents. The source of their power was co-ordination and discipline. Each man literally covered his neighbour with his shield – meaning that any break in the line could be fatal to the collective body. A tight phalanx could withstand a cavalry charge, and, driven by the rows in the rear, was capable of generating awesome forward force. At Leuctra in 371 the Thebans used a revolutionary fifty-deep formation against Sparta, 'to crush the head of the snake'.

In the seventh and sixth centuries *hoplites* had equipped themselves, but as the need for greater numbers arose, the city-states began to manufacture arms and to establish training schools. The demand also led to the large-scale use of mercenaries – men who earned their livelihoods by spear and shield. Notably, during the long and bitter Peloponnesian War (431–404), the profession flourished. The majority of mercenaries originated in the Peloponnese, and therein Arcadia produced the greatest number. Contrary to its idyllic depiction in Western art, life here was particularly harsh: soil was hard won and fiercely defended. Cyrus instructed his garrison commanders to recruit as many of these men as they could.

While inflating his garrisons at home, Cyrus began to put armies into 'cold storage' abroad. To do this he drew on a network of so-called 'guest-friends'. (These *xenoi* were bound by a league of friendship to provide hospitality and material assistance to one another.) Aristippos in Thessaly had asked him for money and men to help in a dispute at home, so he provided both, and told the Thessalian not to disband his force after the matter had been settled. He wrote to Proxenos of Boiotia asking him to organize another army, saying he was planning a second war on the Pisidians, and similar requests were made to Sophainetos of Stymphalos, and Socrates the Akhaian.

Cyrus then wrote to the Spartans, telling them of his plans, and requesting their assistance. Conservative in political matters, they must have been taken aback at the audacity of his proposed enterprise.

Skirmishing with the King on the periphery of his empire was one thing, marching an army into the heart of his kingdom quite another. None the less, it was to Cyrus that they owed their supreme status among the Greeks, and accordingly they instructed Klearkhos, the former military governor at Byzantium, to assist him. This help was more significant than it might appear, for with a Spartan commander Cyrus could be sure of getting the best men, and getting the best out of them.* Using money which Cyrus supplied, Klearkhos recruited 1,000 *hoplites*, 800 Thracian *peltasts* (light-armed infantrymen) and 200 Cretan archers. He based this force on the Hellespont, keeping it occupied by attacking Thracian tribes north of the water. Once the expedition was under way, it was envisaged that Spartan ships would shadow the army along the coast, and a force of *hoplites* would disembark at Issos to join the march inland.

In the early spring of 401 Cyrus sent word to his armies to move. Xenias, who was in charge of the garrisons, came to Sardis with 4,000 *hoplites*. Proxenos brought 1,500 and 500 light infantry. Sophainetos had 1,000 *hoplites*; Socrates 500, Pasion of Megara 300 and the same number of *peltasts*. The armies of Aristippos and Klearkhos were to join the main body at two assembly points along the way. In all Cyrus would have some 14,000 Greek mercenaries in his service, though history would come to know them as the Ten Thousand.

In addition to the mercenaries he had a large contingent of native troops, assembling to the east on the Kastolos Plain, and a personal cavalry guard of 600 Persians.

To all the men, the objective of the expedition was to expel the Pisidians from Cyrus' territory. Nobody outside of the Spartan leadership, and Cyrus' personal counsel, knew of the true object. But Tissaphernes, who must have long suspected the prince's purpose, now had enough evidence of a threat to take to the King. With his 500-strong bodyguard, he galloped off along the Royal Road to Susa.

---

* 'What the Spartans instilled in others was not just prompt obedience but a positive desire to come under their command and submit to them. It was not ships or money or *hoplites* that other Greeks would ask Sparta to send them, but just a single Spartiate commander.' Plutarch, *Life of Lykourgos*.

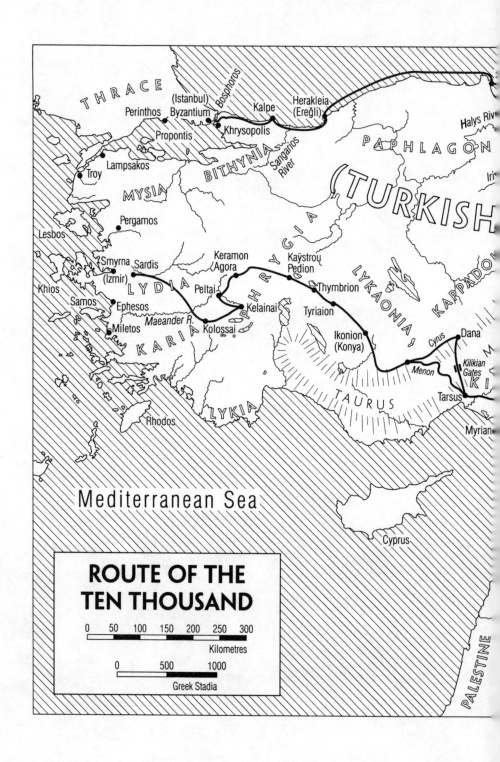

THRACE

(Istanbul)
Perinthos
Byzantium
Bosphoros
Kalpe
Herakleia
(Ereğli)
Halys Riv

Propontis
Khrysopolis
PAPHLAGON

Lampsakos
BITHYNIA
Sangarios
River
(TURKISH

Troy
MYSIA

Pergamos

Lesbos
FRYGIA

Smyrna
Sardis
Keramon
Agora
Kaÿstrou
Pedion
LYKAONIA
KAPPADO

Khios
LYDIA
Peltai
Thymbrion
Cyrus
Dana

Samos
Ephesos
Maeander R.
Kelainai
Tyriaion
Menon
Kilikian
Gates
KI

Miletos
KARIA
Kolossai
Ikonion
(Konya)
Tarsus

TAURUS
Myrian

Rhodos
LYKIA

Mediterranean Sea

Cyprus

ROUTE OF THE
TEN THOUSAND

0   50   100 150 200 250 300
Kilometres

0   500   1000
Greek Stadia

PALESTINE

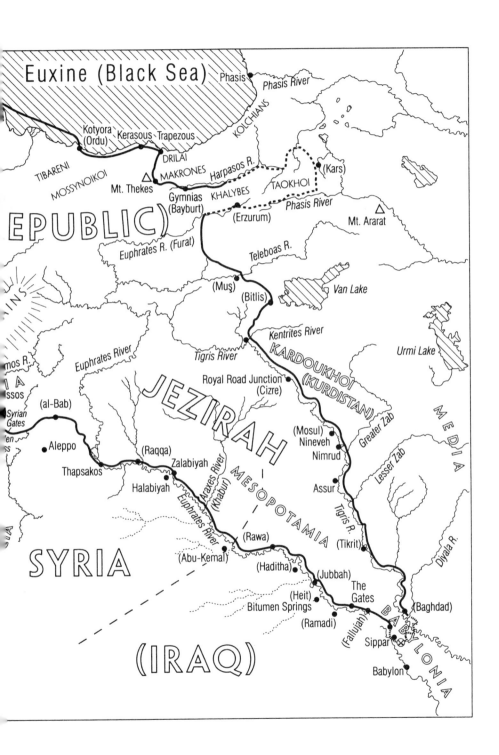

1

Athens

Beginnings

Among the Greeks there was one Xenophon, an Athenian, who followed the army neither as a general, nor a captain, nor a common soldier. Like his fellow countrymen, Xenophon did not know the true purpose of Cyrus' enterprise, but on his way to Sardis from the port of Ephesus, he received a sign. As he left the city he saw an eagle sitting on the shore, on his right, and it called out to him. A soothsayer in his company interpreted this to mean that the journey he was setting out on would bring him into great danger, for the eagle when sitting is vulnerable: small birds can swarm it, or a snake can strike. Neither would there be much reward, as the eagle gets its food on the wing, not hunting by foot. But, said he, the journey would bring him glory and fame, for the eagle is the bird of Zeus the King.

Xenophon had been invited to join the expedition by an old acquaintance, Proxenos, who was a guest-friend of Cyrus. The Athenian had heard much about the prince and was impressed by his character, so when the letter came, he thought that this would be an opportunity to be in the service of a man who was both strong and virtuous. He could see neither of these qualities in his native city any more. By his reckoning democracy had debilitated the state, and ultimately caused her defeat by the Spartans in the recently ended Peloponnesian War. He saw that their finest men had been exiled or executed at the whim of the general mass, who had no competence in either war or statesmanship. Following the ignominious surrender of 404, Xenophon supported an oligarchy of thirty leading citizens, but to his dismay the regime was short-lived and democracy restored.

Before he made his decision on whether or not to accept Proxenos' invitation, Xenophon went to consult the philosopher Socrates. They were friends of long standing, having met when Xenophon was a youth, and, it is said, highly regarded for his handsome looks. The story told of their first encounter is that one day Xenophon was walking down a narrow lane near to the market place when the philosopher leapt in front of him and barred his way with a stick. He demanded to know where a variety of different goods could be bought, and Xenophon answered where in the market each could be found. Then Socrates asked where men acquired virtue, and the youth didn't know. 'Follow me then, and learn.' And from this time he became a follower of Socrates.

When Socrates read Proxenos' letter he was concerned, for the *demos* blamed Cyrus for their defeat by Sparta, and involvement with him could have consequences for his friend. He therefore advised him to go to Delphi and ask the oracle whether or not he should join Cyrus. Xenophon did so, but it seems his mind was already made up, for instead of asking whether or not he should go on the expedition, he asked to what god he should sacrifice in order to ensure the success of the journey he had in mind. Socrates was annoyed when he told him what he had done, and reprimanded him for not doing what he had been advised. 'However, since this was the way you put your question, you must do what the god has told you.'

So Xenophon sailed from the Piraeus in the spring of 401, not knowing that he would never see his mentor again. In 399 Socrates was charged with impiety and corrupting the youth of Athens, and was sentenced to death. In later years Xenophon would write extensively about his life and teachings, but he would be best remembered for his account of the expedition of Cyrus, the *Anabasis*.

*

I had an early introduction to the *Anabasis*. Fr Felix, a polymath Franciscan at Multyfarnham College in Co. Westmeath, taught Classics to my father, and had chosen the text to illustrate the rules of Greek grammar. Long after he had forgotten these, my father retained a vivid memory of the story. He told it to me one day when we were sitting in the car, waiting for my mother and sister to return from the shops. We were on holiday in Co. Kerry and it was driz-zling, as it had been since we arrived in the 'Kingdom' a week or so before. My mother had left saying that next year we were going to France, and even then I grasped that my father was being blamed for the washout. I climbed into the front seat and toyed with the switches on the dashboard. He had a newspaper in his lap and was staring blankly at the windscreen. The wipers came on and the broiling Atlantic appeared before us. 'The sea, the sea,' he sighed, and then he told me the story of the ten thousand Greeks who had gone upcountry with Cyrus the Younger.

Years later, in an antiquarian bookshop in Athens, I came across a copy of the *Anabasis*. It was a nineteenth-century translation by a Reverend J.S. Watson, who had also included Xenophon's *Memorabilia* of Socrates. Watson had taken it upon himself to translate the latter, as no worthy copy was then available to the reader. 'The best previous translation,' he wrote in the preface, 'was that by Sarah Fielding, the sister of the novelist; a performance, however, extremely verbose and licentious. Its authoress had not sufficient knowledge of Greek to justify her in undertaking it. Harris of Salisbury gave her some help, as she says in a note near the commencement, but assuredly not much.'

Leafing through the worn copy, I discovered that there was appended an abridged version of a commentary on the route of Cyrus by William Ainsworth. Ainsworth was one of dozens of nineteenth-century British explorers who had dedicated themselves to investigating the detail of the classic texts. By identifying the places described by the authors, their aim was to bring to life for a contemporary audience the great events of antiquity. Ainsworth was one of Xenophon's first and most enthusiastic commentators. Over a period of seven years he searched for him along the high roads of Asia Minor and Mesopotamia, shedding in the process considerable light on the tracks of the Ten Thousand.

At the time I didn't have enough money to buy the book, so I put down a deposit and waited for my first pay cheque to arrive.

I had gone to Athens to see a girl, but things had changed since I had met her the previous summer on Crete, and she greeted me with less enthusiasm than I had expected when I arrived on her family's doorstep one hot July day in 1999. The plan had been that I would get a job, and we would be together until she finished her photography course the following spring, whereupon we were bound for Alexandria.

I decided to stay anyway, and take the chance to discover the city. Athens had always occupied a prominent place in my mind: it was the backdrop for heroic history and compelling myths, stories I had absorbed from my father's bookcases while growing up. Myth, especially, exerted a fascination. One of my earliest memories is being told the story of the Pied Piper in playschool; the very first story I read on a random opening of Graves' monumental *Greek Myths* was of a contest between Poseidon and Athena for the ownership of Attica. He, the burly god of the sea, thrust his trident into the Acropolis, and a well of sea water sprang from the rock. Athena, being gentler, planted an olive tree; the people judged this to be the superior gift, and they named their city after her.

Later, as a teenager, I heard someone on the radio say that the poet W.B. Yeats had written once that each life corresponds to a myth, so if you could find the character whose story matched your own, you'd know what was going to happen to you. I remember for days after that I trawled Graves and Bullfinch, and although I never found any striking resemblances, the idea remained with me.

Finding work in Athens did not prove to be easy, but after a month I got a job teaching English to young Greeks who were preparing to study abroad. Like much of the public system, third-level education in Greece is poorly resourced and managed. There are too few places and only the top few per cent by grade have a chance of getting into university. The rest make do with courses in technical institutes, or if their parents have the money, go to colleges in Europe and America.

Athens, I discovered, was not a particularly pleasant place to live. Outside of what has been preserved of the Classic city, it is ugly, dirty and packed with aggressive cars and surly people. Horns and irate voices conduct dialogues all along the arteries radiating out from Omonia, the neon heart of the modern city. I rented an unfurnished apartment in the Kerameikos, near where the ancient cemetery used to be, where Pericles delivered his funeral oration at the start of the Peloponnesian War. In recent times the Greeks have moved out and immigrants from Albania and Eastern Europe have taken over the soulless 1970s housing blocks. Belligerent policemen regularly sweep down on the streets, dragging girls from brothels and clubbing youths who fail to produce their papers. 'We throw open our city to the world,' said Pericles, 'and never by alien acts exclude foreigners from any opportunity of learning or observing, although the eyes of an enemy may occasionally profit by our liberality.'

A compensation for life in the seedy inner city was being located at the centre. The roof of our nine-storey building must have had one of the finest views in Athens. Way to the south, smog permitting, you could see the sea at the Piraeus; to the east was the Acropolis, almost in touching distance; and to the north, dominating the skyline, the giant spiralling rock of Lykavitos. I was looking at this through a zoom lens one afternoon in early September when the building shook, and then it started to sway, and I could hear pieces of it crashing to the ground. Tripod underarm, I raced down the nine flights of stairs and out onto the street. Residents from our block and others stood around until nightfall, and then one by one went back inside. The terror which earthquakes cause comes after the event, in the form of aftershocks. For those inside, especially, it's a case of thinking of the straw that broke the camel's back. Some days later a yellow X was sprayed on the front of our building, meaning structural repairs were needed, but nobody could afford to pay for them so the people stopped talking about the *seismos* and secretly prayed it wouldn't happen again for another twenty years.

In October I returned to the bookshop in Plaka and picked up the *Anabasis*. I dusted it and checked the pages as I strolled to a nearby café to meet a colleague from work. Andreas taught mathematics at the school, a way of subsidizing a doctorate in the subject at the Athens Polytechnic. He was in his early forties, a portly man with a flowing black beard. In both appearance and speech, I thought him remarkably like Orson Welles.

At the time he was dressed permanently in black, a traditional mark of mourning for a dead relative. His father's death that summer in a traffic accident had brought him back to Greece from Canada; he thought that if he was ever going to return permanently, this was the time. But he had difficulty in assimilating to what was a different system to the one he had lived in for twenty years. The bureaucracy, and what he saw as pervasive corruption, angered him. His bitterness was underlain by the way the authorities had handled his father's death. He had been riding home to their village outside Alexandropolis one night on his motorcycle when a vehicle smashed into his rear. 'They took the alcohol sample from my father, as he lay dying on the road, and they let the driver of the car go home.'

Andreas believed that philosophy and women were the most worthy subjects a man could discourse on, and it was these which occupied much of the time we spent together. Mostly this was in cafés and bars, but occasionally we would strike out in his car for Mount Parnitha, or stroll through one of the city parks. On that day, a sunny autumn afternoon, we took a table looking across at the Thisseon in the old market place. Andreas had finished his first ouzo by the time I joined him from the bookshop. He asked me what I had bought, and caressed his beard as he examined the book. He handed it back to me and cleared his throat. 'Dareiou kai Parusatidos gignontai paides duo...'

I felt a tingle run down my spine. He continued through the opening paragraphs of the *Anabasis* without pausing.

It had been more than ten years since I had first read the story, but the detail came back to me quickly as I turned the pages. Xenophon's descriptions are vivid, and his accounts of events compelling. Literary critics of the day dubbed him the 'Attic bee' for the ease and sweetness of his prose; Plutarch, in his biography of Artaxerxes, defers to him when he comes to describe the great battle between the brothers at Kounaxa: 'He [Xenophon] brings it all but before our eyes, and by the vigour of his description makes his reader always a participant in the emotions and perils of the struggle, as though it belonged, not to the past, but to the present.'

Over the following days, as I shared again in the adventures of the Greeks, I began to wonder if it wouldn't be possible to follow the same route today. Would there be anything of what the author saw – peoples, landmarks, monuments – still to be found? The story, as I had witnessed with Andreas' recitation, and with my father's recollections twenty-five years before, was still very much alive in people's minds.

I thought that if I travelled the route on foot, as the soldiers had done, I might also absorb something of the original march. I much admired these men: Cyrus for his ambition; Xenophon for his adventurous spirit and contempt for democracy; and the soldiers for their ruggedness, and their faith in each other. I admired Ainsworth as well, a man who had sacrificed his career as a physician to pursue his passion for the event. Xenophon had followed Cyrus and Ainsworth had followed Xenophon. There seemed to me too to be something powerful in the idea of 'following in the footsteps'. Pilgrimage, the literal interpretation of texts, pursuit of the right path: all of these things involve a form of retracing. To retrace is to look for something. I wasn't sure what I was looking for – a place, a person, a myth – but great journeys hold the promise of self-discovery.

The detail of Cyrus' route from Sardis, in the west of modern Turkey, to Babylonia, in what is now Iraq, is recorded in the first book of the *Anabasis* ('March Upcountry'). The remaining six parts tell the story of the Greek retreat from Mesopotamia to the Black Sea, and hence along the coast to Byzantium and Thrace. The author gives a point-to-point record of the journey, supplying for most stages the distance covered and the number of days taken. This is high-quality information, and it has afforded historians the opportunity to reconstruct the course of the expedition. However, as I was to discover in the early stages of my research, there are some problems. For example, many of the places Xenophon mentions have been lost over time, or cannot be identified for lack of descriptive detail. There are omissions of figures on some stages, and some commentators think that the record is incomplete. Then there is the unit of measurement which Xenophon uses, the *parasang*. Not perfectly understood by modern scholars, this Persian measure seems to have been time-based, a single unit equalling perhaps the distance an army covered in one hour's marching. It would thus have been a variable measure, the distance actually covered being dependent on terrain – and, according to Andreas, on the season, as the ancient hour varied with the length of day.

A further difficulty was that, although two points might be known, there was no certainty about the route taken between them. However, from my own experience of walking, I had a sense that this would not be as big a problem as it seemed. Human nature is to find the easiest way of doing things. Roads since they were first developed have always pursued the course of least resistance. With the right topographical model, a learned eye might predict the path of a route between two places. There might in fact initially be several, but over time, in a kind of natural selection, the most efficient endures while the others fade away. Roman civil engineers, projecting imperial power by means of straight lines, altered to a degree this natural order, but as yet the technology to truly change landscapes did not exist. Today engineers can tunnel through mountains, drain lakes, and bulldoze valleys out of existence. In the near future finding ancient ways will be harder, but for the present at least a person travelling on a country road can be fairly sure that, notwithstanding its modern glaze of tar, beneath is a path that has been trodden for thousands of years.

My starting point for trying to put a route together was Ainsworth's commentary. Watson's volume had only an abridged version, but I found the complete one at the Gennadius Library, a rich repository of Hellenic heritage on the slopes of Mount Lykavitos. I also encountered there an elderly woman who proved to be invaluable in getting the project off the ground. She was Dutch, born in Indonesia, and married to a Greek. A linguist by training, Andriette had an interest in Xenophon herself, having once studied the phenomenon of what is known as 'whistled speech'. As the name suggests, this is communication by whistling. The vocabulary and grammar are based on that of the verbal tongue, and in principle there are no lexical limitations: any word, however long or complicated, can be whistled. There are only five places in the world where whistled speech is practised, one of them being in the Eastern Black Sea mountains of Turkey. Andriette's opinion was that Xenophon was the first outsider to record the phenomenon. As we drank coffee on the steps of the library on the day of our first meeting, she located the passage in Watson's text: 'These places were distance from one another about 80 stadia, some more, some less; yet the inhabitants could hear each other calling out from one town to another.'

I learned quickly that the material value of the *Anabasis* was not restricted to language students and historical geographers. People as diverse as botanists, military instructors, and sociologists, all found something relevant to their disciplines in the 2,400-year-old text of the Athenian.

In the course of my research in the winter of 1999, it struck me that there could be a practical element to my trip – important if I was to be able to finance the adventure. An issue that has divided scholars in the field for years is whether or not Xenophon kept a diary on his journey. No direct evidence of such a document has ever come to light, yet, the argument runs, how else could the detail of the journey have been recalled, especially if, as is thought, the story was not written until thirty years after the event? I thought that in trying to maintain my diary over the course of the long journey, I would get an insight into how feasible such an exercise would have been for the Athenian.

Andriette put me in touch with the publisher of *Archaeology and Arts* magazine, to whom I sent a summary of the project. I had a message from the secretary at the school a couple of weeks after to say that she wanted to see me.

The editorial office was on the top floor of a nondescript modern block close to the Plaka. A receptionist led me to a desk in the middle of a quiet open-plan office. A casually dressed woman stood up and greeted me. She was tall and elegant, and spoke English with a trace of a French accent.

She had my summary and route map beside her, and I gave her more detail about what I was hoping to do. I had decided that I would focus on the *Anabasis* stage of the journey, from Sardis to Babylon. The route of the *Katabasis* – the retreat up along the Tigris River into Kurdistan and Armenia – I would consider travelling if and when I got to my first destination. This seemed to me to be the most realistic approach, and I thought as well that it was in keeping with the spirit of the original, for when the battle of Kounaxa was over, the Greeks had no idea what they would do next.

'How long do you think the journey will take?' she asked, turning to the map when I had finished.

I estimated that the 2,500 kilometres to Babylon would take about five months to walk, the return journey somewhat longer.

She had no other queries, and after thanking me for coming in, she handed me a large white envelope. I wasn't sure what to say, and volunteered to report my findings on the diary. She replied that she wasn't looking for anything in return.

I resisted the temptation to open the envelope in the lift on the way down, but as soon as I got home, I unsealed it, and discovered a small fortune in drachmas.

Later the publisher arranged for me to meet an official at the Iraqi embassy. A significant part of the route goes through Mesopotamia, and I was concerned that, given the situation at the time, getting permission to walk in Iraq would be difficult. From what I knew, the ruling Ba'ath Party was suspicious of outsiders, and careful about where it let them visit. The embassy, it turned out, was very helpful. The ambassador himself wrote a letter of introduction for the home authorities, and in my passport it was written that I was a *rahhal*, a venerable Arabic term for a person who travels on foot.

As I soon discovered, their enthusiasm for the project was not founded so much in a wish to further science, as a keenness to exploit the position of my sponsor. 'If you write anything for *Kyria* Lambrakis' newspapers,' the consul told me on the day I went to collect the papers, 'this should reflect the effect of ten years of sanctions on our country.' I answered him that I would write what I saw.

*

I had planned to start the journey in March, as the commentators believe Cyrus did, but a host of things conspired to delay me. One of them was an episode concerning the girl who had brought me to Athens in the first place. One day in February, when I was still hoping to make the original date, Andreas came up to me in the staff room and said we were going to Plateia Klafthmonos after school.

There was a biting wind coming down Stadhiou, and we walked chins in chests, hands in pockets, along the arrow-straight boulevard. Half-way up, we came to the square, and Andreas led me across to a row of shuffling vendors. They had their wares displayed on foldaway tables and upturned boxes. One of them was selling old cameras.

'If you want to have her again, you will buy this.' He picked up one that had a square lens and a short, concertina-shaped body. It was a solid apparatus, and apparently took exceptional photos: a functioning antique. Photography was Anastasia's passion, and I knew this would delight her. But I wasn't sure if I wanted to reopen the affair. Maybe we hadn't been meant to be together, and the time we had spent would always be a special memory. Andreas noted my hesitation.

'It will be easier for you to walk to Babylon and back again twice than to find the right woman.'

He waited with the camera in his hands while I hurried across to a cash machine for the asking price.

The camera was delivered to her mother's shop in Plateia Attikis and I waited to hear from her, but by April there had been nothing. It transpired that she had written to me, but to my address in Ireland, thinking I had returned there. Her letter was one of several in a parcel I received from my mother early on in the journey.

On 11 May 2000 I sailed from Athens to the Aegean island of Khios. A group of the students from the school came to the Piraeus to see me off, as did my friends and those who had helped me in organizing the journey.

Andreas was more upbeat than usual. 'This is the right thing for you,' he assured me, arm over my shoulder, as we posed for a photo on the quay. I had lost some of my confidence in him after the Anastasia episode, but his words and his friendship still meant a lot to me. He didn't know how instrumental he had been in launching me on this path.

The ship arrived in Khios the next morning at 4 o'clock and at 9 I was on a much smaller craft headed for the Turkish coast. Within an hour I was through customs at Çeşme and on a coach to the city of Izmir. Izmir – Zmir, Zmirna, Smyrna – lies 90 kilometres due east of ancient Sardis, the starting point for my journey. If all went to plan, for the next three months I would be trekking across Mediterranean Turkey.

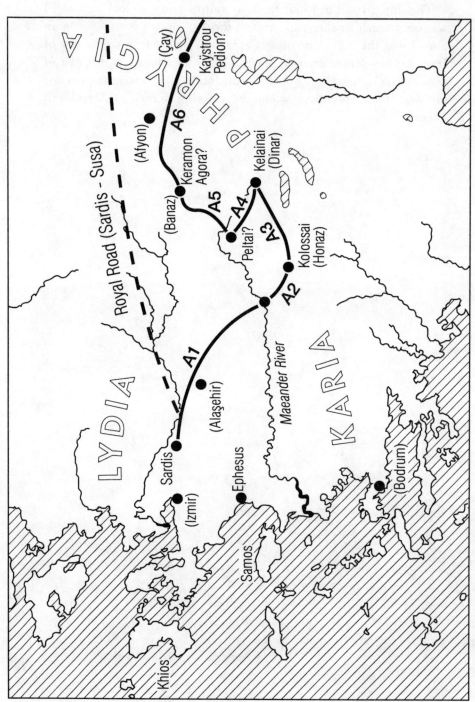

Anabasis 1-6: Sardis to Kaÿstrou Pedion

2

The Royal Road

A1: Sardis to the Maeander River

As soft Maeander's wanton current plays,
When through the Phrygian fields it loosely strays;
Backward and forward rolls the dimpled tide,
Seeming at once two different ways to glide:
While circling streams their former banks survey,
And waters past succeeding waters see;
Now floating to the sea with downward course,
Now pointing upward to its ancient source.

Ovid, *Metamorphoses*

The Turkish Republic encompasses the entire area of ancient Anatolia. This is a geographically diverse landmass which is dominated by a vast, elevated plateau in the interior. Mountain ranges bound its northern and southern fringes, dropping steeply to seas the Turks call 'Black' and 'White' respectively. These heights intercept the rain-bearing clouds from the seas, and what escapes the barriers falls mostly on the edges, precipitation decreasing steadily towards the centre. This outwardly changeless landscape rests on a tectonic plate which is constantly being pushed westwards. The fault line dividing the Anatolian and Eurasian plates runs across the north of the subcontinent, and when the two lock, pressure builds until the tension is released. Usually this is sudden and violent. In the last 2,000 years almost 600 major earthquakes have shaken the region.

The history of Anatolia, to quote the traveller Robert Byron on a different region, 'is almost too profuse. It gives one a sort of mental indigestion.' The modern state might be thought of as a thin crust resting on a mantle of rich civilization. At the core are the Hittites, a warlike, literary people, who flourished on the High Plateau for the whole of the second millennium BC. Following their sudden – and as yet unexplained – demise, a patchwork of kingdoms emerged on the Asian appendage, Phrygia, Lydia, Paphlagonia, Urartu and Armenia among them. Greeks also came at the start of the first millennium BC. An increase in the domestic population and a meagre stock of tillable land set in train a process of colonization that would see Greek satellites spring up around the Mediterranean and Black Sea coasts. The concentration of their settlement was along the rugged western coastline of Anatolia. Two distinct confederations emerged here: Aeolia, extending from the Hellespont to the Hermos River valley, and Ionia, which continued thence as far as the Maeander. The Ionians, colonists of Athens, were the most industrious of the seasiders, and their polity was to become the engine of Hellenic civilization: architecture, geography, mathematics, philosophy, literature, Anaximander, Thales, Homer, Hecataeus, Pythagoras, Heraclitos of the Fire: 'The road up and the road down are one and the same.'

Because of the Ionian achievement, Greek influence spread out over the landmass, and their culture came to be adopted by many of the new regional powers. King Croesus of Lydia was the most renowned of these Phillhellenes. Herodotus speaks of the splendour of his offerings at Delphi, and of his generosity toward his Greek friends. Seeking gold for the erection of a statue of Apollo at home, a party of Spartans travelled to Sardis, 'but although they came to buy it, Croesus gave it them for free'.

By the time of Croesus, Lydia was the largest and most prosperous kingdom in Anatolia. Its legendary wealth derived from its control of the trade routes between the sea and the interior, and probably also in part from the gold reserves of the Pactolos, the river of Sardis (the Lydians suitably, though perhaps not accurately, are credited with the invention of coinage). An aetiological myth retold by Ovid has it that the Phrygian king Midas, 'loathing what he had lately desired', travelled to Sardis on the advice of Dionysus, and retraced the Pactolos to its source. Following the instructions of the wine god, he plunged himself into the foaming spring, thereby 'transferring his power to change things into gold from his person to the river'.

In the end, Croesus was repaid harshly by the Greek oracle for his patronage. Seeing benefit in the further expansion of his kingdom, the

Delphic priests advised him that if he crossed his eastern border and attacked his neighbour, he would destroy a great empire. His neighbour was Cyrus the Great.

The battle they fought in the autumn of 546 was inconclusive. Croesus pulled back across the Halys and decided to retire for the winter, having in mind a fresh campaign the following year. This time he envisaged having a much larger force, with Spartans, Egyptians and Babylonians in his ranks. But he had hardly arrived at his capital when Cyrus appeared in the Sardian plain. The Lydians defended their city fiercely, but after a two-week siege, it fell. Just as the oracle had foretold, a great empire was destroyed.

Anatolia was now in Persian hands, and would remain so for the next two centuries, with Sardis as the seat of governance.

*

My first sight of the ruined city was from a rise on the road 7 or 8 kilometres to the west. From my seat in the front of the inter-city bus taking me from Izmir, I could just make out the jagged outline of the 300-metre-high Acropolis. Already at this distance, signs of the city's necropolis were evident. Into the light brown foothills of Mount Tmolos (Bozdağ) were cut several of the distinctive native rock tombs, while to the north of the highway, sitting eerily on the plain, were the great bulging tumuli of the Lydian kings. The signalled fertility of this plain, as productive now as it has always been, accounts for the modern settlement of Sart. Farmers driving tractors and motorcycles with unwieldy sidecars, buzz in and out of lanes around the village, sending dust skyward and oncoming traffic into the middle of the road. The bus stopped on the outskirts to let me off. The Ankara-bound passengers looked curiously through the windows as I struggled with the straps on my pack. A shop owner beside the stop directed me to the path leading up to the Temple of Artemis.

The sanctuary setting was as idyllic as I had imagined: as I neared the end of the kilometre-long trail, I could see the temple's trademark Ionic capitals bobbing against waves of green hills that rolled into the slopes of distant Tmolos. A colonnade of trees lined the approach, and from alongside on the right came the sound of a stream, the Pactolos, running the final stage of its course to the plain.

Depositing my gear in a clearing on the bank, the sweat pouring down my face, I approached the temple foreground. A light breeze, and a water bottle doused over my head, cooled me somewhat.

The unearthing of the temple columns had been a remarkable feat of excavation. Soil to a depth of nearly 10 metres had to be shifted by the American team who came here in 1910 to uncover the site and its detailed architectural history. The job took four years to complete, yielding in the process a large quantity of jewellery and artwork, most of it now on display in the Metropolitan Museum of New York. Thanks to the Americans the visitor today stands almost on the same level as the devotees who would have come to the sanctuary to worship, possibly from as early as the time of the first Lydian kings.

As I surveyed the deserted complex, I tried to picture the scene 2,500 years before, when the mercenaries of Cyrus were streaming into the city. Most I guessed would have come over the mountains from the south-west, having disembarked in boats at Ephesus, the hub of Greek activity on the coast. Reaching the pass beneath Kel Dağ, a checkpoint in the time of the Persians, they would have had their first sight of the fabled city. Even after Ephesus, this must have been impressive. Eyes would first have looked for and found the awesome, sheer-faced Acropolis; the busy *agora* (market place) would then have come into focus, teeming with the merchants of Asia. Other landmarks catching their attention from the height might have been the tumuli out on the plain, and the *paradeisos* that Cyrus, their new employer, had designed.

The Temple of Artemis as it is today would not then have existed, though on the same site the goddess would have had an altar. This, a square, stepped monument of limestone blocks, remains *in situ*. Cyrus is said to have given thanks here on his return from Susa in 404, and he is sure to have made an offering prior to the commencement of his great enterprise. Doubtless many of the soldiers also prayed at the altar, reverence to the Olympians being their only surety in matters of uncertainty. Circling the appealing edifice, I couldn't help thinking that few of those who made offerings here in the spring of 401, could have imagined the places and extremes to which they were destined to be taken by the ambition of Cyrus.

On the east side of the sanctuary, a soft hill rose above the sprawling ruins of the settlement. I climbed this to get a better view of the site, and of the citadel, perched on a mighty pinnacle of rock away to the east. From his apartments here Croesus would have first seen the army of Cyrus the Great arraying out on the plain. Herodotus wrote, 'He himself was the messenger through whom Croesus learned of his arrival.'

Croesus considered this fort impregnable, and not without reason, for the artificially steepened sides make any approach breathtakingly difficult. It was finally taken by Cyrus thanks to a Mardian called Hyroeades, who had noticed that one side, that facing Tmolos, was only lightly guarded. The Mardian had some experience of climbing; he gathered others with the same skill and one night led a daring assault on the height. Like the Greeks in the belly of the wooden horse, they sprang on the unsuspecting defenders and gave the signal for the army to attack.

Turning again to the temple side, I directed my gaze from one end of the Pactolos valley to the other, trying to mark the way Midas might have taken on his journey to reach the source of the river. I ended at the summit of Tmolos, two raw masses of rock spiking the heavens above Anatolia. In their shadow, free from the curse of his wish, the king is said to have turned to a life of asceticism. Now hating riches, he made his home in a cave and lived on fruit and nuts, with only the animals for companionship. This, I reflected, would have been a transformative story of some power, were it not for the fact that Midas did not really change. The story goes that one day while out picking berries, he happened upon a divine musical contest: Pan had boasted to a nymph on Tmolos that his pipes made the most sublime sound in the universe, and in an instant, Apollo was before them, lyre in hand. It was an unequal match, for heaven had invested Apollo with the gift of music. Midas, however, thought differently, and in disgust the victor changed his ears to those of a donkey. The moral of the myth seemed to be that Midas never lost his capacity for stupidity.

Thinking of Yeats as I made my way slowly back down to the river, I hoped his story would not turn out to be my own. There was no helping it anyway. Midas that day could have taken any of a hundred – a thousand – paths through the mountain forest, but he was fated to do otherwise.

On the riverbank, I took from my pack a bottle of retsina Andreas had given me the evening before, and crossed again to the temple altar. Twisting the cap off, I poured a libation over the stone, drank the remainder, and recited a short prayer:

O Huntress Artemis, daughter of Zeus and Leto,
To whom Agamemnon prayed when he sailed in his tall ships to Troy,
Hear my prayer:
Keep away the evil spirits: no hard task for you, a Goddess,
Great for me, a man.

*

Sardis was the terminus of the Persian Royal Road: 2,500 kilometres of roadway crossing northern Mesopotamia and central Anatolia from the capital of the Great King at Susa. The artery connected the centre to one of its most important extremities. The tribute from the Mediterranean provinces was substantial – as was the propensity of the various subject peoples to revolt. Having the means of a timely, if not instant, response was as valuable to the Persians as the size of the army they could call up. Along the route there were 111 way-stations, *katalusies*, which facilitated maintenance of the road and enabled the operation of the extraordinary courier system. When Xerxes mounted the burning Athenian Acropolis in September 480, a beacon was flashed across the islands of the Aegean to waiting horsemen, and inside a week his triumph over the West was known in Susa. 'Then shalt thou know, then shall it become known to thee, the spear of a Persian man has gone far; then shall it become known to thee, a Persian man has delivered battle far indeed from Parsa' (inscription of Darius I).

Intact sections of the Royal Road have been uncovered near Persepolis, Gordion (near Ankara), and Sardis, and bear witness to the skill of the empire's engineers. The stretch east of Gordion is made of packed gravel, is six metres across, and bordered on either side by kerbstones. The modern highway into the interior more or less follows the course of the former Royal Road.

I had intended to start my journey at this very pronounced point of beginning, but amidst the acres of ruins piling over the southern fringe of the Hermos valley I was unable to locate the excavated stretch. A picture shown to locals at a shop on the highway produced only glasses of tea. The refreshment was welcome, for the heat at Sardis in May is intense, and I was already feeling the strain of carrying my pack. I had thought I had pared my equipment down to the essentials, but in light of my initial ramblings, I knew that the situation would need to be reconsidered.

The traffic on the trunk route – Izmir to Ankara – was heavy. Buses and lorries belted along in both directions, leaving trailing clouds of black smoke in their wake. I was careful to stay well in to the side, mindful of the warnings I had been given by Greek friends about the quality of driving in Turkey. Like most of the advice I had received from the same quarter, however, it did not prove to be well informed. Certainly, a firearm proved unnecessary in the countryside, and nobody in the first hour attempted to rob me at knifepoint. In this time one driver stopped to see if I was lost, and another offered me a lift, but other than that my presence was largely unmarked.

On that first afternoon I made barely half a dozen kilometres. It felt like much longer, but my map seemed to confirm what an attendant at a garage was insisting.

'Sart–Salihli ten kilometre. Here half way Sart–Salihli. *Vallah billa.*'

It was while I was scrutinizing the map on the forecourt that I realized I no longer had my walking stick. It was that sinking feeling you get when you discover outside an exam hall that you've not answered one of the compulsory questions. Leaving everything with the attendant, I hurried off back along the road.

The stick was extremely important to me. On previous treks it had proved to be my most valuable piece of equipment; apart from its function as a walking aid, it could be used to measure the depth of streams, to fend off dogs in the mountains, to rest a pack on while reading a map on the trail, and even to tie a fishing line to. The pole was made of aluminium and was in three parts, allowing it to be collapsed for transit, and the length to be adjusted according to terrain. Its tip was made of steel, and a plastic rim circled a few centimetres above this to enable the pole to be planted upright in snow or soft ground. Over the years the manufacturer's markings had worn off and now only traces of metric measures were visible on the black coating.

I found it in the grocery shop where I had stopped for directions. The owner recognized me at once, and I thought there was a faint look of disappointment on his face as he took it down from a shelf over the counter. I thanked him, put my hand through the loop and tightened it around my wrist. In time it would become like an extension of my right arm.

I camped a short way from the petrol station. A dry riverbed ran under the highway just beyond it, and I hiked up along this until the sound of traffic was faint.

By tradition the Persians began their expeditions in the evening. The idea, it is supposed, was that a man would be able to return home to pick up a forgotten item. My experience that afternoon showed how practical this tradition was, although it struck me, as I emptied the contents of my pack onto the ground, that it could have as likely been intended to enable people to return stuff they weren't going to need.

Much of what had seemed essential only days before now looked decidedly dispensable. In the space of five minutes I had formed an impressive pile of non-essentials: wool sweaters, head-torch, a week's supply of conserved meat, reserve gas canisters, a hefty Turkish dictionary and an Arabic language book. What was worth the post, I stuffed into a liner bag for sending home; the rest I dumped in a skip by the garage the next morning.

As I was replacing the reprieved items, I noticed on the ground what looked like a small silver coin. Holding it to the fading light, I saw that on the face there was a relief of the Virgin Mary. I couldn't figure it for a minute – a 'miraculous medal' in the stony soil of Lydia? It dawned on me then that my mother must have slipped it into my bag before I left home. Dismissive of her superstition, I was tempted to throw it into the riverbed, but on second thoughts restored it to the bottom of the pack. If chance were to play a role in my journey, I reasoned, I couldn't afford to disregard any form of divine help.

Whatever the power of the assorted charms on or about my person (besides the medal, I had a tiger's eye and a sacred stone from Africa), it was to be a remarkable statistic of my journey that of the dozens of objects thrown at me during the course of it, not one of them ever hit their target.

*

I didn't stay long on the Royal Road. After a visit to the post office in Salihli, I left the highway for a country road bound for Alaşehir. This was the way Cyrus would have gone. In leaving the main route at the first junction, his intention was to dampen any suspicions that he was headed for Susa. Actually he had in mind an alternative, quicker route into Mesopotamia, one which would involve crossing the Taurus Mountains and the Syrian Desert. Such a route would be impractical for a large expedition, but possible for a smaller force able to move rapidly over the uninhabited stretches. For the time being he might be thought of as loading a catapult; he had more armies to collect, and while he meandered about his provinces doing so, his true intention was in doubt.

Traffic on the Alaşehir road was light: mainly tractors and minibuses ferrying villagers back and forth from Salihli. This comparative remoteness had the effect of increasing the curiosity of the drivers, who would frequently stop to offer me a lift, or to give lengthy advice in Turkish which I didn't understand. In either case I would wave at them with my stick and carry on walking.

Frequent tea stops at villages, and the lighter load, made the walking less taxing than on the previous day. By midday I had covered about 20 kilometres, and decided to rest for the afternoon in a cemetery shaded by cypress trees. Their careful arrangement let in a measure of light, and I imagined the gravestones bathed in the warm glow of sunset in summer evenings. I remarked that the Turks seem to have inherited something of the Persians' taste for natural beauty. As I lay there, I thought it might have been the ancestor of one of these trees that Xerxes saw 'a day from Sardis' on his way to Greece in 481. It struck him as so beautiful that he decorated it with gold, and assigned one of his 'Immortals' to stand guard over it for ever.

Alaşehir loomed just after sunset, a dark outline against the foothills of Tmolos. The city did not exist in Xenophon's time, though it nevertheless has a long past. A Pergamene king, Attalus Philadelphus, founded it in the second century, and it quickly prospered, profiting from its location on the trade corridor to the sea. Today the fertile plain that stretches away beneath the high acropolis is the source of prosperity. Grapes are the main crop, and a factory on the outskirts of the city uses the harvest to manufacture raki, an aniseed-flavoured spirit drunk throughout the Mediterranean. An uninspiring sculpture of a bunch of grapes suspended over a dry pool at a T-junction in the lower end of the town acknowledges the debt of the Alaşehirlis to the vine.

Philadelphia was one of the 'seven churches of Asia' named by St John the Evangelist. Unlike the other early Christian communities, this one remained a vibrant centre throughout Byzantine and Ottoman times. A visitor in the early nineteenth century, the Reverend F.J. Arundel (chaplain at Smyrna from 1824 to 1840), counted twenty-five churches in the city, among them the ruins of St John's, believed by the faithful to be the 'church' spoken of by the evangelist. Shown the site by the resident Greek bishop, Arundel remarked: 'It would have been useless to have attempted to convince him that such a structure would only have been erected after the empire became Christian, and that the early followers of a crucified master had not where to lay their heads, much less magnificent temples to worship in.'

I visited it the next morning, having stayed the night in a friendly hotel around the corner. Hemmed in in a small, fenced off plot in the upper town, the site today is pretty much as Arundel would have seen it. Actually there isn't much at all to see, just three colossal stumps rooted to the earth. It does none the less remain as the only substantial relic of the town's disremembered Greek past. In 1923, along with the rest of the new republic's Christian population, its Greek inhabitants were 'repatriated', so ending 3,000 years of Hellenic civilization in Asia Minor.

A day and a half from Alaşehir I crossed the eastern extremity of the Tmolos range. The long ascent offered truncated views behind to the plain, a vast, shimmering plot of agriculture. The Kastolos Plain was the assembly place for Persian levies in western Anatolia, and it is somewhere here that Cyrus would have collected his native troops.

A remarkable feature of Xenophon's narrative is how little attention he pays to the 'native' element of Cyrus' force. For all the detail he provides on the make-up of the Greek mercenaries, he tells us practically nothing about the levies. We have no idea for instance who their leaders were (Cyrus' second-in-command, Ariaios, had overall charge), what districts of Asia Minor they came from, or indeed how many of them there were. At a review in Babylonia Xenophon throws out a figure of 100,000, 'and twenty scythed chariots', but the former is huge, and best understood in the tradition of exaggeration that is common to all Greek literature on conflict with 'barbarians'.

Going beyond the sources, however, it is possible to arrive at guesses. Cyrus' exceptional command covered the old kingdoms of Lydia, Phrygia, and Kappadokia, and Xenophon says he had horsemen from Paphlagonia and Thrace, so it must be the tribes from these territories – many of them named by Homer in the *Iliad* – who made up the contingent. As to their numbers, we know that the natives were levies – subjects under obligation to report to the satrap when required – and that each satrapy had its own quota based on population and tribute figures. Cyrus had been appointed by his father as 'commander-in-chief of all the forces that muster in the Plain of Kastolos', probably the assembly place for all of the satrapies of western Asia Minor. A figure of 15,000 – 20,000 has been suggested as a realistic range for this large and prosperous area, and this number is supported by later evidence from the march.

The road beyond the crest wound through a hilly terrain before dropping down towards the floor of another valley. Soon after reaching the height, I stopped to refill my water bottle at a fountain. This was more basic than the ones I had drunk from the previous day on the plain, and there was a handwritten sign hanging from the tap that said something about the water. I thought it said it was safe to drink, though I wasn't sure. The tap made a deep gurgling sound when I turned it on, and after a minute I heard the water rushing through the pipe. It burst out in hot spurts, but gradually formed a cool flow.

A scan through my grammar book that evening suggested that the form of the verb 'to drink' (*içmek*) on the sign was conveying a negative sense. I had been spending short spells in the evenings with Lewis' grammar, but concluded as I emptied what was left of the water out of my bottle that I would have to apply more effort than this if I was to be able to get by. The language, I had been assured by a Turkish lexicographer in Athens, was not difficult. 'You just take a word,' Farouq used to say at the start and end of our lessons, 'and add bits on to make sentences.' Learning the endings he had admitted was not easy, but actually I found once you did, and established a working vocabulary, the language barrier began to lower.

I suffered no ill effects from the water, though I spent that night uncomfortably with sunburnt arms exposed to the cool air. My sleep was upset too by images of slain tortoises on the road. The last stretch, a new section rolling down to the valley, had resembled the scene of a crude cull. Every hundred metres or so the remains of a tortoise were strewn, some flattened beyond recognition, others with gruesome holes punched into their armour. Once, seeing a pair crossing the hard shoulder, I had flagged down an oncoming van and carried them one at a time to the other side. (From later observations I was surprised to discover that, contrary to their proverbial slowness, they could actually move quite fast. One ahead of me on a quiet section before Derbent went across the road at the walking pace of a pensioner, the shell raised and the four legs pounding the earth like pistons. Their problem – apart from new roads bisecting their breeding grounds – is that they are programmed to stop whenever they sense vibrations beneath; and following the passing of a predator, it takes them ages to come out of their shells.)

The Maeander, which I came to the next afternoon, was something of a disappointment. It passed meekly under the bridge and continued in an unexpectedly orderly fashion across the plain. It wasn't as Ovid had told.

In Xenophon's scheme, the river was the terminus of the first stage (A1). His figures for this are 22 *parasangs* covered in three days. Following Ainsworth, I was taking the *parasang* to be a spatial measurement of 30 stadia, or around 5 kilometres. His and his fellow antiquarians' calculations seemed complex (based on 'the earth's true meridional circumference'), but the figure is supported by an examination of the actual distances between known points of the *Anabasis*, and it is to be added that a number of ancient scholars also equated the *parasang* with 30 stadia.

The experience of my own journey was to be that the relationship between time and distance could be fixed quite accurately, and in time I was able to estimate how far I had walked in the course of a given day. Typically I would cover about 5½ kilometres in an hour, 5 with a five-minute stop. Factors affecting this rate included the type of terrain being traversed, weather conditions and the time of day (afternoons were slowest).

Xenophon reports that the Maeander was 60 metres wide, whereas its width at the bridge where I crossed was no more than 20. The damming of the great river upstream, and the use of regulators to divert its waters into canals, are no doubt the causes of this marked discrepancy.

There was some consolation for me in the statistics of the stage. Adding the ultimate leg to the figures in my diary, I arrived at a total of 112 kilometres, a figure closer to that given by Xenophon (at the fixed rate) than I would have expected. On the other hand it had taken me six days to get here. Pitching my tent upstream of the bridge, I realized that I would have to substantially increase my rate of progress if I was to keep pace with the army.

3

Kelainai

A2–3: To the sources of the Maeander

Here [at Kelainai] *Cyrus had a palace, and an extensive park full of wild animals, which he used to hunt on horseback whenever he wished to give himself and his horses exercise. Through the middle of this park flows the river Maeander; its springs issue from the palace itself; and it runs thence through the city of Kelainai. There is also at Kelainai a palace of the Great King, strongly fortified and situated near the springs of the river Marsyas, under the Acropolis. This river too runs through the city, and empties into the Maeander.*

Anabasis I.2

Cyrus crossed the Maeander on a bridge of boats and marched in one day to Kolossai, a distance of 40 kilometres (A2). This was a long stage, but the men were fresh and the road they were travelling along was good.

I wasn't in great shape at this point. Together with sunburn and blisters, I had newly acquired a strain in my shin. It had happened shortly after I had started that morning. I was walking along one of the concrete canals which burrowed across the plain when I felt a sharp pain in the lower front part of my right leg. Taking off my boot, I could make out no sign of swelling or bruising, and concluded it was a light sprain. After some testing on the track I found that by swinging my right leg in an arc, the discomfort was minimized, and so in this awkward fashion I continued.

By what seemed like a fine stroke of luck, in mid-morning I came upon a sign advertising a sulphuric health spa. Surveying the empty canal track ahead, I noted a short distance out on the plain a set of buildings which I would otherwise have taken for a farm complex. Thinking a treatment here would be beneficial, I left the canal and hobbled across the fields.

'*Tureest! Tureest!*' A waiter who had previously been preparing tables in a marquee ran out to the car park as I was negotiating a fence on the perimeter. A couple more joined him and they stared as I tried to free my shirt from the wire. Unable to get over I had tried to slip under, and had become snagged on the barbed wire. Giving up, I crawled forward, tearing a sizeable patch out of my shirt.

The staff greeted me warmly. I asked for water, and was duly obliged with a large jug from the marquee fridge. Removing my boot for the fifth or sixth time that morning, I poured the ice water onto the sore area, and was surprised by the relief this provided.

There wasn't much chance of therapy, an affable English-speaking receptionist informed me, as the spa was block-booked for the entire summer. I gathered from him on a tour of the bubbling sulphur pools that there were numerous such springs in this area, most now harnessed for the lucrative 'therapies' market. More usefully, from another source I later learned that geothermal scientists are working to develop ways of harnessing the energy produced by the springs, the drawback being that, as a by-product of the process, water in excess of 200°C has to be disposed of. Current research is focusing on ways to cool the water sufficiently to allow it flow harmlessly into the Maeander.

Visiting the ruins of nearby Laodikeia on his pilgrimage to the 'seven churches of the Apocalypse', the Reverend Arundel invoked the expertise of a Dr Chandler to explain the phenomenon of the hot springs:

It is an old observation that the country about the Maeander, the soil being light and friable, and full of salts generating inflammable matter, was undermined by fire and water. Hence it abounded in hot springs, which, after passing underground from the reservoirs, appeared on the mountains, or were found bubbling up in the plain or in the mud of the river; and hence it was subject to frequent earthquakes; the nitrous vapour compressed in the cavities, and sublimed by heat or fermenta-tion, bursting its prison with loud explosions, agitating the atmosphere, and shaking the earth and waters with a violence both extensive and destructive.

Instead of going back the way I had come, I picked up a second canal on the east side of the valley, and continued along this side. While I was keen to keep as close as I could to the army's route, there was an unusual sight hereabouts that had entranced the earlier travellers, and I had decided to make a slight detour in order to see it.

From a distance it looked like a great white tooth embedded in the hillside. A picture came briefly into my head of an elderly dinosaur lunging for its last supper. As I slowly drew closer, the object became more distinct, being finally revealed as a grand white crust spilling over the ridge of a plateau. This was Pamukkale 'Cotton Castle', one of Anatolia's most extraordinary natural features. Dr Chandler explained in some detail how it was formed. In summary, layers of calcium were deposited on the hillside by warm water flowing from a mineral-rich plateau above, and hardening by exposure to the air, these deposits variously formed ledges, stalactites, and miniature waterfalls.

The road passing by was as close as I ventured to the travertines. I kept hobbling until I came to a small village, where I took a room above a teashop. After plastering my shin in anti-inflammatory gel, I tended to the blisters on my feet, one of which was steadily growing along the sole of my left foot. Draining it, I cut away the skin and applied a series of heat plasters designed to act like a second skin.

I declared myself unfit for travel the next day, and spent most of it watching Turkish television, with occasional forays into Lewis' grammar. The next morning, feeling more roadworthy, I set off for the other side of the plain.

Around midday I crossed the ancient Lykos River (Çürüksu), and shortly after came to the main road. Beyond this, several slanting plateaus tiered above the valley. The heavily wooded terracing ended abruptly beneath a high mass of rock that I identified from my map as Honaz Dağ. Somewhere in its shadow were the ruins of Kolossai, described by Xenophon as 'a populous city, wealthy, and of considerable magnitude'.

Until recently the precise location of the city was unknown. Over time its monuments had been toppled by earthquakes and removed for use as building material elsewhere. The traditional starting point for explorers was a description given by Herodotus, who located it, somewhat enigmatically, 'where the river Lykos disappears underground into a chasm'. Now on the trail of St Paul, the travelling pastor Arundel and his group spent two days in the vicinity trying to spot this *khasma*. It was the subject too of much investigation by early commentators on the *Anabasis*, for whom the city had especial significance as the place where Cyrus' nemesis, Tissaphernes, finally met his end.

I went first to the town of Honaz. Situated at the apex of a raised triangle formed by its distributor roads and the highway down in the valley, it lies directly beneath the intimidating mass of Honaz Dağ. Honaz is famous in Turkey for producing some of the finest cherries in the country (Napoleons). Its rich *kiraz* fields fill much of the sizeable triangle, the remainder being held by pockets of dense green wood and the odd grazing field. A couple of kilometres from the town it started to rain, the first time it had done so since I had started, and it struck me that the cherry crop likely owed its richness to an anomalous level of rainfall, this in turn being accounted for by the height of the mountain range.

Calling at a pharmacy for directions, I was disappointed to discover that neither the owner nor any of the customers who trickled in for prescriptions from a clinic opposite had any idea of where the ancient city was. A sketch of a river disappearing into a hole generated more positive responses, but it was clear from cross checking that several different places were being referred to. At the suggestion of the pharmacist, I decided to leave my gear in the shop and investigate more freely the accuracy of my map.

On the map Kolossai was due north of the town. I followed a minor road that disappeared into the triangle in this direction. After about forty minutes a lane appeared on the left; taking my bearings, I guessed that somewhere along its route there should be a glimpse of the marked site, or of the river that famously vanished within it. I followed the muddy lane westward until eventually it opened out into a green field. There was no sign of any ruins, but as I stood there in the rain, the faint sound of gushing water came to my ears. Five minutes through an adjacent field strewn with pottery shards brought me to the edge of a peculiar crater-shaped valley. The sound, now like a waterfall, was caused by a river that was rushing through a sluice-like gorge just ahead. Peering down at it, I had the impression it was too precisely defined to be the work of the river. Taken with the sunken appearance of the surrounding valley, it wasn't too fanciful to imagine that the whole area had been set in its current form by seismic movement, perhaps one catastrophic moment which ended the life of a city, and discreetly closed a chasm into which this river had once disappeared.

At any rate, there was no hole that I could find into which it vanished, and no trace either of any stub of masonry that might mark the site of Kolossai. Only an undisturbed mound to the north, and the ubiquitous shards, offered hints of Xenophon's laconic description.

With the rain still relentless, I halted my searches and returned to the town. My experience, it transpired, had not been dissimilar to Arundel's. I read his account as I warmed myself by a stove in the chemist's: 'We returned to the village, heartily tired, and sufficiently wet, about half past four o'clock. It was a severe disappointment to leave Honaz without ascertaining the actual existence of the chasm in which the Lykos disappears.'

Cyrus stayed one week at Kolossai, and was joined here by a contingent of 1,500 troops led by Menon the Thessalian. From here they turned north-east towards the city of Kelainai, a march of 100 kilometres completed in three days (A3).

It had taken me three days to reach Kolossai, but on the next stage I got to grips with the pace. On the first day I descended through the cherry orchards; on the second I passed acres of poppy fields; and on the third, north of a large salt lake, I came into a vast, undulating plain. The scene presented a striking contrast to the fertile valleys of the previous week. Not a house, fence, or a single head of livestock were to be seen on the windswept steppe. With no reference points to fix on, it seemed like hours before I came to the first village, hidden in a hollow in the midst of the emptiness. I took my lunch in a teahouse there, busy with idle males unemployed by the poorness of the soil around.

*

The Persians used to say that from the bottom of a deep well you can see the stars even in daylight. The Turks say that the deepest wells have the coldest water. If you drink enough from one on a hot day it will cool your body from the inside; if you place the back of your neck under the spout, it will lower the temperature from the outside. The Turks have an intimate relationship with water. They discuss it by a spring in the way other peoples talk of wine at a dinner table. They name their daughters for it – Pınar (spring), Nehir (river), Şelale (waterfall) – and remember their dead by enshrining springs in the countryside. These *çeşmeler* are ubiquitous. You meet them along the road just as the thirst is growing again: a concrete casing, a trough, a metal cup and an inscription remembering a loved one: 'In memory of Ayşe, born into paradise on this day.'

There are estimated to be 12 billion cubic metres of underground water in Turkey, a reserve replenished annually by rainfall percolating into the water table. The distribution, however, is not uniform: parts of the country are parched, while in others, you can strike a rock like Poseidon and it will gush from the earth. One such place is Dinar, a small town in the province of Afyon.

I spent much of the third day of the third stage searching for it on the horizon. Over every rise in the rolling steppe I expected to see a spot of green in the distance. Sometimes I would leave the road and hike to a crest; to the north, there was a range of low mountains, but nothing else lent definition to the panorama. A wind strafing across the stony soil added to a sense of desolation.

It appeared late in the day, suddenly: a green gorge at the base of a prominent spur. Parks, and pockets of tall trees, dominated the sloping townscape, and a river flowed from its bottom corner. Even from this remove, it was apparent that this was a place which must have greatly appealed to the Persians, a natural *paradeisos* in the wilderness.

Inside the town the sound of water was everywhere: trickles and torrents of it finding their way to a common beginning. The river they form makes its way to the sea from here in such a manner that its name has become a byword for wandering. The bards had many explanations for the behaviour of the Maeander (*mai-andros*, 'search for a man'), but in the age of reason its circuitous course is accounted for by high volume and low gradient.

Science has also established that the springs of Dinar – the Suçıkan, Ilıca, Düden, Beşpınar ('the five springs'), İncirli, Pınarlı, and Hüdaverdi – are fed by a huge basin, the Dombai Plain, high away to the east. Accumulating here in large depressions, 'eyes', the water finds its way through the porous rock to points in and around the town. The largest of these depressions is the Pınarbaşı ('spring head') Lake, thought to be the Aulokrene of antiquity, famous as the place where the nymph Syrinx was turned into a reed. The story is that Pan, driving a flock through Phrygia, caught sight of her and fell in love. Managing to free herself from his grip, she ran towards the lake screaming for help – and some deity heard, and transformed her into a reed as she plunged into the water.

Pan was heartbroken. He waded through the lake calling her name, and was driven wild in turn by the sound of her voice, which was carried by the wind as it blew across the tops of the reeds. Even for a god it was impossible to figure which stalk of the thousands was her. Plucking a handful at random, he sat down by the edge of the lake and carefully stuck them together with wax. From then on, whenever he played this instrument, he imagined his lips were touching hers, and the sound was her voice singing to him.

Up until the nineteenth century not much was known of Dinar's past, although there was much evidence to suggest that it was long and rich. Antique coins were forever being turned up in the fields, and blocks of masonry bearing faded inscriptions were a feature of many of the houses. The Classical explorers sought these out with great enthusiasm, invading homes and buying up hoards of coin in the market. Most of them had some grounding in the infant sciences of numismatics and epigraphy, but inevitably there were errors. The Reverend Arundel deciphered one inscription found behind a wine press and sent news to London that he had discovered Apollonia. The cleric's find made him something of a celebrity at home, and his account of the journey quickly became a bestseller of the day. However, a number of years later, the same inscription was examined by Colonel Leake, the leading explorer in the region, and was found to refer to a dedication sent by the people of Apollonia on the Rhyndacus, a town some 250 kilometres from Dinar. Learning the news, Arundel graciously retracted the assertion, but he never again took to the high roads of Anatolia.

By this time Leake was already confident that Dinar was the site of ancient Kelainai. Although no traces of the monuments spoken of in the Classic texts had been found, these documents also referred to the extraordinary hydrography of Kelainai, and this was a physical imprint that had not been erased by time. While the authors sometimes used different names, their descriptions of the rivers were largely consistent, and there was no other place in the region that matched these.

Establishment of the waterways in turn permitted speculation on the whereabouts of several of the important historic locations. The source of one, a cave beneath the height dominating the town, seemed very likely to be near the place where Xerxes had his palace. Xenophon describes it as being, 'strongly fortified and situated near the springs of the river Marsyas, under the Acropolis'. The Athenian's description of Cyrus the Younger's residence was equally helpful: 'Through the middle of this park flows the river Maeander; its springs issue from the palace itself.' However, even in gestation, the Maeander proved to be evasive, and to this day there is no agreement on which of the several spouts is the true source.

The cave of Marsyas was the first place I visited in Dinar. It wasn't hard to find: I just followed the course of the river that rushed past my hotel door to the eminence at the north end of the town. For the final half kilometre it ran alongside the main road, which climbed in a straight line to a pass beneath the height. From here, as in former times, the road continued north-east to Afyon and the highway across the interior.

The location has undergone some change since Leake's day. The pass has been blasted by modern engineers to allow a bigger road through, and more recently, a large space has been levelled on the eastern side to make room for a motel. A gap between its gable end and the rock face allows access to the cave where Apollo competed with Marsyas in one of the great musical contests of myth. The story was told by a placard in the motel forecourt. A local shepherd, Marsyas, found a magic flute that had been discarded by a goddess. He didn't know how to play it, but as soon as he put it to his lips, the instrument started to play itself. Great fame came upon him in Phrygia, and some said his tunes were sweeter even than Apollo's.

Not hearing this praise contradicted, Apollo made a point of seeking out Marsyas. He found him one day entertaining the locals at this spot. Marsyas accepted his challenge to a contest, and indeed, so mesmerizing was his playing, that the muses – summoned from Helicon to be judges – could not declare a winner. Marsyas might have gone on to win a deciding second round, had not Midas, who was passing on his way to Sardis, picked up the flute while its custodian was refreshing himself at the spring. Even as he admired it, the instrument, divinely crafted from stag bone, changed into solid gold. The contest was dramatically over, the prize to the victor being a punishment of his choice. Apollo, with the cruelty of a god, flayed the shepherd alive and nailed his skin to a plane tree that grew at the entrance to the cave.

Child of the peak of Kelainai – what fatal folly thine!
Never again shall we listen, we nymphs, as thy fluting thrills,
With its wood-notes sweeter than honey, across the Phrygian hills.

I was sceptical about the placard's involvement of Midas in the plot, and mentioned this casually to the waiter who brought me tea in the plaza. He hurried into the motel, and maybe ten minutes later, a car spun into the grounds. The driver of the aged Mirafiori hopped out, leaving the door swinging on its hinges. He was short, middle-aged, and of a light, agile build; he wore sunglasses and had a thick moustache, and a cigarette hung from the side of his mouth. It could have been Richie Ferguson, a bank robber who had been my mentor on a building site in Boston years before. I remembered the last time I had seen him, in Gurty's Bar on Allston Street, Cambridge. He was drunk. He had breached his parole the day before and his girlfriend had walked out on him. 'Irish,' he said, pausing to order a round for Gurty's Saturday morning clientele, 'you know what my secret is?' He leaned right into my face, his eyes swimming from narcotics and alcohol. 'I don't *give* a fuck!'

This man called out to the waiter, who indicated that I was the one. I stood up rather nervously and wished him a good day. He didn't smile back, but he extended his hand and shook mine firmly. 'Welcome. My name is Mehmet Özalp, the historian.'

I invited him to sit and ordered more tea. His English was at times hard to follow; but I gathered that he had written a book on Dinar, that he was a solicitor by profession, and that he felt it his duty to assist any foreigners with an interest in the town's past. My quest was an easy one. He stubbed another cigarette and nodded towards the Mirafiori. Fifteen minutes later we were bumping up a side road towards the village of Bülüçalan.

Bülüçalan is set in the rear of an L-shaped valley, and a river of the same name rises here. We pulled up at the point where the road first touched the watercourse. I was at once struck by the tranquillity of the place, and the fact that much of the expansive valley was wooded. Mehmet slipped down the riverbank to drink from the stream. 'This is *Menderes*,' he announced, wiping his mouth. 'From here it flows into Dinar, and joins the Suçıkan [Marsyas].'

This was just as Xenophon had described, and it was hard not to concur with the historian, and take this to be the place where Cyrus the

Younger had his palace and royal park. Removed but not remote from the city's citadel, the large and sheltered space would have given him plenty of scope to indulge his passion for landscaping; and by preserving some of the natural forest, he would have had an environment suitable for the introduction of the wild animals he is said to have hunted at his palace.

The only archaeological find of significance in the valley was made by Mehmet himself. Following a conversation with a farmer at the courthouse, he uncovered an inscribed flagstone in a cave behind the village. His excitement rose when he made out the word *MEΔIA* – a province next to Persis, but then, averting an Arundelian blunder, he discovered the prefix *NIKO*. This led him to conclude that the cave had been the retreat of a Byzantine hermit, and indeed on a prominent hill above the valley, there are the remains of an early Christian church. Mehmet suggested this was a good place to get a fuller impression of the area.

I had my doubts as to whether we were going to make it: my guide wheezed ever harder as we ascended the north slope. His legs were up to the task, but his lungs, inhaling five and six packets of cigarettes a day, were not. I began to make frequent stops to compose photographs.

In one pause, he told me, in agonizing snatches, that Alkibiades had once lived here under the protection of Cyrus. I sat him down to hear more. Alkibiades was the outstanding Athenian of his age, a charismatic leader and brilliant general who had fallen foul of intrigue by his political enemies. He was also widely mistrusted by the *demos*, who, Thucydides remarked, 'feared him for the extent of the lawlessness of his lifestyle, and his attitude towards every single thing in which he was involved'.

Alkibiades was born into a wealthy Athenian family around 450. His father was killed in battle in 447, and the boy was raised by Pericles, a relation of his mother's. Wealth, privilege, and handsome looks made him in his youth the uncrowned prince of Athens. Even then, though, his behaviour was winning him enemies among conservatives in the city. Recognizing his abilities, Socrates famously tried to avert him from a life of debauchery, but without any success. The two fought side by side as *hoplites* at Potidaia in 432, and when the young man was wounded, the philosopher stood over his body until the enemy had been beaten back. Alkibiades' shield was said to have been gold plated, and instead of *alpha* for Athens, had emblazoned on its face the love-god Eros wielding a thunderbolt.

In 420 he was elected as one of the city's ten generals. He had proven himself to be an inspirational leader on the battlefield, even if sometimes his plans were extraordinarily ambitious. In 415 he persuaded the citizens to back an expedition against Syracuse, in Sicily. Syracuse was an ally of Sparta's and the chief supplier of grain to the Peloponnesians. Her subjection would certainly change the course of the war, and some feared too that it would bring Alkibiades great popularity.

Just before the huge armada sailed in late spring of that year, the populace awoke, literally, to a monumental scandal: during the night, the genitals on all of the city's Hermes statues had been broken off. Suspicion at once fell on Alkibiades and his companions, whose drinking bouts were known to often end in high mischief. The expedition departed as scheduled, but soon after the commander was recalled to answer charges of impiety.

A fair trial by the mob was out of the question, so Alkibiades slipped his escort at a port in southern Italy and sailed to the Peloponnese. He had ancestral ties to Sparta and was welcomed there, albeit warily. The caution of his hosts was not misplaced, for it was discovered that while a royal guest, he had seduced the wife of King Agis.

Now wanted in both Athens and Sparta, he fled to Asia and the court of Tissaphernes. The Persian, seeing that he could be useful in his grand design of 'allowing the Hellenes to wear one another out', invited him into his circle. Alkibiades assumed the role of confidant, and came to consider himself so influential that he told his countrymen that 'if they would give up the democracy, and make it possible for the King to trust them', he would be able to bring the Persians over to their side.

In 411 he was granted his long-wished-for reprieve, although he did not return to Athens until four years later. The interval he spent brilliantly warring in the Propontis, winning a string of naval victories and ensuring that the channel was kept open for Athenian grain ships. Xenophon, in his history, of Greece described the exile's return:

Dense crowds of people, not only from the Piraeus but from Athens itself, gathered around the ships as he sailed in. Everyone wanted to see and to wonder at the sight of the great Alkibiades. He, it was said, was the best citizen they had, and he alone had been banished not because he deserved it but because of the intrigues of people who were inferior to him in power, who lacked his abilities to speak, and whose only political principle was their own self-interest.

Hellenica I.4

Alkibiades was elected supreme commander and sailed off four months later with all the hopes of his countrymen on his shoulders. But his enemies again succeeded in undermining him: he was blamed for a defeat of the navy under his second-in-command, and the people voted him out.

Despondent, he sailed to an estate in the Hellespont, and then, on the capitulation of Athens in 404, took refuge in the interior. It is at this point that he would have come to Cyrus, a young man no doubt greatly impressed with the deeds of this larger than life character. Mehmet believed the prince had set him up on a nearby estate called Çölova. As I listened, I was captivated by the thought that the pair might once have ridden in the valley beneath, the general perhaps being sounded out on the great enterprise being contemplated by the prince. Whether or not Cyrus sought to enlist him in his cause is unknown, for he was murdered soon after, probably by the Spartans, who were fearful of his influence over their defeated enemy (and no doubt still annoyed over the affair with the King's wife).

The place of his assassination, Mehmet said, was marked by a monument erected much later by the Emperor Hadrian, though this has never been discovered, and the whereabouts of Alkibiades' dwelling in Phrygia are disputed.

Cyrus stayed 30 days in Kelainai, and was joined here by the remainder of his Greek forces. His leading general, Klearkhos the Spartan, arrived from the Chersonese (Thrace) with a 2,000-strong force; Sophainetos of Arcadia came with 1,000 *hoplites*, and Sosis of Syracuse with 300. Cyrus held a review of the Greek troops in the park, and their number was around 13,000, giving him a fighting strength of over 30,000. His catapult was now loaded. But to keep the King in doubt, he faced it away from Persia, and proceeded to march north-west.

4

The Xenophontic Question

A4–8: Kelainai to Tyriaion

The study of Xenophon is a slippery business. He will stand when his critics have fallen. He was not a man of great intellect. One has only to compare his Socratic dialogues with those of Plato to see that. Nor did he have the lofty detachment or intellectual rigour of a Thucydides. His philosophy is second-hand and second-rate, his history moralizing memoirs. He was at his happiest when far removed from what he regarded as the debasing trivialities of sophists' talk. But though plain, he is never transparent. His fate has been to be read by schoolboys and to be puzzled over by scholars ... the Anabasis *is his least perplexing and his most enthralling book. If we had Sophainetos and Ktesias, much would be clearer. But we may be sure that, unlike Xenophon, they would be read by very few.*

George Cawkwell

Cyrus had declared at the outset that his intention was to expel a troublesome tribe, the Pisidians, from his territory. According to Xenophon, no one outside of his personal counsel, and the Spartan general Klearkhos, was aware of the enterprise's true purpose. To underline his deception the prince now set a course north-west towards the province of Mysia: had it been his intention to march against the King – an aim suspected by Tissaphernes, already on his way to Susa – he would have been expected to proceed north-east from Kelainai to meet up with the Royal Road.

There was, besides the imperative for secrecy, a second reason why Cyrus judged it necessary to mislead his own army, the Greeks especially. Had the Westerners known what his real object was, it is likely that most would not have taken up his offer of employment. To them, the idea of marching into the King's backyard would have seemed like a foolhardy exercise, one most likely to end in death or slavery. Such a conviction would not have been based solely on logic – an assessment of the formidable power commanded by the 'Great King', as the Greeks called the Persian monarch. Vivid still in their collective memory was the image of the smouldering Athenian Acropolis, burned to the ground by Xerxes during his brief occupation of Hellas three generations before. Indeed, the shock of this violation engendered a fear so profound in the Western mind, that it would never go away.

When exactly Cyrus planned to inform his soldiers of his plan is not clear. He may have been thinking that the closer he could get them to Babylon, the better the chance he had of persuading them to go on. But he would find that the Greeks weren't easy to dupe, or to persuade.

The first stage from Kelainai – the fourth of the expedition in the scheme of Xenophon – took the soldiers out along the Maeander Plain to the city of Peltai, a distance of 50 kilometres. Here the Greeks celebrated a religious festival. Games were organised by Xenias the Arcadian, and Cyrus attended them with his entourage.

Pausanias, the author of a second century AD guide to Greece for Roman pilgrims, speaks of this festival being observed in the Peloponnese. He says it was initiated by an early king of Arcadia, who founded a city dedicated to Zeus on Mount Lykaios and celebrated games there in his honour. Human sacrifice seems to have been involved for he goes on to say that the King slit the throat of a baby at the altar of the god, whereupon he was transformed into a wolf. 'Ever since ... a man has changed into a wolf at the sacrifice to Lykaian Zeus.' No mention is made of this happening at Peltai, only that athletic games were held, and that the winners were awarded the prizes of golden strigils, instruments used in bathing to remove dead skin.

The fact of the Lykaian Festival having being observed, and Xenophon's statement that Cyrus was in attendance at the games, highlights in the first instance how important the Peloponnesian mercenaries were to his cause; it additionally shows that religion played an important part in the lives of the soldiers, a fact repeatedly borne out in the narrative of Xenophon.

From another perspective, the marking of the festival is valuable in that, if its celebration date were known with certainty, a precise dating of Cyrus' departure from Sardis would in turn be possible. A German scholar of the nineteenth century, Karl Koch, came up with a date of 6 March for the start of the expedition, and though his chronology has generally been accepted by commentators, it is not based on any fixed date. A recent objector has linked the Lykaian Festival, via the Lupercalian of the Romans, to the vernal equinox, suggesting a departure from Sardis in early February. But Tmolos is covered in snow at this time, and the auxiliaries would surely not have come from Greece in the midwinter.

After three days at Peltai the army marched north to the Keramon Agora ('potters' market'), a distance of 60 kilometres covered in two days (A5). Xenophon says this was a populous city, close to the Mysian border.

From here they turned east and marched 150 kilometres to the Kaÿstrou Pedion, an inhabited city. The text says that this stage (A6) was completed in three days, but this must be an error, as the terrain in this region would have made such a rate practically impossible for a large train. Nor is it clear why Cyrus would want, at this early stage, to push his army to such a limit. On balance the likelihood is that there is a transcription error – a case perhaps of a later transcriber recording three instead of, say, five days. This anomaly does none the less raise the question of Xenophon's recording method, if indeed there was one at all.

From the *pedion* (a 'common') Cyrus skirted a low range of mountains fronting the plain (A7), and continued east to Tyriaion (A8), where he put on a display of arms for the Queen of Kilikia.

*

I stayed in Dinar a week. Mehmet insisted that I move into his home, and he had a new place of interest to take me every day. He lived in a new block of apartments on the east side of the town. This, and a series of others, had been built by the Government following a devastating earthquake in November 1995. The Kandilli Observatory in Istanbul – whose first recording after its opening in 1925, incidentally, was of a tremor in Dinar – registered the quake at a massive 7·8. Mehmet looked hard at the ceiling of his living room as he tried to find words to describe it. 'A bomb exploding slowly' was how his eventual comment translated.

Mehmet's wife, his second, was called Pınar ('spring'). A good deal younger than him, she was an attractive, warm-spirited woman. The marriage had produced one child, a precocious four-year-old girl called Nehir ('river'). She was the centre of attention, and adept at getting her way; if her father forbade her to do something, she would retire to a corner of the room and stand there with her head bowed until Mehmet said 'Tamam', whereupon she would race over and throw her arms around him. I found her a good subject on which to practise my Turkish. So long as I kept her in sweets, she wasn't at all fussy about word endings and seemed to understand everything I was saying.

Mehmet had two sons from his first marriage, one a professional footballer in Izmir, the other a student in the same metropolis. Neither of them spoke to him any more. Walking out on a marriage for love has not yet become socially acceptable in Turkey.

On the day I left, Mehmet walked with me out along the Maeander. We departed on a rise in the road overlooking the river, now enormous and assuming its character. It was the first time I had seen it out on the open plain, and regretted having doubted Ovid.

Mehmet was still waving on the road when I turned around for the last time. I found it hard to leave him and his family and friends. They had all looked after me so well, I felt like I had been at home.

Leaving the town I also left behind a group of travelling companions who had been with me since the start. The Reverend Arundel and his party were heading south for new discoveries, while I was off north-west along the river with Ainsworth. He had his work cut out. Cyrus' decision to take a roundabout way from Kelainai to the Konya Basin meant that his movements on these stages were always going to be more difficult to follow for future historians. Less well-travelled areas of the ancient world were less well attested in the texts, and Xenophon's descriptions alone rarely provide enough for researchers to go on. Today, only one of the places named in this part of the narrative (A4-8) has been positively identified: a fountain on the roadside before the village of Ulupınar ('great spring').

An early solution to the problem of recovering this portion of the march was proposed by a contemporary of Ainsworth's, William Hamilton. His method was to work backwards along the main road from Ikonion (modern Konya), the terminus of the ninth stage, using the distances given by Xenophon for the various marches. The single fixed point, the Fountain of Midas, which occurs near the end of the seventh stage, confirmed that his figures were reasonable, and that the army had passed along the base of the Sultan Mountains.

Extending the line back from the fountain almost the whole length of the seventh stage brought him to the fringe of an expansive flat wetland (the Bolvadin Plain), a striking feature of the landscape which might have earned a local city the epithet *pedion* (Kaÿstrou Pedion).

Hamilton next jumped to Kelainai and fanned out along the Maeander Plain looking for another *pedion*. Games were held at Peltai, where the fourth stage ends, and this suggests the presence of a common near to the city. There are a few in the area: Hamilton selected one near Işıklı on the north of the plain; there is another which I passed through beyond the village of Dedeköy in the centre of the plain.

With coordinates for Peltai and the Kaÿstrou Pedion, in theory it is possible to pinpoint the whereabouts of Keramon Agora, the city about which least is known. Hamilton's lines, taken the requisite distances along the main roads, intersect just north of the modern city of Uşak, which he judged to be a good candidate for the missing city. '[It is] a place of considerable commerce and traffic in the present day; many of the high roads of Asia Minor pass through it, and it is therefore well deserving the appellation of *Agora*, given to it by Xenophon.'

For all its neatness, however, this is an imperfect solution to the problem of locating the lost city. As has been noted, the value of the *parasang* is not certain, and Hamilton's method of arriving at a figure – he calculates a global rate based on local means – is flawed, even if the result, 4 kilometres, is reasonable. Subsequent commentators using the same approach have thus come up with different results, though the distribution of 'X's marking Keramon Agora is roughly concentrated along a busy corridor between Uşak and Banaz, a town 30 kilometres to the north-east. According to my own figures for the stages, the site would have been in the vicinity of Susuz, a village 10 kilometres south-west of Banaz. South of Banaz itself there are numerous *tells*, and the farmers hereabout seem to possess abundant quantities of ancient coin.

*

In walking the route I had little expectation of shedding any light on the more obscure locations of the march. I wasn't seeking to do this, but rather to discover what remained, and to try to see the world through the eyes of the soldiers. That I was having some success with the latter occurred to me quite early on, when I noticed that I was developing an ability to read the landscape – a gradual shift from an aesthetic to a practical appreciation of natural features. After several months I could judge with some accuracy the distance across a valley, and work out the most efficient way to get to the other side. Before I started, if asked these things on the ground, I might have guessed a number of kilometres and pointed in a straight line. Now I'd look for elevation, or the line of a ridge that would avoid soft ground in the sump, and judge the distance in time.

Walking brought out the meaning of places in a way just visiting them could never do. The barren approach to Dinar, for example, invests that town with an aura of mystique and power long before it comes into view. To the soldiers it must have felt like being on a grand processional way – the earth cleared out of deference to the Great King.

A booming fountain opposite a petrol station in the shadow of the Sultan Mountains makes for an impressive sight: if you arrive at it on a hot afternoon after a 30-kilometre walk, it's an unforgettable sight; and the experience of bathing in it is equally memorable. '*Buz gibi!*' a youngster shouted as I swanned off the edge of a concrete pump casing. It was as he had warned, ice, somehow in unfrozen form. I shot up to the surface and left the pool with much less grace than I had entered. Xenophon's inclusion of this fountain in his narrative is widely thought to be on account of its mythical association with King Midas,* but I'm inclined to think it stood out in his mind for the same reason it does in mine.

An area I was hoping my journey would shed some light on was the question of how Xenophon remembered things. Did the author record detail of the march in a 'diary' or construct the narrative from memory?

Given the considerable time lapse between the events and the publication of the *Anabasis* (reckoned by some to be as much as thirty years), the argument for a diary seems compelling. Certainly the early commentators

---

* He says that the Phrygian king, Midas, captured Silenos here by mixing the water with wine. This story, repeated by Pausanias, may be a variant of the better-known one, where, as a reward for helping his wayward tutor, Dionysus granted Midas his wish of a golden touch. The former version seems to suggest that Silenos was ransomed to the god.

were of this view. Bunbury in his authoritative *History of Ancient Geography* (1883) wrote:

> It seems absolutely necessary to suppose that some such notes were preserved by Xenophon, otherwise it would have been impossible for him to have given the details of the march with the care and accuracy which distinguish them in all those parts of the route where we are able to verify them with any certainty. We know that the *Anabasis* – at least in the form in which it is now preserved to us – was not composed until many years after Xenophon's return to Greece ... It is however probable that the work may have been in great part composed long before, or at least that he may have committed to writing some brief commentaries concerning the events which he had witnessed, while they were still fresh in his memory. But the whole series of marches and distances traversed could hardly have been preserved otherwise than by being committed to writing at the time; and there is certainly nothing improbable in such a supposition.

A thousand years before the Greek golden age, war reporting was an established practice of the Egyptians. Scribes accompanying a pharaoh's army would record in a 'day-book' details of each march – where the army started from, where they finished, events of note during the day – and after the campaign's finish, these documents would form the basis of a summary which would be inscribed on temple walls. So there is nothing improbable in the suggestion that Xenophon kept a diary. And if he didn't keep notes, as many modern scholars contend, how could the journey have been remembered in such detail?

One answer is that he could have used extant sources to find information on subjects such as the Persian road system. Ktesias, a wandering Greek who became the personal physician of the King, penned a history of the empire in his spare time, and one of his books gives details of imperial routes. He must in turn have based this section on some pre-existing imperial document.

Those in favour of the diary hypothesis counter that these writings would have been confined to the subjected areas of the Persian Empire, as large tracts of its outer regions were not under the control of the centre. Bureaucrats or travellers could nevertheless generate statistics on the outlaw territories, and in any case, books were not the only possible source of information. Opposed by a barbarous tribe on the far bank of a river the army needed to cross in the foothills of the Pontic Mountains (*Anabasis* IV), Xenophon wrote that he was approached by one of the soldiers: '[He] said that he had been a slave in Athens, and that he knew the language of these people. "I think," he went on, "that this is my native country. If there is no objection, I should like to speak with them."' Slaves were a commodity in which the Greeks traded extensively: there would have been no lack of them for Xenophon to interview during his long retirement in the Peloponnese.

The positive arguments against a diary include the incompleteness of the narrative (some commentators now believe there is information missing from the record), and the author's use of 'standard' descriptions in relation to cities, a fact which points to a published source, or at least to the lack of any recollected detail.* Another, altogether more telling instance of this is the figures he gives for the widths of rivers. Unless there has been a dramatic reduction in volumes, the sizes are consistently too large. Even if the army had crossed at the widest points, at the time of the highest volume, they would still be excessive. In this case it seems probable that the culprit is an unreliable gazetteer: Xenophon sometimes has a lazy, but never a careless geographical eye.

Finally, there is the practical point that a diary in the circumstances would have been difficult to maintain. My own experience was that a diary could be kept, but it was hard to maintain regularly, and without a map (which I would try to mark every evening regardless), the details of previous days could easily be blurred into one another. For example, you could recall almost step by step the route of a particular day, but not the actual day, even though the memory may be recent. This is important as it suggests that if statistics are not noted at the end of a hike, or very soon after, the integrity of the record is liable to be undermined.

For the admirers of Xenophon who do not accept the existence of a diary, an uncomfortable matter has to be confronted. Granted that all the route detail he supplies could have been derived from existing sources, what of his column for rest days? Whenever the army halted, he tells us for how long: a week in Kolossai, thirty days in Kelainai, three days at Peltai, five on the Kaÿstrou Plain, three at Tyriaion, twenty at Tarsus. If there was no diary, the inference has to be that they are a fiction. Personally, I'm tempted to view these as arbitrary 'measures of delay': he recalls a long stay at Tarsus, a longer one at Kelainai, there were games at Peltai, and a review at Tyriaion, and so on.

One suggested compromise on the diary issue is that somebody else did record the march details. It is quite possible that Cyrus assigned

---

*Cities along the route are described by either one or a combination of set adjectives: *megale* (big), *oikoumene* (inhabited) and *eudaimon* (prosperous).

someone to do so, perhaps envisaging, like Darius before him, his deeds being immortalized on the walls of Persepolis: 'I...I...I...I...I the King.'

More mundanely, some type of record would have had to be kept for payment of the mercenaries. In either case, it is not inconceivable that Xenophon could have made a copy for himself, annotating it on his review for recollections that must have rushed into his head.

5

The Queen of Kilikia

On the Road

On Kaÿstrou Pedion he halted five days. At this time more than three months' pay was due to the troops, and they went to his tent to seek it. Cyrus had to put them off, and was evidently upset; for it wasn't like him to hold back pay if he had it. Then Epyaxa, the wife of Syennesis the king of Kilikia, came to visit Cyrus, and it was said she presented him with a large sum of money.

Anabasis I.2

O ur sense of place – our ability to orientate, and to judge speed and distance – has probably been in decline for some time; the commencement might be traced as far back as the end of nomadism, when settlement rooted communities. Undoubtedly many of our most sophisticated survival instincts began to weaken at this time; indeed, there is a view that at this critical point, evolution itself may have begun to stop.

A link between rootedness and disconnection imposed itself on my mind following an experience at a small town called Tınaztepe. This sits on a low eminence at the end of a fertile plain west of Afyon, and is separated from that city's hinterland by a long set of robust hills. The location is distinguished by a mountain stack which stands away to the left as you approach from the plain, a prominent landmark that I guessed had for centuries guided traders and armies through the range. Cyrus and his force would have slipped through a gap in the shadow of the stack (through which the modern road winds), but I was planning to cross the remoter middle section, it being a more direct way to the plain at the stage end (A6). On my map there was a village, Büyükkalecik ('big little castle'), on the other side, and I was using this as a waymark. However, according to those I asked in Tınaztepe, there was no path there, and it was thought the village, which some had never heard of, was impossible to reach in a day.

I wasn't convinced. On the map – which had not proved to be infallible, which was why I was asking – the direct distance was no more than 10 kilometres, double this at most by a *keçi yolu* (goat path). Looking at it, I had guessed that I could get onto the ridge in a couple of hours, but I didn't know what the terrain would be like on the other side, or whether there would be any settlement at hand should I run into difficulties.

The odd thing was that when I asked about the distance to a village mapped a way south of their town – thinking I might walk there and start over the hills early in the morning – I was told that it was a short stroll, 'a cigarette smoke' away. It wasn't; and nor, it transpired, was Büyükkalecik nearly as far as they had made out. I came in sight of it the following afternoon, after what had been a circuitous hike down a gorge and up into the hills. I recognized its relative location from the high stack, and after persisting, learned that there was a path leading over the range. Its very obscurity was enough to make clear that few people ever used it, and consequently that there was little contact between the neighbours on either side of the divide: to each, the other might as well have been in a different province. Similarly, the village south of Tınaztepe was very familiar to the Tınaztepelis, and because of this, they had a tendency to underestimate the distance to it. These perceptions were two aspects of the same unnatural phenomenon. I had no doubt that if the people hadn't been settled for so long in the one place, their sense of distance would have been that much more real. An early understanding of the phenomenon, which I came to know as 'Tınaztepe's Law', was to save me much energy and time in later stages.

With the hills crossed it was a lazy day's walk east to the plain of Bolvadin. This part of the country is low-lying, marshy terrain, a vast bowl that had once been submerged. On the map the Eber and Akşehir lakes, surrounded by waterlogged flats, have the appearance of large puddles drying up after a downpour. Xenophon's Kaÿstrou Pedion will probably have been located on the slightly elevated ground that extends from the foothills. Cyrus camped here for five days, as there was a problem with money.

Since they had enlisted with Cyrus, the Greeks had received no money. Most had paid their own passage to Sardis, and had to maintain themselves on the march, buying provisions from the traders who followed in the wake of the expedition. With their savings running low, they now approached the prince and asked about their wages. Cyrus, however, seems to have run out of money; or rather he was probably experiencing what accountants today would call a cash-flow crisis. With a sizeable income from his satrapies and the patronage of his mother, money was not in short supply, but he was not a man to hold on to it for long. He never spared on expenses, and his generosity was renowned: if somebody sent him a gift he would send one back of twice or ten times the value, and anyone who did him a service could be sure of a handsome reward.

As luck would have it, while they were encamped on the common, the Queen of Kilikia came to see Cyrus. She arrived in a covered carriage, like those used by Persian royalty, and was escorted by Kilikian and Aspendian guards.

Kilikia was a small but prosperous kingdom on the southern Asia Minor coast. Enjoying the natural protection of the Taurus Mountains, it had for centuries resisted attempts to subject it. Within the Persian Empire it had autonomous status, its ruler being called Syennesis (the hereditary title of the native rulers) rather than satrap. The current Syennesis' wife, Epyaxa, was reputed to be of great beauty, and perhaps this was a factor in her being chosen for this mission, for Cyrus – though he was much devoted to his Greek mistress, Aspasia – was known to have a weakness for fine women. Syennesis' concern must have been that if the prince were to pass through his territory, and then march on the King, as was being rumoured, he would be compromised in the eyes of the latter. What he therefore was probably hoping to do was persuade Cyrus to turn onto the Royal Road, which was just a day's march north from the common, and to complete his journey by this way. (From Ktesias, the King's doctor, we learn that he simultaneously sent his eldest son to Artaxerxes, warning him of his brother's advance.)

When the Kilikians had set up their quarters, Cyrus went to the Queen's tent and did not appear again until morning. Then the soldiers were paid their arrears, and one month in advance. But whatever talks might have been held between them, Cyrus did not change his course; on the recommencement of the march the army headed in a south-easterly direction toward the Taurus Mountains, and the Queen travelled alongside. Some said she had fallen in love with him, and proof of this came a few days later at Tyriaion, when she begged him to show her his army. Cyrus, beholden to her for the gifts, gave the order for the men to muster.

The native troops were reviewed first. In their various tribes they streamed past the gallery, brandishing their weapons, and chanting the war cries of their countries. The size and bearing of this diverse host much impressed Epyaxa.

When they had passed, Cyrus led the review party out to where the Greeks had been arraying. They had ordered in a four-deep formation, so that their line extended for some 3 kilometres across the plain. The men were fully armed and armoured, their red dress tunics flowing in the wind. The prince and his guests rode along the front line, and when the inspection was completed, he sent word to the generals to have the troops present arms and prepare to advance.

The phalanxes acted on their instructions at the one signal. A forest of spears shot into the air and mighty shields lifted from the ground. At the second sounding of the *salpinx*, the Greek trumpet, they moved forward, each rank in step with the other, spears lowering for attack. Then somebody quickened the pace, and the war-cry to Ares spontaneously rang out. Chaos ensued ahead. The review party broke: Epyaxa was thrown to the floor of her chariot as the driver gave speed; the native troops at the camp downed weapons and ran, and even the traders abandoned their stalls. Only Cyrus and his guard remained on the field.

Just as they were upon the Persians, the Greeks broke off their charge, demobbing in laughter and general high spirits. In spite of the embarrassment their feigned mutiny caused to the commander, he was reported to have been delighted at the panic they instilled in the natives. Epyaxa, too, when she returned was full of praise for the splendour and discipline of the army.

*

Walking as a means of travelling exposes you to the world in a way we're not used to. In a car the driver has the protection of his or her metal shell, and the respect that comes from the prosperity which owning this implies; the cyclist can rise on his pedals and be off when he sees a group of young men idling outside a teahouse in the middle of nowhere; but on foot there's no escape, and on your own you're more likely to be approached than if you are in a group. In fact there's no doubt at all that once spotted you will be approached. People from as far as ½ kilometre away will down tools and hare across a field to thrust their hand in your face: *Nereye?* ('to where?')

In my early days in rural Turkey I found this behaviour vaguely welcoming, but in time it became more and more like an invasion of personal space. I might have accepted this intrusion as a cultural difference, but respecting other people should be a universal value. And I knew besides that if I were in a car they wouldn't be so presumptuous as even to disregard a greeting.

I learned to deal with this situation in different ways. One was to avoid making any eye contact. Looking at another person is an invitation for communication. Without it, even the most burgeoning curiosity can be stayed. A whole mob can be held in check by an individual who ignores them and does not give any indication (such as quickening pace, or trying to act the big fellow by pausing) that he is aware of their presence. In general I didn't like doing this because, in rural Turkey at least, there were hardly any mobs, and the people were only curious, albeit they could have a very direct way of expressing it.

Another, more positive, way was to take the initiative. For example if I saw a farmer in his field, and especially if he didn't see me first, I might pace towards him and call out a greeting and ask what he was planting. Next I'd barrage him with questions about directions, and even as he answered would be on my way again. This also worked with groups, the trick here being to choose the right individual to engage. Actually as a rule of thumb anyone would do except the leader (who could feel obliged to befriend you), or, if there was one, a dozy-looking character on the periphery, the selection of whom for advice called your whole judgement into question. And the object was to get their respect, so that they wouldn't feel at liberty to treat you as a nonentity, such as the lack of any means of transport implied you were. In most cases the bond held long enough for me to be out of sight, at about which time I imagined it would be dawning on them that they knew nothing of who I was, and that another foreigner might not pass by their doors for several years.

My relationship with drivers was always an uneasy one. Living with them meant noise, danger, and intrusion – in what measure largely depended on the place and the type of road. Highways only had the benefit that you were largely ignored, save for the odd trucker who felt obliged to blast you with his horn and flash the lights as he passed. Urban traffic in Turkey (Istanbul excepted) is more civilized than in other Mediterranean countries, Greece especially. Greek drivers operate on the principle that pedestrians are inferior, like bugs that deserve treading on. They think this because the car is bigger, and like any stronger beast it has the natural right of way, anywhere and everywhere, even on pavements should a jam prove intolerable.

On the backroads a passing vehicle would invariably slow, and then sometimes stop a short way ahead, not to offer a lift, but to find out exactly what was going on. '*Nereye? Nerelesi? Niye?*' Once it was established that I wasn't on the road from poverty they might gesture to the back seat, even though I had just done my best to explain that I was purposely walking. The reaction of the Arabs, I would later discover, was notably different. In general they were more appreciative of my aims, and readier to try to imagine the scale of the journey.

I was only involved in one accident. It happened about 3 kilometres outside the town of Çivril on the fifth stage of the journey. I had spent the previous night on a plain to the south of the town, and, as usual, had risen early to take advantage of the cooler hours. Ideally I'd walk from 5 to 11 a.m., and then if I had the urge I might go another hour in the evening. In the beginning at least this was rare; as soon as I had my tent pegged, or had got a room in a teahouse or a hotel, I would flop down and stay there until hunger forced me up.

It was after 7 a.m. when I left Çivril. I'd had breakfast in the market and had spent some time afterwards examining the sizeable fish that had come in from the Maeander. I imagined that the soldiers had feasted on fish during their three-day festival on the plain at nearby Peltai, and I was thinking that they were probably the same species.

The road out of the town rose steeply and then levelled away in a straight line towards Uşak. For a provincial road it was quiet. None the less, I was alert because there had been a heavy shower and the sun was shining into the oncoming lane. I saw the vehicle, a white minibus (*dolmuş*), a long way off. It was travelling too fast. I could hear the noise of the engine rise as the vehicle hit bumps on the uneven surface. The driver didn't see me until almost the last second: he swerved slightly and touched the brakes, the effect of which was to send him aquaplaning towards the far side of the road. I turned and watched as the vehicle went on and on, and finally slid into the side ditch.

Dropping my pack, I raced back down the road. Several times I glanced behind to see if there were any cars coming, but there was nothing in either direction.

The minibus had kept its wheels: it stood at a right angle to the road, its flat front square against the ditch floor. I jumped into the trench and peered through the windows. It was empty except for the driver, who was trying to wind down the window. I yanked open his door and helped him out. He was mumbling away but appeared to have suffered no injury.

Once he had gathered himself, we made a cursory inspection of the vehicle. I opined that the road was dangerously slippery after the rain, and that it was lucky he'd had no passengers with him. He agreed, adding he had just been on his way to collect a group of factory workers.

Climbing back onto the road, we flagged down the first car that passed. This took the driver in to Çivril, while I continued on towards Banaz.

*

Walking made me more alert to the natural world. Sheltering under trees from the midday sun prompted me to learn their names, and to note the sort of places they liked to grow. The poplar (*kavak*), tall and thin, has a great thirst and if it gets enough water grows at an extraordinary rate. Two varieties are grown in this part of the world, oddly, known as Persian and Greek. Inverting the old stereotypes, the latter is said to grow at a faster rate, but the wood of the oriental is of a better quality. Farmers plant the *kavaklar* in regiments on marshy ground, and also by rivers, where they double as sunscreens for workers in the fields. Of a summer's evening you often see the landowner strolling like a king through the long colonnades of whispering leaves.

Plane (*çınar*) trees have an even bigger thirst than poplars and grow to be much bigger, and they say they can live for many hundreds of years. Their trunks are huge, their barks smooth, their leaves like green ghosts flying in the breeze. Turks like to plant them in town squares, by a pool if there is one, a practice borrowed by the Greeks from their Ottoman governors. In both cultures the tree is seen as a sign of prosperity.

The cypress (*servi*) is like a slender hedge reaching to the sky. 'Egyptian obelisks' was how Van Gogh, a great walker and lover of trees, described them. Their fate through much of history was to carry Mediterranean sailors to battle, and now they have an equally noble function, encircling the graveyards of Anatolia. Even in death the Turks like to be surrounded by beauty.

Like the trees, birds were ubiquitous, and it became a habit of my walking hours to observe them. By far the most eye-catching was the stork. Enormous, with long, pink legs trailing beneath a huge wingspan, they would fly low over the plains in pairs in search of prey. Coming upon a likely spot, they would land and trawl the fields on foot for insects and small creatures, which you could occasionally see dangling from their beaks as they headed back to the nest. Of a relaxed, almost arrogant temperament, they were remarkable for both their indifference to humans – it wasn't unusual to see one strolling past a farmer weeding in his field – and to heat. Indeed, it was when the sun was at its hottest that they seemed to be most comfortable. While other creatures at midday sought shelter, they basked in their open nests on the tops of telegraph poles and minarets. The birds are held in high regard by the Turks, who may preserve some belief about a link to fertility.

Turks hold dogs in less esteem, or perhaps it's just that we value them too highly. In the villages everyone has one, mongrels with lots of sheepdog in them. They're lean animals, fit from exercise and hardened by exposure to all weathers. They don't have name tags or collars, although sometimes an owner will attach a leather nail-strap to the neck of an aggressive male to protect his throat in rows. One of these animals bounding towards you with fangs bared is one of the unforgettable sights of rural Turkey.

In many of the mountain villages, where the studded collars are popular, they shear the ears off sheepdogs in the belief that it makes them hear better. My experience was that this wasn't necessary, for I found the non-mutilated ones to be highly effective the way they were. Long before I entered a village they'd appear beneath lopsided gateways, or on top of mud walls, ready for action. (I suspected after a while that the tap of my walking stick was giving me away, and found that putting it away as I approached did sometimes forestall an unpleasant welcome. But once one was alerted, they all were.)

It was rare to be hounded out of town by a pack. Most dogs stuck to their own patch, snarling at a respectful distance until they had forced you into their neighbour's territory. Only if you paid too much attention might one be tempted to pursue, believing that you were afraid of him because of his fearsomeness. Volatile situations usually only arose where there was a surfeit of young dogs, yet to acquire the discipline of their craft. These, and certainly the mature canines would rarely, if ever, risk a nip at flesh, although it's not unheard of. The Bolvadin Plain in the west of Anatolia is one place travellers on foot should be wary of.

*

The army of Cyrus would have faced a different set of problems on the road. Maintaining sufficient supplies would have been the biggest. To make this job easier the commander may have timed the march to coincide with the grain harvest, and he may also have established food dumps at certain points along the way. In addition the baggage train is known to have included 400 wagons of flour and wine, kept aside for the eventuality of a severe shortage.

Drinking water was another concern. Rivers rather than wells will have been the main source, and in summer many of these will have been dry. However the ancient soldiers were more durable than their modern counterparts, and could march for long periods without it; and bad sources had little effect on their insides. Similarly the sun posed few problems: the Greeks in particular were renowned for their indifference to heat. They were hard men.

Ancient soldiers were normally responsible for looking after themselves. There were no cooks to feed them, or quartermasters to conjure new clothes or footwear. Most of what they needed they bought from a 'travelling market' – an army of traders who tagged onto expeditions offering for sale an array of goods and services. The soldiers were given a supplement for this, a sum in addition to their monthly pay.

The market was typically the biggest component of the large non-combatant group that accompanied all expeditions of the time. Other followers included the baggage carriers, entertainers, carpenters, spear makers, and soothsayers. The size of the group tended to increase or decrease depending on the fortunes of the army, but would usually, as an expedition progressed, be swelled by numbers of slaves taken from enemy territories.*

Cyrus' expedition would not have been typical given his concern for speed. His care for the food supply would have discouraged many

---

*An indication of the possible size of the 'camp-followers' is given by Diodoros, who describes an expedition by King Agesilaus of Sparta against the Persians in 396. 'Here [at Ephesus] he enlisted 4,000 soldiers and took the field with his army, which numbered 10,000 infantry and 400 cavalry. They were also accompanied by a throng of no less number which provided a market and was intent on plunder.'

traders, whose prices were determined by supply and demand; nor would the ostensible object of his mission, the tribal Pisidians, have inspired hopes of extraordinary profits. He may also have imposed some limit on their numbers. Though this would have been unusual, later in the march the soldiers were ordered to abandon their possessions, including mistresses and boys, so as to make the fighting body more efficient. It was the case as well that the Persians disliked petty traders. Famously, when Cyrus the Great conquered Asia Minor in 546, the Spartans sent a messenger to warn him against harming Greek settlements. He enquired who these people were, and how numerous they were, that they addressed him in this way. On learning they were themselves Greeks, he told their messenger: 'I have never yet found occasion to fear the kind of men who set aside a space in the middle of their town where they can meet and make false promises to one another.'

An element of the non-combatant group Cyrus would not have sought to limit was the baggage carriers. On ox carts and mules, these transported the common and personal military equipment from one camp to the next. Their use allowed the troops to move practically unencumbered, and hence to complete the frequently lengthy daily marches required. This was especially important for the Greek *hoplites*, whose field armoury was substantial: a *hoplon*, two or more body-length spears, a sword and an assortment of protective armour which included a bronze breastplate and helmet. The *hoplite* panoply has been estimated to have weighed in excess of 30 kilograms.

The Greeks and the native troops would have marched apart from one another, the latter under the command of Persian officers, the former under the men who had enlisted them. In another of his works, Xenophon describes how an expedition proceeded:

The several companies marched for the most part with their own baggage next to them, for orders had been given to those who had charge of the baggage to march each near his own company … and the baggage captain of each centurion carried on the march his own ensign, known to the men of their several companies; so that they marched in close order, and every officer took great care of his own men's baggage, that it might not be left behind; and, by observing this order, they had no need to seek for each other, and all things were at hand and in greater safety.'(*Cyropaedia* VI.3)

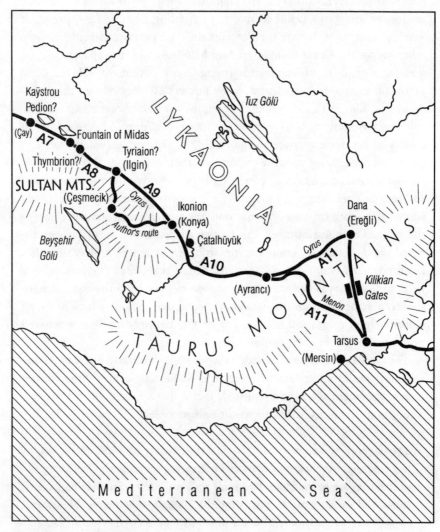

Anabasis 7-11: To Tarsus

6

Straying from the Path

A9: To Ikonion

I knew what he was going to do. Without pretending I did, I pulled
the stick in off the floor and placed it flat along the wall behind me.
Ramazan's eyebrows furrowed and he nipped his bottom lip.

It happened every time I came into the company of men. As soon as
they spotted the stick they had to hold it; and no sooner were they
holding it than they were trying to dismantle it or test its strength. The
telescopic pole was light and strong, but mine was already a seasoned
traveller, and I was concerned for the moving parts. Watching men stab
it into the ground and press their weight on it from different angles
didn't do my nerves any good. I couldn't understand how it inspired so
much fascination. There were other gadgets in my possession – a luminous compass, a Swiss army knife, a water filter – which I would have
thought would have been of more interest to them, but this seemed to
arouse some primal urge whose origins I never figured out.

Ramazan was the *muhtar* (headman) of Çeşmecik ('little fountain'),
a village in the hills south of Ilgın. He was responsible for the lives of
1,600 people, he told me, running a finger along one half and then the
other of a pencil-thin moustache. He was short and slightly built but
projected an air of confident authority. I gathered power had rested in
the Türkan family for generations. There were framed portraits of him
and his forefathers on the walls of the village meeting room, faded
black and white ones with the subjects in a rigid pose. It's still the case
that if you point a camera at a villager he will stand to attention and
stare at the lens.

The *muhtarlık* is the bottom rung of the Turkish governmental
system. The *muhtar* is elected by his co-villagers for a period of five

years, and is responsible for procuring the necessary services from the local district council (*belediye*), which is in turn answerable to the elected provincial government. There are eighty-one provinces in the country, and these are headed by centrally appointed governors. According to their population size, each province returns deputies to a National Assembly (TBMM), and the leader of the largest party usually becomes prime minister.

I had been taken to the village by Halil, a young man who had joined me on the track into the hills earlier that afternoon. By right I should have continued around these, as the army had done, but I was weary of the plain, and tempted by the prospect of a few cool days in the heights.

I had started the stage, the ninth, from near the town of Ilgın, a market centre whose western approaches may harbour the long-lost remains of ancient Tyriaion. A dipping plain a few kilometres before the town fits as a possible site for the martial display Cyrus put on for his Kilikian patron. From the site of the review, Xenophon reported, they marched for three days, a distance of 20 *parasangs*, to the city of Ikonion.

An hour's walk south-east from the plain had led into the hills, a dense range which, on my map, eventually rolled down onto the flat frontiers of the Konya Basin. A kilometre above sea level, and covering over 10,000 square kilometres in area, this is one of several steppe regions which make up the great Anatolian High Plateau. Geologically recent, this arid plateau has played a significant role in the development of human settlement and relations. Across its vast surface tribes since time immemorial have swept between continents and seas, not encouraged to settle here for its dryness, saline soils and the vulnerability which its openness imposes. For these reasons, in history it has assumed the character of barrier, a natural divide between east and west, north and south.

The *dolmuş*, making the return trip to the village from Ilgın, pulled alongside me to allow passengers to stare. It moved on a short way, and then stopped to let Halil off. He stumbled out clutching a plastic bag of purchases. I guessed that he was in his early twenties. He was of average height and build, had straight brown hair and wore a dark blazer and white open-necked shirt.

He greeted me, in reasonable English, as if we were acquainted, and apparently our paths had crossed a few days before at a petrol station in the foothills of the Sultan Mountains. I couldn't recall the encounter, though I remembered the place well enough.

*

The modern service station, despite its projected image of newness, has a lineage stretching back into the history of roads. Already in the Persian *katalusie* (way-station) its essential functions were evolved: shelter, sustenance, supplies. A unique and quintessentially Turkish addition to the architecture of travel was the *kervansaray*, the 'caravan palace'. Built along the main trade routes of Anatolia during the thirteenth century AD, these were distinguished from what went before (or has come after) by their attention to comfort and order, and their conception as monumental rather than merely functional structures. The construction and maintenance of the palaces were paid for by the sultans, at whose expense the unwieldy wagon trains refreshed themselves on their long journeys across the continent – a case of enlightened capitalism perhaps, for the state will have more than recouped its considerable outlay in the taxes levied on traded goods. (Lest a merchant had it in mind to tarry in one of the medieval motels, a limit of three days was normally set on a stay. Hence maybe the Oriental saying, 'You're a king in my home for three days.')

The Selçuk *kervansaray* had the appearance of a fortress: high walls enclosed a rectangular area, which was divided into a large open courtyard and a vaulted hall that contained stables and accommodation quarters. In the centre of the courtyard there was typically either a small mosque, or a *köşk*, a freestanding stone structure built on arches and having an external staircase to the suspended prayer room. Access to the complex was through a grand portal at one of the narrow ends. This was the defining feature of Great Selçuk architecture, its muscular quality being set off by intricate honeycomb carving and coloured tiles. Giant wooden doors, decorated with the same artistry as the surrounding stone, completed the sense of permanence.

At the very outset of my journey, on a short ramble through the port of Çeşme after my arrival there from Greece, I had come across a *kervansaray* built by Süleyman the Magnificent in the sixteenth century. Now a hotel, on my impressionable first day it had evoked a strong sense of Ottoman splendour and achievement. In particular, I recall being greatly impressed at the system which had placed this exquisite way-station at the terminus of dozens of similar ones, which I envisaged as once having formed a chain back to Armenia and the Caspian Sea.

The next one in my path was the Sahip Ata Kervansaray, a Selçuk creation situated on the busy corridor running between the Akşehir Lake and the Sultan Mountains. The army had funnelled through this way, and I thought it might have been possible that the Turkish way-station had been founded on some earlier structure, perhaps even a Persian *katalusie*.

In spite of some effort, though, I was unable to find any remains. Several locals insisted that what I was looking for was the *Kirazlıbahçe* ('cherry garden'), a themed service station that may have been inspired by the presence of the old halting place. I returned to it after a fruitless search of the foothills to the south. Disregarding the homogeneous convention, the Elf garage had been designed as a miniature castle, complete with fibreglass turrets and defence walls. Inside the façade was a homespun fast-food restaurant which had balconies looking out on the forecourt. The rear of the complex offered quieter vistas over acres of cherry orchards that sloped down to the Akşehir Lake. Relieved to find this more natural setting, I took off my boots and sat down at a table, becoming more inclined to believe as I relaxed that this might have been the site of the former halting station.

Whether it was or not, the garage was evidently a big draw for commuters. Half a dozen intercity coaches stood next to one another on the forecourt. Attendants in rubber boots and wielding hoses and brushes washed down the thoroughbreds, while the passengers refreshed themselves and explored turrets and caves. The biggest attraction was a sculpture at the front of the forecourt of Nasreddin Hoja, an Islamic teacher who, Turkish tradition has it, lived in the area in the thirteenth century. A link with Nasreddin is claimed by many communities across the Islamic world, testimony to the appeal of his rustic manner and unique brand of 'foolish wisdom'. I had come across him once before in Bukhara. He was back to front astride a donkey, with enormous feet swaying, and his mouth open as if he were about to say something profound. A Russian man passing had no idea who he was, but an Uzbek drinking tea in the square told me he was a religious figure who had come from Turkey to settle here in the time of Tamerlane.

The Elf statue was greatly inferior in quality to the one in Bukhara, but the small groups who gathered about it, drowsy from 24-hour journeys, did not seem bothered about aesthetics. As I passed a couple asked me to pose for a photo in front of the religious man with my stick.

Others enquired after my journey, and I explained I was trying to follow in the footsteps of an ancient army. Among the onlookers, on his way home from the nearby town of Çay, was Halil.

*

In the villages they have rather a narrow view of outsiders. I came to observe that three things come to a Turkish farmer's mind when he sees a person from abroad: *tureest*, Antalya, and money. Putting these in an order, his assumption is that you are a tourist, have lots of money, and are headed for Antalya (a long strip of sandy coast on the Mediterranean, the 'Turkish Riviera'). This view of a decadent infidel is strongly reinforced by the popular press, whose pages in summer are filled with semi-naked foreign women lounging on the country's beaches. I recall once in Dinar, when I was working on my reading, picking up a copy of *Güneş* ('The Sun') and finding on the front page a tall blonde woman with enormous breasts pouring a bucket of water over her chest. The caption read: 'Dutch tourist cools down in Antalya.' (I suspected that these women were models hired to fuel the fantasies of villagers the length and breadth of the country – which is not to say that foreigners don't come to Turkey in the summer months and provide some grounds for this stereotype.)

The urban view of foreigners is more balanced. They can be tourists or travellers or business people. *Yabancı* ('stranger') is a description as likely to be heard as *tureest*. The city dweller in general holds foreigners in high regard, though among some I detected early on an undercurrent of resentment towards Europeans. Given the public hand-wringing in some countries over the question of Turkey's admission to the EU, this is hardly surprising.

Regardless of how they see foreigners, Turks treat them well. A high standard of helpfulness and courtesy is to be found in all parts of the country, among all strata of society, across the ethnic divides. Invitations to eat and drink are extended to strangers with far greater frequency than in older, neighbouring civilizations. What I gradually came to see was that Turkish hospitality was informed by quite different traditions: in the cities they subscribed to a civic model developed by Atatürk – citizen as representative of the republic – whereas in the countryside behaviour was determined by cultural factors that predated the founding father. The inference might be that while his total revolution took firm hold in the urban centres, it never enjoyed the same success in the villages.

No sooner had I arrived in Çeşmecik with Halil than I was summoned to see the *muhtar*. A youth on a bicycle waiting at Halil's gate was the messenger. The *köy odası* ('village room') was situated above a shop on the raised side of a sloping square. Off the lower end was the mosque, and in front of this, a large fountain. Women, and children swinging buckets, stood about this awaiting their turn.

The shop was owned by the *muhtar*, Ramazan Türkan. His brother was the driver of the *dolmuş*, so the Türkans were, I imagined, one of few families in the village not dependent on agriculture for their livelihood. Wheat, coaxed to grow in slanting fields, was the cash crop, but with the rugged terrain, and many mouths to feed, disposable income cannot have been high. This, I remarked, was a distinct shift from the relatively prosperous life of the lowland valleys.

Soon after I had been introduced to Ramazan, a stream of village high-ups began to arrive in the meeting room. The headman greeted each one and invited him to take a patch of the floor. A samovar and large silver tray ringed with upturned glasses were subsequently brought in by two of his sons. While the tea was brewing, rolling a set of beads between his fingers, Ramazan directed questions at Halil, who relayed the story of our initial encounter and subsequent providential meeting.

They all looked as though they had burning questions of their own, but adhering to protocol, they allowed the *muhtar* to conduct the interview. In between drawn-out sips of his tea, he enquired variously as to the purpose of my walking, and the state of my financial affairs. I answered as best I could in Turkish, showing them on my map the route I was taking through the country. My immediate destination was of greatest interest, and there was much conversation about Tepeköy ('summit village'), a place I gathered none save the *muhtar* had ever been to. Tınaztepe-like, they imagined that it was some far-off destination, and I took some pleasure in proving by way of the map that it was only a matter of hours on foot from their homes. One or two shook their heads and withdrew back to their cushions, but most were convinced by the cartography.

It was decided by the *muhtar* that I would be his guest for the night. Not long after the senior men had left, dinner appeared. As with

Turkish cuisine in general, it was highly agreeable, except for one dish which I took to be a soup, but which may have been a relish or spicy sauce. Ramazan made no comment as I spooned this down my throat, washing the mild burning sensation with a jug of water. In fact he said very little during the meal. Away from his subjects he seemed an altogether less imposing character. He picked fussily over the food, and at one point tussled playfully with his youngest boy over a chicken leg.

After the meal Halil came as promised to take me on a tour of the village. There wasn't much to see. I admired the fountain and then we crossed to the mosque. Though it was several years old, it had not yet been finished, the reason being that the villagers were building it out of their own funds. No money for such projects was supplied by the Government, Halil told me, its resources being earmarked for more material things, like dams and roads.

With a drove of teenagers in tow we scaled the rickety scaffolding to get an overview of the settlement. The sun was setting as we arrived on the top rung, and we seated ourselves in a line along the wooden plank, front row for the spectacle. It's not a sight country people normally pay much attention to, and the silence of the entourage was curious rather than awed.

The chatter sparked again when I lit a cigarette.

'Are you looking for gold?' Halil asked.

'Gold?'

'Yes. They say you've come to search for hidden treasure.'

I laughed, and asked if he'd noticed a shovel amongst my equipment.

He smiled awkwardly. I could see his suspicion had not been allayed.

'It must be your interest in the ancient period, and the map.'

I now recalled how much attention they had paid to the map, and their curiosity about the hand-drawn line marking my progress. This, coupled with the likelihood that they had turned up artefacts from the soil over the years, had doubtless led them to conclude that my real purpose was not what I had said.

Halil called for me early in the morning and we went to his home for breakfast. A battery of chained dogs heralded our departure from the village just after sunrise. Halil descended as far as a dry riverbed with me. The trail finished here but by ascending the opposite slope I would meet up with a rough track that wound south over the hills.

Instead of going this way, I continued up the riverbed, into what I could see was becoming a deep gorge. I was thinking that if anyone were following me, this way I'd have a good chance of spotting them on the climb out. This climb was more challenging than I expected. The gradient was steep, and the ground overlain with a light film of gravel. Tenacious scrub provided occasional handholds, but often it was a precarious scramble from one incline to the next. Once I lost my footing, and my sunglasses flew off: I managed to retrieve them, though one of the lenses was damaged.

At length I reached a small meadow, and from there was able to move at a gentler angle towards the horizon. It was as I closed on the ridge that I realized I wasn't well: my forehead was hot and a great lethargy was creeping over me. Actually I had not felt well since that morning, but I had thought it was just tiredness, and that it'd shake off with the exertion. I was just concluding that it couldn't be food poisoning when my bowels began to churn and I had to hastily relieve myself on the spot. I suspected that the spicy sauce I had taken for soup at Ramazan's the previous night was the cause. After a short rest and a long drink I continued upwards onto the track. This was easier on me, although I could feel my body weakening with every kilometre.

The first dwelling I came to was a wooden hut situated at the apex of a side ravine. A woman hoeing her hard-won garden plot made me a bowl of *ayran*, a salty yoghurt drink that is said to be good for stomach upsets. I had only asked for water and wondered if she had seen me squatting back on the track. It seemed to work, too, for a while; but after an initial burst progress became painfully slow. My disorder meant I was stopping every twenty minutes, and each time it got more difficult to raise my pack again. I could feel my body temperature steadily rising with the morning sun.

Around 10 or 11 a.m. Tepeköy appeared beneath a ridge. It was a comparatively large settlement. Its heart was heaped up over a circular height, and on the far slopes, homes and farms spread down into a valley. Descending towards the citadel, I tried to devise a plan. My thinking was that if I got a few hours' rest, I could perhaps push on in the evening, so as to be within a (long) day's walk of Konya, where I would be able to recover properly.

Near the centre I asked a man for the *köy odası*, and assumed he was taking me there until we entered a barber's. I sat into a vacant swivel chair and accepted a glass of tea, hoping that we'd continue our journey afterwards. Questions flew at me from the patrons but I only shrugged and patted my forehead. At length a man who I thought might have been the doctor hurried into the salon. '*Sprechen sie Deutsch?*'

I shook my head. '*Nein.*'

He repeated the question in a louder voice, enunciating the syllables. '*Nein!*'

The man embarked on a rigorous attempt to disprove that I had no German. Probably this was done for the benefit of his neighbours, an unexpected opportunity to show that his years in Germany had not been totally wasted, but at the time I couldn't see beyond the annoyance of his persistence. I chose to ignore him, and finally he went away, shaking his head.

Everything after that happened quickly. Someone rushed into the salon with news that the milk lorry had arrived. It apparently came every Friday after midday prayers to collect urns and take them into the city. The German speaker appeared at the window. '*Fahren sie Konya?*' The van rattled past the shop, and I nodded. A wolf-whistle halted it, and minutes later I was lodged between two creamery employees, and on my way to the city.

It was a big disappointment to have had to interrupt the stage. Only once before, on the Bolvadin Plain, had I been forced to break off the walk – this for a short distance on account of unruly dogs. I felt, though, that if I had had to stay any longer in the barber's, I would have lost it. I had in this regard been realistic from the outset. I knew that it would be difficult to follow an orthodox point-to-point route for the entire journey, and that there would be occasions when I might have to walk stages in pieces, as I would now have to this one. But trundling towards Konya, I couldn't help thinking that if I had stuck to the right way, this wouldn't have happened. I resolved to be more disciplined on the forthcoming stages.

7

The Celebrated City of Ikonion

This, as one of the most ancient and remarkable cities of Asia Minor,
requires little notice at our hands. Pliny calls it Urbs celeberimma
Iconium; *Strabo speaks of it as small but well built.*

Ainsworth, *Travels*

I konion is one of only a handful of places mentioned in the *Anabasis*
that have been continuously inhabited since Xenophon's day.
Settlement in this city in fact goes back at least another two and a
half millennia from the Athenian's time, so it was ancient already when
the army of Cyrus encamped on the sweeping plain in which it is set.

Location has given Ikonion its longevity. Lying on the fringe of the
High Plateau, it became a strategic staging post for routes south over
the Taurus Mountains to the sea. The first to develop it were the
Hittites, the dominant power in Anatolia in the second millennium BC.
Possibly dormant after their demise, when belligerent nomads from the
west roamed the plains, the city rose again under the Phrygians. One of
their legends has it that 'Kowania' was the first place to emerge after a
great flood which destroyed all of mankind. This story may be linked to
the vacuum left by the Hittite collapse, though it is more likely to be
rooted in some cataclysmic natural event, such as those that inspired the
'flood myths' of other cultures in the Middle East. The Konya Basin
was, at one time (15,000 years ago), covered in water.

The Greeks knew the city as Ikonion (from *eikon*, 'image'), believing
that it was founded by the hero Perseus, who, they say, used the head of
the Gorgon to turn the aboriginals to stone.

On the division of Alexander's empire after his death in 323, Ikonion
became capital of the Seleukid-controlled province of Lykaonia, and
Greeks dominated its life for the next 1,400 years. Paul also found

numbers of Jews here on his first visit in 47 AD. Hostile to his teachings, they stirred up the Gentiles and drove him away in a hail of stones. Undaunted, he returned again on two subsequent missionary voyages.

Following their defeat of the Byzantine army in 1072 AD, the Selçuk Turks took control of the city. They renamed it Konya, and embarked on an impressive phase of building. The city became a showcase of Islamic vigour, and religious scholars from as far afield as Arabia and Central Asia were drawn to its mosques and madrasas. Among them was a Tadjik theologian called Baha ad-Din Valad. His young son, Jala al-Din, would grow up to write sublime poetry, and establish a mystic religious order that inspires to this day. His followers, the dervishes, knew him as the *Mevlâna* ('our guide').

The Selçuks afforded religious and cultural freedom to minorities, and this practice continued under the Ottomans, though in the larger empire the city greatly receded in importance. The Republicans threw out the Christians and proscribed the dervishes, converting their founder's shrine into a museum. The faithful, though, still come to worship, and seek inspiration from the guide's spirit.

> *Come, come, whoever you are:*
> *An unbeliever, an idolater, or a fire-worshipper, come.*
> *Our fraternity is not one of despair,*
> *Even if you have broken*
> *Your vows of repentance a hundred times,*
> *Come, come again.*

*

A visit to Konya today, insular and prosperous on the High Plateau, brings to mind the oppressive regimes of the Arabian oil belt: rows of checkout counters in supermarkets are staffed by men in aprons; alcohol is not stocked in these premises, nor is it easy to find; women are scarcely to be seen on the streets after dark, and rarely at any time in fashionable clothing. This state of being has its roots in a long religious tradition, and in the recent ascendancy of political Islam and right-wing politics. In 1999, the far-right MHP (Nationalist Action Party, a.k.a. the 'Grey Wolves') took control of Konya in local elections, and in 2002 the AK (acronym, meaning 'pure') Party swept to power. But with the army constantly monitoring democratic health, to survive all parties have to take care to remain within the bounds of the Kemalist faith. So those of a puritanical bent focus their energies on keeping the streets clean, providing affordable housing for the steady stream of migrants who come to work in the factories, and promoting and safe-guarding family values. 'ALL TURKISH CITIES SHOULD BE LIKE KONYA', a placard declares across the length of a municipal bus.

My first days in the city were spent in bed, recovering from the stomach upset I had picked up in the hills in the last stage. This was the first occasion on the journey that I had been overtaken by gastric poisoning. This good fortune was partly accounted for by a resilient stomach, and partly by the general native concern for cleanliness. Even kerbside *kebapçıs* observed some standard of hygiene, and in the coun-tryside, suspect water sources were always appropriately labelled.

The small hotel was in the centre of the city. It was run by a skittish character who I thought did his best to annoy me on my arrival. However, his establishment was cheap, and I was too ill to go elsewhere. On the plus side the place was quiet (situated on a side street off the main bazaar), and seemed to be well kept. Large Tourism Ministry posters in the reception area and on the walls of the stairways lent it a bright air. The rooms on the third floor formed a semicircle around a lounge, off which was a pleasant communal balcony. On the first morning on which I felt well enough, I went out here to take the sun, and ready myself for the bustle of the streets.

Xenophon stayed here three days with Cyrus, his only comment being that it was 'the last city in Phrygia'. It wasn't much to go on. Ainsworth seemed to have been similarly stumped by the prospect of trying to uncover some surviving sign of this briefest of visits. Departing from his habit of rigorous field investigations, he offered a cursory comment, and then set off to explore the Selçuk heritage of the city. I was of a mind to do the same thing, but I first had to make arrangements to finish the last leg of the ninth stage.

The owner pointed me in the direction of the bus station, and said I'd find a phone box on the street. I had promised a friend in Athens that I would look up an associate of his living in the city. I wasn't quite sure what he did (something in the food industry) but had been told he was friendly and keen on meeting people from abroad. The hotel wasn't far from the main post office, and I thought this would make for a conven-ient meeting place. However when I called he insisted on coming to collect me, even when I indicated that the place might be awkward to find. 'I know all hotels in the city.' To prove the point he began to list a series of names, none of which sounded similar to Ali's Dervish Pansiyon. I had to repeat this name several times over the phone, and in the end left him with the address on the card, arranging to meet at two the following afternoon.

Drifting into the adjacent bazaar, the hub of the old Ottoman city, I made my way westward. There was a distinctly oriental feel to it. Aromas from spice shops filled the air; ox carts laden with electrical goods scattered all before them in tight alleyways. On a street corner I ate a kebab and fended off a gaggle of shoeshine boys who seemed not to notice that I was in hotel-issue plastic sandals.

Coming at length upon no sign of a bus station, I enlisted the help of a man selling books outside a mosque. He stroked a white beard and frowned. There were two bus stations, one for inter-city coaches, out on the northern ring road, and the other for services within the province, south along the Karaman road. His hand twirled to impress on me his view that this could not be reached on foot. Already feeling tired after the short excursion, I took his advice and crammed into a *dolmuş*.

Most of the vehicles spluttering in the compound of the local terminal were bound for the large towns of the province. Village connections, I learned, were much less frequent; in some cases there was only a single service, departing early morning from the village, and returning again in the afternoon. The Tepeköy bus went at 2 p.m., which I figured would work out all right, as it was at least a day and a half's walk from there back to the city. It was Wednesday, so I thought I could rest the next day and meet Selim, and go on Friday, a week after I had first arrived there.

Back at the hotel I found Ali seated at the reception desk, doing his best to persuade two girls to stay. They were of Eastern European origin, tall and attractive. One of them spoke Turkish, and Ali waxed lyrical to her on the merits of his establishment, while casually knocking the reputation of a neighbouring one. 'The owner is Kurdish, you can't trust.'

Looking at him in earnest for the first time, I noted an instability in his character. Sentences were frequently separated by childish laughter; big brown eyes dilated when he became animated; and his hands were wont to paint the air in royal gestures of condescension. These traits were embodied in an ordinary middle-aged appearance.

I moved forward to get my key and he greeted me in English.

'This my friend from Ireland. Also speaking Turkish. *Nasil otel?*'

I thought this was a bit cheeky, given the confrontation we had had on the first day, and the carelessness of the directions he had given me that morning. I said hello to the girls and expressed satisfaction about the accommodation, qualifying my endorsement with a humorous reservation about Ali's sense of direction.

'I give correct direction.'

I disagreed. He reached for a map and unfurled it irritably over the desk.

'*There* is bus station.' His index finger rapped the desk like an auctioneer's hammer.

'And where are we?' I demanded.

The finger came down heavily again, this time with only a glance at the map, and I rightly suspected he was pointing nowhere near the hotel.

His face reddened as he scanned the map for our location. I saw the young Poles eyeing one other, and then they scooped up their backpacks. Ali hurried down the corridor after them. 'I give first night free. No pay for shower.' I could hear his treacly voice trail onto the street as I bounded up the stairwell.

*

Selim arrived at two the next day. I was just rising from a rest when one of the staff knocked at the door to advise me he was outside. The door was ajar to allow cool air to circulate and I saw him through the gap, running his gaze over the rudimentary furnishings of the lounge.

He was a bit younger than I had expected, in his late thirties perhaps. Sturdily built, he wore cream-coloured trousers and a tight-fitting flower-print shirt. Sunglasses acted as a headband for a crop of sleek brown hair. His complexion was fair, although his eyes and bony facial features betrayed a trace of Central Asian ancestry. A broad smile came over his face when I addressed him. He shook my hand in a forceful grip. 'Welcome in Turkey.'

A barrage of questions about my journey followed. He had an idea of what I was doing from our mutual acquaintance in Athens, though he seemed unsure about certain things. 'You walked from Izmir? Why you didn't come by car?'

Having cleared up the misunderstanding, I outlined my recent progress on a map of the province, and gave him a copy of Cyrus' route. Pleased with this, he suggested we take a tour in his car.

This, a sports model of German manufacture, was parked on the footpath at the entrance to the post office. A group of villagers whose business in the city was done for the day had gathered around the machine. They stepped back as the high-powered vehicle roared into life. Selim lowered his sunglasses and activated the air-conditioning. 'Put on belt please.'

I clicked in the buckle and put on my own sunglasses, which I had managed to repair with tape after the mishap in the hills. Selim frowned when I looked at him. 'You must have replacement,' he declared, before engaging first gear.

Other cars slowed as the Mercedes prowled onto the main street. Expectant of a surge, I settled back and gripped the leather door handle, but there was no sudden acceleration, only a gentle movement up through the gears.

Mercedes was Selim's favourite make of car. He had two other models at home, one for his wife, and another for trips to Ankara. Novel features of this one were described and demonstrated as we cruised up the central thoroughfare of the city. At the lights in front of Alâettin Tepesi, the ancient and modern heart of Konya, he switched to the major landmarks. His arm pointed sharply to a minaret on top of the mound: 'Alâettin Camii.'

We circled the hill a couple of times, before pulling up in front of a religious building facing it. 'This is the İnce Minaret.'

He opened the window, as if suddenly unsure about the identification, and then threw a glance over his shoulder. 'No, I believe İnce's on the other side.'

The building we were parked outside was under repair, an understandable cause for confusion. Selim whistled at one of the workmen, who hurried over to the vehicle.

'This is what building?'

The youth looked at him blankly.

'Get the foreman.'

With this curt order Selim manoeuvred his car closer to the site to allow traffic on the outer lane of the roundabout to flow more easily. He got out to talk to a burly man in a hard hat who approached hesitantly.

As he did so I consulted Ainsworth, reading under 'Iconium' that the Injami Minareh Jami was known as 'the mosque with the minaret towering to the stars'. This was a feature, I thought, that should not have made it easy to confuse with other monuments.

'Yes, this is the Karatai Museum,' Selim announced on his return. 'İnce is on the other side.'

There was not much of a minaret on that one either, and I wondered if Ainsworth, like my guide, had been confused by the number of holy sites in the vicinity. The mystery was cleared up later back at the hotel, when I read in one of the guidebooks in Ali's library that the İnce's minaret had been severed by a lightning bolt in 1900.

I thought we might have gone in to visit one of the sites, but that seemed to be the end of this part of the tour. Accelerating into the wide-avenued commercial district, he told me the history of the company his father had founded in 1965. As part of a post-war industrialization drive, the Government had promoted the large-scale growing of grain in the vast plains around Konya, a successful enterprise which led to this region becoming known as the 'breadbasket of Anatolia'. The bigger acreages required bigger machines, and Selim's father, an engineer with an entrepreneurial eye, set up a combine harvester factory. His product range soon expanded to include a variety of heavy machinery, such as roller mills, pneumatic equipment and screw conveyors.

'We are only one of three countries in the world that is net exporter of food. Now we are in the top five of wheat growers. And one quarter of all our grain is produced *here*.' Though he had studied in the United States – as a designer of machines like his father – to my ear Selim spoke English with a slight German accent.

In the 1990s Molino Inc. set up plants in North Africa and Eastern Europe, and there were plans to expand into South America. They also had what he called a 'trading operation' in New York, and, more intriguingly, there was a concern outside Ankara which made guns for the Turkish military under licence from US makers. More than this he chose not to divulge, answering only when I enquired, that the business was managed by 'retired generals'.

After stopping for ice cream we pulled up alongside a tall office building, part of a centre that had been developed by a cooperative of Turks living in Germany. The forecourt was cast into a sort of cultural theme park, with uninspiring re-creations of national landmarks standing next to one another. I recognized straight away the travertines at Pamukkale, and Selim pointed out the Kappadokian caves, and the Düden waterfalls in Antalya.

Underneath the plaza there was a shopping area composed of a hypermarket and a clutch of stores selling high-quality Western goods. Descending by escalator, still licking our ice creams, Selim asked if there was anything I needed. I thought for a moment and shook my head.

'I will take you sunglasses.'

I thanked him but said I could have the old ones repaired.

'I don't think so. Also, you are friend of Mr Voudouroglu.'

The handful of assistants on duty in the jewellers sprang to life upon our entry. Selim led the way through to the optical department, where trays of eyewear were presently spread like speciality dishes on the glass tables in front of us. I expressed bewilderment at the choice.

'What was your last mark?' the proprietor enquired, trying hard at an American accent. I wasn't sure, as these had come as part of a two for the price of one deal with ordinary spectacles, but I thought they could have been Italian. The trays were speedily reshuffled, and my face was adorned with a succession of designer frames. Selim suggested I consider a wrap-around model from the sports selection, but apparently these couldn't easily be adapted for a prescription, so I settled for a Gucci pair that were light and close-fitting.

Taking advantage of the visit, Selim purchased for himself one of a range of Cardin diving watches that had just come in. He thought it might be useful in Antalya during the forthcoming family holiday.

Admiring our new products, we took a lift up to the rooftop restaurant. Selim ordered lightly, as he had a gym session that evening. Weights, I had gathered, were his thing. He had every sort of lifting apparatus at home, and even had equipment in his office. 'Lifting is about exercise for the body, and also for the mind.' He asked me how much I could lift, and I answered I carried up to 20 kilos on my back every day.

'For meagre frame, this is OK.'

I thought this comment was unfair, as I had lost a good deal of weight on account of my illness, but I said nothing as it made me feel less guilty about indulging in the house dishes while he nibbled on salad. Towards the end my stomach rumbled, and fearing a mighty gastric explosion, I excused myself and hastened to the toilet, but it was only wind.

Konya was comparatively prosperous, he agreed, when I ventured over coffee that for most of the people below in the theme park, it was not beyond their means to experience the real thing. He attributed the city's well-being to what he called 'order', a quality apparently brought by the political party in control of the region, the MHP. He explained that he didn't especially like this party; it was their fixation with social order that appealed to him. 'The streets are clean, there is little crime, everyone has home.'

Selim was not fond of politicians in general. Forums in Ankara and trade delegations abroad had brought him into contact with most of the leading figures over the years: Ecevit, Erbakan, Özal, Çiller. 'All politicians are the same,' he mused, as the waiter totted the bill. 'They have the same ways of thinking, the same personalities. And they are all liars.'

At the hotel in the evening Ali tried to hide his curiosity about my visitor. 'What you do today?' he asked, seating himself beside me in the lounge.

'I went out with a friend,' I answered, handing him back the guide-book I had borrowed.

'You have friend in Konya? Who is name?'

I smiled at him and took myself out onto the balcony, where other guests were relaxing after the day. The two Polish girls had hurried past while I was engaged by Ali, and I guessed that they must have been seduced by the proprietor's desperate discounting the day before. I approached them at a table at the far end of the balcony. They were both sucking on cigarettes and one was trying to open a liquor bottle. I offered to help and a plastic chair was quickly emptied of shopping bags. 'Such a terrible day,' the long blonde-haired one who spoke Turkish sighed. The other, whose name was Anya, exhaled hard. 'They follow us *everywhere*. On bus, in market … terrible!'

Having observed their less than modest dress, I wasn't that surprised by the news, though I thought it better not to lecture them. I advised instead that they learn to ignore unwanted suitors. 'They attack us!' Anya exclaimed, squeezing one of her breasts tightly in a hasty re-enact-ment of a chaotic scene near the Mevlâna Museum.

The day had so upset them that they were now having doubts about continuing with their itinerary. They had intended to go to Lake Van in the east, and from there to Nemrut Dağı, a mountain in the remote south-eastern region of the country that had a spectacular archaeological site on its summit. I could offer them no advice on these areas, though I ventured that from my experience of rural Turkey they would not encounter the same degree of harassment as here.

Their adventurous itinerary was partly accounted for by Katya's having studied Turkish in Warsaw. She had an intimate knowledge of the country from her books, but this was the first time she had visited, and she was determined to see as much as she could. Up until now it had been as she had imagined: they both concurred that the first phase of their journey, two weeks aboard a *gulet* sailing along the coast from Marmaris to Antalya, had been wonderful. 'So many people from everywhere and party on beaches,' Anya recalled, her face lighting up for the first time. We drank a toast to the sea, and then one to international friendship.

They were curious to know about my own adventures, and I produced one of the photocopies I had of Cyrus' march to show them what I was doing. The idea of traipsing through the country with all their gear instantly appealed to them. They chattered excitedly in Polish, while thoughts came into my head of intimate campfires in the wilderness.

'Yes,' Anya exclaimed, getting off her seat to hug me, 'we return to Antalya to make trek on Olympus Mountain.' Taking her onto my lap, I concealed my disappointment about this decision and refilled the glasses. Our revelry however proved too much for Ali, who had been brooding behind a newspaper at the other end of the balcony. He strode forward with his head lowered and his hands clasped behind his back.

'We have celebration, my friends?'

Anya released herself and returned to her chair. The girls stared at the owner who, following a minute of this, took his leave. (He had apparently tried to gain access to their room the previous night, and had been threatened with harm by Katya if he came near them again.)

The cold intrusion was fatal to the chemistry of the evening. The girls dipped into a Slavic melancholy which deepened the more they drank. I began to feel a little the same, and we parted for the night with sorrowful embraces.

The next day, after accompanying the Poles to one bus station, I took a *dolmuş* to the other and waited for the service to Tepeköy. I didn't linger in the village: my second appearance would doubtless prompt more questions than the first.

The winding descent from the hills was scenic and quiet: poplars, springs, birdsong. I camped for the evening by a huge reservoir, which I guessed had been engineered for the city on the plain. In the night it had a marked beauty. The blasted rock that cradled it lost its rawness, and the moon shimmered on the surface of the water.

Early the next afternoon, from way above it, I came in sight again of the celebrated city of Konya.

8

Nomads

A10: Through Lykaonia

He then went forward through Lykaonia, five days' march, a distance of 30 parasangs. This country, being that of an enemy, he permitted the Greeks to plunder.

Anabasis I.2

Cyrus' territorial control extended over Lydia, Kappadokia, and Greater Phrygia. Without the permission of the King, he was not allowed to take an armed force outside his satrapy. By crossing into Lykaonia, he was therefore challenging the authority of his brother. This, combined with the fact that they had not so far come upon any sign of their quarry, the elusive Pisidians, must have been a matter of some concern to the Greeks. Probably to divert their thoughts, Cyrus gave them permission to plunder his neighbouring territory.

Early on their traverse of the Lykaonian land, the Greeks would have passed a remarkable sight, though in all likelihood they would have had no idea of its significance. Separated by a dry river bed, the two overgrown mounds would not have suggested anything out of the ordinary. 2,362 years later, a team of archaeologists exploring the Konya Basin turned their shovels on Çatalhüyük ('fork hill'). Decapitating one of the two adjacent mounds, they found settlement remains that dated back almost 9,000 years. It was an astonishing find, but as the dig progressed, it became apparent that it could be even more than this – that Mellaart and his team may have hit upon nothing less than the holy grail of archaeology. The size of the original community, 6,000 and more people, was unprecedented, as was the level of its cultural development: there was evidence of ritual burial, of a fertility cult, of sculpture and painting. Here, in an area decidedly remote from the Fertile Crescent, were all the rudiments of civilization.

One of the things which struck me first about Çatalhüyük was that it is not an isolated phenomenon. Reading had left me an impression of a chance happening upon the site by a vigilant archaeologist, but the flat plains around Konya are dotted with such mounds, each holding the promise of immense archaeological wealth. Before the village of Abditolu, a day's walk south-east from the city and within a day of Çatalhüyük, I traced the considerable circumference of one such hill. For such a size, I guessed it must have been occupied over several millennia, one city founded on the ruins of another. This seemed to be confirmed by a man building an extension to his house just beyond the mound. He hurried to his gate as I passed, jangling a bagful of coins that had been harvested from the slopes. At his prompting I scooped out a handful. A small silver one had *ΑΛΕΞΑΝΔΡΟΣ* (Alexander) embossed on its face; another, *VICTOR*, with a figure clasping a cross. I ventured explanations of their origins but the man wasn't especially interested in their history: were they worth much? Did I want to buy the coins? Couldn't I take them to Ireland and sell them for him?

Failing to conclude a sale, he invited me for tea. The hill's name was Domuz Boğazlıyan ('the pig strangler') he informed me while stoking a samovar in the belly of the enormous hut he was erecting. Some Italians had pottered about the site a few years previously, but so far as he knew, there had never been any major digs.

After the tea I was pressed into valuing his horde. He and his builders knelt expectantly on the floor while I, without any scientific basis, picked out items of high value (besides coin, there was an assortment of rings, seals, earrings and bracelets). I was half hoping I'd come upon a daric, the currency of Persia. These were gold, and had an image of the King, in bent-knee posture armed with a bow, stamped on their faces, although sometimes there could be a figure of state (I had seen a photo of one dated to 400 that had Tissaphernes on it). The soldiers were paid one of these per month – the equivalent of four Greek drachmas – which was the normal rate for mercenary pay. Thanks to the Kilikian queen, over 50,000 would have been in circulation among the soldiers as they left Phrygia, so I thought the chances of one ending up in the stomach of 'the pig strangler' were not astronomical.

However I didn't notice any in this horde, nor in a second brought shortly after by a neighbour of the farmer's. I left a little disappointed, and thinking that half the wealth of ancient Anatolia must be in the hands of Turkish farmers.

*

I heard a feminist writer say once that having sex for a man was 'a charged return to the birth-source', or some shite like that. Yet, drawing closer to Çatalhüyük, that was how I felt: I was suffused with a strong, almost electric sense of anticipation.

I could see the low hump in the distance, fringed by trees, and left the dirt track to head directly for it. A labyrinth of half-filled canals delayed me longer than the dog-legged track would have done; I should have known better by now, but my mind was racing with other thoughts, chief of which was: what had prompted the nomads to stop? The site presumably offered clues as to why they had chosen to stop *here* (a silt-depositing river running by the mounds in prehistoric times provided one explanation), but I was less sure it would provide an answer to the greater question. Intuitively, I felt the answer to this mystery could only be found in ourselves: somewhere in memory there had to be a record of the cause. The enormity of the decision is hard to overstate. Our condition is to be averse to permanence. A moving target is harder to hit.

The final canal was a big concrete one, empty of water save for puddles. It had recently been built, probably intended to divert heavy rainwaters from the hill. I dropped into it and climbed out the other side, coming face to face with a mass of brown soil bulging from the earth.

Inside the compound there were a handful of administrative blocks: offices, a museum, quarters for archaeologists. A caretaker snoozed in a wooden cabin, and apart from a dog collapsed under a tree there was no other sign of life. I left my gear at the cabin and strolled tentatively onto the mound.

A series of worn paths crisscrossed its surface, which was further marked by spoil heaps and the indentations of earlier digs. I followed a track to a covered excavation on the north side. There was no sign of any work in progress here, and, peering through a plastic panel, I guessed that it was an exhibit showing a section of an original ground plan. The buildings of Çatalhüyük were packed together in a single mass of architecture. There were no streets: access to homes was by ladders through the roofs. These were no troglodyte holes, however, but open courtyards, off of which were rooms and storage areas. The interior walls of the houses were plastered and frequently decorated with paintings. Bulls featured prominently in these, as they do in the other art forms dug out. As it would be for future civilizations, the bull for the first settlers was the supreme symbol of animate power.

From the small marquee, I drifted over the folds of the mound, coming on the south side to a sounding well. It was closed off. A sign advised care so I crawled forward to peek down into the past. Each metre down was literally a giant step back in time. Fourteen building levels were identified by Mellaart over the four years of his excavations in the 1960s, and the deepest have yet to be explored. A long-term project to investigate the site more fully was begun in the mid-1990s, and will doubtless enlighten us further about our original configuration. I wondered, as I lay there under the sweltering midday sun, if somewhere deep inside this giant vaginal object, there didn't lie a magnificent set of murals which told the story of the Fall.

*

Xenophon was the first writer to record the name of Lykaonia. By his time the rivers that had fertilized the plain at its heart had dried up, and the natives had again reverted to nomadism, grazing goats and wild asses on the upland pastures. A hardy people skilled in archery, they supplemented their livelihood by attacking wagon trains bound for the Kilikian Gates, the traditional crossing point of the Middle Taurus. Like other tribes of the interior, such as the Pisidians Cyrus was supposedly seeking, their ultimate fate was to become extinct through assimilation and the settling of their territories.

One of the last historical appearances of the Lykaonians is in Roman times. The Acts of the Apostles records that Paul came to preach among them at a town called Lystra in the west of the province. He and his assistant Barnabas had just been driven out of Ikonion, and were probably hoping to find a more receptive audience in the smaller community. The Lykaonians, who still spoke in their native language, were effusive in their welcome, and when Paul apparently healed a cripple, the pair were hailed as gods. 'They lifted up their voices, saying in the speech of Lykaonia, "The gods are come down to us in the likeness of men"' (The Acts 14:11). It took great effort to dissuade them otherwise, and to prevent oxen being sacrificed in their honour. (Curiously, they took Paul to be Hermes, the messenger – maybe because he was doing most of the talking – while Barnabas was revered as Zeus.) The mission at any rate was ill-fated. Jews from Ikonion began agitating among the natives, and succeeded in turning them against the disciples. Barnabas fled and Paul was stoned and left for dead outside the town gates. Regaining consciousness during the night, he scrambled away from Lystra. No doubt the experience was still in his mind when he came to pen his moving letters to his followers.

I have been constantly on the road. I have met dangers from rivers, dangers from robbers, dangers from my fellow countrymen, dangers from foreigners, dangers in towns, dangers in the country, dangers at sea, dangers from false friends. I have toiled and drudged, I have often gone without sleep. Hungry and thirsty, I have often fasted; and I have suffered from cold and exposure. Corinthians II.11

In the end the Lykaonians may have taken to Paul's message, for the region became an early stronghold of the new religion. On Karadağ ('black mountain'), a mammoth inselberg 75 kilometres south-east of Konya, cavities were taken over by bands of holy men inspired by the ascetic example of the Desert Fathers. In the ninth century AD, with the threat of Arab destruction hanging over Anatolia, fortified monasteries were built in the valleys. The Turks today call the place Binbirkilise, 'a thousand and one churches'.

The course of Cyrus' march through Lykaonia was probably determined by Karadağ. A natural focal point in the region, the terrain to its north is marshy, lessening its value as a more direct route to the Kilikian Gates. Then, as now, the basin was poor, and there would have been little booty for the soldiers to take.

*

On the third day from Konya I rounded Karadağ. Shortly after I had emerged from its shadow, way in the distance to the east, the Taurus Mountains rose. They were less imposing than I had expected: a low ridge bounding the length of the plain.

This corner of the plain was more populous and more prosperous than the bleak tableland surrounding Çatalhüyük. There were paved roads, and the villages had a more modern feel to them. Gone were the mud huts and archaic wooden water pumps. The cause of the change was sugar beet, which supplied an assortment of chocolate and biscuit factories in nearby Karaman, the confectionery capital of Turkey. My informant, a farmer busy trying to confine cattle to a patch of green by the roadside, added that many people hereabouts had relatives in Holland. The number of cars I subsequently encountered registered in that country testified to the connection, as did, rather disconcertingly, the accents of the emigrants, returned for the summer months to assist with the harvest. Young men on tractors and mopeds speaking English with lisping Low Country accents invited me to drink beer, and were not at all put out if I declined.

The fourth morning brought a sharp change in the landscape. Soil and evenness suddenly gave way to an undulating carpet of scorched stone. Early on, mud brick warehouses appeared by the silent roadway, flocks of unattended sheep huddled in their shadow. At the last one in the series, I stopped to refill my water bottle, and confirm on my map that there was some habitation between here and the mountains. All I could see were distant, dainty whirlwinds dancing over the surface of the desert.

An oasis in this long strip of desert is the small town of Ayrancı. As all oases should, it emerged as a shimmering green haze far in the distance. I had marked this as the terminus of the tenth stage, a point not named by Xenophon, but one deducible none the less from the details he gives. He wrote that on this stage Cyrus sent the Kilikian queen back to her country with an escort of Thessalians, 'by the quickest route'; and that hence he advanced through Kappadokia to Dana, a four-day march of 25 *parasangs*. Working backwards along the high road from Dana (modern Kemerhisar), a line of this length finishes a short way beyond Ayrancı. A line from Konya, taken across its basin via Karadağ to Ayrancı, amounts to just over 150 kilometres, the distance given for the tenth stage. Supporting the mathematics, and disregarding the difficulties of the passage, the most direct route east over the mountains to Tarsus from the basin would begin somewhere around Ayrancı.

From the initial sighting of the town it took around two hours to reach it. For the last few kilometres I joined the road, a straight, undulating line of asphalt which saw little activity. I arrived thirsty, covered in dust, and with my lips chapped by the dry wind. So I was pleased to see a farmer hurrying towards me from a lemon grove. Once his curiosity had been satisfied, he led me to water, and then to the municipality.

There is actually very little water in Ayrancı. Up until a decade ago its meagre supply was drawn from a network of scattered wells, and now it flows from a newly built dam 4 kilometres to the east. This is also intended to enable an expansion of the citrus orchards which at present prosper only on the outskirts of the town.

For years in the time of scarcity a German called Karl used to come to the town every summer to search for water. Armed with geological surveys, he roamed the desert on his motorcycle, noting any telltale signs of aquifers far below. As if they were digging for gold – and in a way they were – teams of volunteers under his guidance would sink wells in the hope of striking the life-giving strata. Even if his genius had lately been made redundant, he was much missed by the residents.

As the town's mayor, Mr Sevimli, a tall, distinguished-looking man of mature years, reminisced about the German, I searched Ainsworth for a description I recalled he had included by Strabo of the Lykaonian territory. Locating it, I read the passage: 'The plateaus ... are bare of trees, and grazed by wild asses, though there is a great scarcity of water; and even where it is possible to find water, the wells are the deepest in the world.'

I could see he was pleased, and as he copied the lines out from the book, I sensed that the history of Ayrancı was being rewritten.

The purpose of my visit to the municipality was to try to check my route across the mountains on their map. My map – part of a series covering the country on a 5-kilometre scale – had, with a few exceptions, proven to be quite accurate, but suffering from errors on the plain was one thing; in the mountains it could mean being lost for days.

The man I needed to see, the Forestry Officer, was in the field, so I was referred instead to the District Prosecutor. 'He speaks English and knows everything,' the mayor assured me as I was led away by his assistant.

The DP's office was more austere looking, as was the incumbent – a balding, portly figure seated behind a large desk. On first glance I put him in his mid-forties, although after another look I revised this guess down a decade. A Turkish flag stood on a pole beside his chair, and a photograph of Atatürk hung on the wall behind. He introduced himself as Mr Erkal Özkan.

'You know who this is?' he asked, seeing me studying the picture.

When asked by Turks about the leader, one of my favourite responses was to pause for a moment, as if the name rang a bell, and then nod my head, remembering him as a useful wingback who played for Trabzonspor in the eighties. I felt, however, that in this company such humour might be out of place, and could damage my chances of reviewing the official cartography. The test was passed and he asked me to tell him about what I was doing.

Starting from the beginning, I explained that I was retracing the route taken by a Persian prince and his army to Babylon 2,400 years before. A Greek on the expedition had afterwards written an account, and I was using this as a guide. At this preliminary point he politely interrupted and asked if I was referring to Xenophon and the Ten Thousand. I could scarcely hide my surprise: this was the first person I had met since beginning the journey who had heard of the *Anabasis*. Taking from my folder a copy of the route, I joined him at the desk, and was further impressed as he proceeded to describe events on the army's retreat along the Tigris River.

After he had taken us to the Black Sea, and without raising his eyes from the sheet, he reached to a jar near the edge of the desk and extracted a pencil. Chewing momentarily on its edge, he scribbled on the map, blacking out the name 'Armenia'. 'Some people might be offended if they see this name.' He returned the map and I resumed my seat, unsure of how to react to this bizarre defacement.

We sipped our tea in silence. I decided that I wasn't going to be the one to speak first. I ran my gaze back and forth along the rows of legal manuals that were stacked tightly on the metal bookshelves behind his desk.

'I understand you wish to see our map.'

I nodded.

'Don't you have a modern one of our country?'

I nodded again, and explained the reason I wanted to see theirs.

The DP asked for the sheet that covered the Taurus. He studied it for some time, though on this occasion he did not make any amendments. The case I had put to him must have seemed reasonable, as he raised no objection to my being allowed to review their maps. He suggested, however, that I wait until the morning, when the Forestry Officer was on hand to assist.

The mayor's assistant had arranged for me to stay as a guest of the municipality in the town's solitary hotel, and had already transferred my luggage there. It was situated on the main road, above a teashop, and was basic.

Turks tend to classify their hotels in three categories: *pis, normal* and *lüks*.* A city will typically have a plentiful supply of all, but in the smaller centres, the first category predominates. As with any feature-based classification system, the standards within each division are variable: the best are friendly and clean, the worst neither.

In the lower rung the rooms are generally small, like a shoebox, and unfurnished except for the bed. The walls are painted a dark colour (for some reason nearly always dark green), and there may or may not be a window. A low-watt light bulb without a shade hangs from the ceiling, and at night, a strip light in the corridor floods beneath a gap in the door.

In the *normal* class the rooms are more spacious. There might be a carpet, and certainly a window, and a washbasin, and possibly a fan or a television. *Lüks* rooms have all these things, are *en suite*, and should have a balcony.

The Ayrancı hotel was unusual in that, while *pis* in every other respect, the rooms had televisions. Mine was a colour portable that had a clothes hanger for an aerial. It produced a hollow sound, and the same low droning seeped through the walls from the rooms on either side.

In the evening, while I was watching the news, two officers of the Jandarma, the paramilitary police, called to see my papers. In this part of the country this was unusual. They examined them briefly out in the corridor and thanked me for my assistance. Shortly after, Erkal knocked on the door to invite me for dinner. He had with him a young companion who introduced himself boisterously as Tom. He was tall and lithe, and had wavy blonde hair and striking blue eyes. The offer seemed to be a genuine effort at hospitality, and in spite of some reservations about the earlier map incident, I accepted. I was curious as well to learn more about Erkal, and how he had come to be introduced to Xenophon.

They took me to a *pide* salon, or a 'Turkish pizza parlour' as Tom preferred to call it. The basic *pide* is a length of leavened bread kneaded into a narrow boat shape and baked with toppings – ground meat, eggs, cheese – in a wood-fired oven. Served with salad and *ayran*, the salted yoghurt drink, it rarely fails to make for a tasty meal.

---

* International hotels, such as those found in the major cities and resorts, occupy a fourth class, *süperlüks*, but these are foreign owned and almost exclusively patronized by foreigners.

Once we had ordered, Tom hurried off for beer. We watched through the salon window as he pedalled up the main road on a moped which eventually ignited.

'He is a Tatar,' Erkal answered, when I enquired about his friend's ethnic background. Many of Ayrancı's citizens, he went on to explain, had their roots in the Crimea. Displaced by wrangling over the peninsula by tsars and sultans, the less well resourced of them had ended up in desolate patches of the Ottoman Empire such as this. The majority eked out a living on the land, grazing sheep and coaxing fruit-bearing trees to make do on recycled water. In more recent years some had migrated to the cities, and a few returned to the post-Soviet East.

Erkal didn't volunteer much information about himself, and after the peculiar events of the day, I didn't want to give him more cause for paranoia by talking of Greeks in Anatolia. From our exchanges I knew he had studied in Ankara, and had worked in half a dozen cities and towns about the country. He had been in Ayrancı for two years, but in another month he would be moving on again, to Enez, a small Thracian town on the Greek border. He insisted that he didn't mind the regular uprooting, and I got the sense that he considered his work as something akin to a vocation: bringing justice to the remote regions and peoples.

Tom breezed back in and clicked his fingers for glasses before sitting down. 'My bar no have wait,' he complained as he opened the cans and handed some change back to Erkal.

'Where's your bar, Tom?'

'I many bar – Antalya, Bodrum, Çeşme – every summer I work different one.' I felt I was getting closer to solving the mystery of the name and the slight Scouse accent. 'I suppose Tom is the English version of your name?'

'English people no able to pronounce name. Byoulent.' He skewered an olive and gripped it between his teeth. 'One harlot there is calling me Tom when I try to teach how, so I am using this. Easy for them.'

We gathered from him over the meal that my arrival in the town had caused some excitement. The shopkeeper had heard a rumour that I was Karl the German's son, returned to continue the search for water in the hinterland. Another, which he had heard earlier in a teahouse, was that Karl had secretly been searching for treasure, and that I had bought his maps, and was here to look for the gold. I laughed aside both theories, but realized later as I was readying myself for bed, that the fact that my maps were German must have given some weight to the gold one.

Neither of them could say what had become of Karl. According to Tom, he had objected strongly to the new dam, and some said one year he drove to Ankara to protest and was arrested for physically threatening the head of the water agency. In any event, a bit like the stork whose water source has been tampered with, he never returned.

9

The Taurus

A11: Across the Mountains

The Taurus forms a partition approximately through the middle of this
continent [Asia] ... the mountain has in many places as great a breadth as
3,000 stadia, and a length as great as that of Asia itself, that is, about
45,000 stadia, reckoning from the coast opposite Rhodos to the eastern
extremities of India and Scythia.

Strabo, *Geography*

The mountains the Greeks called the Taurus, we know today as
the great Himalayan belt. Modern geographers break this into
numerous ranges, the westernmost of which is the Toros
Dağları. The Taurus begin on the Turkish Mediterranean coast, and
muscle eastwards across the country as far as historic Armenia, where
they merge with a denser, more remote system of fold mountains. Here
stands Mount Ararat, where Noah's Ark came to rest, and Lake Van,
formed when an eruption blocked the outflow of a river. The other
streams in this area, fed by prodigious amounts of melt water, drain
south to form Mesopotamia.

The Taurus form a rim around the southern and eastern extents of
the Anatolian High Plateau, one of the chief effects of which is to block
the rain-bearing winds from the Mediterranean. The mountains are
composed largely of limestone, and on the exposed face especially,
erosive action results in a characteristic karst landscape of grikes and
underground streams and caverns.

Another effect of the barrier is to limit communications. There is
only one major route across the Middle Taurus – the highest section of
the range – and this is by way of the Külek Boğazı, the Kilikian Gates

of ancient times. This is the way Cyrus and the main body of his army crossed in the summer of 401.

The strategic value of the pass in antiquity can be gauged by the estimation that even a small force stationed here could prevent an army from penetrating into the plain. Alexander the Great considered its abandonment before his approach in the summer of 333 to have been his greatest stroke of good fortune.

When Cyrus approached the pass it was being guarded by Syennesis, the Kilikian monarch. Xenophon says the prince waited for a day beneath, and that on the next a messenger came to say that Syennesis had gone, having learned that Menon's Thessalian force was on its way across the mountains by a lower route, and that a fleet of Spartan ships under Cyrus' command was sailing towards the gulf. The lush Kilikian Plain and the route to Syria were now open to the prince.

The apparent smoothness of these events suggests that Epyaxa may have been more successful in her mission than the narrative admits. Cyrus' decision to send her ahead with Menon could be seen as part of an arrangement aimed at deceiving the King as to Syennesis' loyalty; Menon's appearance in the rear with the Queen as hostage, together with the arrival of the fleet offshore, would leave him little choice but to abandon the defence of the Gates.

Travelling with the main body, Xenophon has no detail of Menon's route, other than it was the shortest possible one over the mountains to Kilikia. This information, however, taken with what he tells us about Cyrus' progress on the eleventh stage, does make it possible to reconstruct a route for Menon and the Queen. It was their trail I was planning to follow across the Taurus. It was now late July, and in terms of the season, I still had time to make up on the army.

*

As I had feared they might, the municipality maps revealed several shortcomings on my own: a number of villages were misplaced, and none of the marked 'summer tracks' was familiar to the Forestry Officer, whom I called on early the next morning. With a green marker he drew on my map the path I was to take, annotating this line with the names of various summer camps where I could find shelter. These temporary settlements are called *yaylalar* (*yayla* in the singular) by the Turks, and are to be found in all the highland regions of the country. Normally, they are inhabited from late spring each year; in a ritual that recalls an earlier time, farmers and their families and livestock make the ascent to the heights from valleys below, and they remain on these idyllic pastures until the cold nights of autumn force them back down again.

The DP, Erkal Özkan, joined us as we were winding up shortly after 8 a.m. He had said the previous night that he would walk with me to the Ayrancı Dam, but a case had come up which required his attention, and he had asked Tom to accompany me instead. He was waiting for us on his motorcycle at the municipality entrance. I shook hands with the DP and we wished each other well.

It was a short walk, forty minutes, to the base of the dam. Tom made an art of keeping level on the crackling moped: one hand coaxed the throttle while the other kept my pack balanced on the pillion seat. Several young men approached us on the road out of town, and from the loudly delivered snippets of information – '*Antalya ... İrlandadan geldi ... büyük bar ... arkadaşım*', I formed the impression that he was suggesting our friendship went back further than it did.

Rising no more than a couple of storeys from the earth, from the front at least the dam seemed by no means the worst example of these engineering eyesores. This sense was reinforced on the road running alongside: with the bridgehead low in the water, the reservoir might have passed for a small glacial lake. I suspected that if he ever saw it, Karl wouldn't be too disappointed.

After composing several auto-photos and exchanging addresses, Tom and I departed: he in a cloud of pungent two-stroke oil, me with a tap of my walking stick, and a prayer to Artemis.

For the rest of that morning I followed the sleepy road along the side of the valley. At its bottom, small rectangular plots of land had been levelled either side of an invisible stream, while above these, reaching up onto the road, were slopes of high-yielding apricot trees. At several places the heavily laden branches drooped onto the roadway, inviting the passer-by to indulge himself in the ripe fruit. Flat rooftops, designed perhaps with a drying function in mind, were covered every centimetre by the disembowelled fruit. The work of picking and pitting them fell to the younger and older generations, who could be seen below on the terraces with their baskets.

Before Üçharman the valley began to narrow, and I picked out in the encroaching rock face on the left an uneven row of caves. According to Erkal, these had been hewn from the limestone by early Christian worshippers, much like the warren at Karadağ on the Konya Plain. Numerous Byzantine relics had been found here over the years, suggesting that the caves had remained in use long after the era of proscription. Today, some of the more accessible ones are used by locals to store fodder for the winter. Wooden palates tied together close off their entrances to goats or any adventurous cattle that might be grazing in the vicinity.

The road crossed the stream in the heart of the village, and immediately after zigzagged upwards onto a gaping, undulating plateau. Parts of this were swathed in wheat, and I imagined that the height and aridity must have made this a precarious endeavour for the farmers from the valley. Like the apricots, the crop was now ripe, and the odd tractor could be seen labouring slowly and soundlessly out on the plain.

A lonely traverse of the plateau brought me late in the afternoon to Çatköy, the last permanent settlement on the western side of the divide.

It was exceptionally quiet. Most of the inhabitants, it seemed, were up in the *yayla*. I lay down beneath a tree close to the mosque, a basic building in need of repair, and was woken some time later by its custodian. He stood above me looking displeased. '*Bisiklet yok mu?*'

It took me a moment to orientate myself. I dusted my trousers and stood up. He followed me across to the ablution taps and repeated his question as I splashed myself. When I had done, I turned to him and replied that I was walking and did not have a bike. He wasn't quite middle-aged, wore a skullcap and gown, and sported a bird's nest beard such as those favoured by the more ascetic religious men. His face was still configured in the way it had been when I opened my eyes, and I realized now that it wasn't a look of displeasure, but one of contempt.

I had had a similar experience in Greece the year before. An elderly early-morning stroller had spotted me asleep on his village green and had demanded to see my passport (I had arrived on the night ferry and, after a few drinks, had decided it was too late to go looking for accommodation). I was quite sure then, as now, that had I chanced to erect my tent – even though this was just a patch of material tightened over a simple frame – I would not have been disturbed. To be without shelter is the ultimate mark of destitution, a state that inspires revulsion in the settler mind.

We were joined at the water shed by the *dolmuş* driver. He greeted us, and said that he had seen me walking earlier in the day. This seemed not to be as big a problem for him and he invited me to his home. I faced the mullah as we left but did not say goodbye.

My host's house was in a corner of the village. Besides driving the bus, Ahmet helped his teenage daughter manage the households of *yayla*-departed relatives. Their principal chore was tending to bands of unruly chickens. Taking advantage of the flight of other animals, they flapped about the streets and generally made the place their own. One of them was picked for dinner by Ahmet, who cooked the bird himself, serving it with olives and boiled potatoes.

After the meal another Çatköylü joined us for tea. He was a teacher in Istanbul and had just returned for his summer holiday. These days, he said, many of the young people went to the cities: Izmir, Ankara, Istanbul, Berlin. It struck me, listening to his story, that what took them away was essentially the same thing that lured the farmers onto the heights: greener pastures. The nomadic instinct was still very much alive in the mountains.

As it had done at Üçharman, the track from the village began to rise beyond the last houses. This time the ascent was gentler, but longer. After an hour and some the track levelled off and straightened along the base of a low range on the left.

At 16 kilometres I passed the Çatköy summer pasture. Known as the Kilise Yaylası ('church pasture'), it was situated in a hollow far away to the right of the trail. Ahmet had invited me to call on his family there, but I was enjoying the walk, and as I didn't have to pass through, I decided to press on.

The Kilise Yaylası was the first one marked on my map by the Forestry Officer. The next one was hidden in a green cleft in the shadow of Yıldız Tepesi ('star hill'). I hadn't intended stopping there either but my advance along the track was checked by two black-faced sheepdogs returning from duty on the mountain. Young and keen for action, they bared fangs and growled, as if daring me to raise the stick. Conscious that against powerful animals like these it would be useless, I removed my pack and sat down on the ground. This had been the advice given to me by a hunter in Ayrancı who had a line in canine psychology. He said that once the dogs perceived that there was no threat, they would get bored and leave.

To me they looked more disgusted than bored. They glanced at one another and then back at me; and then the one on the left slumped down. A scar ran the length of his prominent square muzzle. He began to lick a front paw, but was unfussed about the dirt and grass which clung to his splendid coat. The ears of both dogs had been cropped and they wore the traditional nail-studded collars. In spite of their unkempt and intimidating appearance, they were beautiful animals – powerful, graceful, free. These weren't in any way like the smaller sheepdogs at home, which would do handstands if you sounded the right note. The *kangals* operate independently, free to roam as they like. Their instinct is to guard the sheep, and they don't need training or whistles to do this. The dogs are fearless when faced with predators. Though it may mean certain death, one will confront a pack of wolves, or race to intercept a lone one before it can strike. The sheep themselves, I came to observe, were not at all put out by the presence of their 60- and 70-kilogram guardians. Probably this was because the *kangals* spend a lot of time with them. Most, I got the distinct impression, were happiest when bounding in the midst of a large flock headed for new pastures.

After about five minutes on the track, this pair did indeed become bored and leave. The one that was standing went first, and the other, without even a glance at me, followed suit.

Pleased, I rose quietly to my feet, but had hardly gone 10 metres when they sped out from behind a crest to the right of the track. I was afraid now that they would seek revenge for my mind-games and shouted warnings at them. The commotion drew an audience of children from behind the same hillock. Waving sticks they dispersed the dogs and led me away.

Followed by the *kangals*, we skipped down a slope to where there was a small encampment of felt tents. Several choring women hid any surprise they might have felt at seeing me being escorted like Gulliver into their hearth. After taking tea, at the invitation of an elderly man I set up my tent beside theirs. I remarked to myself that it was like a poodle compared to their sheepdogs. They were concerned that it would blow away if there was a wind, but I was able to assure them that this wouldn't happen.

The mystery of where the menfolk were was cleared up after dark: one by one they emerged from the tents, yawning and stretching in the cool air. Their workday was just beginning.

Following dinner, each was accoutred in a body-length coat made of the same material as the tents. The garments looked incongruous, but these heavy casings would shield them from the biting winds that can strafe the mountain slopes at any time. With flasks of strong tea to keep them alert, and the giant dogs cheerfully in tow, they set off into the darkness.

The stars were still glittering when the shepherds returned for breakfast. The faintest light entered the sky as we ate and, as it grew, the celestial objects which had been almost within reach, faded away.

One of the men walked with me out onto the trail to ensure that the dogs did not follow. He put the distance to Tırtar at not less than 100 kilometres, but I strongly suspected the operation of 'Tınaztepe's Law', and was confident of reaching the eastern slopes before the day's end.

The new day brought signs of recent orogeny, in the form of spectacular nappes, masses of compressed rock sheared from their roots by tectonic pressure. Their geometric shapes and huge size, combined with the absence of any pastures, created the sense of being in a cold desert. An icy wind which blew up early on and pressed against me for the duration of the morning reinforced this feeling.

Turning south-east off the central spine shortly after midday, I entered a less alien terrain. The *yaylalar* began again, speckled over the moonscape on threadbare patches of green.

The crossing of the range was not what I had expected. The Taurus are a notable chain of fold mountains with several peaks in this middle section above 3,500 metres, and I had expected snow-capped heights to rear into view as I mounted one plateau after the other, but it wasn't like that at all. Instead, the plateaus, beginning at the 1,000-metre Konya Basin, represented a series of giant steps that rose steadily to the height of mountains.

Further to the north by all accounts it was more dramatic. A contemporary of Ainsworth's, Colonel Chesney, who undertook the first complete survey of the Euphrates and Tigris rivers, thought the Kilikian Gates were one of the most difficult mountain passes in the world. Ainsworth himself remembered at the windswept location, 'high precipitous cliffs towering up on both sides'. Such descriptions made it easier to envisage the Taurus as part of the cause of the High Plateau's aridity. With the Pontic Mountains in the north, they form part of a virtually unbroken horseshoe around the steppes, forcing the rain-bearing winds to drop their loads on the exposed faces. Up to 300 mm per year falls on these, with only a fraction of that surmounting the barrier, and most of that on the edges of the interior.

In its own way, the exit to Kilikia on the lower route was marked and spectacular. In late afternoon the scree plateau began to narrow into a defile. For an hour the track crept towards it, the walls of limestone on either side pressing in and becoming steeper. At the bottleneck, the path suddenly dropped into a pine-clad gorge, corkscrewing its way towards the bottom. On a clear day the sea from this gusty spot would be visible away to the south. In the space before the coastline, the whole panorama now was green: rolling fields and ridges clothed in trees fading into the haze of evening.

I set up my tent at the pass. There was a well here, and a small cemetery which held the remains of successive generations of the same family. The last one had been interred some years before, and now there was nobody left to maintain the plots. A little further back on the trail I had passed the shell of a house, and I guessed that these people had been its occupants, stationed at the pass perhaps on some official duty that had ceased with them.

*

It took three days to get from the pass to the city of Tarsus. A bit like a dendritic drainage system, all the trails which had their beginnings in this part of the mountains eventually, by way of roads and highways, filtered to one outlet. This was Mersin, so to get to the Tarsus catchment, I had first to cross a range of high forests.

Reflecting the more agriculture-friendly climate, the villages on the east side of the range were notably more prosperous. There were also more of them, high on steep hillsides, and strung along dipping ridges which partitioned the valleys and added to their isolation. The low mud-brick structures of the arid plateaus were replaced by multi-storey houses, capped with red tiles as in the Balkans.

Market gardening and cattle rearing were the main occupations, although I learned that many of the residents were seasonal, and did little or no farming. You could see these people in the mornings on the balconies of their homes, and in the late afternoons, strolling down vertiginous lanes to the village square. Out of season they would be living in the burgeoning cities of the coast, or on the fertile plain behind, which the Turks call the Çukurova. The heat and humidity on this enclosed plain in the summer months are oppressive.

The hamlet of Atlılar, which I made in a pleasant day's walk from the pass, was unusual in that its inhabitants were virtually all temporary. Once they had all lived in the secluded mountainous cul-de-sac, but the rapid development of Mersin on the coast gradually lured them away. Fifty years ago Mersin was a fishing village: now it is the largest port on the Turkish Mediterranean, and boasts the tallest building in the country. The success of their lives in the new world was evidenced by the number of newly built chalets, and the four-wheel drives parked on the narrow side tracks.

From the *muhtar*, who put the long-disused village room at my disposal, I learned that the people of Atlılar had distant roots. They were Circassians, originally from a ring of close-knit villages in the mountains of the north Caucasus. Along with other Muslim mountaineers, during the Russo-Turkish wars of the second half of the nineteenth century, they were suspected of sympathies with the Turks and expelled. The elderly people still spoke the native tongue – an impenetrable language of the north-west Caucasian group – though in tandem with the traditional way of life, this was in terminal decline. I wondered aloud if any of them spoke Russian. The *muhtar* shook his head, but said that there was an old man in a cabin above the village who spoke Greek. He didn't know where he was from, but he wasn't Circassian. My mind turned over as we ascended the slope: was it way too fanciful to think that this man somehow might be descended from a company of Menon's men who had become detached from the main party on the crossing of the lower route, and were never seen or heard of again? Remote pockets at the other end of this huge mountain belt are said to harbour direct descendants of Alexander the Great's army; if there were anything like a live link to the Ten Thousand, it would be in an area like this.

The man, frail, and reputedly more than ninety years old, was seated on the porch of his cabin with one of his granddaughters.

'To your health,' I called out to him in Greek.

'*Yia sou!*' He replied, gesturing to a seat. '*Apo pou esai?*'

I introduced myself and got quickly to the matter on my mind. '*Apo pou eiste?*'

Mr Gökçimen sighed, and there was a wistful look in his eyes. He was born on the island of Rhodos, and had lived there until 1942, when the ethnic Turkish population was forced to leave by the Greeks. He was eighteen at the time and arrived in Izmir speaking hardly a word of Turkish. He married in this city, as later did his daughter, who had fallen in love with a Circassian. On the death of his wife he went to live with them in Mersin, and now, like the other Athlarlılar, divided his time between the city and the heights.

He had never heard of the Greeks I was following, but listened keenly as I did my best to recount the story in his language. As I did, I felt in a way that I was re-embedding the story into the long history of the mountains.

Literally straddling the divide between the Mersin and Tarsus catchments was a place called Boztepe. After a long haul through a pine forest, it appeared above a quiet meadow. Overshadowing the settlement was an imposing pinnacle of rock on the right side. I was told in the teashop where I took a room that there had once been an Ottoman castle on the rock, and a Byzantine one before that. I wondered if it weren't the same as the Castle of Nimrud mentioned by Ainsworth. He described it as a fastness in the mountains near Tarsus, and believed it was where Syennesis and his subjects fled on the approach of Cyrus. However I was too weary to attempt an exploration of the site, and contented myself with the view from my bedroom window.

The passage to the lowlands from here is by way of a mighty spur. Even today, tamed by engineers for the vehicle, the road in places is little more than a ledge chiselled out of the rock face. Twisting round the jagged spur in pursuit of the least-resistant course, it offers breathtaking views out on the valleys fronting the Kilikian Plain. Below, now on the right side, now on the left, the earth falls away into bottomless gorges.

Eagles grace the sky in these parts. Stopping at a spring an hour beyond Boztepe, I spotted directly above me a group of four, a family perchance getting ready for the hunt. They dispersed in different directions, and I lost all but one. With hardly a twitch of its wings, it descended slowly from the clouds in wide circles, its eyes scanning the gorge far below for the faintest signs of life.

*

Xenophon says that Menon arrived in Tarsus five days ahead of the main army group. From the detail he gives of the latter's journey, this implies a week's walking for the advance guard through the mountains. By the same account, this had not been an easy transit.

> Two companies [100 *hoplites*] of Menon's army were lost in crossing the mountains to the plain. Some said they were cut to pieces by the Kilikians when they were on a plundering expedition; others that they had been left behind, and unable to find the rest of the army or the right tracks, had been destroyed while wandering about.

Enraged by the loss of their comrades, Menon's men sacked the city and the royal palace, filling their pockets with whatever booty they could find. By this time Syennesis and most of his subjects had fled to a haven in the mountains, leaving only the shopkeepers to face the Greeks.

This evacuation was inconvenient for Cyrus, who was facing another cash-flow problem. He must have been expecting to receive money somewhere from his mother (possibly at an estate belonging to her beyond the Amanos Mountains) but had not budgeted sufficiently for the interval. Thinking Syennesis may be able to help out, he now sent messengers to ask him to return; however, the Kilikian steadfastly refused to leave his shelter. Cyrus called on Epyaxa to help, and she, still moved by passion or ambition, undertook to get her husband down from the mountain.

Syennesis met Cyrus and transferred to him a large sum of money. Out of gratitude for this gift, the prince presented him with a robe and a horse, and promised as well that his land would no longer be pillaged. Xenophon says nothing more of Epyaxa, but she may have waved Cyrus off believing that soon she would be Queen of Asia.

10

Tarsus

Mutiny

Cyrus and the army stayed here for twenty days, because the soldiers refused to go any further. They already suspected they were marching against the King, and said that they had not been hired for this purpose. Klearkhos, first of all, endeavoured to compel his own soldiers to continue, but as soon as he confronted them, they pelted him and his baggage animals with stones. Klearkhos, indeed, on this occasion, had a narrow escape from being stoned to death.

Anabasis I.3

At first sight Tarsus was unimpressive, an impression that didn't change over the course of the few days I spent in the city. I discovered that in places it was not unpleasant, such as at the tea gardens about the rapids on the River Kydnos (Tarsus Çayı), and around parts of the old district, where two-tone wooden houses and narrow lanes obscure the cheap architecture of the centre, but there was nothing otherwise inspiring about the place.

It wasn't always like this. Rebuilding the city in the early seventh century, the Assyrian king Sennacherib is said to have modelled his plans on Babylon. The Kilikian kings added their palaces, and Alexander thought enough of the place to send a task force ahead of him to prevent the retreating Persians from burning it. Ironically, he subsequently almost lost his life here, and in the most unlikely of circumstances. The Roman historian Curtius recounted the peculiar event on the Kydnos River that nearly changed history:

It was now summer time [333], when the blazing sun parches Kilikia with a more searing heat than any other coastline ... The King [Alexander] was covered in dust and sweat, and the clear water induced him to have a bath while his body was still overheated. So he undressed and went down into the river before the eyes of his troops, thinking that it would also add to his prestige if he showed his men that he was satisfied with attention to his person which was plain and unelaborated. Scarcely had he entered the water when he suddenly felt his limbs shiver and stiffen. He went pale, and the vital heat all but left his body. When his attendants took hold of him, he appeared to be dying, and he was barely conscious when they took him to his tent. A deep anxiety that bordered on grief descended on the camp. In tears the men complained that, in such a sudden and swift-moving train of events, a king who was the most famous of any period of history had been brought low not even in battle and not by an enemy – had been snatched from them and had lost his life taking a bath!

No significant archaeology from the early period has come to light, but recent excavations in the city centre have revealed sections of a Roman road and parts of the imperial *agora*. Tarsus is another of the cities visited by Xenophon that has been continuously inhabited since his day. It also retains the same name the Athenian recorded 2,500 years ago.

For most of its long history, Tarsus was prosperous, its wealth deriving from its position on the route into Syria, and from the hugely fertile plain for which it acted as clearing house. The alluvial soil and moist climate still result in prodigious crops of sugar cane, fruit, and cotton. Stretching for over 100 kilometres from east to west, bounded by mountains and sea, this is the richest agricultural plot in Anatolia.

Things seem to have started to go wrong for the Tarsians when their harbour began to silt up. This natural strangulation – the death for many other great cities on the Mediterranean coast – caused the city to slip into a long but not fatal decline. Buoyed by trade across the mountains, it soldiered on through the centuries, clinging to regional importance right up until the emergence in the twentieth century of the neighbouring industrial centres of Mersin and Adana. Its modern isolation seems to be reflected in an attachment to lost causes. In the heart of the city a Rauf Denktaş Park celebrates in kitsch the life of the truculent Cypriot, while one of the major streets has been renamed in honour of the late Chechen warlord, Dzhokhar Dudayev.

Perhaps because of the absence of any striking monuments from the past, the historical fame of Tarsus rests today on its association with

The Temple of Artemis, Sardis. Starting point of the journey

The Maeander River beyond Yenicekent (Tripolis)

Sunset on the Maeander Valley

Cave of Marsyas, Dinar

Fountain of Midas, Ulupınar

Wheat field on Konya Plain

Turkish girl, Alaşehir

Making bread in the Taurus Mountains

Yayla, summer meadow

Mountain valley, east side of the Taurus

Antakya Gate, Aleppo

View of Aleppo from citadel

Desert road
east of al-Bab

First sight of
the Euphrates

Euphrates at
Balasem village,
Raqqa

Upstream view of Halabiyah, fortress on the Middle Euphrates

Arab girl, Jalabiyah

two people: St Paul, who was born here in 10 AD, and Cleopatra, who sailed up the Kydnos on a floating palace in 41 BC to meet Mark Antony. Her arrival was immortalized by Shakespeare in *Antony and Cleopatra*:

> The barge she sat in, like a burnisht throne
> Burned on the water: the poop was beaten gold;
> Purple the sails, and so perfuméd that
> The winds were love-sick with them.

The harbour at Rhegma has long been covered over in mud, but a Roman arch, the Cleopatra Kapısı, which now forms a traffic island near to the intercity bus station, purports to commemorate the arrival of the Queen of Egypt.

Providing a focus for the past may also be the function of the site of Senpol Kuyusu ('St Paul's well'), a fenced-off pool in the heart of the city's old quarter. It was closed for the day when I visited, and because the information placard was on the inside, I couldn't make out the tent maker's link with the spring. His picture held me for a while. It was the Orthodox depiction: a gaunt, Goyaesque figure staring out at the suppliant. I had grown up with the more wholesome ones produced by Renaissance painters, and went away wondering to myself what a holy man looks like.

I came by the well another day only to find it closed again. There was a man, a foreigner judging by his appearance, behind the wire, and I enquired how he had got in. Accents and a couple of questions established that we were from adjacent counties back in Ireland. He directed me to the far end of the compound where there was a stepladder propped against the fence. Having gained access in this way, I soon found myself part of an operation to ship out litres of the holy water.

When this job had been completed, he returned the stepladder to its owner at a restaurant opposite, and invited me to have a drink. His name was Paul, and his visit was only a brief one, which was why he had taken steps to get in to the well. Early in the morning he was off to Antakya on the penultimate leg of a whirlwind tour of Anatolia's religious sites. He had already been to the Virgin Mary's house near Ephesus (Meryemana), and had visited several of St John's 'seven churches of Asia'. A health crisis, he told me, had been the catalyst for this journey of faith: two years before, a day after his forty-fifth birthday, he had suffered damage to a heart valve and had only recently recovered. It wasn't, he explained, that he had become 'religious' during his illness; rather he had concluded there was an emptiness in his life, and he wanted to fill it with things and places that held meaning for him (the holy water was for his mother).

What had taken him here was a series shown on national television in the 1960s called *Paul of Tarsus*. He remembered rushing home from school to watch it, and repeatedly asking the Christian Brothers where this Tarsus was. One of them finally brought an atlas into the class and located it somewhere on the coast of Spain. It was years before he learned of the mistake and the true whereabouts of his namesake's birthplace.

*

The crossing of the mountains had been a significant event for the soldiers. With the passing into Kilikia, the pretence of Cyrus' stated purpose had faded. In three months they had not had any engagement with the rogue Pisidians, or encountered any evidence of disruption on their part. At the same time the loss of Menon's men had brought home the dangers of marching in hostile territory, and they were now well beyond the sphere of Cyrus' official power. Suspicions that had hitherto been voiced in private were now openly discussed by the men. They said that not only was Cyrus deceiving them, but so were their generals; the conviction grew that the Great King was the object of the expedition. Believing thus that they had been duped, and afraid of what lay ahead, the soldiers refused to continue.

Xenophon says that, with one exception, the generals were not aware of any mission other than the one for which they had been hired. What suspicions they may have had at this stage they kept to themselves, for none wanted to be seen as disloyal to the prince.

Klearkhos was the general who was privy to Cyrus' secret plans. A man of over forty years, he had served his country with distinction in numerous campaigns. The impression of the Spartan from the sources is that he was an accomplished soldier and an uncompromising leader – not one to lend a ready ear to a soldier's grievances. Even those who were his admirers did not seek to conceal the harshness of his method and approach to war. In a later encomium Xenophon wrote:

He achieved this result [strict obedience] by his toughness. He had a forbidding appearance and a harsh voice. His punishments were severe ones and were sometimes inflicted in anger, so that there were times when he was sorry himself for what he had done. With him punishment was a matter of principle, for he thought that an army without discipline was good for nothing; indeed, it is reported that he said that a soldier ought to be more frightened of his own commander than of the enemy.

Klearkhos' last posting had been as governor of Byzantium, a Spartan dominion which had become fractious and to which he had been sent 'to bring order', which he did. Some reports say that his methods there resulted in him being exiled; others that he was condemned to death for disobeying a command of the Spartan governors to return. However, these are likely to have been fabricated to disguise Spartan support for the prince. The generally reliable Plutarch wrote that in response to Cyrus' request for their help, they 'sent a dispatch roll to Klearkhos ordering him to give [him] every assistance'.

It was Klearkhos who now moved to deal with the unrest among the men. Taking a characteristically robust approach, he confronted his own army. Rousing the baggage handlers, he began to manhandle them onto the road; but instead of following them into line, the soldiers threw stones. A mob gathered and the Spartan was said to have been lucky to escape with his life. Some reports say he was not the only one to be attacked, and that the soldiers turned on other of the commanders, and attempted to kill them too.

The other generals of the Greeks were Xenias, Proxenos, Menon, and Sophainetos. Xenias the Arcadian had command of the largest force, 4,000 *hoplites* drawn from Cyrus' provincial garrisons. He was a former head of the prince's bodyguard and was considered his most loyal commander. He had accompanied the young prince to Susa three years before when the dying King had summoned his son to be near him.

Proxenos of Boiotia was a guest-friend of Cyrus. Around thirty years of age, he was outwardly ambitious but is said to have lacked the resolve necessary to realize his goals. Training with the philosophers had imbued in him the conviction that honour and wealth should be won by noble deeds or not at all. He was a great admirer of Cyrus, and wrote once that he valued him above his own country. He made every effort to encourage his friends to take the opportunity of serving with him in the expedition against the Pisidians. There were 2,000 men in his charge, but he was not strict enough to be a good commander, and his authority was regularly undermined by soldiers who exploited his desire to be seen as a fair leader. It was Proxenos who invited Xenophon the Athenian to join the expedition and he introduced him to Cyrus at Sardis.

Menon, who led the advance party across the mountains to Tarsus, was the most ambitious of the Greek generals. A young, educated aristocrat from Thessaly, he had joined Cyrus with 1,500 men at the request of Aristippos, another guest-friend of the prince. Like Aristippos, his own family had ties of friendship with the Persians, a result of Thessalian 'medizing' (accepting the King's rule and adapting to Asiatic customs) in the earlier part of the century. Possibly for this reason he was disliked by the patriotic Xenophon, who indeed regarded him as the worst knave that ever walked the earth.

> He thought that the shortest way to the satisfaction of his ambitions was by means of perjury and lying and deceit; consequently he regarded sincerity and truthfulness as equivalent to simple-mindedness. It was obvious that he felt no affection for anyone, but if he said he was anyone's friend, it was clear that he was intriguing against him.

Elsewhere in the literature of the ancients, however, the impression of the man from Larissa is less severe. Plato even has him as the protagonist of a dialogue: 'Can you tell me Socrates, is virtue something that can be taught?'

The oldest of the generals, and one of the few leading figures who ultimately survived the adventure, was Sophainetos from Stymphalos. Like Xenophon, upon his return to Greece he wrote an account of the expedition. This has not survived, but it may have been used by the fourth-century historian Ephoros, whose *Universal History* (also lost) was in turn used by Diodoros in the first century. One suggestion about Xenophon's motivation for writing the *Anabasis* is that he was dissatisfied with his own portrayal in Sophainetos' account. Evidently we will likely never know what Sophainetos had to say about him, but in Diodoros' epitome of Ephoros, he is not mentioned at all. (A third contemporary account of the journey was written by Ktesias of Knidos, the Greek physician to Artaxerxes. This version of events, fragments of which survive, was probably drawn on by Plutarch for his biography of Artaxerxes in the first century AD.)

After an interval to allow heads to cool, Klearkhos called a meeting of the soldiers under his command. He took his position among them, and for a long time stood in silence, weeping. The men were amazed at this sight, and they too fell into silence.

At length the commander spoke, beginning by telling the men of his friendship with Cyrus, a man who had a deserved reputation for being just and generous. As they were aware, it was he who had given him the money for this army, and when the prince had called him, he did not hesitate to bring them all to Kelainai, ready to act in whatever scheme the satrap might have in mind. Yet for all the respect and admiration he had for Cyrus, he said that his first loyalty was to his fellow countrymen, and if it were to come to a choice between the two, he was willing to sacrifice his friendship with the prince.

Hearing this the soldiers broke into applause. There was a great number of them, for men from other camps had come to hear what Klearkhos had to say.

Informed of what was happening, Cyrus sent for Klearkhos, but he refused to go. However, he secretly returned a message to the prince, telling him not to be concerned, and to send for him again in the evening. This was the beginning of a series of intrigues which were devised by the Spartan to undo the defiance of the men.

After he had disobeyed for the second time, Klearkhos called another meeting of the soldiers, and this time a number of the troops also spoke, some of whom had been put up to it by their commander. One of these argued bluntly that the men should pack their things and leave straight away, asking Cyrus to provide them with ships and supplies. The absurdity of this proposal was promptly highlighted by another speaker – as if, he derided, the man whom they were deserting should care to help them return home! The same soldier reasoned that the best course was to go to Cyrus and find out exactly what his purpose was. If it was something reasonable, and did not put them in any more danger than the present expedition had, then why should they not proceed with him as before?

It was agreed then that this was what should be done, and a delegation of the soldiers was elected by the men to go with their commander to see Cyrus.

Of Cyrus' reasons for keeping his intentions secret, the first had become redundant: now that he was *en route* to Syria, the King could be in little doubt about his purpose. The second reason for his dissembling was that he feared the Greeks would be afraid to engage the Great King in battle: the current events bore out his concern on this matter, and forced him to maintain his evasiveness. When the party of Klearkhos came to him, he thus told them his target was the Syrian satrap, Abrocomas, who had become his enemy. He said that reports he received had put him on the Euphrates, twelve days' march away. If he was there, they would meet him in battle, 'but if he has fled,' the prince said, 'we must make our plans on the spot to meet the situation.'

This answer was taken back to the men, who were still not convinced that they weren't marching against the King. None the less, contingent on an increase in their pay to account for the new objective, they agreed to resume their former loyalty.

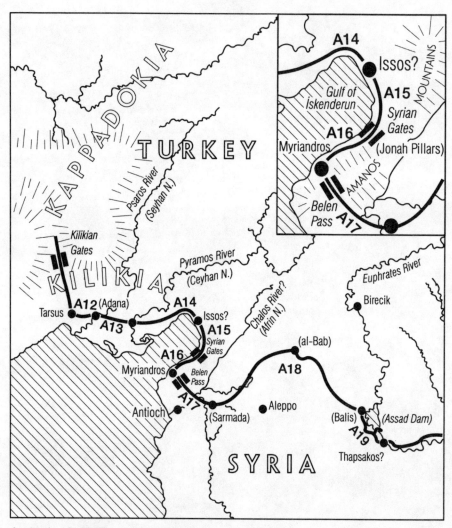

Anabasis 12-19: Tarsus to the Euphrates

11

The Gates of Syria

A12–17: Tarsus to the Chalos River

Seeking and learning are in fact nothing but recollection.

Socrates

I have seen a photograph of Kilikia taken from above the earth and it's exactly as Xenophon described: 'A chain of mountains, strong and high, encompasses it on all sides from sea to sea.' The wide rivers he mentions, the Psaros and Pyramos, can be seen trickling from the Taurus and winding over the plain to the sea. On the right of the picture, a southerly spur of the range, the Amanos, extends down into the Mediterranean, forming the very north-easterly corner of that sea. A sliver of land sits between its western edge and the water.

Not visible in the image is the highway running the length of the Kilikian Plain. This bends around the gulf and skirts along the base of the Amanos; halfway down a rib of rock juts from the spine and abruptly severs this unseen communication line. These are the 'Gates of Syria', the historical boundary between Kilikia and Syria.

After twenty days in the stifling heat and humidity of Tarsus, the army, their pay increased from 1 to 1½ darics per month, set off towards Syria. Two days and 50 kilometres took them to the Psaros River (A12); one day and 25 kilometres, to the Pyramos (A13); and two days and 75 kilometres, to Issos (A14). Issos was the last city of Kilikia, and Xenophon says it was a large and prosperous port.

Here the army was joined by the fleet that had been hovering in the gulf. This naval force consisted of sixty ships: thirty-five from the Peloponnese and twenty-five from Cyrus' own fleet based at Ephesus.

The purpose of the navy was to assist in turning the Syrian Gates, which the army was about to approach along the coast. The ships also brought with them a fresh unit of 700 Spartan *hoplites*, under the command of Xeirosophos, a renowned general of his country. His brief was to aid Cyrus, who was now in pursuit of Abrocomas. The Spartans were still careful not to link themselves to any intrigue against the King – and not without good reason, for the risks were high. The failure of Cyrus' attempt, and their implication in the plot, would almost certainly result in their dominance of the Hellenic world being ended.

These reinforcements, together with a contingent of 400 mercenaries who deserted to Cyrus from Abrocomas, brought the total number of Greeks under his command to about 14,000.

The site of Issos has never been satisfactorily identified. Certainly, no ruins corresponding to Xenophon's 'large and prosperous' city have yet been uncovered. The plain of Issos subsequently became famous as the place where Alexander, renewed after his illness, inflicted a great defeat on Darius III. The flight of the Great King from here in 333 in effect marked the end of the Persian Empire. Within three years Darius was dead and Babylon, Susa, and Persepolis were under the control of the Greeks.

In the context of uncovering Cyrus' route, the failure to pinpoint Issos is not a matter of critical importance, as it might be said to be for Alexandrian commentators. Ironically, the march details supplied by Xenophon are among the best historical clues to the whereabouts of the site: 'From here [Issos] a day's march of 5 *parasangs* took him to the Gates of Kilikia and Syria.' Tracing a line backwards from this prominent landmark – the present day Pillars of Jonah at Sarıseki – and drawing another the requisite distance (75 kilometres) from the Pyramos River at Misis, the two meet in the region of the modern Deliçay, quite probably the Pinaros River, along whose banks the imperial armies of Macedon and Parsa clashed.

Cyrus' plan was to land *hoplites* on either side of the Syrian Gates, and in this way to dislodge their defenders. His men, however, found the position deserted, the garrison of Abrocomas having been instructed to leave the post and join a larger force on the Euphrates. So Cyrus entered Syria unopposed; filing down the bumpy corridor between mountain and sea, he and his army passed through the Gates (A15). From there they marched in one day to Myriandros, a city on the sea inhabited by

Phoenicians (A16). Like Issos, this city has also not been positively identified, though some have tried to link it with İskenderun (Alexandretta). This, however, lies only a short distance beyond the Pillars of Jonah, and the geographer Strabo for one is clear the two were separate cities.

During the army's stay at Myriandros, an event took place that threatened to seriously undermine Cyrus' standing. Two of his commanders, Xenias and Pasion, taking with them the slaves and other booty they had won, slipped away on a merchant ship. Xenias had been a long-serving senior officer of Cyrus, and had gone upcountry with him as chief of his bodyguard when the King was dying.

When he learned of the desertions, Cyrus called the other generals together. Contrary to their expectation, he said that he would not pursue the men with his warships, even though his triremes could easily overtake them. 'No one shall say that I make use of a man while he is in my service, and then, when he wants to leave, that I arrest and ill-treat him and take away his property. No, let them go, with the knowledge that they have behaved worse to us than we have to them.'

The soldiers when they heard what Cyrus had said were impressed; and some who had been contemplating a similar course of action were said to have been dissuaded by this response from leaving.

As it was no longer of any use to him, Cyrus sent his navy back to Ephesus, and began his march into the interior (A17). On the fourth day the army came to the River Chalos, which was 30 metres in breadth, and full of large, tame fish. The Syrians regarded these as gods, as they did pigeons, and would not let anyone harm them. The villages where the army encamped at the end of the stage belonged to Cyrus' mother. She and others in her circle knew of his plan, and there were likely to have been provisions and gold set aside for him here.*

*

Walking through the humid Kilikian Plain had been taxing. Five minutes' toil here is enough to soak your clothes, and it takes hours to dry them even in the middle of the day.

---

* Persian royal women were given lands to furnish them with their own incomes. These they managed themselves, appointing stewards for each holding, and fixing the taxes to be collected. Parysatis owned lands in Persia, Media, Babylonia and Syria.

The sea breeze coming off the gulf brought a welcome respite. For a stretch of maybe 15 kilometres I was able to walk along a wide, flat beach. Holiday huts lined many of the fields behind, though this wasn't a place likely to appeal to any other than local tourists. At one end, a handful of kilometres apart, there were two huge oil terminals, fed by pipes coming from Kirkuk (Iraq) and Baku (Azerbaijan). Tankers hovered in the gulf awaiting their turn to be filled. At the other end of the beach a series of industrial complexes commenced, among them İsdemir, the largest steel factory in the Middle East. You could see these things because the beach, receding into a thin white line, was bending around the corner of the Mediterranean. This geography was probably the cause too of an eerie acoustic effect: the drone of heavy machinery constantly vibrated the air, and the sound was regularly punctuated by deep puffing noises.

This was the first chance I'd had to swim since the start of the journey, and it was also the first time I was able to walk without boots. My toenails had become black from the walking, although the soles of my feet had toughened sufficiently to make blisters a distant memory. In fact the problem had ceased quite early on, not long after I had taken up my father's parting advice and begun urinating on them.

The Gulf of İskenderun is named after the city. This was formerly Alexandretta, and the modern name retains in Turkish the connection with the Macedonian. The city lies 10 kilometres beyond the Syrian Gates, in the midst of a flat, marshy pocket of land. The British considered landing a force here in the First World War but sent their Anzacs to Gallipoli instead. Possibly they had intelligence of the mosquitoes, a fearsome plague in the city in the summer months.

Leaving the sea at Nardüzü, 7 kilometres south-west of İskenderun, I began the long ascent towards the Belen Pass. This is where the road crosses the backbone of the Amanos Mountains, the 'gates' previously described being formed by a spur that branches perpendicular into the sea.

After an hour I met the highway and scaled a steep embankment to get onto it. Vehicles coasted silently on one side, while on the other the gradient exacted its toll on the traffic: in low gear at high revolutions trucks and buses roared upwards, clouds of black smoke covering the breadth of the road. This bothered me less as I gained height, for the compensation was the gradual loss of the humidity that had made walking so uncomfortable in the previous stages.

A few kilometres before the Belen Pass, the town of the same name begins. Having limited room for lateral growth, over the years it has rolled down the highway, its upper and lower parts now being separated by a considerable distance. In the older section there is evidence of Roman building, a legacy perhaps indicating that in later antiquity, the southern control point of the Amanos corridor shifted from the sea gates into the heights. The pass itself, once a precipitous track running along the mountainside, has lately been developed to facilitate heavy transport.

Bends on the long pass afforded impressive views out onto the shimmering expanse of the Amik Plain. Ainsworth from one such vantage point picked out the 'Lake of Antioch', though I was unable myself to make out this body of water. Nor was the city itself visible. Today known as Antakya, a comparatively prosperous regional centre, once it was the third city of the Roman Empire. A natural outlet for Mesopotamian traffic, Antioch under the emperors became the gateway to the Orient. The first Christian house of worship was founded here by Peter in the middle of the first century AD, and in this city the followers of the new faith came to be called 'Christians'. Its cosmopolitan character is said to endure today in a subdued mix of Christians, Alawis, and secular Turks.

Weather along the 750-metre-high pass was, I discovered, highly changeable. Strolling along the top of a retaining wall, enjoying the sun and a light breeze, I was almost knocked off by a high wind which blew up on the far section. Shortly after I had begun descending, the sky above the mountains filled with dark clouds, which promptly spilled over the rocks in spectacular fashion, as though they were being sucked into a gigantic vacuum cleaner hidden on the mountainside. A miserly sprinkling of rain followed, so light that I could barely feel the moisture on my face, and don't believe the earth was wetted at all.

The slopes of the eastern flank were given over to olive trees. I dropped through one after the other of these steep groves, crossing at intervals the newly expanded roadway, which defeated the incline by elaborate zigzagging. Just the previous week on the Çukurova, I had remarked to myself that this tree had not been nearly as common in the country as I had expected. Presumably more valuable crops had gradually come to displace the venerable fruit, which in the time of the long Greek residency in Asia Minor would have been ubiquitous. Stopping beneath one tree that looked like two, I took time to photograph some of the more unusual specimens. Many of them were exceedingly old, having thick, twisted trunks with shapes in them that could frighten a man in the moonlight.

To the Greeks, the olive tree has always been sacred, a gift from the goddess Athena that became an integral part of their heritage. Used for a variety of purposes, in a land short on soil it was also a vital export. Ships taking oil through the Bosphoros in former times would return each summer laden with corn and other indigenous produce from the shores of the Black Sea.

On the landscape of the ancient world, the olive tree was a marker of political stability. The destruction of agriculture was always a priority for an invading army, and because of the length of time it took to mature (up to fifteen years), the olive could only prosper in peaceable climes. For this reason there emerged among the Greeks the tradition of offering an olive branch to a foe as a symbol of goodwill.

In a meadow halfway down the mountain, I was invited for tea by a man standing beside a battered pick-up truck in the yard of his house. This was a simple building, not much different in appearance from the ancillary barns that surrounded it. As I was walking through the heart of his property, I felt obliged to accept the invitation.

A crudely constructed porch extended from the front of the house, and inside this, women occupied themselves with household tasks. Leading me into the shelter, the man, an overweight, jolly type of character in his mid-thirties, shooed children away and seated me on a bench. The women, who had been working at a table, packed up their chores and disappeared inside. They were soon replaced by men who hurried in from the fields.

At first I thought it strange that my arrival should have aroused such interest, but then considered that the highway, even coupled with the presence of a new petrol station next door, did not bring them into real contact with the outside world. It just passed them by. An exception I learned was the periodic appearance of truckers from Eastern Europe. *En route* to Syria, the odd one spent a night in the garage forecourt, departing early the following morning for the lengthy ordeal of the border crossing. Football stickers on the windscreen of the pick-up provided evidence of some cultural exchange, as did the persistence of one of the evicted youngsters, who kept putting dual-syllable questions to me in a Slavic-sounding tongue.

Underneath the front window of the house there was an iron bedstead. During the commotion attending my arrival, the figure of an elderly man sat up on it. He looked frail, and odd with a magnifying glass taped over his left eye. We greeted each other and traded histories. He was the patriarch of the clan, the proud sire of eleven children, most of whom were still at home. The plump man who owned the pick-up was his eldest, and with two brothers he worked on the farm. A younger sister, or perhaps a granddaughter, kept attendance on the old man. She emerged from the house with a glass of water and held it to his lips. His agedness was more pronounced than I had remarked. A set of crutches rested against the bedposts, and even with his optical aid, he depended on voices for proper identification.

For a reason which was fated to be forgotten forever, while he refreshed himself I turned to my bag. As I did so my gaze fell on the eldest son, who was slouched in a worn armchair opposite me. He held my walking stick, one piece in each hand. I never dismantled the walking stick. Springing from the bench, I took it from him and put the parts back together. But by brute force, twisting in the wrong direction, he had stripped the worn plastic thread inside. I tried and tried to find a grip for the metal end; I remember my hands trembling, and then I just exploded. There wasn't a name I didn't call this buffoon: the frustration of having watched countless men abuse the stick, and the reality of the final, inevitable result, completely overtook me.

After the initial outburst, I channelled my anger into questioning, trying to learn exactly what it was that had urged him to dismantle the pole. Why did he *have* to try to take it apart? '*Bak,*' I said, pointing to the wreck in front of us, 'you have a car. I come and admire it: I can look at it, touch it – even sit in it; but I *don't* lift up the bonnet and strip the engine. *Bebek!*'

The porch had emptied somewhat by this time. The old man, left by his nurse, looked on in silence, stoically enduring the bad manners of his guest, and the disgrace brought on the family by his eldest son. It was for his sake that I finally forced myself to calm down. I apologized for the outburst, but did not try to explain the reason for it. At that moment I wasn't fully certain of it myself. Lying out on the bench, I breathed deeply and drew my hat down over my eyes.

The next morning I had a strange experience. I had risen early, after sleeping the night on the bench in the porch. A reconciliation of sorts had come about after the son had offered me a wooden stick in replacement for the aluminium pole; I declined it, but accepted his father's invitation to stay and eat with them.

Before sunrise I was on my way down the mountain towards the plain. In the first rays of light, this spread into Syria like a perfectly scaled relief map. I was jotting on paper the canal lines I would follow to take me there, when an image suddenly projected itself into my head. A child, four or five years old, I was clinging onto a fence in a neighbour's garden, and my playmate was calling me.

I jumped down and he pointed to a pile of builder's sand and said that my rifle was buried there. I saw the tip of the barrel and cleared away the sand, revealing the toy in two pieces. I ran home crying to my mother, and she somehow managed to glue it back together. But in those days glue demanded days of patience, a quality I was not blessed with. Every ten minutes I tormented her, and she would wearily go to the shelf in the garage where it was mending, returning to tell me it was nearly ready. Once, when she went to answer the front door, I took a chair from the kitchen and pushed it into the garage. My fingertips just reached the gun. Thrilled to find it fixed, I took aim at the garage door, but it snapped like a matchstick in my hands, and never fired another cap again. What I understood in that moment above the plain, was that my playmate had accidentally broken the gun, and then hidden it in the sand. For all those years I had just assumed it had got broken in the sand.

Walking was peculiar like that. You could be ambushed anywhere by a memory from the past triggered by some random encounter, or for no apparent reason at all you'd remember a face or a place long forgotten. I had the thought once that by the time I had finished, every single memory in my head would have flashed past my eyes.

Negotiating a route on the ground proved to be much harder than charting one from on high. I found my path repeatedly blocked by waterways, and several times became lost in fields of corn that grew to over two metres in height. Another crop in abundance was watermelon. August was harvest time, a labour-intensive process that temporarily brought family units from surrounding towns to live in shacks on the plain. I stayed that evening in one of these with an elderly couple from Kırıkhan, and for their sake the following morning I had to plod a kilometre with two monster melons in two plastic bags. Their concern at least took me on to a meaningful track. Minus the melons, I reached the village of Kumlu before midday, and from there picked up the road to the border.

I was on the lookout for the Chalos River, in Xenophon's day 'full of large, tame fish'. How they had come to be like this I wasn't sure, but I guessed it was related to their status as gods: nobody was allowed to catch them, and presumably they were well fed by the priests. I had identified the Chalos with the modern Afrin River, which rises in Turkey, and flows through Syria on its way to the sea. I came to it in mid-afternoon, although I found it necessary to confirm its identity with two separate locals, so meagre was the flow. Apparently the Syrians were responsible for this, siphoning off the greater volume for their pepper fields in the Afrin valley. I stood on a bridge above it for a while, a bit disappointed.

Instead of proceeding to the border, I diverted to Reyhanlı, a busy, and not particularly appealing, market town. Here I had repairs made to my stick. A wizard of a man trained in the mending of shoes managed to bind the plastic socket sufficiently to allow the teeth to grip the metal screw on the male part. Having felt distinctly odd while walking during this and the previous day, I now felt ready for the new phase of the journey.

*

A couple of twisting kilometres separate the busy customs posts at Cilvegözü and Bab al-Hawa. In the no man's land between them there stands a well-preserved ruin of Byzantine times, the Kızlar Sarayı ('girls' palace'). Engraved on the hill face which cossets it on the west side are giant letters spelling TÜRKİYE, while a short way to the east, the paraphernalia of Syrian statehood is visible. Until recently this area, and the whole Antakya region, was part of Syria. The present demarcation only came into being in 1939, when the French, who held a post-Ottoman mandate to govern the country, gave the province to the Turks in exchange for neutrality in the event of war. Today in Antakya there are still many Arabic speakers (most members of the Shia Alawi sect), and the Syrians insist on including the province in maps of their country.

At the first outpost of the Syrian complex, a uniformed man slipped out of a pillbox to greet me.

'Why you walk my friend, plenty vehicle?'

I said I had wanted to see the castle.

'Where you go after leaving Syria my friend?'

'I plan to go to Iraq.'

He examined my passport, and with what I thought was an air of slight disappointment, waved me on to the customs building.

He may well have been disappointed, for one of his functions was to apprehend people intending to travel to Palestine. Every week, unsuspecting visitors who might only have expressed a wish to see the Holy Land, were turned away by this man and his colleagues loitering in the vehicle bays behind. That the visitor was in possession of a Syrian visa was irrelevant: a hint of suspicion was enough to have entry refused.

The matter was of some concern to the Tourist Officer at the border, whom I found in an office at the end of the Arrivals Hall revising for a forthcoming English examination. A casually dressed man of about my own age, he welcomed me, and invited me to have tea. While it was brewing I took his textbook and tested him on prepositions.

'Grammar is my heel on Achilles,' he admitted with a broad grin after a weak show in the practice test.

Mohammed had been working at the post for three years, juggling it with a degree in English at Aleppo. Over glasses of heavily sugared tea, he spoke about his day-to-day life on this, the busiest of Syria's border crossings. Tourist-wise, things were quiet – commercial trucks made up the bulk of the traffic – although the heavy bureaucracy and the enthusiasm of the guards in seeking out visitors to Palestine meant he often had to get involved in matters outside his field. On the latter subject he was at pains to point out that his feelings on the Jewish occupation were not any different than the majority of his countrymen's, but he was upset by the way people were being unfairly led into corners. 'We are giving a bad first impression in our country.'

At his request I outlined on one of his tourist maps the course I thought my journey would take east to the Euphrates. He liked the idea of walking. 'Two Swiss last year cycle, but to walk, yes, a fine idea.' In what may have been a rush of blood to the head, he decided he was going to come with me. After leaving a note for his deputy on the desk, we set off toward his hometown of Sarmada.

12

Aleppo

Summer in the city

The city is as old as eternity, but still young, and it has never ceased to exist.

Ibn Jubayr of Valencia, twelfth century AD

To the population of Syria's barren north-western border region, the town of Sarmada ('eternity') is known as 'Paris'. This envious appellation alludes to the fact that many of the small town's inhabitants are employed at the border crossing. As I had gathered from Mohammed, this is comparatively lucrative work, as there is a guarantee to most of them of some share of the hard currency cow that is milked to the maximum by layers of bureaucracy. Jobs here are so coveted, indeed, that they are bought and sold like commodities in a market.

The main road from the border runs to Aleppo, 60 kilometres to the east. This follows closely the stone highway built by the Romans to connect this city to Antioch, and a section of the *via* near to the border has in recent times been uncovered. The extent to which it has been repaired is unclear, though such was the reputation of Roman engineers that it is not hard to believe it could have been unearthed in its present impressive state. Roads laid in other parts of the former empire have been in constant use for the last 2,000 years, requiring as little as half a dozen resurfacings in this time.

Mohammed led the way briskly toward our destination, turning only to check that I was in tow, or to emphasize a point in conversation. His roots were in the Bedouin culture. Had I been an Arab, he said, I would have recognized such distinctive features as his prominent jawbones and nose. It had been several generations since most nomads had settled, yet permanence had not withered their culture. Notably, their tribal system remained intact, and this cohesion ensured that the once powerful group still had influence in the wider society. Although it had smashed opposition to its rule from political factions, the government, Mohammed said, had never attempted to break the unity of the desert clans.

Moving on to religion he told me that he regarded himself as a devout Muslim. He defined one as a person who was intimately acquainted with the holy book, and who lived by its precepts. In his opinion most Arabs were not devout. 'I believe the Arab society is not suitable for Koran. They don't listen to what the words are saying, only what they want to hear from one imam and another – what is compatible with their own traditions.' The veiling of women was cited as an instance of tradition bulldozing scripture. 'There is nothing in Koran to this effect,' he insisted.

As he provided other everyday examples, I got the impression that Mohammed had developed for himself a secularized form of his religion, and that on these terms he was orthodox. I planned to put this to him, but it was hard to get a word in, and my attention was increasingly being claimed by the new world.

It took us an hour and a half to get to the turn-off for Sarmada. A large boulevard ran south from the highway towards the centre of the town. On either side of this there were spacious single-storey dwellings, the odd pretentious villa hidden behind high gates underlining the prosperity brought by the customs business.

In contrast to the residential architecture, the state of the infrastructure was poor. The concrete pavement along the wide avenue was regularly broken into uneven slabs; wires hung loosely from telephone poles planted in the sidewalk; and along the thin traffic island in the centre, a regimented line of street lamps stood without bulbs. Rather than Paris, I had the sense of walking into a remote Soviet settlement that had been earmarked for improvement by the centre. I envisaged unenthusiastic brigades of government workers pawing at the project for weeks before, at the allocated time, moving on to the next name on their list. As in the provincial towns of the former Soviet Union, their efforts amounted to little more than a makeover, an insubstantial exercise whose purpose was to create the illusion of progress.

Mohammed's home lay in the old part of the town, up a narrow side street bounded on each side by high whitewashed walls. Arabs, I came to remark early on, had a liking for walls: even in remote areas men were wont to raise stone walls around their homes. For a race famously indifferent to privacy, this always struck me as a curious paradox.

At the house Mohammed rapped on a metal door, and after a short pause led me into a shaded yard. An olive tree provided the shelter; beneath this, seated cross-legged on a reed mat, was an elderly man. He was short and stocky, had mousy grey hair, and a prominent nose – an older version of Mohammed.

'*Ahlan, Ahlan.*'

'*Salaam alaykum.*'

'*Alaykum salaam. Ahlan wa sahlan.*'

The father beckoned me to join him, and alerted the house to the fact that a guest had come. This proved unnecessary as a glass and pitcher of water were already in transit. Planting the tray on the mat, the same boy heaved on my pack, though I would not let him take away my walking stick. Mohammed took it to his room for safekeeping.

Mr Kandil had no English, and I had no Arabic, but I understood from a series of gestures that he also worked at Bab al-Hawa. Mohammed confirmed this when he rejoined us a short time later. He looked different, having swapped his jeans and sweater for a long robe-like garment, a *jalabiyah*, that almost touched the ground.

'My father is on the commercial section, checking weights of containers. Now he is many years. When he retires, Ahmed will take his place.' Ahmed, the lad who had taken away my gear, was the youngest, and between him and Mohammed there were two other brothers, both employed at the customs. The family was completed by a number of sisters, those not yet married still in the house.

A discreet call from one of them sent Ahmed racing into the open hallway off the yard. He returned bearing a mountain of rice and chunks of sliced lamb. Courses of salad and soup followed, together with a big bowl of yoghurt. Tearing strips off giant flat circles of bread, we dug at the meal until our hunger was satisfied.

In a year or two Mohammed planned to have his own home. The family had a site on the outskirts of the town and this was his to develop. By then his parents hoped he would be married. They had recently been trying to wed him to a cousin across the border in Antakya, but he wasn't going to be pushed into anything. Exposure to the outside world, and a memorable trip to the Lebanon the year before, had left him with a view on these matters different to the older generation's.

Reclining on cushions while awaiting the arrival of coffee, he told me that compatibility discussions had been underway for several months. His uncle's wife – who was the girl's older sister – was acting as the go-between. He had met his prospective bride once before, at the wedding of another uncle, and had found her agreeable. An obstacle at the present time, he revealed, was her wish not to live in Sarmada; she said she wanted to be in a city, preferably Antakya, though it was thought she would agree to a life in Aleppo. A response on Mohammed's part was expected soon, and it was evident the matter was weighing on his mind. After a break in the conversation, he returned himself to the sitting position.

'The true problem,' he confided, 'is that I am not in love.'

This revelation was not what I had expected.

'Maybe you can grow to love her.'

He sighed. 'Maybe I can grow fond of her. Love is or isn't.'

Turning to my freshly poured shot of bitter coffee, I couldn't help thinking that it was probably as much from such notions as this as the reputed wealth of her citizens, that the town near the border had acquired its exotic reputation.

*

The next day we travelled to Aleppo, a journey of an hour by 'microbus', the Syrian equivalent of the *dolmuş*. Syrian buses warrant both descriptions, being small (Asian models), and invariably packed to the gills. There is an added drawback in that women have to sit separately, so a bout of awkward shuffling is nearly always assured on a journey. Drop-offs present their own problems. To let one passenger tucked away in the rear row out at his desired destination can involve virtually the entire passenger load having to empty onto the side of the road. The Syrians, though, hardly give a thought to this inconvenience, and are happy to repeat the ordeal several times in the course of a trip.

Another early observation was that roads in the country had no surface markings. They looked like black streaks of tar painted over the landscape by a giant brush. The drivers treated these not particularly wide roads as dual carriageways, flashing their way past trucks and slower vehicles, oblivious to oncoming traffic. The system works OK until two overtakers meet and someone has to give way. Dogs also seem to get caught up in the disorder, their corpses littering the roadside at frequent intervals.

The terminus for the Sarmada microbuses was located opposite Bab Antakya, the western entrance to the old city. Until early in the last century, most of Aleppo's inhabitants had resided inside the long circuit of ancient walls, which now, as then, enclose a dense warren of *suqs*, workshops and mosques. The French, who governed the country for a brief spell after the Ottomans, laid out a new city beyond the walls, a *nouveau* design of straight boulevards and *jardins* and stolid building. A period of rapid expansion after their departure in 1946 saw it spread uncontrollably in all directions.

Stepping out of the bus, I felt I had arrived squarely in the Middle East. The smell of spices and cheap fuel hung thick in the air; rubbish was everywhere, loads of it heaped into mounds and scattered about the streets. Pools from burst pipes stagnated in the summer sun. Chickens and stray dogs drank from these and foraged for a meal among the food scraps discarded alongside countless snack stalls whose owners competed to out-shout one another.

Mohammed pursued a way through the throng. On his advice, I had decided to spend a few days in Aleppo: 'You must see it, Aleppo the White. See the Great Mosque, and the tombs of the saints, and the citadel that defied all Crusades.'

We skipped across a roaring downtown highway and in minutes were at the Baron Hotel, a grand-looking establishment, famous in the last century as a gathering place for the social elite. Agatha Christie and her husband, the archaeologist Max Mallowan, stayed here, as did Atatürk, and that great hater of Turkey, T.E. Lawrence. It now had a faded air about it, but was still popular among adventurous travellers.

The manager, a burly, campish character, took us up to the room where Lawrence used to stay on his visits to the city. It was on a corner of the building, looking out on what in his day would have been park-land. Compensation for the replacement of this view by office blocks came in the form of satellite TV and air-conditioning. Mohammed set about lowering the temperature while I appreciated the décor.

'Here Lawrence wrote his book,' the manager informed me, pointing to a desk by the door.

After an account of the Arabian's lifestyle habits, he left to see to a pot of tea. Lawrence always took this upon his return from a day out, and then he would shoot ducks from the window and have his batman bring the choicest bird round to the kitchen to be plucked for dinner.

A porter presently arrived with the brew and ushered us into a dining annex. An enquiry about the room rates revealed they were beyond my budget, so we had to return the keys and Mohammed took me to a nearby place run by an acquaintance of his. This was a much smaller and more basic affair, situated on a side street behind the Baron. The street was called al-Ma'arri, after a poet and philosopher who, Mohammed related, had lived in Aleppo a thousand years before. As a child he had been stricken with smallpox and lost his sight, an event that shaped a future sceptical view of the world. Contemporaries called him the 'heretic' for his unconventional outlook on religion, but his free thinking earned him wide respect in the Islamic world. Mohammed, a modern admirer, said that he was buried somewhere inside the city walls, and that his epitaph read:

> *It is my father who did this wrong to me*
> *But I did not commit one against any other.*

The al-Rabih reception was in a recess on the bend of a narrow dog-leg staircase. From his stool, the owner, an intense young man with wiry spectacles perched on a large nose, monitored the comings and goings of his guests. He was shaven-headed, and dressed unassumingly in T-shirt and jeans. His name was Osama, though his friends, I later learned, called him 'the fox'.

He showed me quickly around the premises. Mohammed recommended an *en suite* room at the back and negotiated a deal which the proprietor protested aloud was robbing him.

In his nook on the landing Osama purveyed everything. The 2 × 2 metre office functioned as a communications centre, travel bureau, bookshop, exchange office, and in general, any service that could be provided at a profit. On the first day I rented several books from him and bought an ISIC (student) card. The card wasn't cheap but he guaranteed it would pay for itself a dozen times over in reductions. He claimed to have seven languages, including Japanese and ancient Akkadian, and to have degrees in law and philosophy. He prided himself on running the cheapest hotel in Aleppo, and to maintain this status, he was prepared to undercut any competitor who sought to challenge him. The foreign guidebooks stacked on his shelves had not been kind to him, but this bad press didn't deter customers, mostly backpackers and East European merchants who hadn't done as well as they had hoped. Osama in fact got some satisfaction from his unflattering portrayal. He giggled as he read the entries to me from different tomes: 'It's a dingy little number but costs LS125 per person, or LS75 on the roof'; '... light and air-free rooms ...'; 'electric shocks and erratic plumbing come with the territory'.

A commendable feature not mentioned in the guides was the staff. They were all Kurds from the north, liked by Osama as they were hard workers and easy to replace. The longest serving was a man called Halil. He was from Qamishli, a large town on the Turkish border, and had been in the city for just over six months. His ambition was to study English at the university as Mohammed was doing, and he was using the job as a way to improve his language skills – not that I imagined he had ever much of a chance to get into proper conversation; if he were engaged with a guest on a non-business matter for any length of time, Osama's voice would sound irritably from the nook. '*Yah Halil, Yah!*'

My room looked out on a corrugated iron roof. The hotel adjacent was occupied by Russian prostitutes and the roof was littered with detritus from their lives. On the opposite side, the entrepreneurial-minded owner of a yard had erected a platform, and youths and older men hired spaces on this in the evenings when the girls were getting ready to go out. Occasionally a *diyevushka* would hurl an empty vodka bottle at the voyeurs, or a pimp would threaten them in Arabic, though it was never long before the heads popped up again.

Apart from the window, the advantage of the room was that it was cosseted to a degree from the shattering noise that echoed through the streets at dawn and dusk as the artisans opened and shut their premises. Aleppo the White, the city of a thousand shutters.

*

Aleppo had the feel of the 1950s. I wasn't born then but it was how I imagined life in a city in that period might be like. Giant Ambassador cars (refitted with Suzuki engines) plied the wide avenues; elegant ceiling fans twirled above bank foyers; contented cinemagoers spilled onto the streets beneath mammoth paintings of matinée idols. There were no supermarkets, malls, or fast-food chains to speak of.

Underpinning the anachronism was a near complete absence of tech-nology. I spent an afternoon looking unsuccessfully for an internet café – and few people I spoke to had even heard of the medium. Fax machines, having just been made legal by the government, were at the cutting edge of communications technology, and to have a telephone in your home was considered an elite privilege.

The walled city was a time capsule within this. In the great covered market especially, only the odd camcorder-totting tourist and the sudden roar of a two-stroke engine reminded one that this was not a medieval place. Along its dimly lit thoroughfares veiled women haggled with silk sellers, young couples eyed wedding rings and merchants dug their hands invitingly into open sacks of spices and coffee. Every so often at the narrow, crowded junctions, a poignant clash of past and present would play itself out. Overladen donkeys, *en route* from one *khan* to another, would steadfastly refuse to give way to revving Korean micro-vans, whose drivers tried to intimidate them by keeping their horns depressed. Hail the tattered outlaw of the earth!

In comparison with the Turks I found the Arabs more relaxed about selling. If you showed no interest in their wares, they generally didn't bother you. Turkish traders on the other hand were on top of you as soon as you came near their establishment. *'Buyurun! Buyurun!'* The natives seem to have no problem with this, but to the Western mind its relentlessness can be grating. I often wondered how they thought this harassment was a route to greater sales, until a friend from Izmir explained it to me. 'It's like fishing,' he smiled. 'If you throw the line in enough times, you'll catch something.'

There were other notable differences in trading practices. If you ask a Turk the price of something, for instance, he'll give you the true amount; if you don't, he'll probably cheat you. If you ask an Arab in the market for his price, he'll cheat you anyway.

I liked Aleppo, and ended up staying a month. After falling out with the fox over a fine imposed on a late-returned library book, I moved to another hotel further up al-Ma'arri Street. The Syria was bigger, and slightly more upmarket. It was run by an articulate, bewigged gentleman, who had the skill of making his guests feel they were staying at a more luxurious place. As well as managing the hotel, he told me he was assistant curator of prehistory at the archaeology museum across the road, and had consular roles with several Central Asian states.

I got a room at the rear of the third floor, so avoiding the industrial noises that floated up from the poet's street from early morning to dusk. The room was small, a rectangular box furnished basically with wardrobe, bed, and table. It also had a sink, and a ceiling fan that rotated at an angle, rather like a flying saucer taking off. The wall on the bedside was graced with the names of previous Russian guests, who, together with their personal details, sometimes penned lurid anecdotes of their time in the city.

During my stay in the Syria I became friends with a Moroccan chemist called Raschid. His room was at the other end of the same corridor, facing al-Ma'arri Street. Our paths crossed in the lounge one afternoon and he invited me to join him for tea. He was a tall, heavily built man, with an ample moustache and a thick head of black hair. He stood out for his well-cut suits, and a trilby which he never wore but always had to hand.

At that stage he had already been in the city for six weeks. Like myself, he had started off in the Baron Hotel, but found this one 'plus comfortable'. His family owned pharmacies in Rabat and he had been sent to Aleppo to procure medicines for the business. Aleppo, he told me in that first meeting, was famous all over the Arab world for its medicines.

Raschid had recently qualified in the profession, and this was his first business trip abroad. I didn't enquire how his factory visits were going, as I had previously formed the impression he wasn't making many. He rarely rose before midday, and it was never long before his table in the lounge was surrounded by an entourage. I'd often see them lunching at the open-air cafés opposite the citadel. The next time I was there with Mohammed he sent over coffee and waterpipes. 'From Mr Raschid,' our normally inattentive waiter whispered.

*

Together with Damascus and San'a, Aleppo has claims to be the oldest continuously inhabited city on earth. Not much survives from the early periods, although current excavations on the citadel are uncovering architecture from most of the major epochs. For me the main attraction of the city was its vibrant character: over 2,000 years as an international trading centre has left it with a diverse mix of peoples and a brazen attitude that transcends the restrictions of Arab culture. It is a place that is used to outsiders, and as an outsider, you can be anonymous. The Russian prostitute, French tourist, Armenian shoe salesman, Moroccan chemist, all are absorbed without notice into the hectic rhythm of daily life.

The first settlers, 4,000 years ago, may have been drawn by an enormous flat-topped mound, whose appearance in the middle of the desert is likely to have invited religious association. The twelfth-century AD Andalusian traveller, Ibn Jubayr, heard that Abraham had camped on the windswept summit en route from Ur to Canaan. It was said that he had milked his cows here and distributed the milk as alms among the people, which is how the city got the name that survives to the present (*halib* is Arabic for milk, 'Halab' the Arabic name for the city).

The city grew up around the mound, and from as early as Hellenic times was enclosed by a rectangular wall. While the citadel was always used as a refuge against invaders, it wasn't until the Muslim era that it was developed into the formidable fortress that dominates the city today. Chief patron of the defensive architecture was the legendary Ayyubid ruler, Saladin. After conquering Aleppo in 1183 AD, he appointed his son to be governor, with orders to ensure the fort could not be taken by the Crusaders. Al-Malik al-Zahir Ghazi dug a deep moat around the base, steepened the sides, and fitted them with panels of smooth stone. A bridge was built to lead up to the entrance, a massive barbican containing three heavy iron gates and flanked by a pair of lofty stone towers. Inside he constructed a *dar al-sina'ah* (arsenal), a water reservoir, a grain store, and a tall minaret. From atop this on a clear day a lookout could see north as far as the Taurus Mountains, and east to the hills fronting the Euphrates River.

Circling the perimeter of the citadel, the remnants of its stone glacis capped by a ring of thickset walls, it is hard to pick out any place where an attack might be successfully made. The reservoirs, silos and mosques within meant that a siege could be faced by the waiting defenders with a justifiable air of confidence. Still, when Tamerlane came in 1400 AD, it could not resist. A Bavarian soldier of fortune in the service of the Imperial Nomad, Johanns Schiltberger, provided an account of his assault in his *Reisebuch*.

> He went into his [the Mamluk] territory, and lay siege to a city called Hallapp, which contains four hundred thousand houses. Then the lord and governor of the city took with him eighty thousand men, and went

out and fought with Tämerlin, but he could not overcome him, and fled again into the city, and many people were killed in his flight. He continued to defend himself, but Tämerlin took a suburb on the fourth day, and the people he found in it he threw into the moat of the city, put timber and mire upon them, and filled the moat in four places. The moat was twelve fathoms deep, and cut in the solid rock. Then he stormed the city, and took it by assault and captured the governor, and fully occupied the city.

The citadel's last stand was against the Ottomans in the early sixteenth century. By then the Mongol destruction had been repaired, yet perhaps with memories of Tamerlane still vivid, those inside had not much stomach for the fight. When Selim I (the Grim) entered the city at the head of his army in 1516 AD, no one opposed him. He encamped outside the walls, and in what must be one of history's grandest gestures of military arrogance, sent a lame soldier armed with a club up to the mighty entrance portal of the citadel. Rapping the outer doorway, he demanded, and received the surrender.

In the Ottoman era Aleppo became the principal trading centre of the Levant. Its position midway between the Euphrates and the Mediterranean had always made it an important caravan stop, but now it was a hub in a multinational empire. Silk from Persia, coffee from Yemen, indigo, spices, and peppers from the Far East, all funnelled through here *en route* to the markets and workshops of the West. Aloof from such commerce, the sultans were content to allow Europeans to exploit the resources of the Orient. They built the covered *suq* for them, and so long as they were discreet, and paid their taxes, they were tolerated.

The merchants of Aleppo were not at all shy of profit. They earned fortunes acting as middlemen between the caravaners and the Europeans. Many were Jews and Christians and in the boom period of the seventeenth and eighteenth centuries they invested their wealth in lavish houses. The Jdaidah ('new') Quarter north of the *suqs* remains the most pleasant part of the city, a quiet, compact area of accomplished architecture and narrow cobbled laneways. Most of the houses are still said to be owned by the families of the once powerful traders, though the Jews have gone and it is now a predominantly Christian enclave.

The opening of sea routes to the Far East in the nineteenth century led to a marked reduction in the volumes of raw materials reaching Aleppo. However, the further development of local export industries – textiles, ceramics, glass and metalwork – ensured the city did not suffer excessively.

A further blow came in 1939 when the French gave the province of Antakya to the Turks – a sea and a hinterland were cut off at the stroke of an imperial pen. 'Its days and nights have been long,' wrote Ibn Jubayr in his *Travels*, 'it has survived its rulers and commoners. These are its houses and dwellings, but where are their former residents and the people who visited them? These are its palaces and chambers of court, but where are the Hamdanid princes and their poets? They have all passed away, but the city is still here. City of wonders! It endures.'

13

Vanishing Footsteps

A18: Between the Chalos and Dardas Rivers

In Aleppo the journey fell off the tracks a bit. I had intended to reach the Euphrates by the end of August, just a month after the time Cyrus is thought to have crossed, but a long delay over a money transfer put paid to this. It was also the case that I had become inert in Aleppo, spending days in bed and nights whiling the hours away in cafés. The truth, as I admitted to myself lying in bed one morning, was that I had lost my appetite for the journey. I was struggling to find traces of the army's passing: except at the beginning, at the Temple of Artemis, and at a fountain in Phrygia, there were no moments I had truly had a sense of connection with the expedition. And now awaiting me was a stage for which the route itself was uncertain. Besides all this, walking took up so much energy and focus that I often felt I was absorbing little of my surroundings, just passing over the landscape like an android.

As I hauled myself out of the bed, Yeats came suddenly to mind: I was becoming like Sisyphos. Every morning rising early and toiling until sunset, with no result. Was this my destiny?

It was Mohammed who restarted me on the journey. He had pulled out of marriage talks with his prospective bride and was keen for the freedom of the road.

Over tea at a café beneath the citadel, he produced the sketch I had drawn for him in his office a few weeks before of the route I was planning to take to the Euphrates. This was a smooth arc running from the border through the northern town of al-Bab and down hence to the Assad Dam. Its geometrical purity was a reflection of the uncertainty of the stages on this section of the route. In the crossing of the Syrian Desert, for the first time, the tracks of the Ten Thousand begin to fade.

As I looked at the graceful line, drawn in one deliberate stroke, it crossed my mind that I mightn't have made enough of an effort to discover the way, to try to be on the right path. Perhaps, I thought, a discovery – a place, a person, a myth – could only be possible if the journey was properly done.

When I got back to the hotel that afternoon I took out my notes and maps and sat down at the small table in front of the window. The sun had crossed behind the roof and a breath of air came through the open window. I could feel an impetus returning as I located the passages in the text:

> After these occurrences, Cyrus proceeded four days march, a distance of twenty *parasangs*, to the river Chalos, which is a *plethrum* in breadth, and full of large, tame fish which the Syrians regarded as gods. They allowed no one to hurt either them or the pigeons. The villages in which they stayed belonged to Parysatis, having been given to her for her girdle. Thence he advanced five days' march, a distance of thirty *parasangs*, to the source of the river Dardas, which is a *plethrum* in breadth. Here was the palace of Belesys, the Governor of Syria, and there was a very large and beautiful garden containing all that the seasons produce. But Cyrus laid it waste, and burned the palace to the ground.

When researching the route I had marked the Chalos as the Afrin, and placed the villages of Parysatis in the upper end of the river valley. This seemed reasonable enough, though because of the border, I had been unable to pursue exactly the path I thought they had taken. For the next stage, the eighteenth, I had written in my notes that 'the army probably went across country from here in a direct line towards the Euphrates'.

My thinking now, after having been in their tracks for several months, was that they would have followed some pre-existing trade route, which would have passed through various oases in the desert that served the caravan trains. Aleppo would have been one such halting station; al-Bab, 40 kilometres to the north-west of here, another. Some scholars think that the latter is where the Syrian governor spoken of by Xenophon had his palace. W.J. Farrell, who visited during the war (1941–5), wrote: 'Bab is well watered and full of trees – an oasis in a harsh land – and entirely suitable for a Persian governor's park; indeed the only possible place for many miles. It is also the source of the river called nahr al-Dhahab, which corresponds to the description of the Dardas.'

But as I had flagged in my margin, there was a problem with distances. Assuming the Afrin to be the Chalos, and the Dhahab to be the ancient Dardas, even a meandering route between the two would scarcely amount to the 150 kilometres (30 *parasangs*) given by Xenophon for the stage. They might have criss-crossed the desert, or the figure could be inaccurate: Xenophon – or whoever he obtained the detail from – could have overstated the distance between the stops. As I had discovered myself, it was all too easy to do so on difficult stretches.*

A more imaginative solution to the problem was to devalue the *parasang* because of the harshness of the terrain on this stage.

On the face of it the case for 'devaluation' on this leg is not an unreasonable one. The *parasang* is not a specified measure of distance, but rather the distance that is covered in a given period of time ('an hour's march at the pace of infantry', according to Farrell). In the instance of this particular stage, heat and difficult underfoot conditions would certainly have slowed progress. But if a 'reduced rate' was used here, why then resume the former value for the next stage to the Euphrates (as would be necessary to get there from al-Bab), undertaken in similarly trying conditions?

I had a question mark in my notes next to this theory, and nothing had happened since to make me reconsider my view. My heart, if not my head, told me that Xenophon's figures were no less credible or consistent than previously. I resolved to stick with them unless the trek and visit to al-Bab suggested otherwise. By all accounts al-Bab was a prominent oasis, and whether or not its river was the same as the Dardas, I thought it probable that the army had passed through it on their way to the Euphrates.

My new route thus extended north from Sarmada to the area around the church of St Simeon on the lip of the Afrin valley; then east to cross

---

* The phenomenon is known to military planners. Bunbury in his *Geography* cites the case of a nineteenth-century British expedition into Abyssinia. 'Here the distances traversed by the army were afterwards actually measured, and it was found that a day's march, estimated by experienced officers at 16 or 18 miles, often did not exceed 8.'

the Kuweik River above Aleppo, and on to al-Bab and the Euphrates. The new line, I remarked, while not as aesthetically appealing as the original one, was more meaningful.

*

The day before I was due to go out to Mohammed's I dropped in to see Raschid. His room was on the same floor as mine, and was *en suite* and had TV. This was switched off before he came to the door. He had a *jalabiyah* on, the tracksuit of the Arab.

I refused to disturb him, and extended my invitation without going further than the hallway. Several times he had expressed an interest in walking. His ancestors, Berbers, had spent their whole lives doing it, and often when he had a waterpipe in hand, he would hanker after the nomadic life. However, now he looked a bit down in the mouth, and politely declined to join us. 'I must to confess at the moment, the affairs are many. Perhaps *plus tard?*'

The distinguished manager of the Syria hinted when I went to settle my bill that Raschid's account was not as the hotel would like. I called to his room again that evening saying I had some extra cash. He was offended that I had thought to return his hospitality in this way. There was no problem, he assured me. Money was being sent by his father. We embraced and said goodbye.

Mohammed was waiting at the bus stop in Sarmada. He was dressed as for work, his only adaptations for the trek being a light shirt and a baseball cap. The contrast in our appearances made me feel a little self-conscious; I had boots, lightweight trousers, a long-peaked sunhat and my stick. As we set off, I reflected that however much I walked, I would likely never acquire that oneness with the landscape which was innate to the Bedouin.

On our way out of town we detoured to its most famous landmark, the Pillars of Sarmada. Situated in a walled-off compound behind the homes on the east side of the boulevard, these are said to mark the burial site of a Roman aristocrat, Alexander, who lived here in the first century AD. The two 10-metre-high pillars which formed the monument were joined near the top by a thin wedge of stone, and crowning them were two bulky capitals, one Corinthian, the other something like Doric. The edifice struck me as unconvincing, but in light of it being the symbol of the town, and Mohammed being an employee of the Tourism Ministry, I refrained from airing my scepticism about it having stood on this site for 1,900 years.

In any case, he preferred to concentrate on the excavated tombs in front of the pillars. These, it had to be said, were unquestionably genuine, having probably suffered only the violations of ancient robbers before their opening by twentieth-century archaeologists. There were three graves on the site, each with a simple stone stairway leading down to where the remains were laid. According to Mohammed, similar family tombs were to be found throughout the region; many, like these, were situated near to the highway, where there would have been halting stations and the mansions of wealthy farmers.

Surveying the empty limestone landscape that extended northward from Sarmada, agriculture was not something that came to mind. But as my companion was at pains to point out, it was necessary to imagine swathes of the stony ground covered in row after row of olive trees. For in the Roman era this parched basin was developed as the oil reservoir of Antioch. Where other vegetation would wither here, the olive tree thrived, its tenacious roots creeping deep into the porous rock to find water.

In the early centuries of the successor (Byzantine) empire, another dimension was added to the life of the region. Inspired by the example of the Desert Fathers in Sinai, legions of pious Christians from Antioch and its environs flocked into the wilderness to set up secluded places of worship. In all more than a hundred monasteries and churches are said to have been founded, and thanks to dryness and isolation, many of them survive in a high state of preservation. For this reason they have become known as the Dead Cities.

The most famous of them is the church complex of St Simeon Stylites, an eccentric monk who spent most of his life atop a pillar, haranguing pilgrims who had journeyed from as far away as Constantinople to receive his blessing. We had visited this site on a day trip from Aleppo a couple of weeks before, and I had marked it on my new route as a waypoint for the eastern turn. (From its walls, the Afrin River and the town of Jindairis – an elevated settlement area, possibly where the villages of Parysatis were – were visible away to the north-west.) I reckoned the height to be about 25 kilometres from Sarmada, a good hike by country road after the lengthy lay-off. Mohammed, though, knew of a more direct path used by local shepherds, and not long after crossing the highway, we joined the faintly marked track. In a short time we were in a desert, rolling and filled with an infinite number of rocks.

Simeon was born the son of a shepherd somewhere in this desolation late in the fourth century AD. Little is known of his early life, other than that one night while grazing sheep he had a visitation. Whatever he saw or heard prompted him to enrol in a local monastery, and it is here that his unusual personality began to express itself. From the beginning he relished arduous spiritual exercises, and soon took to wearing a spiked iron girdle. He dressed in it for work in the monastic groves, and tightened the straps at prayer time to increase his awareness of the master's suffering. It is said he even wore the girdle when, with several other novices, he submitted to being buried in the ground up to his neck, an exercise thought to facilitate communion with the Holy Spirit. Most begged for release after a few days, but Simeon remained in the earth for three months. Forty-day fasts were meat and drink to him, and meaningless unless accompanied by daily bouts of self-flagellation.

His quest for disciplinary Nirvana eventually led him onto an exposed, flat-topped hill on the edge of the Afrin valley. It's a conspicuous spot, a bluff rising from the desert, constantly swept by the wind. Following in his footsteps, one can readily imagine the smile forming on the demented face when he discovered a massive boulder on the centre of the summit. Hastening back to the cells for his equipment, he returned and chained himself to it.

After some years, as word of his holiness spread, people began to come to the hill. Unwilling to suffer distraction from his prayers, he had a pillar erected, ultimately to 18 metres, and he resided on top of this until his death thirty years later. By this time he was legendary in the Christian world. Pilgrims from as far as northern Europe were journeying to behold him on the pillar. Keen to preserve the site as a place of pilgrimage, his much-expanded community began to raise money from sightseers and royal courts for the building of a monument. The eventual result was a giant cruciform church with four basilicas, one at each of the compass points, the pillar enshrined in the centre. Today, after 1,500 years of souvenir hunting, this has been chipped away to a stump of rock no more than a few metres in height, possibly something like the boulder that the saint originally happened upon.

Used to the ankle-breaking terrain, Mohammed led the way. Occasionally he paused to allow me take a photograph, or if there was some overhang that afforded shelter, we'd rest in its shadow. We came upon one such at mid-morning and refreshed ourselves.

'What does a holy man look like?' I sprang the question on him after he had satisfied his thirst. He considered it for a minute.

'I think we recognize him from what he does.'

'What does he do that makes him holy?'

'He follows his faith. God's word. For us this is revealed by the prophet, who is our guide.'

He wiped his forehead and handed me back the bottle. 'Do you know the Hadith? These are the sayings of Mohammed, peace be upon him. He says that every good act is charity. Charity makes a person become holy. Helping a blind man cross the road is charity. Giving water to the thirsty is charity. Showing a stranger the way is charity. I think we must all try to be holy men. It is our duty.'

When he started on the subject of religion, Mohammed could go on all day. He preached on as we started over the stones again.

In a way I envied him. He had a solid faith, a conviction, and right or wrong, it gave his life a definite direction. I was raised a Catholic. My mother was a Limerick Catholic, a west Limerick one. Unbeknownst to her, one day I stopped going to mass; then somehow I came into my present condition as a mortalist, a person who believes that the soul dies with the body. The cult of mortalism is about accepting that you are nothing more, or less, than the stones; than the smallest particle of dust that blows out in the cosmos.

I didn't know if this belief was rare – mortalists don't gather for worship, or generally associate with one another on the basis of common belief – but I didn't discount the existence of a god. The difficulty was that if there were gods, they were immortal, an obvious anathema to the creed. But I didn't see them that way anyway. Even the greatest, Helios (the sun), has only finite power, and moreover, Pan is dead. Plutarch records his passing in the first century AD, although the causes of his death were secret to the Delphian priests. So I preferred to think of the forces shaping our lives as demigods, outlasting but not everlasting.

For an hour or more we had not been following any path. Periodic glances at my compass showed that we were headed in a westerly direction. Thinking that at a cairn, or some discrete natural landmark, we were going to swing north, I said nothing to Mohammed. I decided now to ask if there was long to go to a water source. He halted and looked around. His face, normally assured, betrayed mild bewilderment. He took out a handkerchief and wiped his forehead. 'After this hill I think the road will be.'

From the scorched height there was nothing to be seen in any direction, save for what I thought might be a look-out post on the Turkish frontier. I suggested that we head back the way we came. He seemed slightly upset by the misadventure, and did not object when I volunteered to take the lead with the compass.

Less was said on this hike. Wearied by the sun, we concentrated our energies on getting back to the road. Without proper footwear, I realized that the wayward walk must have been especially taxing for Mohammed, but he showed no signs of discomfort.

In mid-afternoon we sighted a sloping grove of olives, and soon after came to a quarry, where we slaked our thirst with a hose. I held it for ages to the back of my neck to cool my body, then I sprayed it on Mohammed, who had been more restrained in its use. He reacted rather negatively, and then admitted that he wasn't feeling very well. I suggested that we take a lift back to Sarmada, but he waved aside the proposal, and led the way himself to Daret-Azzeh, the turning-off point for the Church of St Simeon. At that stage neither of us felt up to going out there, so instead we drank soft drinks in the village and took a microbus back to Sarmada.

I thought Mohammed might have caught too much sun. His eyes looked yellow and his head was sore. He went to bed when we got back to his house, but in the morning he rose looking much more like himself. He wanted to continue with me, but I thought it would be better for him to take it easy for a day or two. I reasoned that he had my route, and could catch up by bus if he felt up to it later in the week.

After breakfast, we caught the microbus back to Daret-Azzeh. We left each other on a hill just outside the village.

'Keep on the path,' he called after me.

I waved back at him with my stick.

This road into Aleppo was quiet. Microbuses, and vans overloaded with red peppers, were the principal users. Most took no notice of me, although several people in roadside villages wanted to know why I was walking. The Arabs like gestures. For many everyday communications they use them instead of words. This language is intuitive and you pick it up quickly. A finger pointed downwards and twirled rapidly is an offer for tea (teaspoon in the glass); hand to mouth is food. The twisting wrist is an enquiry, a gesture I became especially familiar with. There are several different types. Done close to the chest, it's respectful. 'Can I help you?'

As the arm extends, the register of the question becomes more severe. Fully extended, it's impatient and possibly aggressive. Speed and the ambit of the twist are the important factors here. An arm flung out with a full turn of the wrist means you've most likely seriously upset somebody.

The number of plastic bags littering the landscape took me aback. Snared on stones, they fluttered in the wind like industrial prayer-flags. They were the small black ones shopkeepers dished out for even the smallest of purchases. The blight, I was to discover, worsened near areas of settlement. In some patches I thought they were almost as numerous as the flies, the more traditional plague of the desert.

Making good progress on the smooth black surface, I came in sight of the city just after midday: Aleppo the White.

A pick-up van pulled alongside as I took in the scene.

'I give lift my friend. No much money, no problem.'

I looked in the window at the driver, a fat man in a stained grey *jalabiyah*. A cigarette burned between the fingers of his gear hand. He looked like the border guard who had quizzed me on my onward itinerary when I entered the country a month before. Besides the physical resemblance, he had the same anticipatory glint in his eyes. I had an urge to wind him up.

I straightened and regarded the city. Aleppo the White.

'Friend, would $100 be enough?'

He shrugged indifferently.

I unclipped my pack, but then had a change of mind, and thought I'd go over the hills toward al-Bab instead.

'Too far friend. No walk this direction. Nothing.' The van attempted to follow as I crossed the road but cut out in the hasty pursuit. The engine turned over repeatedly as I mounted a ridge and headed north. 'Come friend. *Ta'al! Ta'al!*'

*

Al-Bab, 'the gate', lies 40 kilometres north-east of Aleppo. The conditions in this area are even harsher than around the Dead Cities: soaring temperatures and a persistent dry bluster make eking a living from the rocky terrain especially precarious. The principal occupation is sheep rearing, a job which entails youths escorting small flocks about the hills in search of scrub and other extreme vegetation. Settlements in this region are fewer than in the western hinterland of the northern capital.

Being a day's camel ride from Aleppo, and two from the Euphrates, al-Bab was ideally located for a caravan stop. The existence of an ample water supply here ensured that it developed as an important way-station, a gateway to both east and west. Little archaeological work has been carried out in the city, but a conspicuous *tell* on its northern side suggests that habitation goes back a long way.

I was taken to the mound by an English teacher, Hussein Kassar, who was summoned by a helpful shopkeeper from whom I had sought information on my arrival. I explained to him as we travelled in his car that I was really interested in seeing the river, and if possible, the place where it rose.

'There was a river,' he told me, after a discussion with his brother-in-law, also Hussein, who was in the rear, 'but it stopped many years before.'

The men had no personal memories of it, although Hussein in the back thought it had flowed up until the early 1970s. An elderly neighbour of theirs confirmed this. He painted a picture of a lively stream, the al-Dhahab Nahr, 'gold river', whose banks were lined with tall trees. This would have been the sight that Farrell saw during his military reconnaissance in the 1940s. The pressures of increased population in the independence years seem to have been the cause of the river's death. Water now comes to the dusty city of 40,000 by pipe from the Euphrates.

Our enquiries that afternoon also unearthed memory of an ancient palace, Qasr al-Zuhur ('palace of flowers'). This name evidently invited a link to the residence of the governor referred to by Xenophon, who he said kept a very large and beautiful garden. Taken with the fact that the name of the dead river in Arabic culture is associated with beauty, it seemed certain that al-Bab had historically been a lush oasis in the wilderness.

However I left Hussein's the next morning not wholly convinced it was where the eighteenth stage ended. Whilst the previous existence of gardens and a bucolic river in this desert location made a strong case for the contention, accepting it would mean either 'correcting' Xenophon, or devaluing the *parasang*. Granted there was a reasonable basis for the latter, taking this course would introduce problems down the line: given that the same conditions prevailed on the remainder of the route to the river, it wouldn't make sense to resume the regular value for this next stage. And if it wasn't resumed, whatever route east was taken from al-Bab, would, by virtue of the reduced rate, fall well short of the river. As the nineteenth stage took Cyrus, 'to the river Euphrates', such a situation would be problematic.

If the 'standard' 5-kilometre rate was maintained for A18, then continuing through al-Bab and heading south-east across the desert towards the elbow of the river would lead to the ruins of ancient Balis. Balis was a Roman garrison town that might have been founded on the site of an earlier city. The problem with naming it as the terminus of the eighteenth stage is that in Xenophon's time it stood within a few kilometres of the Euphrates, and he was clear that the next stage, a three-day march of 15 *parasangs*, took Cyrus to the Euphrates.

14

Cyrus Reveals the Truth

A19: The Crossing Place

I know a discontented gentleman
Whose humble means match not his haughty mind:
Gold were as good as twenty orators,
And will, no doubt, tempt him to anything.

Courtier to Richard III

Thapsakos derives from a Semitic root, *psh*, meaning 'ford'. In Achaemenid and into Seleukid times, the place so-called was the principal crossing place for the Middle Euphrates. A branch of the Royal Road ran south-west to it, and numerous trade routes from east and west converged on it. The Hellenic geographer Eratosthenes considered the location so pivotal that he chose it as the point from which to make his measurements for all Asia.

Given its prominence in the Classic Age, and the fact of the city itself being spoken of in impressive terms by the ancient writers, it is surprising that no trace of Thapsakos has ever been found. Some have tried to identify it with Karkamish (Farrell, Engels, Brunt), a Hittite fortress in the north of Syria that controlled the middle river in the second millennium, but this fusion of the two places has not been widely accepted by philologists. Other sites suggested for the ford include Birecik (Manfredi), Bir Khallo (Lendle), Balis (Barnett), Qalaat Dibsi (Herzfeld), Anazah (Ainsworth), Raqqa (Bury) and Dayr Ez Zor (Rennell). The spread of these sites – 450 kilometres from Birecik to Dayr – is a reflection of the uncertainty, and also, it has to be said, of the academic propensity for pure speculation. In this regard, the modern commentators are the more indulgent. The best of them is a German called Otto Lendle. Exhibiting the finer traits of the national stereotype, he succeeds in producing some remarkably simple solutions to problems of the march. His siting of Thapsakos at Bir Khallo, though in the received view too far upstream, has the merit of being located at one of the widest points of the river, and is near where a ferry service has operated since at least the beginning of Islamic times. As I progressed I found myself referring regularly to his hand-drawn sketches of the stages.

Regrettably, and in spite of all the scholarly effort, there is now the real possibility that the mystery of the crossing place may never be solved, for a colossal dam built at Tabaqah in the 1970s has quietly submerged hundreds of square kilometres, and thousands of years of human heritage.

My first sight of the Euphrates came as I approached a stone tower situated on a plateau high above the artificial lake. The deep blue expanse of water, striking against the desert brown, backed northwards up the valley, gradually narrowing into the natural form of the river. Looking at it, my immediate feeling was one of disappointment; it was like looking at a once peerless athlete who had become cruelly blown up on steroids.

Signs of the river had appeared long before it did: a gradual greening of the landscape, a massive concrete canal, a chain of gangling pylons relaying high voltage west toward Aleppo and its industrial hinterland.

Before this, for a day and a half beyond al-Bab, it had been hard walking through desolate terrain and villages whose menfolk did long stints on the building sites of Beirut. Poor directions and a mapping error had resulted in a dehydrated night in the wilderness. The prayed-for appearance of a shepherd the next day (on a motorcycle) brought me by way of a lingering dust cloud to his settlement. The people there would have had me follow a road south-west to the highway, but I chose to follow the nearby canal, and that evening came close to its source. I was prevented from getting there by a man in an isolated dwelling who insisted I couldn't pass without first availing of his hospitality.

In the morning he took me to a hill from where a stone tower, a minaret, he said, was visible in the distance. To ensure that I didn't get lost on this final stretch he escorted me to the outskirts of a small township away to the right. Dozens of these were built at minimal expense on the hills above the Euphrates valley to house the communities forced from their homes by the flood. I was struck by the soulless character of this one. The functional grid design, unpaved streets and lack of recreational amenities did some for this effect, but there was a sense too that being settled in this ordered environment was not at all suited to the free-spirited Arab condition.

The stone tower, a square structure with Arabic engraving around its base, had presumably been transported from a town in the valley and planted on this conspicuous height as some sort of regenerative symbol. Rescue operations did manage to save a number of monuments in the 650-square-kilometre lake area, but many more – and surely dozens of unexcavated sites – have been lost. One which barely escaped this fate is the city of Barbalissus (Balis). Visible far below the tower, it is protected from any sudden wash by a causeway which bends round it like a jetty sheltering yachts. Barbalissus was a major Roman garrison in the later years of the empire, part of a line of fortifications defending the territory against Persians from the east.

For those commentators keen to place the Dardas River at al-Bab, the ruins at Balis present themselves as the most likely candidate for Thapsakos. The distance between the points, at the 'standard' 5-kilometre rate, is a close fit to the 15 *parasangs* given by Xenophon for the stage.

Interestingly, though now Balis sits precariously on its bank, the expansive site would originally have stood a kilometre from the river. In theory, this slight remove from the right bank permits a case to be made for Balis being the location of Belesys' palace. The distance of 73 kilometres from al-Bab, added to the 80 taken up on the march there from the Afrin River, makes for a good approximation to the 30 *parasangs* recorded by the author for the eighteenth stage, while the condition for the next one, 'to the Euphrates', is (technically) not violated. As for the matter of the sources of the Dardas – the problem that a river of this size is unlikely to rise beside another – a theory put forward by Ainsworth is that what Xenophon actually saw was a canal, cut from the Euphrates to supply the city. This idea is not quite as damaging to Xenophon's reputation for observation as it may seem, for the man-made channels of ancient times would not have been as distinctive as they are today, and this one, moreover, would have carried a high volume of water. He says that the breadth of the Dardas was 30 metres – problematic for a river at its source, but feasible for a major canal.

Taking Balis to be the location of Belesys' residence, Ainsworth pursued the next stage (A19) in sight of the river until the town of Hammam. 'The 15 *parasangs* given [for the stage] corresponds to the overland distance from Balis to the ford celebrated among the Arabs as that of the Anazah or Badawin ... The remains of a paved causeway are still to be observed on both banks of the river, which is here 4 stadia in width.' The presence of this causeway, the numbers, and a collection of brooding mounds nearby, led him to conclude that this was the site of Thapsakos.

I was unable to ascertain whether or not the features remarked upon are still to be seen, for my course, slightly broader across the arid uplands fronting the lake, brought me to the Assad Dam, the modern crossing place of the river. One thing that was clear at the dam was that the river at Hammam, 20 kilometres downstream, would be a mere shadow of what Ainsworth had seen. The barrier secretes water in such meagre amounts – to form lifeless, braided channels – that it is hard to imagine the river ever reconstituting itself, let alone attaining the dimensions spoken of by the author and the commentator.

I recall thinking at the dam, not for the first time, that Xenophon – or whoever the source of his figures was – had had a unique method of measuring river widths. Notwithstanding Ainsworth's verification of the distance (he may have seen the river at its highest), 4 stadia – 710 metres – is an enormous reach. One commentator has estimated the widest span of water in the pre-dam configuration, including side channels, to have been no more than 450 metres. I wondered if Xenophon (or his source) were not, for example, measuring from one bank to the other, rather than from the respective shores. He could also have been citing the maximum width instead of the width at the fording point, although in light of what has just been said, this is unsatisfactory for the Euphrates. A possible, if not fully convincing, explanation is that formerly our climate was wetter.

Something else was to strike me later – a mystery of geography possibly solved by divine intervention. An extraordinary thing happened at Thapsakos: the army crossed the Euphrates on foot. The people of the city were amazed at this sight, as never before had it been possible to cross other than by boat. Assuming a regular enough rhythm to the annual cycle of the river, this information, it seemed to me, could be useful in establishing a start date for the march. Conventionally this has been taken to be early spring (Karl Koch, a nineteenth-century German philologist, came up with the widely used date of 6 March), which would imply from the stage details provided by Xenophon that Cyrus crossed at Thapsakos in late July. But at this time the river should have been at, or very close to, its maximum height. In summer the flow of melt water from Armenia peaks; with this source exhausted, and no rain, the level gradually starts to reduce, reaching an ebb some time in mid- to late autumn. If this was the case, then Xenophon's account of events would be better suited to, say, September than July – unless, as the Thapascenes believed, the river had given way to Cyrus as the new king.

The great dam may have created a microclimate. The air on the littoral is moister, and the temperature range less marked than inland. Mosquitoes and biblical quantities of scorpions thrive near the rocky shores, and there is said to be an abundance of snakes too. On the first night that I stayed beside it, a dramatic lightning storm broke overhead; I half expected my tent to be washed away, but there was no rain at all, only the flashes, and the noise.

As I set myself up on higher ground the next evening, a man appeared on a motorcycle and invited me to his house. In five minutes I had packed up and was on the pillion seat. Where there was the opportunity, it was the habit of the Greeks to billet themselves in villages around the halting place.

The man was an olive farmer and had a small flock of sheep which his daughters brought in search of scrub every day. There were eight of them, aged from four to seventeen. The oldest kept to themselves but everyone else settled on the floor of the guest room to watch as we ate dinner. Mohammed had only a little English so communication was limited. It had been my intention to learn the basic Arabic phrases, and eventually I did, but the sacrifice of my books at the beginning of the journey set this back. Fortunately it turned out that there were more people in these lands who spoke European languages than in rural Anatolia, and at any reasonably sized village, one was nearly always found.

There was as much attention focused on my gear as on my person. My sleeping mat was of great interest to the girls. After the meal I undid the straps and they unfurled it on the ground like a royal carpet. They liked the compartments on the bag as well, and the folders I had for my maps and papers. I noted that they paid little attention to my walking stick, a further confirmation of my belief that the pole-dismantling gene was only present in males.

Mohammed's wife, through her husband, expressed surprise that I didn't have a headscarf. I showed her the long-peaked desert cap that I considered my most important piece of equipment after stick and compass, but none of them was very impressed with it.

In the morning, as I prepared to leave, Mohammed removed the cap and replaced it with a red and white chequered *shamag* (cloth). He wrapped it around my neck with the care of a father doing his son's tie for the first day at school. When I was out of sight, I undid the arrangement, though I later found that this light cloth had a far greater utility than my own headgear.

It took about two hours to get to the dam from the house. I arrived in the town of al-Thawrah at 11 a.m. and recorded the moment in my diary. Over the four months to this point I had covered 1,550 kilometres.

The Assad Dam is of great economic importance to Syria. The regulation of the water flow has enabled the area of cultivable land to be increased, while the giant turbines meet a high proportion of the country's power needs.

The dam is also a potent political symbol, its construction (with substantial Soviet assistance) being a major milestone on the nation's path to industrialization. Such is the strategic importance of this facility to the Syrians that it operates as a military zone and access to the complex is tightly controlled. Vehicles wishing to use the road running over the dam are searched at either end, and are forbidden to halt at any place on the spine. Needless to say, there is no provision for pedestrians to use the crossing, and my request to be allowed to walk was politely refused by an official in the administrative area.

'The chance of Zionist attack is always present,' he grimaced, as we sipped tea in his office. 'We must be on 100 per cent guard against it.'

Browsing the fact-sheet he had handed me, I ventured that any act of sabotage would require a mighty blow to the mammoth structure – effectively a mountain of earth with a concrete finish: 2½ kilometres long, ½ kilometre thick at the base and 60 metres high. He seemed surprised by this observation. 'Probably you are right. Actually,' he added, rising from his desk, 'our biggest threat is not coming from the Zionists.'

Facing a relief map on the wall, he traced the course of the river northwards, circling several points in eastern Anatolia. With one fist (the Atatürk Dam) already around the throat of the river, the Turks were building again. According to this man their aim was to be able to exert complete control over the river, to be in a position that they could literally turn on and off the supply like a tap. They had attempted this in the early 1990s – a riposte against Syrian support for Kurdish rebels – and the two countries had come to the brink of war. The success of the Turkish tactic on this occasion (Assad eventually expelled the rebels), I imagined, was one reason behind their latest round of dam building. I left the complex in no doubt that water was a deadly issue between the two neighbours.

The official drove me himself to the other side. 'I am sorry we could not give more help. Your army anyway would have gone on boats.' They hadn't, but I didn't stop to explain the detail. I thanked him and hauled my gear from the back of the jeep. A high wind had blown up and clouds of sand thick enough to completely block out the sun swirled above the road ahead.

*

Assyrian reliefs of the ninth century show soldiers swimming across rivers with the aid of inflated animal skins. The method is likely to have been used long before this by inhabitants of the Mesopotamian river valleys. Xenophon, recounting how the soldiers crossed the Euphrates at Charmande to get provisions, describes how the buoyancy aides were made: 'They stuffed the skins which they used as tent-coverings with dry grass, and then drew them together and stitched them up so that the water would not reach the hay.'

As economies developed, wooden boats came more into use, and ferry services sprang up, though the skins endured as a type of economy class. Thapsakos, described by Xenophon as 'a great and prosperous city', must have owed much of its wealth to the transport business. An ever-increasing flow of traffic, to include armies and entire peoples, needed to be conveyed in and out of Mesopotamia. The ferrymen seem also to have inaugurated a service downstream to Babylon: Diodoros reported that the Persian admiral, Konon, went by boat from here to see the King in 396.

A concurrent development was the construction of bridges. The Persians were among the first to build these, and are likely to have had one here since the time of Cyrus the Great. Properly they were pontoons: a line of adapted longships tied together, with the ends anchored inland. At the outset of his march Cyrus crossed one 60 metres long at Kydrara on the Maeander River. Some were quite extraordinary feats of engineering. In 480 Xerxes strung two of them, each 1¼ kilometres long, across the Hellespont.

> With these bridges in place across the straits [between Europe and Asia], they sawed sleepers equal in length to the width of the pontoon, laid them neatly on top of the taut cables in a row, and then tied them down. Next they put brushwood on top of the sleepers, evened it out, put soil on top of it, and stamped the soil down. Then they ran a fence along either side, high enough to stop the yoke-animals and the horses looking over it and being frightened by the sight of the sea. (Herodotus)

Reckoning by Xenophon's own figures: the breadth of the Euphrates (710 metres) was twelve times that of the Maeander, where a pontoon of seven ships was in place, suggesting the one at Thapsakos must have consisted of around eighty-four ships. Abrocomas, the Syrian satrap whom Cyrus was pursuing, set fire to the structure after he had crossed.

Upon arriving at Thapsakos, Cyrus stood the expedition down and withdrew to his tent with his advisers. Recalling what he had told them at Tarsus – that if on reaching the Euphrates, Abrocomas had taken flight, 'we must make our plans on the spot to meet the situation' – all the talk among the soldiers was of what he would do next.

Cyrus could have kept up the pretence of his vendetta with the Syrian satrap, but instead, he decided to reveal his true object to the army. The purposes of the original deception had been served: the King to some degree at least had been caught off guard, and the men had been taken almost to the point of no return. So he informed the generals of his intention to march against his brother, and asked them to tell the soldiers, and to try to persuade those who wavered not to give up the enterprise. (Diodoros gives a different account to Xenophon, writing that Cyrus addressed the army himself, and only won them over by fantastic promises of riches. 'Thus the soldiers, soaring in their expectations, were prevailed upon to follow him.')

The soldiers, when they were told the truth, were angry. They believed that the generals had known of this plan from the outset and had deliberately misled them. There was a unanimous belief that the new object was perilous, and the Greeks said that they wouldn't even consider going on unless there was a hefty rise in their pay. Cyrus promptly responded by saying he would give each man a bonus of five *minas* of silver (1 mina was equal to 4 *darics*) at Babylon, and would meet their wages in full for the return journey to Ionia.

While this lucrative offer was being digested by the armies, spread out in their separate camps along the banks of the river, Menon called his men together. He advised them to pack their gear straight away, and to go with him across the river, 'for if they vote in favour of following him, you, by being the first to cross the river, will get the credit for the decision. Cyrus will be grateful to you as being the most enthusiastic of his supporters, and he will show you his gratitude. And if the others vote against it,' he went on, 'we shall go back again, but he will look upon you, the only ones to obey his orders, as the most reliable people for garrison duties and promotion from the ranks.'

His soldiers were impressed by this reasoning and hastened to gather their equipment. When the others saw them wading into the water, they too packed up, and a general urgency seized the camp. Cyrus mounted his horse, Pasakas, and led them himself into the river. On the crossing, no one was wetted above the chest. The people of Thapsakos said this was extraordinary, as never before had the river been passable on foot. They took this to mean that the river had given way to Cyrus, as he was destined to be the new king.

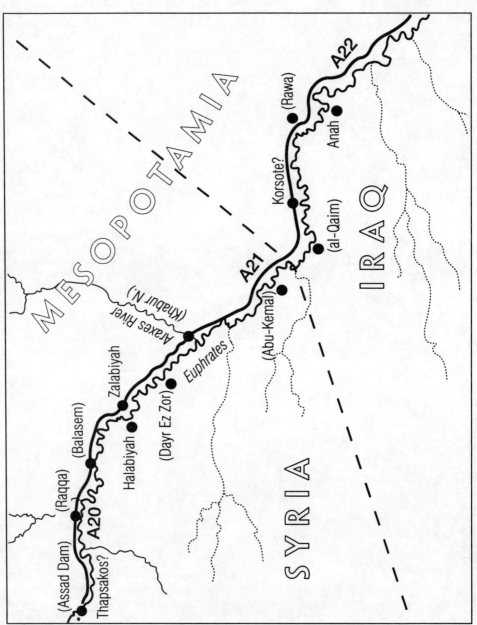

15

Along the Euphrates

A20: Thapsakos to the Araxes River

Mesopotamia contracts in shape, projecting to a considerable length. In outline it resembles somewhat a boat; and the greatest part of its periphery is formed by the Euphrates. The distance from Thapsakos to Babylon, as Eratosthenes states, is 4,800 stadia.

Strabo, *Geography*

When Abrocomas crossed at Thapsakos he proceeded north-east along a branch of the Royal Road to a junction on the Tigris River. This lay in the plain beneath Mount Judi, where the modern states of Turkey, Syria, and Iraq meet. The main route from Sardis continued from here to Susa, while branches went east to Ekbatana, the Achaemenid summer capital (modern Hamadan in Iran), and south to Babylon. Uncertain of which route Cyrus would take, Abrocomas installed himself in the foothills above the junction, ready once again to obstruct the prince's progress. Time was critical for the King, who was awaiting the arrival of armies at his capital.

But Cyrus had another surprise in store for his brother. Instead of marching up to the junction, upon fording the Euphrates he turned east, and hastened along the left bank of the river towards Babylon. By taking this famed city in the heart of the empire, he believed he would strike a significant first blow against the King.

For their part, neither the King nor his generals gave any serious thought to the defence of this route: beyond the Araxes River (a sizeable tributary of the Euphrates 250 kilometres downstream from Thapsakos), there were no roads to speak of, and no Persian expedition could do without roads. Much of this region, besides, was barren, with little for man or beast to forage. Xenophon is to the point: 'In this march [A22] many of the baggage animals died of hunger, as there was no grass or anything else growing. The ground was completely bare.' Getting through the desert proved to be a matter of determination. Marches, the author says, were made extremely long by the commander, and there was no quarter given to slackness or poor discipline.

*

The road from the dam seemed to lead nowhere. On the left, after 2 or 3 kilometres, a handful of mud huts appeared, but after these the desert landscape rolled away as before, empty and bleak.

The sandstorm that had been brewing on the left bank on my arrival became gradually more intense. To shield my face from the swirling sand grains, I covered my head with the *shamag*, and in stretches took to walking backwards. In an hour one vehicle passed. Its headlights suddenly shone through the haze, and just as quickly it was gone, the noise of the engine drowned in the howling of the wind.

Occasionally there would be a lull in the tempest, and at these times enough of the sand fell to earth to allow the shape of the sun to be seen: a dim disc hanging low in the sky. As I pressed along the road during one such interval, I made out the shell of a house away on the right.

It had been abandoned many years before. Three and a half walls and three-quarters of a roof survived. Inside, the floor had been raised by the encroachment of sand, entering through the door and spaces where there had been windows. There was a faint smell of urine and a sprinkling of cigarette butts, traces of refugees past. The wind rose again as I ate, and I decided to stay for the night. I unrolled my sleeping mat and kindled a small fire. As I wrote up my route diary in its flickering light, I couldn't help wondering whether the storm was an omen for the coming days on the Jezirah.

When I awoke it was dark. Everything was quiet and the stars were peeping in through the hole in the roof. I stretched out and watched them until the sky began to shed its blackness. The transformation is quicker in the lower latitudes: dark blue, then a yellow circle pops up, then azure.

To counter the great elbow of the Middle Euphrates, the road from the dam goes north for about 15 kilometres; it then veers east towards the city of Raqqa, and from there runs south-east along the bank to the Khabur River. The main road, coming from Aleppo and the Mediterranean, bypasses the dam and keeps to the south bank all the way to Fallujah in Iraq.

Passing into the catchment area of the river, the colour of the landscape changes from brown to light green, and small settlements begin to appear. They gradually become more frequent, and in places the impression is of walking through a vast, ramshackle suburb.

The people on this side of the river were even friendlier: shopkeepers shouted 'Ta'al! Ta'al!' ('come, come') and made the sign for tea on their doorsteps, while schoolchildren danced alongside me as though I was the Pied Piper. In the evenings numerous offers of hospitality were made. At first I declined, but seeing that this was causing bewilderment, if not offence, I became more sociable. Self-interest thereafter began to take over, and I eventually gave in to the temptation of accepting invitations only from the finer style of house. (Without great conviction, I justified this to myself by reasoning that these people were better able to afford to feed an extra mouth.) There were occasions when I even picked places from a distance, slowing myself on approach to ensure that the owner of the mansion had enough time to get himself up the driveway. Once, near Abu-Hammam, I spotted a villa that had several satellite dishes on the roof. It was set in a spacious compound and had a well-maintained garden at the front. As luck would have it the owner was at the entrance when I strolled by. He greeted me warmly and I didn't have to think long before accepting his offer. Locking the gates he took a bicycle from the wall and patted the rear carrier.

For twenty minutes we bumped along a track towards the Euphrates. I finally had to insist on dismounting, and we did the last kilometre on foot, he wheeling the bicycle and balancing my pack on the carrier, while I trailed behind massaging the feeling back into my backside.

His village was exceedingly poor. Mud houses with small yards shared by farm animals were packed together. He had two homes, a wife in each, one adjacent to the other. The woman in the house I stayed in was about to give birth again, though this didn't seem in any way to lessen the demands on her. A teenage daughter provided energetic support, even if her toiling was not much appreciated by her parents, who blamed her for anything that went wrong. The dinner was not memorable but every effort was made to see that I was comfortable. We slept in the yard and in the morning my host escorted me back to the road.

The first major centre along the line of settlement I came to was Raqqa. Said to have been founded by Alexander the Great, the city became an important station in the Roman defence line against Parthian Persia. The Parthians were the successors of the Achaemenids, and when the Hellenic empire which had vanquished the Great Cyrus' dynasty itself began to buckle, they reasserted Persian control over Mesopotamia. In 224 AD, much as the Medes had been by the Achaemenids eight centuries before, the Parthians were displaced by another native tribe. The Sasanids challenged the Western presence in Syria up until the seventh century AD, when Persian power was finally ended by the Muslims.

In 772 AD, ten years after he had begun work on Baghdad, the Abbasid Caliph al-Mansour chose Raqqa as the site of his Syrian garrison. Dwarfing the existing architecture, he raised a 5-kilometre-long outer wall studded with 132 defensive towers and ringed with a moat filled from the river. Under the great al-Rasheed it briefly became capital of the Abbasid Empire (796 – 808 AD), and in this time a series of large palace complexes was constructed.

Today hardly anything from this illustrious period remains. Mongol destruction undid the refinement of the Abbasids, and the Ottomans, way off on the Bosphoros, saw no reason to revive it.

Independence, and more recently the construction of the Assad Dam, have given the city new vigour. Evidence of modern urban planning is apparent in the residential western districts, although this attempt at order crumbles as one moves into the centre: the roads narrow and became congested, and generally everything becomes noticeably more shabby, noisy, and dirty.

Raqqa's central square is dominated by a towering telecommunications mast. The space itself is filled with cramped retail outlets – barbers, jewellery shops, fast-food grills – and seems to be constantly enveloped in a haze of cheap oil, burned by scooters and the packs of growling buses that ply between the nearby station and random points about the city.

There were supposed to be a couple of graded hotels in the vicinity but buffeted by the crowds, I wasn't able to spot signs of any. The same tourist brochure I had been given by the official at the dam, which referred to this place as the 'Pearl of the Euphrates Basin', provided directions to Bab Baghdad ('Baghdad gate'), so after consuming a chicken and a jug of water, I continued on my way.

*

It often happened that at the end of the day I started to walk faster. As the air cooled, tiredness fell away, and the load on my shoulders seemed to lighten. But I came to think that there was more to it than that. It was as though the departing sun was exerting a pull; something instinctive, the fading of the light triggering an urge to seek shelter. The Arabs retain a fear of darkness: lamps glowing in every sleeping-quarter are a testimony to their nyctophobia. Perhaps because of this they used to come for me every evening before night enveloped the world.

On that evening the sun was behind me, huge and forbidding. I kept turning to watch it as it descended towards the horizon. Close to nightfall I mounted a hill off the side of the road and hunkered down. The thought came into my head that a farmer 5,000 years ago might have sat on this same spot and watched this same spectacle. The Akkadian word for sun was 'shams', as is the Arabic, and the Babylonian sun god was Shamash.

Watching me behold the cosmos were two girls standing at the gable of a mud hut on a plateau adjacent. When I looked they waved and scampered round to the front. They were sitting outside on a carpet when I arrived five minutes later, their heads lowered out of shyness. I said hello and drank a glass of water that was presently brought for me by a third girl. She gestured to the carpet: '*S'il vous plait.*'

She was eleven or twelve, had long black hair and big dark eyes. The others, who were around the same age, stood up and giggled. I should have been off, but the setting was wonderful and the cushions enticing. Removing my boots, I eased onto them and lay out on the rug.

On the opposite side of the flat hilltop there was a second house, of a similar basic design but longer than the one we were outside. A slanting wooden shed with chickens on the roof sat to the left of this. Beyond, scattering south towards the river was the main body of the village. One by one dim lights were now coming on in the homesteads.

'*Comment tu t'appelle?*' Disregarding the propriety of her peers, the young French speaker knelt in front of me.

'*Je m'appelle Shane.*'

'*Comment tu t'appelle Mama?*'

'*Elle s'appelle Celine.*'

'*Quelle couleur aimez-vous?*'

I pointed to the base of the sky, where traces of the landed sun were to be seen as great vertical streaks of rouge. We watched this sight, and observed the appearance of a second god, Aphrodite. As though they had passed in the mid-heavens, she rose just to the left of where the sun had sunk, becoming higher and brighter as the sky darkened. Zahra the Arabs call her, which can mean a blooming flower, or a witch.

An excited shriek and the rapid disappearance of the two other girls alerted us to the arrival of menfolk. They came over the lip of the plateau from the fields, carrying hoes and pitchforks. The French speaker retained her poise, rising gracefully from the carpet and striding with her head aloft into the house.

'*Ahlan wa sahlan.*'

'*Salaam alaykum.*'

'*Alaykum salaam!*'

The two men sat down beside me and smiled. One introduced himself as Shou'ayb. He had a handsome face, carefully groomed moustache, and rather camp hairstyle. The other man, in contrast, was dour and unkempt. Shou'ayb, I understood, was a teacher in Raqqa, but was here to work on the cotton harvest. The house, he signed, belonged to his parents, and the girls were his sisters. I tried to explain with a diagram in the dirt that I was walking along the river. I next produced a photocopy of Cyrus' route, and walked my fingers along the Euphrates to Babylon. They took the photocopy and studied it in silence.

The news of my arrival spread quickly, and a group came hurrying across the plateau from the direction of the village. Their leader was a retired English teacher, Mr Mohammed. Standing before us, he wiped his forehead and accepted a glass of water. Unlike the other males, he was attired in the Western style: an open white shirt, grey slacks, and polished shoes, which he removed before getting onto the carpet. He was about fifty, fat, bald on top, and had a kindly face. We introduced ourselves.

'Mr Shane, you are welcome to Balasem village. We have honour because of this visit. Please give me your request.'

I told him everything was fine, although my hosts must have got the contrary impression, for he immediately furnished them with a list of things required for my better comfort.

First I was issued with a *jalabiyah*, for complete protection against the mosquitoes; my clothes were then whisked away for washing, and a barber was sent for. He took such great pains over his work that I felt unable to object when the hand-mirror revealed a light quiff on top of my head. He had also neglected to erase a week-old moustache, and was perplexed when I asked if he could shave it. Intervening, Mohammed assured me it was the fashion among young men, so it remained for the time being.

The centrepiece of the meal that had been laid out in the Shou'ayb family's guest room was a tin of canned meat. It sat unopened on a plate surrounded by local dishes. Mr Mohammed did the honours. 'This will be softer for European palate.' Upending the container, he allowed the soggy contents to fall onto the plate. Nostrils flared in an attempt to savour the delicacy that had come from Belgium via Saudi Arabia, where the English teacher had worked for two years after he had retired from the local school. I ran my nose over the dish and feigned approval.

Mohammed was planning to return to Saudi Arabia the following year to perform the hadj, the pilgrimage to Mecca. Shou'ayb hoped to accompany him, with a further view to seeking a teaching post in the kingdom. Mohammed said that they would marry him off before he left, otherwise a foreign woman would have him. 'He loves ten but forty love him.'

Tea was taken back out on the plateau. The first time it came prepared in the traditional way, sugar mixed in. Mohammed discovered this just in time; words were exchanged with the house and a few of the men went indoors to supervise a fresh brew.

The second time it came on a tray with a bowl of sugar in the middle. Mohammed poured a glass for everyone, before carefully sprinkling two spoonfuls of sugar into his own. I put half a spoon in mine, but discovered my taste had become much sweeter over the preceding weeks. Similar processes of trial and error were embarked upon by the others, so that the plateau for a short time rang to the sound of rattling teaspoons.

When we were relaxed on the cushions, Mr Mohammed asked me about my journey. He had the photocopy of the route I had earlier given to Shou'ayb in his hand.

I told him the background to the story, and how Cyrus had secretly raised an army of Greeks, and had led them to the Euphrates, and then revealed that his true aim was the Persian throne. Having absorbed this and questioned me on a few points that hadn't been clear, he relayed an account of the expedition to the gathering. Several more had appeared for tea, and men had to hunker around the large carpet as the story was told.

'This is the path they have gone Mr Shane?' When he had concluded, Mohammed held up the photocopy and drew his pen along the Euphrates to Babylon. After I had confirmed it was the way, he passed the paper around.

'Can we say Mr Shane, that the Greeks stayed here in Balasem?'

'They may have done,' I answered, 'and they certainly passed by. The problem is that there isn't much information, and often the places and features Xenophon describes have been lost or have changed with the passing of time. I'm afraid that in Syria,' I added, 'I'm finding it especially hard to find any traces of them.'

Mohammed translated this sombrely, and a subdued mood came over the evening. I instantly regretted having said Syria: it wasn't strictly accurate – east from the Mediterranean the whole journey moves to a higher level of uncertainty – and they may have taken the comment personally.

'Is there anything we can do to help?' Mohammed asked before I could attempt to clarify myself.

I took out my map. I had been looking out for the Balikh River that afternoon. Some modern route commentators, Lendle among them, have taken it to be the Araxes of Xenophon, the river which marked the end of the twentieth stage. This view depends on the army having forded the Euphrates high in its middle course, a view which, in line with Ainsworth, I didn't share. None the less, I was curious to see it if I could.

The name circulated briskly among the gathering.

'It's here Mr Shane.' Mohammed straightened up and pointed in the direction from where Shou'ayb had come earlier. The mood lifted again and a second round of tea was ordered from the house.

In the morning we made our way through the fields to the Balikh River. The cotton was in full bloom. Farmers felt its texture between their fingers and traded opinions across ditches. For the rural population this cash crop is a vital source of income, and all along this stretch of the Euphrates they were now waiting for the harvest to begin. Normally this happens in the last week of September, when every family member capable of work is drafted into the fields. Once picked and stuffed into giant 200-kilogram sacks, the cotton is carted off to regional markets, where it fetches around $100 per bale.

The Euphrates valley, from the great bend on the middle river, lies just below the so-called Fertile Crescent, and successful agriculture here is dependent on irrigation. In this regard the construction of the Assad Dam has been of significant benefit to the farmers. The water supply to the fields is regular, and they no longer have to fear their crops being damaged by flood.

Shou'ayb led us through the white-speckled landscape for about twenty minutes, halting abruptly before a swathe of reeds which formed a thick line that wound like a snake through the cotton fields. This wasn't what I had expected. Suffocated by the reeds, and bled practically dry by a succession of pumps whose snouts burrowed deep into the greenery, the Balikh was now, it seemed, nothing more than a rivulet. Even in late spring, and in a less thirsty age, it was hard to imagine it ever having a size that would have warranted notice by the not easily impressed Xenophon.

Mohammed beamed as I noted its dimensions in my diary. When I had done he slapped me on the shoulder, and led me by the hand towards the river's outlet.

There I had another surprise. Since I had last seen it at the dam four days before, the Euphrates had grown mightily. Reaching over 50 metres across, it moved with a palpable sense of power. Our party sat together on the bank for a while, not saying anything, just watching this enormous force pass by.

*

Two days south-east from Balasem stand the ruined forts of Halabiyah and Zalabiyah. Situated on either side of the Euphrates, about 2 kilometres apart, they were once a part of the strategic line of fortifications that defended the Roman and Byzantine empires from barbarian attack.

The present fortresses were built by a Palmyrene king who was the local muscle for Rome in the third century AD. He fought several battles with the Sasanid Persians (successors of the Parthians) and managed to keep them at bay across the river. Upon his murder in 268 AD, his wife, queen Zenobia, assumed power as regent for their son. Her ambition was ferocious. She raised a huge army and marched west, conquering the provinces of Syria, Arabia, Egypt and Kilikia. She then declared herself Augusta, and minted coins stamped with her image and the supreme title. Aurelian dispatched legions over the Taurus, which defeated the empress successively at Antioch and Emesa (Homs). The Palmyrenes retreated to their capital, and a siege of the desert city followed, during which Zenobia fled with her son. But they were captured by soldiers, ironically while trying to cross the Euphrates, and taken in chains to Rome.

The fortress walls as they appear today probably date from the mid-sixth century AD and the reign of the Byzantine Emperor Justinian. Though at the height of its power in this period, the empire was under constant pressure in the east. The Euphrates was a long, and in places difficult, line to defend, and the Sasanids were restless neighbours. The Treaty of Endless Peace was signed in 533 AD, but seven years later they stormed across the river and overran Antioch. Taking more concrete steps to secure the frontier, Justinian had the garrisons rebuilt and fitted for sustained defence.

Of the two here, Halabiyah on the right bank is much the better preserved. I crossed to it on a pontoon bridge, leaving everything behind except my stick.

It was designed in the shape of a triangle: two thick walls, a couple of hundred metres apart, climb up a steep hillside from the riverbank, their ends converging around a commanding citadel. I hadn't intended to go all the way up, only as far as a bastion a quarter of the way, but when I got there I thought I might as well go to the next one, and by the same law of travel found myself in a short time panting on the summit. This just peeped above the narrow river valley, revealing nothing but stretches of broken upland on both sides.

In spite of the efforts of Justinian, the Persians managed to capture the fortresses in 610 AD, and again they rampaged onwards to the Mediterranean. Heraclius subsequently restored the dimensions of the empire, but its days as a great territorial kingdom were now numbered. The fearsome quarrelling between the old enemies had made it much easier for another power to impose itself. By 640 AD, Syria was under Islamic control.

Zalabiyah, downstream, was less impressive. From an ugly quarry beneath I failed to make out any notable ruins on the bluff where it was situated. Closer inspection revealed decayed mud walls and the outlines of former defences. The river on this stretch is fordable at certain times, which is why the forts were situated here, but I wasn't altogether sure why this one had been necessary. Open to the enemy, if it fell it would have provided them with a base for incursions across the river. It seemed to have been smaller in scale, so perhaps it was nothing more than a look-out post which was intended to be evacuated in the event of attack.

Absorbing the views on a sharp ridge, I imagined a bleary-eyed sentry in a tower seeing a cloud of dust rise at dawn in the desert; then the silence broken by the roar of Pan, his comrades alerted to the terrifying advance of some barbarian horde. Tumbling down the embankment they untie boats and row to the boundary of civilization: 'BARBARIANS! BARBARIANS!'

*

It took almost an hour the next morning to cross the desert and meet up with the road, which took the most efficient route along the river, pursuing a more or less straight line across the tops of the widest meanders. Cyrus would have tried to follow a similar course, though the need for drinking water would have required him to stay fairly close to the bends.

The first village appeared not long after I had gained the road, and thereafter the familiar pattern of settlement resumed. The distances between the villages gradually decreased until, a dozen or so kilometres before the city of Dayr Ez Zor, habitation became virtually continuous.

The walk to the city, a day and a half from Zalabiyah, was marked by the number of times I had stones thrown at me by youngsters. It had happened before around al-Bab and Raqqa, but not with the same frequency or vigour. The probable cause I realized during a conversation I had with a chemist in one of the villages, was the outbreak of another *intifada* in Palestine. He told me how the Temple Mount had been violated, and how a young boy had been shot dead in his father's arms.

At tangential points on the approach I could see the emerging outline of Dayr Ez Zor, the last city on the Syrian Euphrates. It seemed to be compacted on the right bank: on this side the villages continued until a tree-lined university campus opposite the centre, and they resumed again on the other side of a highway signposted for Turkey.

In the evening I left the river and walked across barren fields to meet

up with the quieter Iraq-bound road. Well before I reached it, I picked
up a strong smell of diesel in the air, and then, quite unexpectedly,
spotted in the distance a blazing oil stack. More of these came into
view as I progressed towards the embankment. Spaced at intervals of 3
or 4 kilometres, in the darkness, they gave the impression of a great
Stygian colonnade.

Householders near the road were upset to see me walking at night.
Leading me to his home, a man reasoned that I only had to knock on
any door and they would shelter me. We ate, and then sat quietly in the
yard, watching the flare stacks lick the black sky.

On the eighth day of the stage I came to the Khabur River. Even
allowing for the season, it was pitifully small, though there was more
water in it than there had been in the Balikh. The distance from the
Assad Dam by my calculations was 240 kilometres, slightly under the
50 *parasangs* Xenophon recorded for the march from Thapsakos to
the Araxes.

After half an hour following the stream from the dusty market town
of Busayrah, I came in sight of the place where it flowed into the
Euphrates. Somehow, as if recognizing its moment, it expanded before
the point of confluence and gracefully glided towards oblivion.

As I approached the junction over a flat bed of sandy soil, I had the
same positive feeling I had experienced way back at the Fountain of
Midas in Phrygia. It was one of those rare moments of connection with
the past. Resting on the sandbank, I cooled my feet and watched the
currents form at the point of union.

The Khabur nurtured the very earliest of our civilizations. Its banks
are peppered with *tells* that contain settlement layers as old as 7,000
years. On account of its converging tributaries, the upper course of the
river is known to archaeologists as the Khabur Triangle. Adequate rainfall in this more northerly area made it suitable for agriculture, and the
earliest sites are concentrated here. In time, population pressures forced
settlers into the drier valley of the lower Khabur, where they developed
the basics of irrigation. By Xenophon's time habitation in this area was
still prospering. He speaks of numerous villages 'well supplied with
corn and wine'. The army stayed at the confluence three days to rest and
supply themselves with provisions for the next stage.

16

Arabia

A21: To the Maskas River and the deserted city of Korsote

Cyrus now advanced through Arabia, having the Euphrates on his right,
five days march through the desert, a distance of 35 parasangs.

Anabasis I.5

The land east of the Araxes is called 'Arabia' by Xenophon. This designation has upset some commentators, who think he may have confused the north and south banks of the Euphrates. However, the term (probably coined by Herodotus) is closely tied to the nomadic peoples of the eponymous peninsula, and in the ancient literature has consistently been applied to places inhabited by them. Pliny and Strabo both refer to Arabs in Mesopotamia. The latter says: 'The parts of Mesopotamia which incline towards the south and are farther from the mountains are occupied by the Arabian *Skinitai* [tent-dwellers], a tribe of brigands and shepherds, who readily move from one place to another when pasture and booty fail them.'

Xenophon had a vivid recollection of the long stretch between the Araxes and Maskas rivers. He described the land as a treeless wilderness, vast and level like the sea. The area he said was plentiful in wormwood and aromatic plants, and abounded in exotic wildlife. He was known to be a keen huntsman, and perhaps it was this which served to preserve his memory of cavalrymen chasing ostriches, wild asses and gazelles.

The wild asses, when anyone chased them, would start forward a considerable distance, and then stand still, for they ran much faster than the horses. And again, when the horses approached, they did the same, and it was impossible to catch them, unless the horsemen, stationing themselves at intervals, kept up the pursuit by relay. The flesh of those that were taken resembled venison, but was more tender. No one succeeded in catching an ostrich. Those who tried soon gave up the pursuit, for it made them gallop a very great distance when it ran from them. It used its feet for running and got under way with its wings, just as if it was using a sail.

The Athenian's record has a unique value in that it affords a glimpse of the Mesopotamian environment as it was before concentrated, if not widespread, human settlement. Originally much of the vast area was steppe, host to an extensive variety of flora and fauna. The natural environment was underpinned by the annual flooding of the rivers, a process which created teeming bogs and caused thick woodland to grow near the banks. Beasts native to the region besides those named by Xenophon included lions, elephants, deer and aurochs, now extinct wild oxen that were the ancestors of domestic cattle.

The advent of civilization rapidly began to transform the steppe. Farmers adapted it for agriculture, and as populations expanded, began the first attempts to harness and control the rivers. Success in this field fuelled further colonization of the wilderness, and so the steady decline of its ecosystem. The observation of Xenophon by then represented a greatly reduced habitat for these creatures. In a matter of hundreds of years, the last of them would have been driven away forever.

Today in the remoter regions there are wolves, foxes, jackals and hyenas. There may also be the odd lion roaming; Uday Hussein reintroduced them to Iraq in the 1980s for big-game hunting, though most were kept in pounds in his private pleasure parks.

To the Arabs living in this region today, the area between the rivers is known as al-Jezirah ('the island'). They distinguish it thus from the Shamia, the rocky desert rolling away from the right bank of the Euphrates.

The Arabs have had a presence in Mesopotamia longer arguably than any other civilization. Though considerably divided on the subject of their ethnic roots, and seemingly unable to form any united political entity, they share a culture that is among the world's richest and most durable. The strength of their civilization has been said to derive from the traditionally close relationship of the people to the surrounding landscape. A meagre nourishment in the desert, hard won and precarious, seems to have instilled in them the values of moderation, community and independence. The simplicity and harshness of their lifestyle itself produces morality: in the purest Arab villages, there is civilization before education.

One of the major differences I noted between travelling in Turkey and Syria was how people in the countryside reacted to me on first encounters. 'Are you hungry? Do you need to drink something?' a Turkish farmer might enquire if I met him at the gate of his home (this after he had established that I was not walking because I couldn't afford a bicycle). An Arab when he saw you coming would approach and invite you to his home, not put out by the fact you were under your own steam. Once seated in the guest room he watches closely to see what is needed: he prides himself on being able to anticipate a request in advance. Food and drink are brought as a matter of course; the Arab doesn't ask.

This comparison is not in any way meant to be a slight on the Turks; after all, it is hard to think of many other European countries where a stranger would be taken off the road and fed and watered, bike or no bike.

One inference, I thought, that could be made from this, is that the Turks are closer in spirit to the East than the West. The two peoples, Arabs and Turks, in fact, share much more than a period of common (Ottoman) history, for Turkish origins also lie in nomadism, in the steppe and deserts of Central Asia. They too embraced the Islamic faith in their original state. When their time came, they were the natural successors to the Arab raiders of Mohammed, their prowess as mounted warriors extending ever further the boundaries of the Muslim empire. It is the demise of this empire that led to the schism: upon taking the reigns of power, Atatürk immediately began to drive the New Republic away from the heritage of Islam and the wilderness.

*

In the countryside, Arabs very often have big families. In the villages I went to, ten, fifteen or twenty children was the norm. Establishing an exact figure could be difficult. I asked a man once for his brood's size as we relaxed on cushions in the yard of his house. He thought for a minute, names in chronological order whispering off his lips. 'Seven.'

I was surprised. I thought when we were eating dinner the yard had been fuller. There was that number alone playing about us.

'How many boys and how many girls?'

He smiled knowingly and stretched out on his pillows. 'Ah, we don't count the girls.'

Though the holy book allows Muslims to take up to four wives, it's rare for an Arab to have more than two. Dowries have to be paid to the girl's family, and are expensive. Marriage and property are closely linked. A man without a home – or at least the prospect of a room in the family house – is unlikely ever to be married. If per chance a villager found himself owning a second property, he'd have a second wife; three homes, three wives, and so on.

Arranged marriages are the normal practice in the villages. Matches are made by elders on the basis of clan relationships, and the talks do not usually involve consultation with the couple. In the towns, as I witnessed with Mohammed in Sarmada, there was more latitude, but not complete freedom of choice. There may be exceptions. Travelling in the Syrian interior in 1905, the English Arabist Gertrude Bell was told by a guide that women in his tribe wielded much power. 'For if a maiden says: "I would have such a one for my husband," he must marry her lest she should be put to shame. And if he has already four wives let him divorce one, and marry in her place the maiden who has chosen him.'

Segregation between the sexes in rural society is rigid. Women have their own living quarters and are rarely seen in the public spaces of the house. Outdoors they must be veiled, and accompanied by a male member of the family.

Besides raising the family and running the household, Arab women also work on the farm. Theirs is the task of weeding, sowing, irrigation and harvesting. Menfolk are responsible for the organization of this work: they purchase seeds and fertilizer, decide on auspicious planting dates, and ensure the crops get to market on time.

If a tract of land is more than a few kilometres from the home (not uncommon in the fragmentary land ownership systems), they also have to get the women there early in the morning. The better-off take their own tractors, but most have to wait outside the village and arrange a lift with a passing vehicle.

Instead of having to make a return journey, a farmer will often choose to spend the day with his labourers. This also gives him the chance to inspect the land at first hand. Walking across country, I frequently encountered these robed squires, reclined beneath trailers or discussing affairs across the ditches with neighbours. They always invited me to have tea, or if it was near lunchtime, to eat. In these cases the females might be sent to the other side of the tractor, or occasionally they'd have to sit a short distance away, usually without shelter from the sun. If I pointed this out to the husband, he'd wave aside my concern and point to their headgear. They all had some form of head covering. Married women wore scarves, the girls a more elaborate covering, something like a mummy's dressing in appearance. The light material was wrapped repeatedly around the head until only the eyes were visible. I thought that this casing must make them overheat, and certainly make breathing difficult, but they seem to have evolved a tolerance to the condition. I was told that they insisted on wearing these bandages themselves, as they keep their skin soft for when they are married.

My contact with females in the Arab lands I passed through was minimal. It usually happened by chance, walking by the river or crossing a field where they were working. I'd greet them and they'd always reply in kind. If I needed information I'd ask at a distance, although I gave this up after a while, as they seemed not to have any sense of where they were. Collective head tilting or extraordinary numbers of kilometres to the next village were standard responses. I had a feeling that in most cases they must have known the answer and were being deliberately misleading in order to underscore their femininity. Directions and distances, like driving, were in the proper sphere of men, so it was unbecoming in a woman to show a capability in this field.

The Arabs are a proud, free-spirited people. The maintenance of their traditions gives them a high degree of self-confidence. They recognize the value of their own culture, and whatever curiosity they might have about other ones, they have no feelings of backwardness. Attempts have been made to convince them of their inferiority, but without real success.

Political unity has eluded the Arab world for centuries. Their cause is not helped by the presence of oil in many of their lands. Pan-Arab nationalist movements have always incurred the hostility of nations reliant on its supply to drive their economies. Of these movements, the most enduring has proved to be the Ba'ath Party, a secular, socialist organization founded by two teachers in Syria in 1941. Its aim was nothing less than the rebirth of Arab culture and the creation of a single Arab state. The vision of the Ba'athists was comprehensive, idealist – 'unity, freedom, socialism' – and by virtue of this it never had immediate appeal beyond a narrow class of urban intellectuals. None the less, active branches sprouted in several Middle Eastern countries. Each had its own 'regional command', responsible for the promotion of Ba'ath ideology and answerable to a supreme 'national command', a body elected by the regional memberships.

Agitation in the 1950s among students and the officer class of the armies increased the party's power base, while proposals for land reform enhanced its appeal to the peasantry. Slowly, the preconditions for an Arab 'October Revolution' were falling into place.

Within the space of one month in early 1963, the party seized power in both Syria and Iraq. A union was the logical next step, but groups in Damascus and Baghdad loyal to the Egyptian leader, Gamal Abdel Nasser, opposed the talks. The leaderships flew to Cairo to promote a triumvirate, but Nasser was convinced that Arab destiny lay in his hands, and his only. This marked the end of the Ba'athist period of idealism. The Iraqis fell to feuding and were ousted by the military in November of that year; the Syrians purged their government of Egyptian supporters, and to avoid the fettering of their power by the National Command, established their own central committee, in effect, a rival faction within the Ba'ath Party. The two neighbouring powers became estranged, and eventually bitter rivals.*

In Syria, people are not afraid to discuss politics, but they do so carefully. One person I knew in Aleppo was accustomed to preface any comment he made on the subject with the line: 'Our president is a good man ...'

---

* The Syrian Ba'athists are often characterized as the 'left wing' of the party. Since 1970 the Syrian branch has been controlled by the Assad family, who are members of a Shia sect, the Alawis ('followers of Ali'). Alawis dominate the government and apparat. In Iraq a similar situation existed with the al-Tikriti clan, who were Sunni.

The intense personal rivalry between Hafez Assad and Saddam Hussein went back to unity overtures made by the former in the late 1970s. Suspecting that Assad had designs on being the leader of a proposed unified state, Saddam seized power himself and had those in the party sympathetic to the Syrian executed. Assad sided with Shia Iran in its war with his Arab neighbour (1980–9), and supported the 'coalition' in ejecting Saddam from Kuwait in 1991.

During my prolonged stay in the city, I used to meet him occasionally at a café beneath the city's citadel. In time the preface was dropped. One night he took me across to the moat, where a few trees wilted in a thin belt of dust. He had been trying to explain how things worked.

'I might say: "I think this tree would be better over there." Another man hears me and says: "The government planted this tree here. You are saying it should be somewhere else – you are *criticizing* the Government." '

Some Syrians believed that the succession of Bashar Assad (son of the deceased Hafez) would bring about more openness in government. Signs of a *glasnost* though are not obvious; the ubiquitous posters of the leader, hung on lampposts and street corners and on display in every business, now show the son instead of the father. Bashar himself ordered that this practice be discontinued, but the people say they love him, and nobody wants to be the first to take theirs down.

Another decree in the reforming spirit was to have a hotline set up to his office. Citizens dissatisfied with an aspect of public service, or the state of the country in general, can visit their local post office and fax the president direct. The service is free and the procedure comparatively straightforward, though, as yet, it seems the dedicated machines are not being overworked.

*

Something I observed that binds all of the disparate Arab tribes together is their religious faith. Observance in the villages is almost universal. The sound of the *azan*, the call to prayer, marks the rhythms of day and night. Men break casually from whatever they are doing to spread a prayer mat on the earth and bow in submission towards Mecca. The first disciples it is said prayed toward Jerusalem, but Mohammed, asserting the Arab character of the faith, turned them to face the Kaaba.

Jerusalem is still of great importance to Muslims. Their third holiest site is the Temple Mount (al-Haram), location of the Dome of the Rock, and the al-Aqsa Mosque. The Koran says that the Prophet Mohammed was carried here from Medina by angels in the night, and that he ascended into heaven from the rock.

In September 2000, Ariel Sharon, a man held in disdain by many Muslims and all Arabs, forced himself onto the Mount. Surrounded by a rabble of guards, he proceeded to slouch across the hallowed precinct. The provocation had its effect: within hours, another *intifada* had begun.

At this time I was nearing the end of my journey in Syria, and apart from occasional stone-throwing children, nobody showed any hostility toward me on this account. Arabs have become used to humiliation in their own backyard; they bear it stoically, believing that justice is in the hands of the Almighty, and will come. The plight of the Palestinians weighs on every Arab. They despair of their treatment and wonder why the world watches and does nothing.

I found the empathy to their cause nowhere stronger than in Iraq. Wise men would shake their heads, and younger ones rail aloud against the treatment of their brothers. Following the outbreak of the second *intifada*, a million volunteered to go and defend them. On the main streets of villages, in schoolyards on the outskirts of towns, and outside factories in the cities, you could see them in the evenings marching up and down with brooms on their shoulders.

As I was to discover early on, the Iraqis themselves were the victims of a brutal oppression; a less public, more pervasive one. You sensed it in the rawness of the society, inferred it from behaviour, and, on the rarest occasion, heard it spoken of. My journey from entering the country took on a different character. I have to say that my focus on those whom I was following slipped as I tried to make my own way towards the journey's end.

Anabasis 22-24: To Babylonia

17

The Anbar

A22: Through the Desert

Iraq is for all, and her security is the responsibility of all.

Saddam Hussein

The border crossing between Syria and Iraq lies about 6 kilometres from the town of Abu-Kemal, on the right bank of the Euphrates. The river is not visible from the road, but is probably not more than ½ kilometre from the frontier complex. On my arrival there one morning in early October, a number of heavy vehicles were backed up, and movement between the two sides was slow. Crossing under an unmanned barrier, I walked into the customs post to show my passport. I emerged at the other end of the building after about an hour of form filling. On the edge of Syria, a giant-sized, hand-painted portrait of Hafez Assad stared across at an identically sized one of Saddam. Eyeball to eyeball, the old adversaries grinned at one another.

To get to the border post, I had had to switch to the other side of the river at Abu-Kemal. Once inside Iraq, I intended to cross back and continue along the route of Cyrus. The finish point of the current stage (A21) from the Araxes River was a large city called Korsote. Xenophon described it as being deserted, though the soldiers were able to obtain supplies here for their onward journey, and they stayed three days at the site. His statement that a river, the Maskas, curved around the metropolis may be similarly imprecise.

The whereabouts of Korsote are disputed. In the 1930s a Frenchman called du Mesnil du Buisson unearthed a site above Abu-Kemal, revealing occupation from the prehistoric period to the Iron Age. He declared this to be '*l'ancienne Corsôté*'; however, the distance from the

Khabur confluence to this point is only 110 kilometres at most, well short of the 165 recorded by the author for the stage. Today the site is known as Baghouz.

Ainsworth believed that the city was sited on an inland peninsula downstream from al-Qaim, the present-day Iraqi border town. He reconciled the still considerable gap in the distances by suggesting that on this remote stretch the army had followed the bends of the river. The encircling Maskas, he argued more convincingly, may have alluded to the pronounced southerly loop in the river which forms the cliff-faced peninsula. The Bavarian traveller Leonhard Rauwolf, who sailed down the Euphrates in the sixteenth century, recorded that it took him more than half a day to encompass this feature.

The next stage (A22) was the most demanding for the army. It took thirteen consecutive days of pressing marches to traverse the barren waste of desert separating Syria from the plains of Babylon.

*

A guard on the Iraqi side escorted me to a warehouse-like administrative building close to the barrier. My passport was taken, and shortly afterwards, I was summoned to a room where there were several officials talking. 'There is a problem with your visa,' the one behind the desk informed me bluntly. I was surprised by this news, and asked what was wrong. He gestured to a seat, and once again thumbed through the pages of the passport.

'Somebody has interfered with the date of issue. What do you say?'

I said nothing. Thoughts of the trip having to be abandoned skipped across my mind, and then I remembered the letter that had been given to me by the Iraqi embassy in Athens.

The official waved his finger and I stood up to hand him the envelope. As he read it, his demeanour changed. I added that I now recalled that the date on the visa had been altered at the embassy, owing to a mistake in estimating when I would arrive at al-Qaim. He picked up the telephone and relayed details of the letter. Shortly after he replaced the receiver and handed me back my documents: 'Welcome in Iraq.'

A youth with a smattering of English was assigned to take me through the entry procedures. While I was insisting that a fresh needle be used for the mandatory Aids test, he hurried to the bank to exchange money. I gave him $100 and he returned with a carrier bag. 'Are there no bigger denominations?' I asked, peering into it.

'There is none.'

It transpired that there was only about $30 worth of Iraqi currency in the bag, but it was, in any case, weeks after that day before I could spend a single dinar. The Aids test was $50 and I gave the medic another $20 not to do it.

The dusty frontier town of al-Qaim unfolded along the first kilometre of the Baghdad road. It took about ten minutes to get from the border post to a mural of Saddam waving off arrivals on the boundary. The guide suggested he take a photo of me in front of this, and afterwards insisted there was a $10 fee for the privilege. I offered him a bankroll from the bag, but he ignored this and turned back to the customs post.

A short distance further on I heard whistling and looked around to see two soldiers waving. I acknowledged them and kept walking, thinking that they just wanted to chat. In Syria everybody wanted to chat. A car travelling into town veered across the oncoming lane and braked right in front of me. Two men got out and pointed back to the soldiers, who were now toiling up the road. Somewhat surprised by this attention, I accompanied the breathless troops back to their station.

The officer in charge of the barracks was waiting at the entrance and greeted me warmly. He was a portly man with a thick moustache and a soft face. He wore a forest-green uniform with important looking insignia on the lapels.

'Have you time for tea?'

I thanked him and followed him into a dusty courtyard.

A whirling fan cooled his office. The windows were shuttered to keep out the afternoon sun. An assistant went for the refreshments.

He asked me if I smoked, and handed me a fresh packet of Korean cigarettes. In turn he declined my documents and contented himself with a first-hand explanation. He listened attentively until I had finished.

'You want to walk on the *left* side of the river?'

'Yes, this was the route taken by the army I am following.'

'But why on the left? There is no road.'

'I can walk by the bank.'

He sighed and we turned to our tea, which came with sugar cubes on the saucers. I explained the Syrian preference for premixing and he made polite enquires about other experiences in that country.

'You know, it would be better for you to walk on this side. There are cars and towns. On the Jezirah ... our people are sensitive.'

I was relieved. I had feared that he was going to insist on a change of plans. I assured him that I was used to the attentions of locals while walking, and could show my papers to the police or military. We drank another glass, and then there was a disappointment. I saw it coming. He shifted on his chair and dusted the lapels of his uniform.

'The buffer zone along the border is restricted. I am afraid you cannot walk here. However, I can send you to the Jezirah.'

*

The jeep pulled up at the foot of a bridge. The commander himself had come along, with another officer. He stuck a packet of Korean cigarettes into my shirt pocket and we shook hands. I crossed slowly onto the Jezirah, absorbing a fine view of the upstream landscape. I thought it unusual that the bridge was not a fixed structure; apparently there were only two or three fixed bridges between here and Baghdad – all the others were like this one, narrow pontoons bending against the flow of the river.

There were some people standing outside a garage above the far bank. I waved at them and turned to photograph the river and the cliffs that overhung it on the upstream side. As I prepared to start on my way, the natives crossed to meet me. A burly man in overalls stretched out the palm of his hand and drew a diagonal line across it. I thought this might be a national variation on the universal Arab invitation for tea, though his body language and expression said otherwise. When I made no response he repeated the gesture more aggressively. '*Pasaport! Pasaport!*'

The document was hesitantly returned after scrutiny by each one of them in turn. I had gone about 100 metres up the road when I heard a car crunch in the gravel behind. People hurried up from the garage; out of the corner of my eye I saw a youth haring across a field. The mechanic pushed me back against the car and grunted. A more articulate man demanded to know who I was. I produced my letter of introduction and the situation was resolved.

Just around a bend up ahead the same thing happened again. This time there were two cars involved, both heading towards the river. The first driver passed the letter to the second, and without any comment he handed it back to me. They hopped back into their cars and continued their journeys.

After that things quietened. In the next kilometre only one vehicle passed, a minibus, and though several passengers piled against the rear window, it did not stop. I hoped that, away from the river and the buffer zone, things would be more relaxed.

At the head of a straight stretch there was a line of houses, and as I approached I could see people coming onto the road. I passed them, getting a half-hearted response to my salutations. I could hear their voices trailing behind. An elderly man with a wooden cane hurried from a house up on the right and started to shout at me. I ignored him until he lashed out with the stick. I grabbed it from him, and somebody attempted the same with mine: it was snatched from behind, but the wrist strap kept it in my possession.

'Pasaport, pasaport!' the old fellow screamed, repeatedly cutting the palm of his hand. There was a moment in which our eyes met. He was a ball of hatred. I imagined one of his sons being blown to pieces in a trench in some desert of the south and felt no resentment towards him. I was jostled and lost balance. I remember the sound of my sunglasses bouncing along the surface of the road. Two men lifted me to my feet, and another returned the glasses, which fortunately were unscathed.

The crowd pressed around me, some shouting questions, others debating among themselves. Shortly afterwards the jeep that had left me at the bridge half an hour before reappeared. The officer's aide got out and spoke to the locals. As they dispersed, he called two youngsters aside and instructed them to walk with me. This helped over the following half hour: people stared but were stayed by the explanation of my escort. Then, without a word, they left, and the hostility resumed. At one village a man accelerated towards me in a tractor. I leapt aside to avoid narrowly being squashed into the track. I shouted blue murder at him but the vehicle kept moving.

By then I was becoming upset. Beyond the same village a young man in a car pulled up alongside and asked to talk. I told him to buzz off and kept going. He followed on foot and said he wanted to help. I had just stopped and was eyeing him when a truck packed with villagers roared over a hump. They jumped from the trailer and grabbed me, wrenching my bags off. They parted to let one of their number through; he faced me with a rifle. I thought he was getting ready to hit me when the young man from the car stepped between us. The mob relented and I was bundled into the front of the truck and taken back to the village.

Mohammed, the young man who had intervened with the villagers, was the son of the district Ba'ath Party secretary. His father was at his desk in the party office in the heart of Rumana. In appearance I thought he bore a strong resemblance to Gandhi – bald, with a wrinkled forehead and a prominent nose. Wearing the traditional *jalabiyah*, he exuded an air of calmness and assurance, hallmarks, I would come to see, of the organization's governing cadre.

He offered me a chair and then asked to see my papers. Everybody who had been on the truck, together with a throng who had gathered to await the posse's return, crammed into the room. They watched as the secretary affixed a pair of wiry spectacles and reviewed the materials in front of him.

I was surprised that they were there at all. Sensitive matters might be expected to be conducted in private, the better for controlling information. Here the message seemed to be openness: the Party as instrument of justice with nothing to hide from dutiful citizens. The secretary was just one of them. No perks or special status were attendant on his post.

Once his review was complete, he straightened and inclined his head downwards. 'The passport has an entry signature for today. We see you are not an intruder.' He smiled briefly before turning to a neat pile of files on his desk. The matter was closed; work must continue.

The hum about the room faded and the gathering began to break up. Pushing his way through to the front, a big stocky man placed one hand on my shoulder, and the other over his chest. I recognized him as the one who had wielded his gun at me. Another came forward and returned my sunglasses, which had not survived as well this time. Mohammed asked this man to arrange for my other belongings to be brought to his home.

This was a spacious if Spartan dwelling situated within close earshot of the mosque. We sat alone in the guest room and drank tea. He asked to see my papers for himself and perused them while I attempted to refit a lens to my sunglasses (as with an earlier pair I had damaged in Turkey, a plaster finally did the trick). Outside, children stared through the windows. When they became noisy Mohammed made as if to rise, and they momentarily disappeared. 'They are not used to foreigners.' I was the first in his recollection to have come to the village, though in 1991, three Britons with 'electrical equipment' had been apprehended down on the river. One of them, he said, was shot, and the other two taken into custody.

I was curious about this incident, but said nothing for fear of attracting more suspicion.

'Today, you were afraid,' Mohammed said to me after a lengthy pause.

I expected that he would have been as well if a mob had set upon him, but I shrugged my shoulders and said I hadn't been.

In the evening the father came and we ate a rubbery chicken. Conversation was sparse. A television was brought in after the meal, and with it came some of the younger members of the family. Saddam in a white suit and wearing a panama hat strutted about a garden giving a press conference without questions. Then a newscaster in a studio read an open letter from the president to his Egyptian counterpart about the crisis in Palestine. Mohammed translated the main points: Saddam would not be attending an emergency meeting of the Arab nations in Cairo (Saddam hasn't left the country for 15 years; some abroad want to assassinate him); he appealed to the leaders to take action; he appealed personally to President Mubarak (he is the strongest leader, the others are worthless).

The party secretary did not seem to be as interested as his son in what the leader had to say – a case perhaps of the enlightened not being in need of improvement. He glided in and out of the room, attending to family business and the odd caller seeking counsel at the door. I remarked to myself that he had about him an unsettling aura of serenity.

When, late in the evening, my turn came to receive wisdom, he seated himself cross-legged in front of me.

'Our president calls the Anbar the "White Province". It gives him the least trouble. I advise, if you continue, that you seek out the responsible official each day. They are the ones who can help.'

I nodded, and thanked him for his concern.

Shortly after this bedding was brought in and everybody left except Mohammed. He was soon asleep. I stared up at the ceiling for ages, turning the events of the day over in my mind. Pondering the next phase of the journey the night before in Abu-Kemal, I had never imagined the sort of reception that awaited me across the border. Neither had any of the Syrians with whom I had discussed my journey. Indeed, they imagined the country to be as friendly as their own. 'They are our brothers. They love guests like we do,' Mohammed Kandil, the tourist officer from Sarmada, had assured me.

I tried to look on the positive side. Once I was away from the frontier, there would probably be less concern on the part of the locals about my presence. I resolved to try to keep out of their way as much as I could.

Mohammed took me down to the river in the morning, pointing out as we approached the place where the journey of one of the Englishmen had ended. He wished me success for my trip and we parted.

I had chosen to walk along the bank in order to avoid the villages, which were dotted along the dirt track that twisted through the hills above the river. This way I imagined that I'd have less contact with the population. The plan, however, proved to be impractical, for quite apart from the ranging bends multiplying distances, the ground in many stretches was sand marsh.

Changing tack mid-morning I turned inland across a series of irrigated fields, and before long found myself in a wilderness, a tract of rolling desert stretching as far as the eye could see. I kept on a northeast bearing for about thirty minutes, and then adjusted to an easterly course, the general direction of the river's flow in this area. At times I could see it in the distance, a brilliant blue artery shimmering in the midday sun.

I came upon no habitation until early afternoon. The river must have swerved sharply north, for over the rise of a hill there appeared a large village. On the faintly marked track leading down to it I met a shepherd in his early teens. We muttered *salaams*, but once we were a safe distance apart he drew his knife and made murderous jabbing motions. I stood watching him for a moment, and then raised my walking stick, cocking an imaginary high-tech trigger. He hastened off over the hill.

On the edge of the settlement there was a school, and a teacher in the yard waved and beckoned me in. The staff proved to be extremely friendly, abandoning their classes to join us for tea in the principal's office. A female teacher called Nahr presented me with two pictures her pupils had drawn. A burning house was depicted in one, diving aeroplanes in the other. I rolled them up and slipped them into the hollow of my sleeping mat.

A group of them walked through the village with me, ensuring that I found the right track to the next settlement. I only saw one more besides that one that afternoon, avoiding both by taking a wide northerly berth.

Towards evening I decided to make for the river valley to see whether I could get to a house. The advice of the party secretary at Rumana had been at the back of my mind all day, and I guessed that if I didn't look for the officials, they'd come looking for me.

After about twenty minutes heading south I picked out a lush patch of agriculture by the riverbank and proceeded towards this. As I came to within touching distance of the greenery, however, the river appeared between me and it. I had seen it several times on the approach, and it was definitely flowing from the top left-hand corner of the field. From the bank I traced the cause of the deception: a deep loop undercutting the height on this side. The delineation was striking: this side twisted away hilly and rocky in both directions, while on the right bank a neat green carpet covered a more even landscape. Contrasts of the river: the desert and the sown.

I finished what water I had left and continued along the bank. The sun was dipping and, as there were no homes in sight, I thought I had better look for a shelter. I found one, and had started to eat my dinner on top of the overhanging rock, when I heard a motorcycle buzzing along the embankment overhead. I was unsure what to do, but thought it best not to act in any way suspiciously. The machine stopped and the driver shouted down. A frayed *shamag* trailed down his back like a ponytail. Duh-Duh-Duh-Duh-Duh. He roared his name over the noise and pointed ahead to where I guessed his village was. A scrawny dog arrived on the scene and wagged its tail. I mimed that I'd follow, and in a cloud of dust the pair resumed their journey along the ridge.

The place was hardly a village – five or six mud huts on a concave height overlooking the river. Ahmed was bleeding his oil pump and nodded to a reed mat. Once we were seated I showed him my letter of introduction, but I don't think either he or a second man who joined us, was able to read. None the less they were not bothered by my sudden appearance. We sipped tea as the sun set and Zahra rose, brilliant against the deepening blue sky.

A few more men joined us. They drank and stripped a gun and began to trade bullets. As they bargained, a beautiful thing happened. From the hut next to ours, a tall man dressed in a green *jalabiyah* emerged and walked toward the centre of the hollow. A child followed him and ran back to the hut with a towel the man had been drying himself with. He stood for a minute, readying himself, and then called the faithful to prayer. His voice was deep and powerful like the river, carrying the sacred words beyond the limits of the hamlet. Our company was too engrossed in their business to heed the call, but I saw others make their way to a shack on a rise behind. When he had finished, the *muezzin* turned to follow them. It was among the most moving acts of religion I had ever witnessed.

We slept where we were on the mats, but in the middle of the night a pack of wild dogs invaded the camp and forced us inside. Ahmed took up a position at the door with his gun, but either he was afraid of felling one of his own animals – engaged in what sounded like a fiendish brawl – or he was reluctant to waste a bullet.

The small community seemed to be the last in the present line of settlement. In the morning my host took me onto a nearby hill and pointed into the desert. I had thought there would be a track to Rawa, a town further down the river which I was aiming for that day, but Ahmed was clear there was none.

I went back to get an extra container of water. With a good drink in the morning, I had found that I could get through the most arduous of days with just another litre, but in the present circumstances I thought it prudent to take a second. (Earlier experience had led me to discontinue the practice of heavy drinking: moderation, and the training of the body, I found to be far more effective than gluttonous bouts of thirst quenching.)

The only difficulty I faced that day was the flies. I couldn't figure out whether the desert was full of them or whether every fly in this part had homed in on me. In places all I could see was a black haze, and I spent much of my time and energy swatting the air. To counter this annoyance, the Arabs wrap their headgear fully around their faces, but it was too hot for me to wear the garment in this manner for any length of time.

Because of the flies my progress was slow, and I may also have drifted off course. In late afternoon I climbed several hills but could not make out any trace of the river valley. The landscape in this area was breathtaking. Low, round hills, brown and bare, rolled into the distance with no sign whatever of life or vegetation. It was, I thought, the way the floor of an ocean might look if it were to be drained and left to bake under the sun.

After spending the night in a gully, at first light I set off in a south-south-easterly direction. With still no glimpse of the jinking Euphrates, I decided to head directly south, and at around 9 a.m., I sighted a solitary homestead. I feared that the river might trick me again, and that I mightn't come across a village on this side for days, but the house was firmly on the Jezirah.

Dogs alerted the occupants to my approach. Two squinting farmers came out of the mud hut and waited. They might have been father and son. The younger, a tall, skinny man, pushed the door nervously and invited me in.

The dwelling was one long room, bare of furnishings. Flies hovered above the earthen floor, their activity exposed by a thick beam of sunlight shining obliquely through the window. A veiled woman in a loose-fitting purple robe brought a bowl of water. The sun had withered her face, and time had faded tattoos on her chin and forehead. I took her to be the older man's wife.

We drank tea and I filled my canister. I showed the men my letter but don't think they understood it. They stared at me without talking. I was keen to be off but they insisted that I wait to eat, and the younger went to fetch meat. He was a long time so the other ordered his wife to give me a serving of what was in the pot. This was some type of mixture of bread and stew, an unpalatable dish which, if I hadn't been extremely hungry, I would have left untouched. I let it settle for a bit in my stomach and then got up to leave. The man became agitated and shouted at his wife, who was squatting by the stove. Wrapping her hand in a cloth she retrieved the teapot and dropped it beside him. He rattled glasses, as if this would entice me to stay. Failing, he scurried outside and seized my hand. There was a frightened look in his eyes. I felt sorry for him, and at the same time couldn't help feeling some disdain. I took his hand off mine. Overhead the sky was darkening; a gust snorted a tin can across the yard. There was a sign in it perhaps. I went back into the hovel and sat down in a corner.

I heard the dogs barking first, and then the sound of vehicles pulling into the yard. The wind was up and daylight dim. The door swung open and the skinny man who had earlier left hurried in. Two others followed and made way for a short fellow with a detached band of light blond hair. He brushed this across his pate and strode over to me.

'I am Mr Wajid, representative of the Arab Ba'ath Socialist Party. We are here to offer help and take you to Rawa.'

*

Though the town was only 20 kilometres away, in the heavy weather it took over an hour to get there. At times, when visibility dropped, we had to stop to avoid the risk of striking one of the other vehicles (the chain was linked by radios). I sat in the front of a jeep between Wajid and the driver. There was little conversation. As we bumped along, my thoughts remained fixed on the sorry dwellers in the hovel. Their loyalty to country and party troubled me. In the city a citizen might be persuaded to a cause by words and reason, but in the villages they understood only violence.

Pulling in behind another vehicle on the outskirts of Rawa, we waited for the others to arrive. The re-formed convoy moved slowly through the lonely looking town. Passing a statute of Saddam in the centre, we turned into a walled compound. The front doors of a modern two-storey building opened and we filed up the stairs to a large second floor office. Stark strip lighting revealed that everybody was covered in sand and dust. Mr Wajid pasted his hair and seated himself behind a desk. A set of standard procedures was followed. The secretary conversed jovially with someone, possibly at a regional office some-where, and then more stiffly with somebody in the capital. The connection was poor and Wajid had to raise his voice to communicate details of my person.

I spent the next three days in the compound. While they were happy to assist me in completing the interrupted stretch to Rawa, there was disquiet over my plans to continue along the Jezirah. Citing various reasons, including wild animals, and a lack of habitation, they started to pressure me into crossing onto the Shamia. I sought an audience with the secretary to discuss the matter, but he proved difficult to track down.

Life in the compound was something like being in a military barracks. There was a guard at the gates, and a core of five or six armed men who spent the day hanging around the foyer waiting for something to happen. At night a few stayed behind and took turns to patrol the perimeter. I observed that they conformed to no particular type, being of widely varying ages, appearance, and character. They had no uniforms, nor any insignia marking their status.

They looked after me well. One spoke some Russian (as I did) and one night produced a bottle of Moskovskaya vodka; another man wanted to take me to his home and, although this was against the rules, he succeeded in getting permission to take me there for breakfast on the morning I left. Another idea of his was to arm me so that I could defend myself against wild animals, but this one wasn't as well received by the management.

If I ever wanted to buy anything, one of them would take a box of money from the office and take me out to the shops, where everything was available. Once, on the way back from the fruit market, my escort paused before the gateway of the compound. On the metal archway there was a round plate bearing the party emblem, a map of the Arab world. He pointed this out proudly to me. 'Hezib!' (Hezbil Ba'ath.) In time, I formed a grudging admiration for this organization. Whatever its failings high up, in the lower echelons its members by and large were not motivated by self-interest. They believed in the goals of the party – in Arab unity and social equality – and that it would in the future deliver some kind of justice to their countrymen. 'In great endeavours, to want is enough' (Propertius).

On the day that I completed my walk into the town, I collared Wajid in the foyer. It was a custom that at around six every evening he returned to the headquarters to review the business of the day. A fuss would be made when the car pulled up, and everybody gathered in the foyer to greet him. I joined the retinue as it passed. He was pleased to see me and asked how things had gone. We ascended the stairs together. 'It will be difficult for you to continue along the same route. At Haditha, you can cross back to the Jezirah.' The clique followed him into the starkly lit boardroom, leaving me to contemplate a change of plans.

18

Haditha

The Commissar

A single death is a tragedy; a million is a statistic.
Stalin

I imagined that a consolation of being on the Shamia was that there would be less hassle on the road. A trunk route ran from the border to Ramadi, the Anbar capital, and I assumed that the more worldly commuters would be less suspicious of my presence.

This wasn't the case at all. I had no sooner turned onto the road from the Rawa junction than a man had his finger and palm in my face. The traffic in fact was light, but few could pass without performing their duty. The normal scenario was that a driver would pass (in either direction), slow down, look around to check if there was anyone with me, and then turn around and confront me.

Another surprise for me was that the opposite bank was almost as desolate, and no less harsh: brown earth and stones, stones, stones. For long stretches the road was the only trace of civilization. Population pockets seemed to be situated at the end of remote feeder roads, although unlike on the Jezirah they were connected to a transport corridor. Historically, settlement on the middle Euphrates has always been concentrated on this bank. The distribution of ancient sites – Thapsakos, Halabiyah, Dura Europos, Mari, Anah, Charmande, Iz – is predominantly on this side.

Resorting to my earlier tactic of walking across country, at a place where I could see nothing for kilometres, I skipped off the asphalt. I remained a good distance away from it, so that only the most paranoid of Arabs could have picked me out through the dunes. But evidently I was unlucky. I was feeling tired, not having stopped to rest for a number of hours, when I heard the sound of a vehicle behind and looked around to see a white pick-up bumping slowly over the rocky surface. I kept walking – I suppose I just hoped it would continue past – and when I turned around again three men were standing outside it. They were armed and pointing their guns at me. One of them stepped away from the car and moved to his right, the second remained behind a door and the third approached me head on. He stepped cautiously over the rocks, his weapon, a heavy pistol, held in a sideways position. He jerked the gun to indicate I was to raise my hands, which I did, letting my stick fall to the ground. He kept stepping towards me, and when he was close enough, grabbed my arm and twisted it behind my back. The others ran forward: my bags were pulled off and I was made to kneel on the ground. I told them I had documents, and after a search and a short discussion, they let me show them. As they perused the papers, I explained in English the reason I had been walking off the road.

'We thought you were Mossad agent,' the man who had been behind the car door confided. I had to suppress a smile. They would never know just how unlikely this was.

They advised me that I needed to be careful at this time, as the army was moving military equipment to the border. Saddam had apparently made a request to the Syrians to allow him send a division across their territory to Palestine. A national campaign was underway to raise volunteers for combat.

We smoked cigarettes at the car and chatted nervously. They seemed more relieved than me at the outcome. We shook hands and I waited as the car turned around. The man in the passenger seat wound down the window and gestured to the one in the rear, who had apprehended me. 'He says he is sorry a thousand times for pointing the gun at you.' As I turned to gather my bags, it dawned on me that I might never have done so again.

Within an hour I found myself in another unwelcome situation. My way was suddenly barred by a gaping valley, which turned out to be the first in a horrid series of wadis. These steep-sided gorges were a fairly common feature of the landscape, but I had not previously encountered ones so deep. In places, the drop, up to 30 metres, was sheer, a testament to the tremendous erosive power of the flash floods. The floors of these wadis were remarkably smooth, ideal, I thought, for a game of football, or even as a landing strip for light aircraft.

Weight made descent to the beds exacting on the knees. In the afternoon a dense fog enveloped the desert, and the coolness lessened the strain of climbing out. To bridge each wadi, including the initial search for a way down, took me forty to fifty minutes. In all that day I crossed four, halting in the fifth to rest in a shallow cave.

Thinking more clearly in the morning, I decided to follow the floor south until I came to the road. Noise from the traffic reverberated off the valley sides long before it came into view. At about 7 a.m., around a bend, I saw a bridge. Heavy vehicles, some hauling pieces of artillery equipment, crossed over it at short intervals: Saddam making good his promise to camp on Syria's doorstep. I realized that it wasn't a good location for me to be in, so retreating round the bluff, I backtracked down the valley. For another two hours I struggled with the wadi system, but finally it finished, and I picked up a heavy-duty water pipe stretching in the direction of Haditha.

The pipe in fact was buried underground, its route marked by a soft bump trailing across the desert. At fixed intervals there were manholes, and on the covers of these it was written, in English, that the pipe was carrying drinking water. Occasionally the line skirted villages, but far enough away that I was not at any great risk of being spotted by locals. Once, rounding a hill, I came face to face with two girls weeding on the edge of the desert. They straightened and looked at me with expressionless faces. I greeted them and continued, reckoning that it would take them ten minutes or more to get to the village should they choose to report me.

Five kilometres on from this encounter, the pipe turned and bored straight into the centre of Khasfeh, a small, pre-planned satellite town. Wide, empty streets intersected one another at right angles, their ends terminating seamlessly in the desert. I walked onto one and strolled unnoticed past facing rows of rickety houses. The odd rusting vehicle lay carelessly parked between a footpath and a garden; wooden fences attempted to define perimeters but wavered midway and fell into vegetable patches. Order on this scale didn't agree with the Arabs at all.

Two youths approached and I asked for the responsible official. The apparatchiks were away, so after a discussion with others, they took me to the home of a local merchant. He had spent a couple of years in the

Gulf and seemed to be considered worldly wise because of this. His house was situated right on the corner of the grid, and was quite big, having had several extensions made to it over the years. Razan rose above the excitement of my escorts and coolly ordered the group home, after having questioned them in detail on the circumstances of my arrival. He had a shark-fin nose and wore a white turban bunched up in the manner of a sheikh. His belly swelled through the light fabric of his robe.

The guest room of his house was impressive. Like most Arab lounges I had seen, it was spacious, and minimalist. The principal fittings of this one were a stone fireplace and a large water cooler for summer days. A light red carpet covered the floor. At the end opposite the fireplace a quantity of embroidered cushions lay neatly stacked against the wall. Two were taken off the top by a teenager and placed at our sides. I leant on mine while Razan pored over my papers, puffing on Marlboro cigarettes. Two more sons came into the room and joined the other one kneeling in front of us. Once their father was satisfied to a degree, they were sent to fetch refreshments.

In the evening the town's senior men came. Each on arrival was allocated a space along a wall of the guest room by the eldest son, possibly to some hierarchical tribal scheme. I sat next to the host in the middle of the side facing the entrance, receiving the greetings of the guests, but otherwise remaining in the background while he described my journey.

The Iraqis have a custom unique among Arabs. Wherever there is a gathering, the last person to arrive will say after he is seated, '*Allah-bel-kher*' ('may God bring you good'). Each of the others will respond to him in their turn with the same blessing. So as somebody new came, Razan's story was paused; it also had to be restarted, for Arabs like to be told a story from the beginning. Even if a man has the full detail of an event beforehand, he needs to hear it again for himself from the eyewitness.

Quite what Razan was telling them, I wasn't sure, for he knew little about what I was doing other than what he had gleaned from the letter of introduction. His English was poor, and I doubted he understood much of what I had told him over dinner. Occasionally one of the guests would seek clarity on a point, and he would turn and mumble something to me.

'Sorry, can you say again?' I'd usually have to ask. His head would nod a few times, and he'd turn back to the gathering with a reply to the query.

Among those there were a number of cripples: men without limbs, and one with a huge crater in his skull. The injuries I learned (bypassing Razan with my few words of Arabic) were suffered in the country's long war with Iran. The one with the crater had been hit by shrapnel from an exploding shell. Two of the men present, he explained with gruesome animation, had lost their legs in a minefield on the Fao Peninsula. They came forward and revealed the extent of the damage. I was led to understand that it was the fault of their own side, that the men had been deliberately directed into a section of no man's land so as to clear it of mines. The Iranians did this with children, who ran through the front lines shouting the name of God. There were over a million casualties in this war that achieved nothing.

Whether or not it was because he was being sidelined, the host cut short our laboured communication. Places had to be retaken for the serving of coffee. The eldest son had spent half an hour before this alternately crushing grains with a hefty pestle, and stoking the fire to heat a slender coffee jug. Wielding this expertly with two small cups in his other hand, he went around the room pouring a shot for each person. A swift upward motion produced a jet of thick black liquid. The measures were small, swallowed in a gulp like vodka, and bitter too. Afterwards, the cup was handed back, and the second one refused in accordance with custom.

Following this ritual the guests gathered up their coats and crutches and made their way home. I regretted not having had the chance to spend longer with them, to learn more of their stories, and perhaps their views on those who had conducted the Gulf War.

*

There was a dam somewhere above Haditha. Its construction a decade before had forced the people in the affected upstream area to leave their lands. The larger communities were resettled in government-built towns like Khasfeh.

I was hoping I could cross the dam and get back onto the Jezirah without having to go through Haditha. Razan nodded when I asked if this was possible. He walked with me in the morning to the end of his yard, and pointed vaguely toward the river valley.

A heavy fog made the dawn unusually cool. I put on another sweater and wound the *shamag* around my neck like a scarf. The filtered light in the desert produced strange colours: my fingernails appeared bluish, as did my watch face and compass, and the stones had a soft, aquamarine hue. The sun gradually began to assert itself, and by 8 a.m. it had burned off the low cover.

Early on I happened on an empty Bedouin camp, guarded by dogs. The animals were persistent, and I made the mistake of throwing a stone at one of them. In a fury the pack snapped at my heels and harried me for ages over the rolling hills.

Not long after the sun had appeared, I came to a high wire fence which I took to be the perimeter of the dam complex. Opting for the more certain, if longer, way around, I turned right and tracked the fence upwards towards its corner.

This took only twenty minutes to reach, but I was left wishing I had started the day in a different direction altogether, for set up on the plateau, on both sides of the fence, was a military encampment. In front of me I could see soldiers going in and out of tents, while inside the fence, men were oiling a row of large guns. I thought there was no point turning back, as it was likely that I was going to be spotted at any moment. I pulled out my map and began to look around with a suitably surprised expression.

An age seemed to pass before I was noticed. A shirtless young fellow bent over a stove outside a tent on my right looked sideways at me. I greeted him, and he stood up, but then went back to the stove. I crossed to the wire and called out to a group servicing a gun, '*Salaam alaykum.*'

A few hesitant replies echoed back. One of the men nudged an officer, who had his nose stuck in a manual. He put this down and strode over to the divide. I said I was looking for the dam. He stroked his palm. Ordering one of the soldiers on the outside to bring me around, he disappeared with my papers.

The same officer was waiting in a jeep at the entrance to the complex. I squeezed into the front and we sped off down a hill, catching a glimpse on the next rise of the river and the town of Haditha. Descending again we looped into an enclosure. A commander in a bunker surrounded by smartly dressed officers took my papers and shook his head. The obvious questions were asked. I explained that I had been told there was a public road over the dam. The general muttered something to the officer who had brought me in and I was ushered away.

The jeep entered a fortified compound in the centre of Haditha. From the emblem over the gate I recognized it as a party building. My papers were handed to an official who subsequently led me to a waiting room. It was late morning when he returned.

Shortly before this, a jeep and a car had pulled up outside. The driver opened the rear door of the car, and an impeccably dressed middle-aged man stepped out. He was slight, about 5 feet 10 inches in height, and wore a brown cotton tunic and matching trousers. The shine on his black shoes was noticeable even through the grimy window. Pausing to stroke a mat of black hair, he strode into the foyer.

He was waiting for me in a large office on the second floor. A mahogany table complemented by straight-backed wooden chairs ran virtually the length of the room. A desk banked with telephones fitted snugly at the end away from the door. On the wall behind this there was a portrait of Saddam Hussein as a young man, one I wouldn't see often on my journey, and usually in an official context. In the iconography of the organization, I came to understand that it represented the idealism of the party.

'Please have a seat. Will you drink tea, or something cool?' The secretary was standing beneath the portrait with his hands behind his back.

I thanked him and sat down at the table. When he had ordered, he joined me, pulling his chair close to mine. The contrast between his groomed exterior and my own appearance unsettled me a bit, as did the familiarity of his manner. Paternalism seemed to become more pronounced with seniority in the party. After enquiring about my journey, and how I had come to be at the dam, he paused in thought.

'You must try to avoid these areas. We are in a sensitive period.' He looked me in the eye to ensure that I had understood, and then rose to go to his desk.

'Can I ask where you plan to go from here?'

I answered that I was hoping to get back onto the Jezirah and continue in the tracks of Cyrus the Persian. Somewhat to my surprise, he did not object, asking merely that I outline on my map the route I was intending to take. I spread this on his desk and marked a course along the river. He jotted down names, stopping me at Heit, the limit of his power. A bony finger dabbed an area on the map. 'There has been some trouble in these villages. Better that you do not visit.' I didn't enquire as to the nature of the trouble, but made a show of carefully noting their names on the map.

'How else can I help?'

My letter of introduction from Athens was in a state of decomposition, a result of countless inspections *en route*. I asked him if he could write me another.

He replaced his reading spectacles and studied the document. His assistant appeared promptly on the buzzer and took a handwritten note away to be typed and stamped. While we waited, I explained the difficulties I was having in the countryside: any time my path crossed another's, there was a demand for papers, and in a village I could get stopped three or four times. His eyebrows rose as I cut my palm under his nose in imitation of a citizen. Like other senior officials down the line I talked with, he was outwardly sympathetic to this situation, but secretly I suspected that they were delighted at the vigilance of the population, and not at all upset by the psychological bruising I was taking.

*

From the Hezib compound I proceeded upstream to a pontoon bridge. While awaiting the commissar I had calculated that, to this point, I had covered about 195 kilometres from the border, perhaps a dozen of them in jeep rides. The ten-minute drive from the border to the pontoon was the first notable stretch of the journey I hadn't covered on foot. But like the recent ride from the dam, it couldn't be helped. My main concern now was getting through the rest of the 'White Province' as quickly as possible.

My second entrance into the Jezirah was not a dissimilar experience to the first: passage through the suburb on the left bank was heavily punctuated by demands for identification. Sometimes I'd hardly be out of the sight of one crowd when another would be around me. If I asked for the police, as suggested by the commissar, they would knock their chests aggressively: '*Ana polis!*' The prospect of this continuing for the rest of the journey was a demoralizing one.

On the positive side, the new letter at least resulted in shorter hold-ups: whereas the previous one tended to be studied, this was handed back almost instantly, the inquisitors returning smartly to their business. I guessed that the cause of this was either the party emblem, prominent on the letterhead, or the abrupt signature at the bottom.

The city boundary finished near where an impressive new rail bridge ran high above the Euphrates. Together with the dam upstream, it was unexpected evidence of recent economic development. These major civil projects, however, were in marked contrast to the uniformly poor quality of housing, schools, and other public buildings I had so far seen. I guessed that this was socialism from above.

At a jumble of houses beyond the bridge I hailed a boy playing in his yard. I waited outside while he raced in with my container to get a refill of water. His father came out and asked for my passport. I insisted on getting a drink first. There was a stubborn standoff, and finally he shook his head: '*La.*'

His refusal to give water was incredible to me. I waved my hand in his face and walked off.

To beat a severe meander, I followed a direct line inland through the hills. The peninsular area was empty, uncultivatable, uninhabitable. After forty minutes I came in sight of the river again. Along the bank there was a series of low mounds, each topped with a cluster of mud huts. I made my way to a dwelling on top of the first one. There was nobody around so I drank from a bucket in the yard. A dog asleep in the dirt awoke as I left. He circled nervously and then quietly sat down, his eyes fixed on me. I had observed this phenomenon once before on a country road in Turkey. It was dawn and I was pressing along when I came upon an animal sleeping on the road in front of a gate. Out of mischief I shouted in his ear and he sprang up and did a circle. Then he disappeared into the house, emerging moments later in a froth of anger. This one seemed to have been too surprised to make any amends for its extraordinary negligence, but he may also have been thinking that if he did nothing, no one would be any the wiser.

Beyond the last mound a man shouted at me from a forest of palm trees. I ignored him and he raced across the intervening field waving a hand-scythe. We confronted each other in the middle of the track. He was a short, wiry fellow, with big dark eyes. He wore a dark grey *jalabiyah* and had a red and white *shamag* tied handkerchief-fashion on his head. We eyeballed each other for some moments, and then I felt myself being swept aside, as though I had been hit by a wing-forward flying off the side of a scrum. The tackler picked himself up and the two men stood over me, pointing back to the mound. They lessened my humiliation somewhat by indicating we were going to eat.

A pot was heated in one of the huts and some gruel served while other villagers assembled. I didn't eat the food and hardly said anything when they returned my documents. I walked slowly back down the hill, conscious that the will to continue was ebbing away from me.

Al-Qaim, Iraq. Welcome to the Anbar

Camels outside Drema

The western desert, al-Anbar

Harvesting dates, Qsariyat

With Nasser (*right*) and Wazir (*far right*), Qsariyat

Jubbah

Mr Thabet

Um Talid

Kareem (*left*) and Aziz

Safa

With Abdullah and Father Nadheer, the Mother of Sorrows Church, Baghdad

Kemal on Embassy Street

Nassir in his garden

The Kadhimiya, Baghdad

It started to rain in the evening, the first rains of the season. A light, steady patter fell on my flysheet through the night. Reluctant to erect my tent lest it be seen, I had draped the outer shell over a thicket on the riverbank. The water succeeded in finding its way onto me and made the night cold and uncomfortable. Hunger also kept me from sleeping.

In the morning I walked along the water's edge. I was making no real progress, but wasn't concerned, so long as there were no people. Coming upon a dense grove of date palms where workers had broken for tea, I made off with a pile of freshly cut branches, stripping them on the river of their sticky fruit. The only other signs of life I saw that morning were the boats that occasionally plied the waterway. I thought that if I had one myself, I could float like the traders of old all the way to Babylon, with nothing to bother me except the sun. I was sure that Cyrus would have done this too if he could ever have assembled enough boats to take his army.

The density of palm trees increased as I progressed. Ubiquitous from here on south since time immemorial, they were evidently still an important resource for the river people. Fishing seemed to be another source of income. At one place I came upon a small jetty which had several boats tied to it, with others beached on a narrow strip of shore, ready for use perhaps at dusk. I was looking at one of them when a voice called from a concrete shed above the bank. A man came out and stood right over me. I asked if he spoke English.

'I am speaking English. My name is Wazir.'

He was blind and his left hand was a stub. I explained who I was and said I had papers to prove it. He asked me to climb up, which I did, and he took my hand and smiled. 'I am very happy to meet you.'

There was nobody else around so he led me himself through an adjoining palm grove. Women standing beneath the trees watched us in silence. A few gaping youngsters fell in behind.

Wazir had learned English at school, but hadn't spoken the language for years, though he often listened to the BBC for news. His injuries, he told me, were the result of a fishing accident. When it was available they used dynamite to fill their nets. An explosive was detonated beneath the surface, killing every living thing within a radius defined by the size of the charge. It was a delicate business which didn't always go well.

Closer to the village our entourage swelled. I braced myself, but I had already sensed that there was something different about this place. The people smiled, and their expressions were curious rather than fearful or suspicious. A youngish man with a beard joined the troupe and spoke above the chatter to Wazir.

'He wants to take you to his home. This is teacher, Nasser.'

*

Qsariyat was typical of the disorderly settlements found on the Jezirah. Houses stood where the owners had decided to build them, and tracks passing for streets wound around them as they could. The Government paid for a school and supplied electricity, but this appeared to be the extent of central involvement.

Nasser's home was a rickety wooden structure in the heart of the village. He shared it with two elder brothers, Sadoun and Said. Each was married and the place was overrun with playful infants. Chickens, ducks and other farmyard animals moved in and out of the open hallway like part of the family.

Sadoun was also a teacher, though the levels of pay (the equivalent of $10 a month) meant that they both had to spend weekends on the family date plantations. A brother-in-law, Maiad, was the English teacher at the school, and he came soon after I arrived to help with conversation. Like his in-laws, he was tall and handsome; a fine head of dark hair was precisely parted at the side, and a carefully trimmed beard grew down from his high cheekbones. Maiad was more reserved than the brothers, giving his opinion only when asked. When he did speak, softly, his hands resting on a cushion between his legs, the brothers gave their full attention.

He was busy through the evening as a constant stream of neighbours called to meet me. As is the way with Arabs, each in turn had to be told the entire story of my journey. To assist him, early on I laid out my map on the shrinking floor space.

'I see you have written our name,' he commented, while the crowd pressed in about us.

'Yes, your village was commended to me by the chief in Haditha.'

More relief for Maiad was provided by a football match on the television, the first between Iraq and Iran since the war. Midway through the first half, with the game scoreless, the transmission was interrupted for the news. There was no undue annoyance expressed at this, but when the President made his customary post-bulletin appearance, Sadoun crossed from his spot by the door and jerked the volume to zero. He then sat on the floor with his back to the screen and joined a conversation.

When normal service resumed (Saddam's musings on the day could go on for ten or twenty minutes) the national team was a goal down. With a quarter of an hour to go, and the visitors pressing for an equalizer, the power went. What I took to be terms of crude disapproval in Arabic filled the room; oil light illuminated disgruntled faces. This was a nightly occurrence, though the hour and duration of the electricity cut were variable. The official cause of the disruptions was a lack of spare parts in the generating plants, although I could never understand how this could result in cuts of this sort. Either the parts worked or they didn't: was it the case that they had to be repaired every evening? Maiad had no answer to this, but Wazir, who was the least inconvenienced by the daily trial, had his own idea: 'The government likes to remind us of the embargo on our country.'

The final minutes were played out on a transistor radio. There was no change to the score line and the evening broke up on a rather subdued note. I imagined that it was much worse for the team. The country's then head of sport, Uday Hussein, didn't take kindly to defeat. After one poor performance the previous year the players had had their heads shaved and were beaten with baseball bats.

I had been asked during the evening how I found the people in Iraq. My reply had been fairly diplomatic, emphasizing that once they knew who I was, people were very hospitable. When we were alone – Maiad, Sadoun, Nasser and I – the subject came up again. This time I was more truthful, confessing that sometimes people were not at all friendly. The incident of the previous day involving the water was uppermost in my mind. 'In Syria everybody says "*Ahlan, Ahlan*". Here it's "*Jawaz, Jawaz*." '

'Most of them, they are afraid,' Maiad responded, after translating what I had said. 'Even if they see an Arab, an Iraqi who is not from their district, they are obliged to discover his identity. You must try to excuse them. This is the way things are.'

We were joined by the wives of Nasser and Sadoun, and chatted late into the night. Their curiosity was boundless: religion, marriage and families, education, work. Why was I on my own? Was my mother not worried? Did the army eat dates? Maiad toiled to keep up with the exchanges. His eyes squinted as he sought the right words to convey my answers. I encouraged him to keep going. For the first time in the country, I felt I was having a real exchange, something which made me feel that all the hassle was worth while.

The next morning I was taken on a tour of the village. We went first to the school, where I was swamped in the playground by the children. Nasser had them sing songs and persuaded the principal to call a half-holiday. Everywhere I went people greeted me. Shopkeepers hailed us and presented me with the best of whatever was on offer; tractors bumping along the dusty main street blew their horns and waved. I began to feel like a celebrity.

In the plantations behind the village the harvest was in full swing. Felled dates were being carried to waiting trailers on the tracks while a wave of harvesters hacked away in the treetops. A man slid down from one to give a demonstration of his skill. His key tool was a pair of boots that had hooks protruding from their ends: applying these to the bark, he was able to shin up and anchor under the canopy, where he deployed his other essential piece of equipment, a curved hand-scythe.

Down at the river we called on Wazir. He had a freezer in his water-side cabin and he showed us the fish he had gutted that morning. They were bigger than I had expected, some ½ metre long, and fat. A choice pair were wrapped up in paper and handed to Nasser for our dinner.

Murmuring on a shelf above the fridge was his radio, a foreign-made transistor on which, with much perseverance, he was able to pick up international signals. He handed it to me, perhaps expecting that I would instantly locate an English voice. My blushes were saved by one of the fishermen on the jetty, who shouted at Wazir to send me down.

Assured that no dynamite would be used, I boarded the small craft and embarked on my first trip along the river. The pilot sped from bank to bank before twisting the boat full circle to take us back upstream. At a likely spot he cut the engine and took in his hands a long pole. I assumed this was a fishing net – the sort with the hoop-basket at the end you see anglers carrying – until I noticed wires where there should have been a net. Dipping it into the water, he called over his shoulder to his teenage son, who flicked a switch on a large battery that was lodged beneath the middle bench. For a second I thought we were all going to be electrocuted, but there was a fault with the wiring and we had to return to shore for repairs. Wazir explained that conventional fishing methods here were useless: there were too many weeds and floating debris that snagged the nets. He admitted that their techniques were crude, but they had to make a living.

When we got back to Nasser's that lunchtime I went to bed. I had begun to feel unwell and had symptoms of mild food poisoning. A local remedy was administered, and to be on the safe side I excused myself from dinner.

On account of my illness callers did not tarry that evening. One of them, who lived in a village 15 kilometres downstream, left a message to say that he wanted me to stay in his house. Sadoun said he was a friend, and he thought I should go with him when I was fit enough to do so. The next day I felt better, and it was agreed that in the morning I could set off for Jubbah.

19

Jubbah

Outlaws of the Earth

We climbed, he first, I following his steps,
Till on our view the beautiful lights of heaven
Dawned through a circular opening in the cave:
Thence issuing, we again beheld the stars.

Dante, *Inferno*

Aziz turned up at the house shortly after seven and refused to come in for breakfast. He was dark skinned and had a wiry build. He wore trousers and a shirt but did not have any shoes. I guessed that he was in his mid-20s. He seemed of a nervous disposition, his eyes frequently darting, his few words accompanied by orchestral arm movements. He insisted on carrying my gear, even though we assured him that I was well enough to do so myself.

A small crowd had gathered on the main track and came towards the gate of the house when we emerged. They stepped forward one by one to wish me well. Wazir was among them. He gripped my hand tightly and told me to be careful, and said that if I ever came back I was to bring him a short-wave radio.

By the bends of the river the walk took us three hours. There was one small settlement in between, and a number of isolated homesteads. Whenever we came across anyone at one of these, Aziz would volunteer a terse explanation of who I was and brush aside offers of hospitality.

Although I was still a little under the weather, I enjoyed the morning's outing. The dirt track hugged the river, and on rises offered fine views along the valley corridor. Because of the palm trees, this now appeared much less rugged. Sometimes I asked my guide to stop, and while he fidgeted with the straps on my pack, I hunkered on the side of the track to listen to the breeze whistle on the reeds. I reflected in those moments that this was one of the few occasions in the past two weeks that I had been able to appreciate the beauty of the winding Euphrates – eternal, pulsing over the earth.

Shortly before 10 a.m. Aziz left the track and mounted a steep hill on the left. I scrambled up after him and followed his gaze out onto the river, which now widened considerably as it swerved to the south. Ahead in the flow, like a giant sailing ship anchored off the Jezirah, was the island of Jubbah.

*

The island was approximately 1 kilometre in length, maintaining an even width of about 120 metres until two-thirds of the way down, when the sides began to converge. Much of its surface was covered by palm trees, the concentration of housing being at the wide (north) end. Here there were two flimsy pontoon bridges, the one to the Shamia being the longer.

Crossing by way of the Jezirah bridge, we proceeded along a pot-holed track, passing a school and a handful of vegetable stalls. Although this area was full of life, many of the houses were derelict, abandoned at some time before and left to decay. (Chiefly I learned, this was on account of floods that had submerged the island in 1968 and again a year later. The construction of dams upstream had since ended the annual inundation, but many of the families who had taken refuge with relatives on the mainland never returned.)

In sight of the second pontoon we turned left onto a narrow lane, which twisted into the heart of the island, the dwellings gradually being replaced by tall palm trees. About a third of the way along, rising in storeys above the open-side shore, was the wheelhouse of Jubbah. Dogs charged from a gateway to meet us, undeterred in their affections by Aziz's swiping.

Inside we were greeted by the captain, Sheikh Thabet al-Aziz, whom we found reclined on the floor of his cabin. He struggled up and tapped his thighs to indicate he was unable to stand easily. He was nearly bald and wore a faded grey *jalabiyah*. A walking stick by his side contributed to the impression of his being older than he probably was. '*Ahlan wa sahlan.*' His voice was warm, if not vigorous.

I sat opposite him at the place appointed. Cushions were spread around me like I were a sultan arrived at court.

'*Allah-bel-kher.*'

'*Allah-bel-kher.*'

'*Allah-bel-kher.*'

Like Aziz, Sheikh Thabet didn't speak English, so the three of us fell into silence, looking at each other and a large radio set that droned in the corner. Notwithstanding the lack of conversation, there was no sense of awkwardness in the company.

A young man of about twenty broke the peacefulness. He shouldered open the metal door and set a tray of food on the carpet. He knelt beside it and regarded me as though I had been delivered by flying saucer. His name was Bahar, the seventh of ten sons, next after Aziz in the line of succession. Neither of them joined us in the meal, but if the Sheikh thought something was needed, he said so to Aziz and Bahar took off.

Sheik Thabet's eldest son was a genial fellow called Talid. He was a teacher in a nearby town, to which he made a complicated commute every workday. I met him on his return below in the garden, an untended patch of lawn set on a small terrace which was raised a few metres above the powerfully flowing open side of the river. The main body of the house rose in stages behind this, with various appendages spaced along the bank.

Talid was short in stature. He wore a creased suit, and had just a light film of hair left on his head. A big nose and slanted eyes completed a not very handsome appearance. After an introduction by Aziz, he flopped down beside me on the grass, drawing his arm over his face to shield the afternoon sun. An engaging, if long and sometimes hard to follow story followed. English was one of his subjects, but his pronunciation was not very good, and he had a penchant for long sentences. In summary, it turned out that his wife left him shortly after they were married and took their infant son to Baghdad. He formed a plan to take him back to Jubbah but was pressed into military service and spent eight years in a bunker near Basra typing reports. On his return he found that the part of the house allocated to him had been taken over by a younger brother's family. There was a girl on the Shamia he had loved in his youth; his heart still fluttered when he saw her on the street. She had never married, but his father would not allow him marry again.

By the time he had finished his father had been helped back to his room by Bahar, and another brother, Wasfi, had joined us. He listened, I thought, not with the attention an oriental sibling normally granted the eldest. As Talid's story was reaching its denouement, he fell upon him and delivered several light blows to the midriff. They brawled like kittens until Talid managed to free himself. He turned away on his side, muttering in a low voice.

Wasfi resembled his father in appearance, being tall and wiry with a high forehead. Unlike him he had a free-range beard, which, with his traditional garb, made him look like a religious man. However none of the al-Azizs were that way inclined. Theirs, indeed, was one of the very few Arab homes I stayed in where the call to prayer was pointedly not heeded. Atheism had been bred in them by their father out of political conviction. Even their names – 'river', 'star', 'mountain' – strained to avoid religious association.

His first words to me came as a surprise. 'Saddam Hussein. Hezib. *Mu-zein!*' ('not good'). He made a brushing movement with his hand to emphasize his distaste.

I looked around at the others. Aziz and Bahar were undoing knots in a length of rope, while Talid had nodded off, though shortly afterwards he rose and slipped into the house. (As I was to discover, he did this every time the subject of politics came up; there'd be a derisory laugh from the company and playful jeering as he took himself off to somewhere else.)

Between Talid and Wasfi came Aiham, Saffah and Hassan. They were all married and lived with their young families in buildings around the wheelhouse. For a living Wasfi and Hassan reconditioned fridges in a workshop on the mainland, Aiham managed the farm and Saffah soldered appliances in a small shed overlooking the river. He was the most intense of the brothers. Tall and handsome, he spoke like a philosopher: 'I am waiting for the sun to shine.'

One evening in the middle of the first week Wasfi called me out of Thabet's room. I followed him upstairs; then up a vertical ladder that was affixed to the landing wall, and finally through a hatch in the ceiling. People I had never seen before were sprawled across the attic floor, their gazes fixed on a television. The pictures, Wasfi whispered, were coming from a satellite dish set up on the roof. Saffah lay in the prime position in front of the screen, a mound of cigarette butts smouldering by his side. The remote control, I remarked straight away, was like an extension to his arm, imperceptible zaps moving the uncritical audience from one scene to another. Hard news (Al-Jezirah and ANN) and soft porn were the staples.

The dish had come from Kurdistan. A thriving smuggling trade, which included government oil trucks bound for Turkey, brought all manner of goods from the enclave into the country. Watching was as risky a business as unsanctioned peddling. A prison sentence was almost certain for anyone involved in the chain of law breaking. During the day the dish was kept in the attic, giving poor reception and a limited range of channels; but at night it was restored to the roof, where a simple change in direction captured a whole new universe of images.

I was ushered across the floor to a place next to Saffah. We acknowledged one another and I lay back on a cushion. Several English-language channels were flicked through for my benefit. I had the sense that Saffah had seen all there was to see: ten hours of news is the same as one hour ten times. A breast is a breast is a breast. He had reached the stage where the rhythm had become the thing. At short intervals his thumb pressed, and the world passed by.

One night he turned to me and offered me the remote. I was sitting behind him between Bahar and Wasfi. Hassan and Kareem, a neighbour, were also in the attic. I felt a lump in my throat as I took the device. It was more than just the symbolic acceptance into the family; for me it was also a reminder of an entire former life wasted in front of the TV.

In the course of my time with the al-Aziz's I came to see that the older group of sons was inherently more privileged, and not just in the usual sense that in Arab families the younger members are fated to serve their elders. For the fact was that Aziz (next after Wasfi) would probably never be married, and those below him had even poorer prospects. There was no room for another family, no money to pay out on dowries, no means of supporting another raft of young mouths. Indeed, to circumvent the tradition of payouts to brides, all the sons had married cousins.

I wondered sometimes if, in a cruel second blow of fate, the younger ones weren't victims of the longstanding practice of intermarriage. Somewhere around Aziz there seemed to commence a pattern of character instability. Bahar (family cook when the mother was away), a fair-haired lad with the kindest disposition imaginable, suffered from a degree of hyperactivity: even when sitting, he would rock back and forth and mumble aloud to himself. He hadn't advanced beyond primary school, and the army had rejected him after a firing incident on the training ground. Consequently he had never been much off the island, though even here he was never far from trouble. Wasfi told me that when he was younger he used to eat something by the river which would drive him out of his mind for days and leave the family and doctors perplexed as to the cause. Taking turns to keep an eye on him, they finally discovered it was a wild fungus which Bahar himself had no recollection of eating. (A spray was brought from Haditha and the problem resolved.)

After Bahar came a boy called Halla, whom I hardly ever saw. He was said to be unable to bear the company of strangers, which meant everyone except the immediate family. The second youngest, Furat, was a Down's syndrome child. He was much loved by Sheikh Thabet who, along with Bahar, was the only one who could make sense of his speech. He had a ferocious appetite and could finish a stew or leg of chicken more quickly than anyone I'd ever seen. The youngest son was Taif, aged twelve, who was a model of health and intelligence.

In addition to the ten sons in the family there was one girl, Efaf. At the time of my visit she was away with her mother in Qsariyat.

*

The most impressive residence on Jubbah belonged to Mr Tahreer. His terraced dwelling was situated on the port side of the island, 20 degrees north of the al-Aziz's. Bounded by a dry stone wall running alongside the circuit track, the building dropped in levels to the shore, and was clearly the work of an able designer. Tahreer's wife was said to be of a wealthy family in the regional capital Ramadi, and his own family had a sizeable holding of farmland on the Shamia. The couple had seven daughters and three sons, one of whom had been killed in the war with Iran. Tahreer himself had been a military man, an officer in the air force, and it was during his service years that he acquired his now some-what dated English. The training staff in the flying schools at the time were British, and Tahreer still spoke fondly of his instructors, 'Major Farrell, and Mr Rutherford from Kent.'

The cultural contact had left an indelible impression on him. Though his *jalabiyah* and *shamag* marked him as a proud Arab, there was something of the country squire about his appearance as well. He cultivated a twisting moustache, and on social visits wore a cravat and carried a light wooden cane. It had always been a dream of his to visit England, but a series of events in the 1970s put paid to his notions of embarking on a Grand Tour. Like many of his generation, and as was the norm in the military, Tahreer had been involved in politics. He was a member of a group within the Ba'ath Party which supported a proposed union with Syria following the treachery of Sadat in 1977. Saddam had always been sceptical of this venture (a source of his great personal animosity towards Hafez Assad), and on coming to power in July 1979, he immediately set about a purge of the ranks. Hundreds of senior party officials and army officers were executed, and many more, like Tahreer, imprisoned. He was released after six months and told to go back to Jubbah and never to set foot off the island again.

As part of the same amnesty, and under the same conditions, Sheikh Thabet had also been freed. He was not a Ba'athist, but a member of the Iraqi Communist Party (ICP). As the ICP's fortunes had waxed and waned over the years, so Thabet had found himself in and out of detention. The early 1970s had been the era of hope for the party. In 1973 they entered government as part of a Ba'ath-led Progressive Front. The Soviets lauded their involvement. Thabet travelled to the Eastern bloc and upon his return rose quickly through the ranks, becoming the Anbar party secretary in 1975. Heavy criticism of Ba'ath policies, however, led to a deterioration in the relationship between them and the ICP, resulting finally in the shutting down of the latter's offices in May 1979. At this time an estimated 7,000 communists were eliminated by the regime. Thabet, being part of a powerful Anbar tribe, was spared this fate.

In spite of their being neighbours, and having once been inspired by similar ideologies, the relationship between the two men was not particularly warm. During my stay, the one time Tahreer called at Thabet's, there were cordial exchanges but enough in the body language to suggest that social visits were not frequent.

The purpose of his visit on that occasion was to invite me to dinner. 'Splendid,' he declared, when an arrangement was fixed for the next evening.

Bahar, who had got into the habit of escorting me everywhere, took me to the house at the appointed hour, but was not himself asked in when a daughter of Tahreer's answered the door.

'Welcome Mr Shane,' she smiled.

A girl in her late teens, I thought her very attractive. She was without a veil and wore a bright red robe, tightened enough around the waist to define her figure. She had long black hair, sparkling teeth, and a soft, oily complexion. After some moments her father came into the hallway to greet me and she vanished through another door.

The guest room was not what I had expected. A large chandelier hung from the ceiling and the walls were decorated with gold-framed prints of bucolic landscapes. Saddam cross-legged in the desert stared out from amidst these scenes.

Just inside the door there was an elaborate brick fireplace. I had heard this spoken of before. Tahreer had apparently built it himself after a design he had found in an old home improvements magazine. The al-Aziz's were convinced it didn't work, believing that the hearth was too small and the chimney too short. Wasfi had challenged me to get Tahreer to light it, but I wouldn't be drawn into any intrigue. None the less, out of curiosity, I asked him when we were seated if he used it.

'Oh yes, of course. It's very cosy in winter.'

He rose from his armchair and showed me the various paraphernalia that he had purchased for it in Baghdad. A copper bin kept wood, and there was a fancy fireguard, and a shovel and poker.

His daughter glided in to ask what we would like to drink. I asked for water and kept focused on the fireplace in an effort not to be caught staring again. While we waited for her to return, and as I was admiring the rest of the room, I noticed a face pressed against the window opposite. It was becoming dark outside but there was no mistaking Bahar. Seeing my surprise, Tahreer swung round. Muttering to himself, he plucked the heavy poker from the grate and made for the door. An empty bucket clattered across the yard and Bahar was gone.

I gathered that he was not in Tahreer's good books. There was some tension between the leading families on account of a donkey, the only one on the island, which Bahar had the charge of. The animal wasn't the property of anyone, but it was Bahar who used him for his daily chores. Tahreer was threatening to shoot the animal if he ever caught it in one of his plots again.

After drinks we took our places for dinner at a long table overlooking the river. The host sat me at one end and took his own place at the other. The meal did not disappoint. We had herbal soup to start and chicken and rice for the main course. I sent my compliments to his daughters. There were three of them still at home, Tahreer having as yet been unable to find suitable partners.

A chief topic of conversation that evening was the location of Xenophon's Charmande, a city on the right bank of the river to which the soldiers had swum across for provisions. Tahreer, who maintained a gentlemanly interest in the subject of ancient history, had never heard of this place, and was bothered that it could have existed under his nose for sixty years without his knowledge. I sent off for Ainsworth's commentary and when it was delivered less than ten minutes later I read the relevant passage to him:

> CHARMANDE. On this long march through the desert, the troops are described as passing over on rafts of skin to an opulent and extensive city called Charmande. As no distances were given, I was inclined to identify this site with the most important position on the right bank of the Euphrates that occurs within the interval between Korsote and the 'Gates'. This is the city of Iz or Izanescopolis, whose bitumen fountains were visited by Alexander, Trajan, Severus, and Julian; but Colonel Chesney is more inclined to seek for the site at some ruins which occur on the right bank opposite to the island of Jibbah, or Jubbah.

Tahreer rose from his armchair and paced across to the fireplace, his mind roving the well-known landscape facing the island on the Shamia. Upstream on the Jezirah side there were mounds that had been linked to Assyrian civilization, but he was not aware of there ever having been anything discovered near Jubbah.

'This fellow Ainsworth, when do you say he visited?'

I told him he had passed over 150 years ago, and the colonel before that again.

'Well then, we'll have to look into it.'

Historically, Jubbah has always functioned as a refuge. Since the area was settled her inhabitants farmed on the mainland, and on the approach of raiders from the desert ferried their livestock across to the island. Rauwolf, passing on his boat in 1574, noted a wall stretching right around it, which is thought to have dated from the Abbasid era. Long before this, the Assyrians had fortifications in the valley.

With the demise of the threat from desert nomads in the twentieth century, and to avoid the no less destructive force of the annual floods, many natives left the island and built homes on the Shamia. Benefiting from a marginally better infrastructure, and boosted by the establishment of an army base nearby, the colony has grown larger and more prosperous than the mother settlement.

The twenty-odd families who remain on the island today are in the main poor, subsisting on small vegetable and rice plots, and the income that comes from the palm trees growing around them. With the exception of Tahreer's, most of the homes are extremely basic. Made from mud bricks manufactured on site, they typically consist of a single earthen floor space partitioned by sheets hung from the ceiling. A hole made in the roof allows through a metal chimney for an oil burner.

A boon to the residents in the sanctions era were the monthly food packages they received from the Government (by way of a UN-administered 'food for oil' programme). Based on the number of persons in a household, these consisted of a variety of imported foodstuffs, such as rice, sugar, powdered milk, vegetable oil, flour and tea. The difference this made to those on the lowest incomes was significant, and led me to the view – later somewhat modified – that the majority were better off under sanctions than they would otherwise have been. Certainly, the popular view at the time that the embargo hit the people and not the regime was a misguided one. Under the British, and then under the monarchy they installed, and finally under the Ba'athists, little of the country's natural wealth had ever come down to ordinary citizens. The socialists had made material improvements in their early years – dams, roads, universities, hospitals – but the megalomania of Saddam Hussein directed all resources to projects of his design: castles, fancy fighter jets and superguns.

The food packages, it is worth underlining, were paid for by the Iraqis: it was their oil that paid for them – and they paid well for them. The appointed 'purchasing agents' had to cover their costs, as did the UN, which took a percentage of the gross revenue. And in spite of that esteemed organization's efforts, numerous consignments received in their warehouses were spoiled, or out of date; some of the produce never even got that far, ending up in the markets of Baghdad, Mosul, and Basra.

*

The stomach upset I had picked up in Qsariyat persisted on Jubbah. This was in spite of a highly agreeable regimen. I was set up in Sheikh Thabet's quarters, on the side opposite to where he slept. The room was situated in the north-west corner of the house, a level and a half up from the garden. Windows on two sides made the Spartan space bright in daylight, and cool at night, when a breeze off the river would rustle the net curtains. The only furniture was a bookcase set against the back wall. The shelves of this sagged with volumes of discredited political literature and voluminous yearbooks which listed national production figures. In a corner of the bottom shelf there was a series of journals which Thabet had maintained over the years. Once or twice a day he would pull out one of these and pen his reflections of the moment.

After an early morning breakfast, we would usually recline and tune in to the radio. A bulky Japanese system from the 1970s, its short-wave bands put the world at our fingertips: Radio Rossiya, All-India Radio, Austria Radio International, London World Service. The radio had been purchased by the family some years before so that Thabet could listen to the nightly communist broadcast from Kurdistan. Every evening at 8.30 he tuned in to the rebel station and listened attentively to the news. On its conclusion, he would invariably turn to whoever was in the room and nod his head, a resigned expression always on his face.

Besides the radio, our other permanent company was a one-eyed cat, Bassoon, which kept its distance on one or other of the windowsills. He normally sneered at my attempts to lure him inside, but at meal times, when Bahar ducked out for something in the kitchen, he would boldly leap into the middle of the room and screech until one of us tossed him a scrap.

In the afternoons I'd usually take the air with Bahar and Kareem, and whoever else was about. Kareem was a neighbour, an athletic young man whose physique and prodigious work rate had earned him the reputation as the island strongman. This had recently been enhanced by his unexpected return to Jubbah only weeks after being conscripted into the army. Apparently he had attacked an officer at a base in Mosul, escaped and somehow, with no money or papers, made his way back to the island.

On Jubbah he was virtually untouchable. Nobody could approach without being seen or heard by the dogs, and there were always boats on hand to slip an outlaw onto the Jezirah.

His mutiny, however, meant that he could no longer take casual work across on the Shamia, where there was an army base. His family's financial situation was aggravated by the absence of his father, who was also a criminal. Along with ten other locals he had been arrested six months before by the security service on suspicion of conspiracy. It seemed the men had developed an interest in the Dervish (an Islamic mystic order) way of life, and formed themselves a lodge. I gathered from Tahreer that this was prompted more by curiosity than serious asceticism, let alone subversion, but that the act of secret assembly had doomed them.

Our strolls would usually lead up to the 'forward deck'. This began at the end of the middle third of the island, where the edges commenced the steady formation of the 'bow'. The land from here dropped in steps, and narrowed, until just a long finger extended into the water. In a wind it would be washed by the river, but most days you could walk right out along the mud plank to the very tip of the island.

Beyond the last of the vegetable plots, an oval-shaped patch of sand sloping towards the right bank had been developed as a football pitch. Depending on numbers, a game might be started here. It wasn't played in the way I was familiar with, being more of a cross between soccer and American football. A player in possession would root the ball up field and opponents would try to cross his path as he chased for goal. A hectic pace and steady dropout rate resulted in relatively short games. I would always be one of the first to clutch an ankle, my status as guest ensuring that I was not then pressed into the more dangerous position of goalkeeper.

Another leisurely pursuit was attempting to scale the 'mast' of Jubbah – the mosque's minaret. This rose to an impressive height above the palm trees in the centre of the island. Our efforts however were repeatedly thwarted by the vigilance of a mullah who would not countenance the presence of an infidel on the sacred precinct.

One day we fooled him. He was blind but had the hearing of a whale, which was what normally caught us out ever before we came near the crumbling mosque. This time I was vowed to silence, and as a distraction, Bahar went ahead on the donkey. Hearing the alien steps on the stone threshold, the mullah erupted, and the four of us in the group – Kareem, Aziz, Taif, and I – stole right under his open mouth and up the pitch-black stairwell of the minaret.

The aged structure leaned Pisa-like to the starboard side and, worryingly, you could feel it vibrating during pauses for breath on the steps. Halfway up I suggested that we stop where we were and continue one at a time, but my companions had more faith in the resilience of the tower. Minutes later the four of us blinked onto the covered balcony. The views from here were commanding, the sleekness of the island's form much more apparent than from the ground.

By this time Bahar had made his exit. Shuffling round to the north side, we saw him tugging the donkey through a rice field. Led by excited children, the mullah was coming alongside them on the other side of the wall that bounded the field. We shouted warnings to the outlaws, who must have heard, because they jerked to the right and ploughed through a ruined house to make good their escape.

Our meeting place, where we gathered at the end of the day, was one of the island's old waterwheels. In the days before combustion these had lifted water onto the fields: an aqueduct received it from the paddles and carried it to irrigation channels. This one was on the open side of the river, just below the football pitch, and was the biggest of them. Though the giant wheel had long since been carted off for firewood, the stone superstructure to which it had been affixed remained intact. To get out to the platform you had to walk along the high channel, a nerve-testing passage, but with the reward of another impressive view of the island's form.

Water power, I learned, had also been the basis of a local flour-milling industry. Impressive feats of contemporary engineering, the waterwheels driving the grindstones had been constructed on tiny outcrops in the river that occur upstream of the island. The hulk of one of these is still to be seen, though the causeway which linked it to the Jezirah has long been swept away. Fareed, a cousin of Thabet's, thought these had been built in the twilight years of the Ottoman era, to be quickly superseded by the revolution in motor technology. Fareed was the most knowledgeable of all the Jubbans except Tahreer about the island's history. Formerly employed in government in Baghdad, he had recently returned to open a small shop on the Shamia. He called to see me during my first week on Jubbah.

A big man – over 6 feet tall and heavily built – he had studied Semitic languages at university, and had a strong interest in Arab history. Tahreer had already sought him out on the question of Charmande, and found support for his belief that no evidence of the 'large and pros-perous city' spoken of by Xenophon had ever been discovered on this part of the Shamia. Fareed had consulted various texts, among them

Rauwolf's account, and a book by a native scholar, Dr Jaber Khalil, *Pre-Islamic Monuments of the Jezirah*. He left this with me, recommending I look up the section on Heit, a sizeable town two days' walk downstream. This was the Iz mentioned by Ainsworth in his reference to Charmande. Through the ages different writers have given it different names, but the unique occurrence of bitumen springs here means that there is no doubt about the place being referred to. Xenophon does not note such a feature, though according to Khalil, a German philologist has speculated that the name of his city derived from an Aramaic word, *kir*, meaning 'pitch', and a Persian adjectival ending, *-mand*.

It was unfortunate that Xenophon hadn't mentioned the springs; perhaps he didn't come across them, or thought them of insufficient importance to warrant mention in his account. Had he done so the entire march framework would have been put on a firmer footing. I reflected that even in the few places the author mentions that can today be identified – Sardis, Kelainai, the Fountain of Midas, Ikonion, Tarsus – either he tells us very little about them, or there is very little left of what he describes.

20

Heit

Desert Fox

One morning early in the second week, as I was hurrying to the outhouse, I spotted Bahar and his donkey on the riverbank. On my return through the garden, I called out to him: 'How's it going?' 'Good, good!'

The pair of them splashed along the water's edge and came to meet me below the retaining wall of the garden. Bahar had a bucket in his hand and he mimed for me what they were doing. Peering over I could see the water swishing about in the barrels mounted on the donkey's back. I went back inside, wondering whether I had unwittingly discovered the reason for my stubborn stomach ailment.

Wasfi said that everybody was given iodine tablets to purify the water, but the supply was erratic and people had fallen out of the habit. In any case the chemical gave the water a bad taste. From then on I began to use my filter, and in the following days thought there was an improvement in my condition. The islanders were sceptical, regarding the high-tech mechanism with mild amusement. They gathered to watch whenever I produced it, nudging each other as I worked up a sweat pumping from one bucket to the other. Even though at these times I felt a bit foolish, I kept faith with the equipment.

Thabet and I were listening to the radio one afternoon when the telephone rang. I hadn't known that there was one in the house, and Thabet seemed just as surprised to hear the shrill noise coming from the corridor. After a few moments he nodded his head, in the way he did when the nightly Kurdistan message finished, and we reclined back on the floor.

Furat presently came rushing into the room in a state of excitement. His speech was rocket-paced, and he whirled about the floor like a drunken dervish. Thabet started to laugh, and this had the surprising effect of calming the boy down. Through the open door I caught a rare glimpse of the other unfortunate brother, Halla, who was staring in the direction from where the ringing was coming. Eventually it stopped.

We didn't have to wait long to find out who had been calling. Talid came in directly on his return from work. He sat cross-legged on the floor instead of stretching out as usual. A party official in al-Baghdadi, the town where he worked, had called to see him at the school; they had been enquiring after me in Haditha, and were anxious to know all was well.

Bahar brought in tea and Kareem and Taif and other members of our gang tiptoed into the room to learn what the news was. I took the opportunity to say that I was feeling a lot better and would probably be on my way in the next day or two. Talid translated and Thabet shook his stick at him to emphasize his sentiments. 'He says you are to stay as long on Jubbah for ever. You are guest.'

I thanked my host, and said he had made me feel this was my home, but I still had a way to go on my journey.

*

On the morning I left, everyone in the house walked with me to the Jezirah pontoon. Along the way people came out of their homes to wish me well. Tahreer and his younger daughter joined us, and Fareed came over from the mainland. He wrote down the address of a house his family owned in Baghdad, inviting me to stay if I visited the capital. At the bridge we said our goodbyes.

Kareem, Bahar and Taif had decided in secret that they were going to accompany me to Babylon. The plan was revealed after Aziz and a few others had left us at Abu-Tabak, a high, windswept stone hill overlooking the great loop of the Euphrates. Kareem was upset when I dismissed the proposal, and pulled shoes from his pockets to show the seriousness of the intent. Bahar untied a blanket he had been carrying on his back like a sack, revealing bread and biscuits, and potatoes he had boiled that same morning.

My fears for their plan were borne out near the first village we came to after the crossing of the peninsula. A farmer confronted us in his field and started to fire questions. Taif, who in spite of his age was by far the most sensible of the young Jubbans, explained who we were, but the man persisted and Kareem shaped at him. He hastened off towards his farmhouse and the four of us ran into the desert. Thirst brought us back to the river an hour later. The three of them dropped onto the bank and drank like cattle from the river.

Combined with swelling feet, the experiences of the day were enough to convince the group that the plan had little chance of success. Moreover, the attention we had attracted made it clear that Kareem was in danger of ending up with his father in prison. He had no identification, and if we were detained, it would only be a matter of time before his status as an army deserter was discovered.

We parted on the trackside. I sent them back the way we had come, drawing an arc in the soil to impress on Taif the need to give the settlement corridor a wide berth. It was difficult to see them go, especially Bahar, whose simplicity and good nature had endeared him to me from the start. I had hardly gone 50 metres when I heard his voice behind. He came hurrying up with the sack, and became upset when I insisted it was too big to carry. Taif took him away by the hand and I waved until they were out of sight.

Still not feeling a hundred per cent, I had to stop regularly to get my breath. Even in late October, the sun was a menace. I was hoping that my passage through the next village, Meshrubiye, would not be an arduous one, but it was. On the outskirts a car came out to detain me. They didn't believe I was alone and a gun party later went out from the village to search the hills for intruders. A subsequent theory was that I was a downed American pilot, but by evening no such success had been announced by the state media. Feeling decidedly off colour, I wasn't helpful in any of these inquiries.

I took them by surprise in the morning. Before it was light, I slipped from the room where I had been billeted for the night. My host, a Ba'athist who had been designated to look after me, snored, oblivious as I eased the door closed – and my good fortune held even to the dogs. I hadn't planned my departure like this, but during the night I had woken feeling as right as rain, and had an urge to walk.

By first light I had put 8 kilometres between myself and Meshrubiye, and was out of reach of all but the most adventurous of shepherds.

By midday I reckoned I had covered around 35 kilometres and was somewhere west of Heit. I was in two minds about whether or not to visit the town. It was possible that it was the location of Charmande, and even if it weren't, it would be fascinating to see the famous bitumen springs. On the other hand I had a momentum, and enough supplies to last me several days. Tracing a course on my map, it struck me that in as little as five or six days I could be in Babylon. For the first time in the journey through Iraq, I felt I had some control over my destiny; and for the first time in the entire journey, my destination was in sight. For months it had been a place in my mind, an abstract point on an ancient map of Mesopotamia: now it was only a week's walk away.

*

After a nap in the shadow of a boulder, I decided to visit the town. Approaching the boundary of habitation, I paused to track the cloudless progress of a soundless vehicle. This was the first paved road I had met on the Jezirah. The houses, too, looked more like civilization: concrete structures with fenced yards and driveways.

Five minutes along the asphalt I heard a car coming behind. It passed slowly, stopped, and reversed. Before he had a chance to speak I asked the driver how far it was to the town. '*Heit, chem kilometr?*'

He refused to answer and demanded my papers. I pressed my question and finally he lied and sped off. I wasn't surprised to see him again a short time later.

A band of locals had in the meantime detained me. After I had recovered my papers and was preparing to continue, one of them made a discovery. Shouting to his friends, he carefully pulled from inside my sleeping mat the drawings I had been given at the school in Drema a few weeks before. I could see, as they were being unfurled on the ground, that something dramatic was expected, but all they found was evidence of their own misery. I refused to take them back and waved dismissively at the group. The one who had made the find became upset and hurried after me. It was then that the car reappeared. A middle-aged man in traditional dress got out of the passenger seat. He greeted me in Arabic, and then in Russian.

'How are things, comrade?'

'All right, moving along.'

After this short exchange he spoke to the citizens. Then the one with the drawings rolled them up, slotted them into the mat and departed, while the car likewise turned around and left us.

The man's name was Mohammed Latiff. He said he was a local party representative, and that he wished to walk into the town with me. I said that it was too far, but he brushed aside my consideration and said it was his duty to provide help.

I expected him to quiz me on my recent whereabouts, but instead he rambled on about the time he had spent working in Moscow with a state trade association. When we got to his home he showed me photographs, fading Polaroid snaps of him in grinning poses about Red Square, his *shamag* swapped for a *shapka*. The house was situated just beyond a T-junction, the perpendicular arm of which ran to a bridge leading into the heart of the town. After tea a car came and took me across the river. Mohammed said there were some formalities to complete and that he'd expect me for dinner in the evening.

Heit was the biggest Iraqi town so far on my journey, and reminded me of the provincial Syrian centres I had passed through further up the river. Like these, it was dirty, noisy and stocked with buildings of inferior quality. A familiar mix of sharp smells laced the air.

Belying its shabby modernity, the town has a lineage extending back 5,000 years. It owes this extraordinary longevity to the presence of the bitumen springs, still bubbling in waste ground near to the centre.

Bitumen, as I had learned from Dr Khalil's book, is a 'black viscous mixture of hydrocarbons which occur naturally or can be obtained from the distillation of oil'. The tar is impermeable to water, and it is this quality which made it highly valued by ancient engineers. The earliest of them, from Sumer, Akkad and Babylonia, travelled here to harvest the substance. Gangs creamed it off and floated it in booms downstream to the great cities of lower Mesopotamia. There, the labourers gathered the tar by hand, using a swift rotating motion to prevent it sticking, and coated it like paint on ziggurats, palaces, and ships.

On reflection I considered that the existence of the springs probably ruled Heit out as the location for Charmande. Although it would not be remarkable for Xenophon to omit mentioning them, noteworthy natural features did catch his eye, and the activity at the springs would likely have brought them to his attention had he visited the city. He knew what bitumen was, and what it was used for. When the Greeks later come to the Wall of Media, he wrote that the huge structure 'was built of baked bricks, laid in asphalt'.

On the other hand, and assuming he was keeping a diary, Xenophon's focus on his task may have begun to slip. The strains of the march through the desert were beginning to tell on the army. At Charmande a quarrel among the soldiers over provisions resulted in Klearkhos ordering a beating for one of Menon's men. The man's comrades were angry when they learned of his mistreatment, and one of them, spotting Klearkhos riding near their camp later that day, threw an axe at him. He missed, but a hail of missiles from others followed, and the Spartan had to flee to his own camp. There he gave the call to arms. His cavalry mounted and arrayed about him, and the heavy infantry gathered their equipment and fell in behind. Menon's men dispersed and ran for their own weapons.

These two had been the first contingents to arrive opposite Charmande; Cyrus had taken up the rear that day, and in front of him were the other leaders, with Klearkhos in the vanguard. It happened that as the two armies were squaring up to one other, Proxenos arrived with his own men. Informed of what had happened, he immediately ordered his *hoplites* between the two camps, and appealed to Klearkhos to back down. But the Spartan was furious that, after having just escaped with his life at the hands of subordinates, a fellow commander should expect him to give way. He waved him off the field and prepared to attack Menon.

In the meantime one of the Persians had galloped off to tell Cyrus of the disturbance. He was now close at hand, and hastened to the camp with his mounted bodyguard. Bearing his javelin aloft, he rode into the middle of the Greeks and addressed them.

> Klearkhos and Proxenos, and all you other Greeks here, you do not know what you are doing. If you start fighting amongst yourselves, you can be sure that I will be finished off on the spot, and you not long afterwards, for if things between us go wrong, the native troops will prove more dangerous enemies to us than those on the King's side are.

The sight of Cyrus calmed Klearkhos somewhat, and his words were sensible. Eyes fixed on Menon, he stood his men down, and both sides withdrew and piled their arms outside their camps.

Our car honked its way through a busy market area before emerging onto an open stretch which was lined with motor-repair outlets. We turned left at a set of traffic lights, decelerating soon after in sight of a grey office block. In an alleyway at the side there was a guarded entrance, and the barrier rose as we approached. I was taken into a room where a man was speaking on the telephone. I set my pack against the wall and waited. The office was small and windowless; at one end there was a bed, at the other a metal desk. A portrait of Saddam in combats, wearing shades and a beret, hung behind it. The man at the desk was about forty, overweight, and had a bushy black moustache. A cigarette burned in the side of his mouth as he chatted.

Bringing his conversation to an end, he pointed to a chair and introduced himself gruffly as an officer of the Amn, the internal security branch. 'My name Abbas.'

As requested, I arranged my documentation on his desk, and recalled as best I could the places I had been to in the previous three weeks.

While I spoke he pawed at the papers, interrupting me to ask what I wanted in Heit. I said I was hoping to photograph the bitumen springs.

'Bitoomen? What is bitoomen?' His face scrunched as he pronounced the word.

He disregarded my explanation and went back to the papers.

'You have been Qsariyat. It's true? Why no tell me when I ask?'

I protested that I hadn't reached that point yet in my account.

'Don't speak to me so. I am two-star general!' His cheeks puffed and he glared at me. After a minute's staring he eased himself back into the swivel chair.

'There in Qsariyat, teacher Maiad, he is my friend. I call him and you talk?' I shrugged my shoulders indifferently, but was taken aback to learn this news.

He punched a number into the telephone and held the receiver up so that I could hear the ringing tone. There was no answer. 'We try later.'

Following a barked order a guard brought in a tray of food. The dish smelled appetizing and Abbas consumed it with some relish. When he had finished, dabbing his whiskers with a handkerchief, he lit a cigarette and regarded me with a look of benign curiosity.

'You have wife?'

'No.'

'I like the women of your country. Always they are having sex. I have two wife. You like see picture?' He stubbed his cigarette and tugged a wallet from his back pocket.

I sat up in the chair and asked him if we'd be much longer. I wanted to see the fountains and was expected back at Latiff's for dinner.

His thick black eyebrows furrowed. 'Why so angry?'

'I'm not angry. I want to go.'

'Go where? To vitoomin? No, no friend. You go Baghdad.' He scooped up my documents and paced out of the room.

The guard who had earlier brought the meal came in shortly after and took away my pack. I wondered what was going to happen, and tried to figure a line of enquiry from the questions Abbas had been asking. There seemed to be none, and I had a strong feeling that not a single thing he had said in the whole of our interview was true. I rued ever having come into the town. I should have just kept going until I had had to leave the desert.

The guard returned around 10 p.m. My bags sat outside, little effort having been made to disguise Abbas's interference. The guard handed me my papers and I followed him into the night.

Latiff's house was in darkness. The driver blew his horn and some minutes later Mohammed appeared at the door. He walked slowly towards the car, shielding his face from the headlights with his hand. I apologized for the hour. He forced a smile and led me inside.

In the morning we ate melon and olives in his backyard. No mention was made of the previous evening's events, and I had the sense that he just wanted to be rid of me. In the circumstances I thought it best to forget about the bitumen springs and be on my way.

At the first opportunity I left the road. The track I chose rose steadily towards a small village set on a flat-topped mound. The inhabitants watched as I passed but did not approach. The track, becoming fainter all the time, wound on through a series of hills, finally disappearing on an empty plateau. For stretches this appeared to be smooth, but actually it was heavily scarred by deep channels that had been gouged into the surface by the elements. Perhaps it was the tension of the day before, but for the first time on entering the wilderness, I had a bad feeling.

*

Early on I stopped in a trench to eat. The breakfast at Latiff's had been light and I had eaten little the previous day. After some fruit, I cut a chunk of the cake Wasfi's wife had made for me on Jubbah. As I was wrapping it up, my thoughts back on the island, I heard the drone of an engine. I lifted my head over the lip and saw a white truck passing less than 100 metres away. Following it a short way behind were three motorcycles. I guessed that there must have been a quarry of some sort in the desert, and decided to set my course deeper into the interior.

In so far as I could, I kept to the winding runnels that defined the landscape. These were like tunnels in that nobody surveying from the surface had any chance of spotting a prey. At times, such as when the direction was unsatisfactory for a lengthy period or I reached the mouth of one, I had to ascend onto the roof. I was crossing one such stretch in mid-morning, keeping to the base of a clay embankment on my left, when the white truck suddenly passed by its far end. It was travelling back towards the river at an oblique angle, which was probably the reason why none of its occupants noticed me. Expecting the motorcycles, I lay flat on the ground and remained still until I judged that there was nothing else coming. At that moment I didn't believe they were looking for me; I only knew that if I was seen out here, they'd almost certainly take me back to Heit.

My opinion about their purpose changed an hour later. I had crossed a wide ravine and was hiking into the hillscape beyond when I spotted the truck and the motorcycles moving along the dusty floor below. They were far enough away so that there was no sound, and little chance of them seeing me among the rocks. I wouldn't have seen them at all, except that in the preceding weeks I had formed the habit of regularly looking over my shoulder. I decided to stop where I was and wait until nightfall before continuing.

The night wasn't as dark as it could have been. The sky was clear and there was a sliver of moon. Constellations imposed themselves amongst bands of sparkling galaxies. I moved carefully over the plateau, my walking stick leading like a blind man's cane.

At midnight I stopped. I had thought of continuing until daylight, but figured that, with no success that day, my pursuers (if such they were) would have given up their search. I slept lightly on a levelling near the top of a hill, concerned that something hungry would scent my food and come to investigate.

Nothing came that night, but I did have an encounter with a predator the next morning. I had given up plying the gullies and was pacing over the rooftop when I spotted in the distance what appeared to be a fox. It was sitting with its back to me, taking the sun. I stopped and watched; it suddenly turned its head, saw me and bolted. A light trail of dust marked the gentle arc of its path. It stopped again and looked behind, and then disappeared. It was the first time I had seen a wild animal in the desert.

Emerging from the same shallow depression, I came upon a large mound that had a trench sunk through its middle. Beyond, the earth changed into something like a mud flat. Standing in the shadow of the hillock, I thought for a minute about taking the chance of a rest, but decided to move on.

After about ½ kilometre a white truck came into view. It was away to my left, heading towards the river. I figured it could only be a matter of minutes before they saw me, but I stood still and hoped they wouldn't.

It turned in my direction, halting about 30 metres from where I was standing. Two men got out from the passenger side. The first was tiny, like a garden gnome in his robe and bunched-up *shamag*. He edged toward me making soothing sounds. The second man, at a prompting, raised a gun from his side and stepped awkwardly to the right. His left hand was missing and the breach balanced on its stub. He dipped the barrel and several rounds ripped into the sands away to my right. The gnome started to shout and the one with the gun advanced, jabbing it at me as he went. I feared an accident. The atmosphere was incredibly volatile. I concentrated on the gunman, raising my hands and speaking as calmly as I could in Arabic.

'I have come from Heit, from the Hezib. I have papers.'

As I focused on him, the small man ducked in and tried to pull off my pack. I kept fixed on the gunman. At least he now stopped jabbing the weapon, and when the driver arrived with a rope, he seemed to be happier.

The gnome dragged away the bag while the driver tied my hands behind my back. Somebody hit me in the lower back, and I dropped onto my knees. As I made to get up the gnome pushed me onto the ground. His eyes then fell on the walking stick and widened. He grabbed it and leapt about pointing to the small plastic rim above the tip. 'Antenna! Antenna!'

The other two went for the pack and rifled through its contents. Papers hastily stuffed into the bag in Heit were glanced at and flung in the air. The bulkier items came out – jacket, tent, sleeping bag. There was a hush when the cake emerged: they opened the packaging and stared for a moment before discarding it. They were being disappointed. I told them to take me to the party office in Heit. At one point they seemed to decide on this, but then vacillated and began to argue among themselves. I sat up, and at every lull, repeated my request to be taken to the party. Finally they got me up and shoved me into the cab. The one with the gun squeezed in behind the front seat and poked me periodically to let me know he was there.

The gnome also asserted his presence. Once or twice as we bobbed along he turned and punched me in the head. 'You're a British agent – are you a British agent?' Everything from my haircut down to my boots convinced him they had bagged a military saboteur. The Order of Saddam beckoned. I ignored his goading and kept looking straight ahead through the window, consoling myself with the knowledge that he was in for a major disappointment.

After twenty minutes we came in sight of a small village. It sat at the foot of the plateau we were on, and wasn't far from the road. I could see cars passing along this and felt a surge of relief.

We descended in low gear and bumped slowly into the village. The truck stopped outside one of the houses, and after the driver had spoken with the owner, I was taken inside. When they pushed me out again an unfriendly crowd had gathered. They followed us to the road, where a car was turning around. I recognized Mohammed Latiff as one of the passengers. He was the first one to get out, and he raised his hands in the air when he saw me. I think he was genuinely upset at what had happened. He shouted at the gnome to let go of me, and asked why I hadn't shown them my papers. I said they'd seen them, but it transpired that they couldn't read. Mohammed muttered aloud as he tried to untie my hands. The small man, now looking less triumphant, was bumped close to me by the crowd. I sneered at him and he flared up. Mohammed stepped between us and I was bundled into the back seat. The engine roared and the car sped off towards Heit.

I cleaned myself up at Mohammed's house. There were a few bruises on my face, and my wrists were chaffed from the rope, but he agreed that it could have been worse.

'They are simple people. They thought you were an enemy.'

He left me in the lounge with his son while he travelled into town to report the incident.

I felt for a while as though I was floating in the air, and then became extremely despondent. The thought kept recurring that it was only by chance that I had avoided being shot.

From an early stage in the journey, probably because I was alone on the road, I had begun to set great store by the power of my lucky charms: my tiger's eye, my African stone, my mother's miraculous medal. I also said a prayer at the start of most mornings to Artemis, the goddess of the hunt, asking her to keep at bay evil spirits. Whether or not this or the charms had any effect, there was no doubt in my mind that I had enjoyed a degree of luck in the months since I left Sardis. I felt as if this had now deserted me.

Later I went out to the backyard to check my gear. The pack was propped against a fruit tree. With most of its contents back in the village, it looked like an inflatable object that had had the air let out of it.

My walking stick lay on the ground beside the bag. Luckily they hadn't tried to take it apart, though the rim, the 'antenna', had been ripped off. I went to the sink and wiped the shaft clean with a cloth. As I was doing so, the incident replayed itself once more in my mind, but this time beginning before the truck appeared. I was standing in a depression looking at a fox. It ran, paused, ran again, and finally disappeared. I realized then that this may have been a sign, telling me that I too had to be like the fox. And beyond, on the edge of the mud flat, there was the oddly shaped mound which had struck me as being an ideal refuge. I sat down on the ground, tears coming into my eyes. It seemed I mightn't have been forgotten after all.

Mohammed returned in the afternoon with my missing gear, and an offer from the Party to escort me to Ramadi. A car would come in the morning and follow me as far as the city. I guessed that they were keen to avoid the embarrassment of something happening to me on their patch, but I wasn't complaining as I had decided anyway that my days in the desert were over. Now it was a question of getting through the remaining days to Babylon with as little hassle as possible.

21

The Gates

A23-24: Through Babylonia

'I see the man!'
Cyrus, *Anabasis* I.8

Not far from Charmande Cyrus came across the first signs of his brother. Scouts discovered hoof marks and horse droppings, and concluded that a force of around 2,000 cavalry was near. As became apparent, the mission of the King's men was to destroy livestock, villages, and anything else that could be of use to the invading army.

On the thirteenth day after leaving the abandoned city of Korsote, Cyrus arrived at a place called the Gates. Here the rolling deserts ended, and the fertile plains of Babylonia commenced.

Passing onto the fields he marched cautiously for three days, keeping the river on his right (A23). Sightings of the King's cavalry were now becoming increasingly frequent, and Cyrus believed that his brother was at hand. At midnight on the third day he held a review of all his troops. By the light of flaming torches, the soldiers, Greeks and Asians, fell into their units and presented arms. 10,400 *hoplites* were counted, and 2,300 *peltasts*; the native infantry numbered around 15,000, and they had in addition 2,000 horsemen, and 20 scythed chariots. How many waited to oppose them was unknown; it remained to be seen how successful the King had been in gathering the far-flung forces of his kingdom.

At dawn the army went forward in battle formation. Cyrus led in the centre, with his native troops on the left and the Greek mercenaries arranged on the right. Around midday they came to a freshly dug ditch, roughly 10 metres across and 6 deep. This, they believed, had been the work of the King, who they thought must have had insufficient time to complete it, for it stopped just short of the river. The scouts reported that it ran for dozens of kilometres inland.

The army filed quickly through the gap and formed up again in their previous order. As there had been no attempt to meet them at this defensive line, the generals began to think that the King had pulled back to Babylon, and that he would not now oppose them until they came to that city. Cyrus was confident that he would not; he was sure that he would have advanced to meet him if he had sufficient armaments. Eleven days before, a soothsayer in his entourage had foretold that the King would not give battle 'in the next ten days'. Cyrus had replied that if he didn't show in that time, he wouldn't show at all, and he promised the augur 10 talents if what he predicted turned out to be true. Now he summoned him and paid him the money, and the army advanced the rest of that day in a more relaxed fashion.

*

My minders from Heit were not conspicuous, but they turned up at the end of the day and led me to a house in Bahsaf, an agricultural shanty town on the outskirts of Ramadi. After dark the streets were taken over by dogs: packs of them raced up and down the alleyways, their barking and howling rending the night. My host and his own dogs escorted me out of the maze in the morning. A police car was waiting just before the Euphrates and took me in to the Party headquarters. A formal but brief interview with an official resulted in a new paper being issued. Following lunch the car drove me to a checkpoint on the far side of the city. I was meant to be on the other side of the river, but I didn't feel it mattered too much any more.

Being on the highway was completely different from walking on the Jezirah. The traffic was heavy, and largely oblivious to my presence. From time to time cars would pull over, but to offer assistance, not to demand papers. Sometimes they just handed me things through the window: cans of orange juice, fruit, cigarettes, even money. In the four weeks I had been in the country, I had not been able to spend a single dinar, and when they were insistent I produced the plastic bag from the border to prove my solvency.

In late afternoon I came to the town of Kaldiya. Typically shabby, it was divided down the middle by the highway. The businesses fronting each side were all dedicated to servicing the traffic: garages, kebab stalls, teahouses, tyre changers. By far the most numerous were the tyre changers. I was struck by how many of them were able to survive in the one stretch.

Nobody here, amidst the fumes and oil pools and noise, seemed much put out by my passing. Those who happened to notice waved, and the odd shoeless urchin would tag on until I took the stick to him. Past the foot of a high bridge that arced over the Euphrates a man called Shakir, a teacher, pulled up in his car and invited me to his home. I thought I had another hour before dark, but he insisted that I didn't, and had my pack in the boot before I could protest any further.

Ten kilometres beyond Kaldiya, the highway began to rise gently toward a crest. I could see that this had formerly been a bluff, its left side having been sheared away to make a passage for the road. Before the engineers, the feature would have extended almost to the river. On the truncated height there were anti-aircraft emplacements, and these, combined with the topography of the location, brought to mind the Gates mentioned by Xenophon. Some think the term described a natural defence, a place that might control river and land traffic, such as this could certainly have done.

Another view is that the Gates were a symbolic milestone marking the exit from the desert. Something transitional does seem to be required by the name, and here at Sin al-Deban (fly's teeth), the great flat plains of Babylonia begin in earnest. I rested by the crest for a time, watching as the sun climbed high over the new landscape.

According to my diary, from the border town of al-Qaim, a possible location for Korsote, to this point was around 365 kilometres. Xenophon gives 90 *parasangs* as the stage distance, 450 kilometres at the 'standard' rate, though if there were ever to be a case for reducing the value of the *parasang* it would be on this long and arduous leg.

The march to the Gates from Sardis had taken the army five months and covered 502 *parasangs*. My journey from Sardis to this point, by way of the lower route over the Taurus, had taken five and a half months and 2,270 kilometres.

I had a strange encounter at the Fly's Teeth. On the approach I made out some kind of activity on the roadside; closer up, amidst a small crowd of locals, I saw somebody in a gown and turban astride a camel. Behind this the head of another rider bobbed, and then a third.

The caravan was making tardy progress. The lead animal was stationary, and not happy. It periodically spat at the onlookers, and seemed to be trying to angle its rear end toward them. It didn't look a very healthy specimen. Clumps of hair grew wildly in random places and the skin on its legs was discoloured. The rider looked bemused, and was evidently inexperienced as a handler of these animals: he spoke soothingly to it, and nudged his knees gently as though he was on a thoroughbred. The fellow was from Sheffield, though he was too distracted to offer any further information than this.

The second rider was American. He produced a big smile and pointed a camera at me. 'Hey, where you guys from?'

'I'm from Ireland. I'm on my way to Babylon.'

'Yea, we've just been there. We're headed for Bethlehem – to be there for the birth day of the Christ child.'

His camel wrenched its neck, and I moved on through the scrum. There was a shanty settlement on waste ground sloping away to the left and I guessed most of the onlookers had descended from there. A few were trying to sell hot food and one man had tractor tyre tubes over his shoulder.

Following some way behind the camels, moving slowly down the crest, was a convoy of minibuses, alongside them on foot several pilgrims. A tall, well-built man dressed in a flowing white gown led this group. He had a long, amber beard and ranging hair crowned with a baseball cap. I guessed he was in his early thirties.

'Hi, I'm Bob from North Carolina.'

I extended my hand to meet his and introduced myself.

They were members of an organization called the Holy Land Trust, and were retracing the route taken by the Magi, whose journey to find the newborn king of the Jews is described by Matthew in the New Testament. Bob's group had begun their pilgrimage in Ctesiphon, the ancient capital of Parthian Persia just south of Baghdad. Aside from marking the 2,000th anniversary of the event, the object of the trip, he explained, was to highlight to the world the fact that there were Christians in the Orient too. 'We ourselves represent the breadth of the church. We draw from four continents for this project.'

We stood in the shade of one of their minibuses and a bottle of ice-cold mineral water was handed to me. There were two people stretched out in the rear, like casualties from a front. One had caught too much sun and the other had blisters.

'The camels are proving more challenging than we envisaged,' Bob confided, after I reported what I had seen. 'We may have to retire them and continue altogether on foot.'

They were already two days behind schedule, and had only left Ctesiphon on Monday. Their guides, officials from the Ministry of Information, were getting impatient. The leader caressed his beard while pondering the situation. Oddly, given that I had spent the last five months trying to relive the experience of the Ten Thousand, I felt in that moment as though we could have been on the original journey of the Magi. With the train stopped, and people milling about, and the camels, there was a strong sense of being part of an expedition. I said this to Bob and a renewed calm came over his face. He gave the word to stand down for a fifteen-minute break.

As he searched through a satchel in the back of the van, an urchin bothered us with his hand out. In the other he had a bicycle tyre tube and a short wooden stick. He was eight or nine, barefoot, and his hair stood on end from not having seen soap for months. One of the minders shooed him away before I could, and when he was obstinate, another rooted him up the backside. The child backed off like a stray dog: slowly, and ready to bolt. Bob looked perturbed. He approached the boy, and beckoned him gently. 'Son, do you speak English?'

Then this giant of a man placed his hand on the boy's shoulder and got down onto his knees. 'Son, forgive us.'

The lad looked distressed; he stared wide-eyed at us, and when one of the minders flicked his head he ran off towards the collection of huts on the waste ground.

I accompanied Bob back to the front of the line. The numbers of curious locals had grown and we saw a riderless camel entering a field on the other side of the highway. The other two were standing with their mounts in the middle of the road, savouring the disruption they were causing to traffic. A man I took to be their handler lashed at each in turn with a cane and swore liberally in Arabic.

Bob called his people together and they formed a huddle away from the crowd. I kept an eye on the camels while they conferred. They concluded with an invocation: 'Thank you O Lord for the trials you send us. Grant us the wisdom to see your ways.'

There was a lift in Bob's step as we headed back to the van. After I had strapped on my pack he embraced me, and then read from his book. 'Be strong and of a good courage, fear not, nor be afraid of them. For the Lord goes with you: he will not fail thee, nor forsake thee.'

With that he raised his hand and gave the word to move out. The line of vehicles roared into life, and slowly the convoy pressed forward.

I hastened the short way on to the crest and turned, watching the unmistakeable figure of Bob striding towards the Holy Land. I wondered, was this what a holy man looked like?

*

There was now a sense of being in a different country. The river flowed less forcefully, and its valley flattened out into a rich and densely populated plain. To the left and the right, for as far as the eye could see, the land was under cultivation: maize, wheat, rice, vegetables and swathes of palm trees. Apart from oil, dates were Iraq's most important export. Tons are harvested from millions of trees every year, and there are said to be over a hundred different varieties growing in the country. Xenophon observed: 'The sort one sees in Greece, they set aside for the servants, while the ones reserved for the masters were choice fruit, wonderfully big and good looking. Their colour was just like amber, and they used to dry some of them and keep them as sweets.' He discovered too that there was a part of the crown of the tree which was eaten as a delicacy (possibly because once it was cut away, the tree died). He calls it a 'cabbage', remarking that most of the soldiers were 'greatly impressed with its appearance and its peculiarly pleasant taste, though it was also extremely apt to cause headaches'.

The next town in my path was Fallujah. My first sight of it came on top of a flyover: beyond a wide expanse of trees to the north-east, I could see a cluster of minarets, and the rooftops of several tall buildings. The rail track beneath travelled directly to the town, but the highway continued east, before bending sharply north to meet a bridge over the Euphrates.

In ancient times a huge canal cut at Fallujah (Pallughtha) may have connected the Euphrates to the Tigris. The commerce brought by such a waterway would explain the extensive ruins that are still to be seen just north of the modern town. Rauwolf the sailor was so impressed by them that he believed he had happened upon Babylon itself. He described the site as seen from his boat, its focal point a prominent castle in the plain: 'You may still see the ruins of the fortification, which is quite demolished and uninhabited; behind it, and near to it, did stand the Tower of Babylon.'

Even though Fallujah is of considerable size, and almost out of the Anbar, I still felt some uneasiness crossing back onto the Jezirah.

Upon crossing the bridge I volunteered my papers to a traffic policeman, who glanced at them and pointed me on to the Hezib. Their building was ½ kilometre ahead on the left side. A wall ran round the perimeter and guards idled at the gate. They invited me into the gate-house for tea and one hurried up the driveway to report my arrival. He returned a while later, looking rather sullen, and said I had to leave. The cold shoulder was a surprise, but welcome if it marked a more open climate.

A white Toyota pick-up pulled alongside me not far from the town. I knew from the model that its occupants were from some security branch or other, although they said they were tourist officers and wanted to help. We drove back into the centre and they started asking about Sin al-Deban. Had I taken photos? Any of the airbase?

I pretended that I hadn't noticed one, and underlined that I was only interested in the river. We shuffled for an hour between offices and finally I was taken to the Hezib. In the evening a short man with one leg entered the room where I was watching TV. He wasn't in uniform but must have been important as all the guards stood up promptly.

He rested his crutch against a table and sat down. His face widened with a smile, an expression that seemed to require some effort on his part. 'Are you *zein?*'

'Yes, *zein.*'

'*Rahhal entay?*'

Rahhal was how I was described in my letter of introduction. Mohammed in Syria had told me it was a venerable Arabic term used to describe a person who travels on foot. In Syria they chose to refer to me as *hadji*, a pilgrim, and in Turkey, I was a *tureest*.

'*Nam*' ('yes').

He reached for his crutch again. 'You must to eat. *Yallah.*'

A car took us back along the main road towards the bridge. On the right side there was a line of lively-looking restaurants. Scores of chickens roasted on the pavement, while appetizing smells wafted through open windows. I hadn't been in an Iraqi restaurant before and was impressed by the hectic conveyance of full and empty plates. It was one of those places dedicated to eating: no nonsense with décor or table-cloths, just the serious business of eating. We were pointed to a table that had just been vacated and was being wiped clean by a youth in a blue kitchen tunic. I ordered excessively.

'As much you need,' my host encouraged as I asked for things I had dreamed of in leaner times. He didn't order anything except a glass of tea, which he only stirred while I attempted to make inroads into the plates.

'People in Iraq, very love Saddam Hussein. America, London – *mu zein* (not good)!'

In broken English he spoke about the effects of sanctions and the evil of Zionism. I made acknowledgments but did not stop eating long enough for conversation to be possible. Around us they ate a bit like this as well, so there was no embarrassment to the home country, as my mother always predicted whenever I'd set off on a trip.

When I had come to the point that I couldn't eat another morsel, I straightened up on the chair and held my stomach, concerned that I might have overdone it. There was still a quantity of food uneaten: I thought to ask the boy to wrap up one of the kebabs, but didn't know if this was acceptable diner practice.

The Hezib man smiled. This time the expression seemed to come more naturally. 'Saddam Hussein – *zein?*'

I raised my thumbs. It would have been bad manners not to agree.

*

The Fallujah road joined up with a new motorway. The size of this gave the impression that the traffic was very light, and it may have been, for the road had few junctions, so that local traffic probably stuck to their old ways.

From the high embankment, for much of the morning I could see the trees on the left bank of the Euphrates. As the day went on my compass showed that I was diverging; sometimes, where there were only fields, I could see away to the right for kilometres. This stage through the plains of Babylonia was the last for the army on the march upcountry. They moved slowly, expecting the enemy to appear at any time. These must have been the most tense days of the journey, not knowing whether, when or how many would see their homes again.

The approaching end focused my own mind intensely on the journey.

All day I revisited in my head places along the line of the route, and at the same time wondered how closely I had followed in the tracks of the Ten Thousand. The known points of the journey, after all, had been few and far in between. What's the reward for the pilgrim who follows the right path? I should have asked Bob.

Taking stock in a field that afternoon, I looked back with a degree of satisfaction. I felt I had gained an understanding of what life would have been like for the soldiers on the march; I felt as well that in my moments of discovery, wonder, excitement and fear, I had caught something of their spirit. And if I hadn't found that something – a place, a person, a myth – I had hoped to, there was more than enough compensation in the variety of the encounters I had had.

I walked for a long time that day, and continued into the night. I had an urge to keep going until I came to the end; it was as if the something might be revealed there, like the proverbial crock of gold at the end of a rainbow. In fact, like the rainbow, there was no true end at which I could conclude, for Kounaxa, the name given as the place where Cyrus fought his brother, has never been identified. Xenophon made no mention of this place, saying only that the army advanced from the Gates in slow order for five and half days, and that the plain where they fought was 360 stadia from Babylon. By the modern course of the river, this would put it at about the same distance, 65 kilometres, from Fallujah. Because I knew at the outset that I couldn't hope to reach a recognizable spot, my destination had been Babylon.

I left the motorway shortly after 8 p.m. and started to walk towards the river. It was cold and I stopped to wrap the *shamag* around my head. I could see the lights of a village away on the left, and behind, the headlights of the odd car on the motorway.

After about twenty minutes I came onto a tree-lined track and followed its winding course through the countryside. I gave up looking at the luminous points of my compass and just kept walking. The sound of village dogs gradually faded; a breeze rustled through the leaves overhead. More and more stars came out, and became brighter as the night grew.

At some point I heard a vehicle. I wasn't sure from which direction it was coming, or if it was on the same track. The sound rose and fell as it bumped along: I stopped and listened, wondering as it came closer whether to slip into the woods. It appeared suddenly around a bend. The headlights shone directly in my face. Another car came up behind it. The drivers called out to one another. I turned to look at the way ahead, and then slowly took off my gear, deciding that this was the end of the line.

*

In the early afternoon dust appeared, like a white cloud, and after some time a sort of blackness extending a long way over the plain. When they got nearer, then suddenly there were flashes of bronze, and the spear points and the enemy formations were visible.

Anabasis I.8

The following day, the fifth after they had passed through the Gates, the army went forward in loose formation. On the next there was yet more laxness: Cyrus travelled in his chariot, and the soldiers mingled with neighbouring companies. About mid-morning, Pategyas, a table-companion of Cyrus, came into view on the plain. He had been leading a reconnaissance party that had earlier set out from the main body. He was at full gallop, and began to yell as soon as he could be heard. Continuing through the ranks he shouted in Persian and Greek that the King was approaching with a great army.

Confusion fell upon the soldiers. They ran for their weapons, some not knowing where they were, as they had strayed from the baggage trains, others separated from their captains.

Cyrus leaped down from his chariot and accoutred himself. He put on his breastplate, thigh guards and greaves, but did not wear a helmet. Taking his javelins from his arms bearer, he mounted Pasakas and gave orders for the armies to take their positions. As the soldiers were hastily forming up, Klearkhos rode up to him and asked if he would not remain behind the lines in safety. 'What are you saying Klearkhos?' replied Cyrus. 'Dost thou bid me, who am reaching out for a kingdom, to be unworthy of a kingdom?'

It was midday now and Cyrus kept his formations in tight order. On the left wing he had his native troops – Lydians, Phrygians, Thracians, Paphlagonians, Medes, Persians – all commanded by Ariaios. On the right side were his Greek auxiliaries. Klearkhos had his men beside the river, and next to him were those of Proxenos, Sophainetos, Xeirosophos, Socrates, Agias, and on the left, Menon. The *hoplites* were in an eight-deep formation, untouchable by cavalry, and capable of punching through any opposing line. The men stood shoulder to shoulder, spears rooted in the soil, their huge shields propped on the earth.

Cyrus, as was the Persian tradition, was in the centre of the army. With him were his 600 hand-picked cavalry guard. The horsemen were armed with spears and Greek sabres, and wore armour from head to shin. The horses themselves were protected by steel plating around their heads and chests.

From the river the entire host stretched over 3 kilometres into Mesopotamia. For over an hour they stood expectant under the blazing sun. And then they saw it, a faint dust cloud rising on the horizon; and soon they heard it, rolling thunder along the banks of the Euphrates: 100,000 men-in-arms, on chariots, on horses and on foot.

*

Because the King's army was so much larger than Cyrus', his line extended much further out into the plain; his left wing alone was longer than Cyrus' entire front.

His offensive range was also greater: cavalry, scything chariots, spearmen, archers, slingers, and heavy infantry were present in each army group. The scything chariots – named after the barbed metal rods that protruded from their wheels – he had placed at intervals in front of the line, and these were the first of the enemy Cyrus' force saw.

Like Cyrus, the King was in the centre of his army. This position allowed the commander-in-chief to control both flanks, and to react as quickly as possible to the flow of the battle. A heavy ring of bodyguards protected Artaxerxes: they moved as he did, as though they were all part of the same body.

Artaxerxes had placed Tissaphernes in command of his far left, probably having had intelligence of the deployment of the Greeks. None of the Persians had the intimate knowledge of Greek warfare that he did, and few had been as close to the mind of Cyrus in recent years. His force consisted mostly of Egyptian infantry, while about his person he had his own cavalry. The King's other commanders were Gobrias, the Satrap of Babylonia, and Arbakes, the Median satrap. Abrocomas, who had burned the pontoon over the Euphrates and gone up to the Royal Road, did not arrive in time for the battle, nor did the levies from the more distant territories, but given the time and logistics, the King cannot have been dissatisfied with his defence.

The discipline of his men surprised the Greeks. They had expected an unruly mass to confront them, but on the contrary, the barbarians advanced at a steady pace, orderly and silent.

Having surveyed his opponent's line, Cyrus gave his instructions, which were that the Greeks were to join him and the cavalry in an attack on the Persian centre. "'If we win there,' he said, 'it is over.'"

But because the enemy line was so much longer, the King was a considerable way to the left of the Greeks, and Klearkhos feared that if they moved from the river they would be encircled by the Persian left. He sent word back to Cyrus that all would be well.

The brothers were about a kilometre apart when the watchword went along the Greek ranks. Cyrus was riding along their frontline when he heard, and he stopped to ask who had given the word, and what it was. The man who rode forward was Xenophon, and he answered him: 'Zeus the Deliverer, and Victory.'

Cyrus regarded him. 'Then I accept the word. Let it be so.' And he rode away to his own position in the field.

At ½ kilometre the *salpinx* sounded and the Greeks began to move forward. The *hoplites* clashed their spears against their shields, and the war cry to Ares went up. When they came in range of enemy arrows they charged, spears lowered to the horizontal. The Egyptians did not withstand them, and fell into disarray; the Persian cavalry under Tissaphernes tackled the lighter *peltast* formations and, though they managed to break through, they failed to inflict any damage, and did not swing about to engage again. The Greeks slaughtered everyone they caught and gave relentless pursuit along the river.

Cyrus saw what was happening, and realized that his order had been disobeyed. Believing there was still a chance for victory, he signalled to his cavalry, and the 600 charged at the enemy centre. The King's guard, which had been advancing towards the river to link up with Tissaphernes, hastily closed up, but the horsemen cut through their ranks with flying swords. Cyrus himself is said to have slain their commander, Artagerses, a close aide of the King's. As Ktesias tells, he hurled his spear at close range, and then drove its head through his neck past the collarbone.

He was sure now that his brother was at hand. Swinging around on his mount in the midst of the battle, he spotted the royal ensign, a golden eagle upon a spear with its wings spread out. 'I see the man!' Cyrus pointed his sword and galloped at the King.

Those of Cyrus' guard who had heard his cry broke from combat and chased after him. Despite the heavy cover about the King, Cyrus managed to strike him. The blow split his breastplate and he fell from his horse, though not fatally wounded. Almost in the same moment, a javelin struck Cyrus, piercing him under the eye. He too fell to the ground, and his table-companions dismounted and surrounded the body. As the finest of the Persians fought hand to hand, Cyrus staggered to his feet, thinking he had killed the King, and not knowing that his own life was ebbing away. He fell again, for the last time, and one by one the eight nobles who had managed to stay with him were cut down.

22

Baghdad

The City of Peace

I have travelled to many places; I have seen countries from Samarqand to Quirawan, and from Sarandip to the Roman lands, but found no place better or more appealing than Baghdad.

Abu al-Qassim al-Dilami

We bumped along the track until we reached a road that ran alongside the motorway embankment. The car behind emitted a weak honk and disappeared into a wood. We turned left and found our way onto a flyover. This led into a small town which the driver, a farmer, said was called Khandari. It was dominated by a large prison compound. Arc lights flooded the interior like some kind of outdoor arena. The Ba'ath Party office was behind this and was closed. The farmer drove back round to the centre, stopping outside the mosque, a sizeable building on the main street. He got out and spoke to a huddle of men, one of whom subsequently came to the window. He wore a skullcap and had a bushy black beard. 'Do you believe in God?' I nodded my head without great conviction. He lifted my pack from the back and I followed him into a house adjacent to the mosque. In the morning, when the party representatives came, I thanked my host for his hospitality. 'God willed it,' he said, pressing his hand to his chest.

The Hezib brought me to the office and my papers were reviewed.

'You're going to Babylon?'

'Yes.'

'On foot?'

'Yes.'

After some phone calls they took me back out to the car. I thought they might have been taking me to Babylon, until at a major junction east of the town we turned north. Inside quarter of an hour we were driving through the outer suburbs of Baghdad.

There was nothing appealing about the suburbs at all. Low-rise apartment blocks were fronted by waste ground grazed by sheep looked after by kids: the Third World.

Things improved as we moved along. The streets became tidier, and there were shops with display windows and houses with gardens. Mosques of delicate design sat amidst groves of dusty palms. Near the centre we passed a needle-shaped tower that must have risen to 200 metres. 'Saddam Tower,' the front passenger informed me when I asked. I should have known. On the other side of the road, giant casts of the president's head stood guard over the gates of one of his own palaces.

We didn't have much further to go. Rounding a plaza, we turned right onto a busy boulevard. Our destination, the Ministry of Information, loomed at the far end on the left, a soulless modern building among many in the administrative quarter. My attention was caught by an unusual portrait of Saddam on its corner. I had never seen him like this before: Maxim Gorky in his study, an old man, slightly jaded, resignation in his eyes. It seemed to have been intended for a more sophisticated audience, or perhaps the propagandist had not understood his brief.

I was deposited at reception, and a short while later was taken up to what was called the Protocol Department. An official debriefed me here and went through my papers. When the processing was completed another man took me to a media centre on the top floor. He told me that he had studied languages at university, French being his major. He was of medium height and scrawny and had an enormous set of teeth which glistened on the odd occasion he smiled. He did this curtly when he presented me to a journalist.

I explained the journey to her in some detail and supplied her with a series of maps detailing the stages of the route.

'Can you speak of your purpose in doing this?'

'I thought retracing the route might be another way of learning about the past, just as a historian studies documents to get some insight, and an archaeologist digs holes.'

She scribbled away and somebody from the television station came in to do a piece.

Following all this the protocol man came to take me to a hotel. Not long after we had sat into the taxi he turned round in the front seat and said: 'I am famous in Iraq.'

I asked him why, while taking in my first sight of the Tigris, and he explained that he had been a footballer, goalkeeper for the national junior side. He had represented his country at international events and, but for a knee injury, and sanctions, would have earned senior honours. I admitted that I hadn't heard of him, but said I had friends more interested in football back home who might have.

We turned right after the bridge and crept down a lively thoroughfare fronted by shops and restaurants. I was surprised to see so much prosperity in the ostracized city. The pavements teemed with shoppers and there seemed to be markets set up along every side street. Veering off a roundabout the taxi sped up the driveway of a high-rise hotel. A porter hurried down the steps to get the luggage. It wasn't the sort of place I normally stayed in, and I mentioned this casually to my minder.

'Give me money for taxi.'

I found the plastic bag and handed him one of the bundles.

We entered the spacious lobby and crossed to the reception desk, which was busy registering a party of noisy Koreans. The porter deposited my gear and looked in disbelief at the notes I discreetly handed him. We nudged ourselves in at the end of the counter and waited for attention. At every opportunity my minder flashed his teeth at the female receptionist, but the glare was insufficient to distract her.

When the last of the Koreans had received their keys she welcomed us in English. My details were swiftly tapped into the reservation system.

'When did you make your booking, sir?'

I turned to the official; they spoke and she frowned. It was the busiest week of the year in the capital; the annual Baghdad International Fair was about to get underway. She rang round a number of other places. Noting the room rates, I crossed my fingers and enquired of the minder about less extravagant hotels.

'Impossible,' he sniffed. 'They are only for Arab citizens.'

When the receptionist had concluded her efforts, he asked for the phone and rang the office. During a pause in his conversation, having been pondering what might happen next, I mentioned that I had friends from Jubbah in the city who had invited me to visit. The information was relayed to the departmental manager, a Mr Daud, whom I had met briefly earlier in the morning. I was sitting on a sofa in his office when a German in a suit came in and asked me to leave. 'Yoh, you can wait outside.' This instruction was accompanied by a nod and some kind of brushing hand gesture. I ignored him and he turned to the desk where Daud was arguing on the phone. Placing himself between us, the German produced a wallet and placed bills on the table. (I saw this because I moved along the couch to see what was happening.) The manager was visibly embarrassed, but had little hesitation in gathering up the money.

He now asked to speak with me. 'Are they Iraqi? How do you know them? When did you meet?'

I handed him back to the minder who straightened and took instructions.

Baghdad east of the Tigris is known as Rusafa, the west bank, al-Karkh. We crossed back to al-Karkh and made a sluggish traverse through the government quarter. The city centre on this side had a decidedly modern and cold appearance, as if bulldozers had been run up and down it like lawnmowers and then the vision of some brutalist architect imposed on the slate. Curving underpasses and vast civic spaces relieved the monotony of the grid plan, as did the compounds of the president, great walled palaces with forbidding gates. Amidst this modernism, it was odd to see battered cars and donkey carts trundling past one another on the boulevards.

'This is Saddam Tower,' the guide informed me as our car laboured past. I sensed that he was in familiar territory.

'I live here,' he announced moments later, pointing out of the window toward a wide avenue that unfolded away to our right. 'Its name is Mansour, named after the ruler of Baghdad, and presently home to the high officials and foreigners.'

We continued for another five minutes to a busy junction, Nafaq-a-Shorta, 'the police underpass'. We turned off this into another of the western suburbs, al-Qudra. This too looked like a prosperous area. Rows of neat retail outlets faced one another on either side of the main road, while mansions with palm trees lined the side streets that ran perpendicular to this.

With the cryptic address 620/4/71, Fareed's house was straightforward to locate. It was behind a school on a quiet road parallel to the major one. Like all the residences on Embassy Street it was comparatively large, a two-storey building with a driveway and a small front garden.

The house had been built by Fareed's father, Hadji Abdul Ftkhan, in the 1960s. For many years he had worked as an engineer with the oil ministry, but returned to Jubbah after the death of his wife. He had married again, but suffered more misfortune when one son was killed in a tractor accident, and another, I believe, in a shooting in Baghdad. I met him on one occasion in his house on the Shamia. He had a worn face and spoke in a deep voice. He spoke good English, though he preferred to listen rather than talk.

The house in al-Qudra had been rented out until Fareed came to study in the capital in the 1980s. He read Semitic languages, and afterwards worked for a government body. Like his father, however, he was drawn back to Jubbah, where he married and opened a shop.

The current occupants were Fareed's two younger brothers, Firas, aged twenty-two, and Kemal, nineteen, and an eighteen-year-old cousin called Faisal. The brothers were students at an engineering college, while Faisal was studying Russian. He was gone every morning before I got up, but I never knew Kemal to attend classes, or ever saw him take hold of a textbook with scholarly intent. Most of the time he was horizontal on a mattress in the lounge, chewing dates and flicking through the three television channels. Firas, who was taller and leaner than his squat brother, was much more industrious. He ran a stall at the central bus station in Hilla, and was always scheming ways to make money. Faisal was his reluctant assistant. He was a biggish lad but had no spine in him at all. I guessed that this stemmed from a lack of self-esteem, occasioned by several physical disadvantages. He was deaf in one ear, had a stammer, and a lazy eye. He also suffered from acute asthma and was prone to severe attacks. The others forced him to sleep in the hallway, so ferocious was his snoring. And when he went to sleep it was almost impossible to wake him, a factor which made him the object of countless foolish tricks.

About once a fortnight their mother came from Jubbah with supplies, and this I had no doubt served as a check on the more outrageous plans of Firas.

*

As arranged I was ready at eight the next morning, although it was close to ten before the minder called. He kept the doorbell pressed and by the time I got there from the kitchen Kemal was sitting up on the lounge floor rubbing his eyes. I hurried up the driveway after the official and hopped into the waiting car.

He had several newspapers on his lap, a few of which had pieces about my journey. *Al-Jumhuriyah* ('The Republic') had run it beneath a picture of Saddam on the front page, he resplendent in cream-coloured suit upon a throne in one of his palaces. I leaned forward to hear the translation. 'RAHHAL ARRIVES IN BABIL.'

He skimmed through the piece and then briefly summarized. 'It says you walked to Babylon from your country to highlight the effects of sanctions on Iraqi people.'

I fell back in the seat laughing. He twisted to look at me. 'What is the matter?'

Every time I tried to answer, he exposed his teeth, and I lost it again. He eventually returned to the papers and didn't speak for the rest of the trip. Approaching the ministry, I tapped him on the shoulder and handed over the money for the taxi. Before the laughing gripped me once more, I declared in as stern a voice as I could: 'I am famous in Iraq.'

By chance that same morning I came across the journalist who had interviewed me. Her name was Moona, a hefty woman who had once worked as a nurse for an Irish company in the capital. I asked her about her article and she agreed that it mightn't have been entirely faithful to my story. 'We work for the government,' said she, 'everything has to be presented with certain goals in mind.'

The itinerary for that day centred on a visit to the National Museum, where an audience with the renowned Dr Rabiyah had been arranged. Rabiyah was the outstanding figure of Iraqi antiquities, the gatekeeper to the treasures of Mesopotamia, and I was a little surprised that an appointment had been made so easily.

At the museum my minder said that he had to go home and needed money for the fare. I gave him one of the wads, and he said he needed another for the return. I knew that wasn't true as he had only ever slipped two or three notes from the bundle when paying. I asked him why he thought I should be paying. He huffed off without replying and failed to show at the house the next morning.

It transpired that I didn't actually have an appointment to see the Director. A receptionist explained that persons who had business with him were usually seen in turn. He confirmed that he was in residence and pointed me along the corridor to his secretary's office.

She perused my letter of introduction from the ministry and asked what it was I wanted. I said I was looking to locate the battlefield of Kounaxa, and she scribbled a note of this and led me into a waiting room. This was quite small, and full of foreign savants. I sat on the remaining vacant chair beside the door and introduced myself to the man next to me. He was French, an Islamologist, seeking to gain access to manuscripts held by the museum. He was not very old, but he worked hard at cultivating a sagacious appearance: fulsome beard, long hair, pot belly. The room was thick with his cigar smoke.

On the row of chairs opposite there was a contingent of bored Italians. Their leader I took to be an elderly man wearing a bow tie who was seated on the edge of his chair, his hands clasped tightly over a wooden cane. The others were incrementally younger and had assumed less dignified postures.

I figured that it was unlikely I would be seen any time soon by Dr Rabiyah, and I wasn't keen on sitting for the day, so I decided to visit the collections. I arranged with the Islamologist that he was to say I had just popped out for a minute if someone else came to join the queue.

The museum was in a separate building next to the administration block. A diagonal path running across a burnt lawn led from one entrance to the other. I browsed in the lobby while a guide was summoned. The place was deserted. I wandered alone down a hall of glass exhibition cases displaying armaments from the Abbasid era. As I knew, the institution had been founded in the 1920s by Gertrude Bell, the English Arabist and adventurer. She was its first director, and spent the last years of her life arranging these collections. Though plundering at Nimrud and Nineveh (Layard), and at Babylon and the ziggurat cities of the south, had greatly reduced the inheritance of the new nation, the museum still had custody of some of the oldest and finest artefacts of civilization.

I was curious to know if the building, a long warehouse-like structure, was the original repository. The guide when she came, irritable as a *babushka* in a Lenin museum, shrugged and stabbed her watch. I thought it unlikely we would get through the highlights in the hour before lunch and said I'd come another time.

The security guard at the front entrance was also not sure about the museum's history, though he was certain the ceremonial gate nearby was a recent addition. This huge façade – possibly meant to be an imitation of the Ishtar Gate in Babylon – faced out toward the traffic chaos of Hilla, its edges black from pollution.

As I walked toward Hilla to get a photograph, my attention was caught by a striking mosque in the distance. It was a small, colourful construction, distinguished by a giant bulbous cupola flowering on the roof. Adding to its exotic character was a slender hexagonal minaret, decorated from top to bottom in glazed tiles, and crowned with a sparkling ceramic turban. Notwithstanding the pall of diesel fumes hanging over the building, it was, I thought, singularly evocative of the Baghdad of al-Rasheed and the Arabian Nights, the last great flourishing of Mesopotamia.

*

Baghdad was founded in 762 AD by the Abbasid Caliph al-Mansour. He called his new capital, Medina al-Salaam, the 'city of peace', though somehow this never caught on, and it became known by the name of a village that had been sited nearby.

It was situated on the west (right) bank of the Tigris, and was enclosed by an almost 3-kilometre circular wall. A moat fed by the river provided an outer ring of protection. The huge mud-brick wall was pierced by four gates located at the intercardinal points, and from these roads ran to the four quarters of the empire.

It was intended that the 'Round City' would house only the Caliph, his family, and his administrative apparatus. Merchants, the military, foreign missions and the common subjects were all to be kept at a stately distance. The result was that dedicated suburbs quickly grew up around the citadel, even crossing over to the far bank of the river. It was this side, which became known as Rusafa, that was to develop into the enterprise hub of the capital, as it still is today.

Within a hundred years of its establishment Baghdad had become the commercial and cultural centre of the world. In part its extraordinary rise was down to the fact that it was the political heart of the expanding Muslim empire: taxation revenues poured into the city, as did embassies, scholars, and travellers from lands near and far. Trade and the availability of labour for building projects were other factors in the rise. Baghdad had access to the fertile and densely populated

Babylonian plains, it was on the major east–west land routes, and could be reached by merchant ships from the Gulf. In effect it was the successor to the great Mesopotamian cities that had gone before: Ur, Babylon and Ctesiphon. The same factors which accounted for the flourishing of these centres and their civilizations applied to it as well.

History and economic success and political power did not necessarily mean that the city should also become a global centre of learning. The creation and sustaining of a vigorous intellectual life was primarily down to the character of the Abbasid Caliphate. Enlightened yet politically unstable, the leadership in its generous funding of arts and the natural sciences fostered a heady climate of enquiry, and at the same time, because of internal weakness, was unable to influence the free thinking that came with the creativity.

The greatest of the caliphs was Harun al-Rasheed (786–809 AD). His name in the West is most readily associated with the 'Arabian Nights', his court being the setting for many a magical tale, but his historical legacy goes way beyond being a protagonist in fairytales. Harun consolidated the explosive expansion of Islam, and he oversaw the emergence of an Islamic character, a synthesis of Mediterranean and Eastern culture tempered by the revelations of God. Unlike in the Latin scheme, these did not restrict the voice of science; on the contrary, the texts urged Muslims on to enlightenment: 'Seek knowledge, though it be in China.' And they did. Armies brought back whole libraries from the conquered territories, and Baghdad scholars set about translating them for their schools. Ironically, their preservation of the Hellenic heritage – of Archimedes, Euclid, Ptolemy, Plato, Socrates (the 'imam of reason'), Hippocrates *et al.* – was to enable the West to re-emerge after its millennium in the dark.

The golden age of the Abbasid period was brief. Weakened by wars of succession and the eventual reliance on a base of foreign (Turkish) mercenaries, the caliphs gave up effective control of the empire in the tenth century AD. In the end the dynasty and its capital were swept away by the brute force of the Mongols. Beaten back in 1245, the nomads returned reinforced thirteen years later. Deploying boulder-slinging catapults and flame throwers, they pounded the city relentlessly. The Baghdadis resisted fiercely, but it was only a matter of time before the hordes burst the gates. In the course of a single week in February 1258, the army of Hulagu, a grandson of Genghis Khan,

razed the 'Round City' and butchered up to half of the population of
two million people.

*

The mosque in Hilla was a new one, the guard at the museum entrance
informed me on my return. It was named after a wealthy merchant
called Bunnieh, who had commissioned its design and construction.
According to my French Islamologist friend, no architecture of the
Abbasid era remains in Baghdad.

Nobody else had come in the hour I had been away, and in this time
neither he nor any of the others waiting to see the director seemed to
have stirred. On the facing side, one of the Italians had fallen asleep,
while another aggressively flipped pages of an in-flight magazine. The
professor remained tight-lipped on the edge of his seat.

'How long have you being waiting now?' I enquired after a bit, idle-
ness breeding mischief in me.

He lifted his jaw and moved his bottom around the chair before
answering. 'Two hours and a half. We will wait fifteen minutes more.'
He added this last sentence after the slightest of pauses.

They stayed longer than that, but it didn't make any difference.
Shortly after 2 p.m. the secretary came in and coolly announced that
Dr Rabiyah would not be seeing anyone else that day. My neighbour
closed his eyes and exhaled a long '*putain*' ('bitch') beneath his breath.
The Italians conferred and stormed out of the room indignant. Two
others of unknown provenance followed them.

A woman whom I hadn't noticed (she must have been tucked away
in the corner on our side) confronted the secretary. She was clutching a
book and was quite upset. I gathered it was a tome on Sumerian pottery,
and that it was vital Dr Rabiyah see it.

'I will give the book to him,' the secretary assured her repeatedly, but
each time she reached out to take it, the woman drew back and underlined the urgency. From her accent I guessed that she was German. She
was frail and thin, in her forties, and was dressed like an Arab woman
except for hiking boots.

'I go tomorrow. Also, I must give it to him *myself.*'

The secretary said again that no one else would be seen that day.

By way of compromise, I offered to take the book and bring it the
next day to my own meeting.

'Dr Rabiyah won't be able to see you.' The secretary turned to me and handed back my papers. 'You can go to this place without his permission.'

The two women resumed their wrangling and edged nose to nose towards the door. I sat down and returned the documents to my folder, glad at least that I didn't have to wait all day to be knocked back. Out in the reception area I said goodbye to the women but they didn't hear. The guard at the entrance obliged me by stopping a taxi and giving him the address I pointed to in my diary.

*

Across the road from Hadji Ftkhan's there was a half-finished house in which lived a man from Sudan named Abduljalil. He was a big man, over 6 feet tall and heavily built. He was the mildest of men, an uncomplicated character whose life revolved around prayer and Egyptian soap operas.

The house he lived in belonged to a doctor who a few years before had run out of money and had had to stop work on it. It wasn't much more than a shell. Heaps of sand, buckets, planks and other building detritus cluttered the front yard. Entering at night was like re-enacting a temple scene from Indiana Jones. Abduljalil was the security guard, and for his 24-hour cover received a minuscule monthly allowance from the doctor. He had transformed a room at the rear of the ground floor into his living quarters. The holes for the windows were boarded up, and a thick curtain was draped over the doorway to keep autumn breezes at bay. In the winter months a buzzing single-bar heater was the sole source of warmth.

An occasional lodger of his was a compatriot called Abdullah. His real name was Min Allah ('from God'), but he preferred to use the more familiar name. He was to become one of my best friends. I wrote later in my diary that if I had embarked on this journey and nothing of note had happened except that I met Abdullah, it would have been worth undertaking.

Abdullah had come to Iraq in 1985 for education. He had been a student at an agricultural institute in Cairo, and before that had read law in Madras, but funding for both these courses had been cut before he could finish. In the 1980s the Iraqis started offering scholarships to nationals from all Arab countries, a tactic doubtless intended to gain influence for the Ba'ath Party in future years. Owing to difficulties in their own country, the Sudanese were disproportionate in the take-up. Many too were enticed to the country at this time by a shortage of labour. The scale of the country's industrial development, and the biting human cost of the Gulf War, left many sectors undermanned. Some estimates put the number of Sudanese living in Iraq prior to the first American attack in 1991 at almost one million.

Abdullah graduated from the economics faculty of Baghdad University in 1990, but it was not an auspicious time to begin a career in business. Economic sanctions were imposed on the country in August of that year, and with these, and the imminent prospect of war, investment money went to ground and took flight where it could.

Sanctions in the 1990s crippled the already beleaguered Iraqi economy. From having once been the progressive engine of the Arab world, by the agency of Saddam Hussein and the United States of America, it gradually returned to the era of the donkey and cart. In its intended aim of isolating the regime, the embargo, the most comprehensive ever imposed on a nation, was an undoubted success. However, at best it achieved only this; it did nothing to undermine the control of Saddam Hussein. Sufficient 'black' oil was exported via Turkey and the Gulf to enable him maintain his security apparat and armed forces.

For a time on my journey I thought that sanctions may actually have been benefiting the less well off, as they received substantial food packages every month by way of the UN-administered oil-for-food programme. In effect this was an imposed redistribution of wealth: Saddam would never have diverted his oil revenues in such a way. However, I came to see that this was a restricted view. When these same people, for example, needed hospital treatment or medicines, they often weren't available. Worn equipment could not be replaced, and what stocks of medicines there were in the country were not going to those on the breadline. Sanctions were a sort of 'Catch 22' for the poor of Iraq. For the nation as a whole, they were slow strangulation, resulting in broken pavements, delapidated vehicles, queues, blackouts and pain.

Being among the lowest-paid workers, and without land to live off, the position of the Sudanese in the 1990s became precarious. A number managed to migrate to better-off Middle Eastern states – down the Gulf to the oil fields, and to Beirut and its booming building sites. Some, those who had saved and who had had the foresight to convert their savings to hard currency, returned home, while the remainder were stuck.

On the positive side, the relationship between the two peoples is good. The Sudanese enjoy a reputation for honesty, and are implicitly trusted by Iraqis. For this reason many found employment, like Abduljalil, looking after the properties of wealthy natives. An active expatriate network also helped. The Sudanese retain a strong sense of their own identity, and keep in close contact with others from their own regions of the country. They gather regularly to discuss news from home, to exchange phone numbers of potential employers, and to help as they can any of their compatriots in trouble.

When it was clear international trade was not to be his destiny, Abdullah did a course in repairing fridges. Under sanctions, everything had to be recycled, so getting into the repair business was a sure way of earning a living. For several years he worked as an itinerant repairman, touring the neighbourhoods with the tools of the trade. In 1996, when he had enough saved, he hired himself a small premises and bought equipment that enabled him to undertake bigger jobs.

We first met a few days after I had arrived. My guide from the Information Ministry had failed to show on three consecutive mornings and I was unsure of what to do. I was anxious not to get on the wrong side of the authorities, and at the same time didn't want some bored official shadowing me everywhere. Kemal asked Abdullah to come over; years as a semi-outsider in the country had left him well versed on the workings of the system.

He wore a neat blue shirt draped over a pair of jeans. He was above average height, and very thin, with long wiry arms and legs. His hair was closely cut, a mat of short black curls.

Most Arabs like to sit cross-legged, but he preferred to be on his knees, resting on his haunches with his back straight. His voice was soft, and slightly hoarse from nicotine. 'You in Europe,' was how he began every second sentence, until I started to do the same but with the continents changed. He was sharp-witted and quick to see the humour in life. His laugh was infectious, a low rumble that steadily built, but only ever erupted in the most extreme of circumstances.

He didn't know how old he was. Only recently had the Khartoum government began to require this information for passports. 'You in Europe, your system is different,' he said, as I tried to stifle a laugh, and even the normally impassive Firas sniggered. (We later worked out from establishing the year he entered secondary school that he must have been born at some time in 1964 or 1965.)

Abdullah was quietly ambitious. He didn't envisage himself mending fridges for the rest of his days. His dream was to travel to Europe, to work there for a few years and to see all the great cities before finally returning to his homeland. To this end he had been saving for an airline ticket, and had been collecting visa forms from various of the nearby embassies. I didn't want to tell him it wouldn't be easy. I didn't say to him, 'Abdullah, you're black, Muslim, from Sudan and living in Iraq: you have no possibility whatsoever of going to Europe.' He would have replied that whatever the outcome, it was God's will. His faith was strong, and the most important thing to him was to try to live his life within the moral framework of his religion.

Turning late that evening to the question of what to do about my former minder, Abdullah asked me what my plans were. I wasn't sure. I wanted to go back to Khandari, the prison town near where I had stopped, to see if I could find any signs of the ancient battlefield. I was thinking that after that there would be no point going on to Babylon, but I was keen to have a look at what the Greeks did next, even if it was not on foot. I explained to him that after the battle and the death of Cyrus they were faced with the problem of getting home. The Persians agreed to escort them there, but on the way up the Tigris they seized their generals, and harried the soldiers into the mountains of Kurdistan.

Abdullah's advice was that I tell the ministry that I was going to go up the Tigris, and get a paper to say I was doing so; that way if I decided to go, I wouldn't have to go back there again, and because I was leaving, they wouldn't be bothered about a minder. He accompanied me to the office the following morning.

The former footballer, it transpired, had left the service. Daud thought I had gone too, and as he drew up my travel paper, he repeatedly asked when I was departing. I lied that I was going the next day, having it in mind to spend a few more days exploring the city. In the event, I became absorbed in it, and in the lives of my new friends, and it was a month before I finally left.

23

Adrift

Cyrus' head and right hand were cut off. Ariaios, who was being hard pressed by the King's right wing, heard the news and fell back. His forces retreated hastily to the station from where they had started that morning. The King's armaments pursued them until they came upon Cyrus' camp, which they thoroughly plundered, taking away the dead prince's Greek mistress, Aspasia.

The Greeks at this time were about 5 kilometres away. They had pursued the Persian left along the bank of the river, and though they killed a number, most of the enemy had managed to flee. The Greeks suffered not a single loss in the battle.

Word now came through that their camp had been sacked, and that the King was preparing to engage them again. (In fact the King had been taken from the field, and Tissaphernes was in command; moreover the Greeks did not know that Cyrus was dead.) They quickly regrouped and marched in their former order back along the Euphrates. The oncoming Persians, however, kept beyond their right, Tissaphernes hoping to draw them away from the protection of the river, and to disrupt their formations. But the Greeks held their shape, and to prevent their exposed wing being surrounded and cut away, they manoeuvred 90 degrees so that the river was to their rear. The Persians responded by drawing up opposite in battle order. They must have hoped that this display of prompt force, together with the news of Cyrus' death and the plunder of their camp, would have cowed the Greeks, but it was not so. At the sound of the *salpinx* they struck up the paean and charged. For the second time that afternoon the enemy failed to withstand their attack, and again the Greeks pressed their pursuit across the plain.

The Persian centre regrouped on a hill above a settlement, the one to which the King had been taken after his injury, and his standard was seen amidst the mass of cavalry. When they saw that the Greeks were intent on an engagement, they filed off the hill and rode away. By this time it was near sunset. The Greeks halted where they were and piled their arms. There was surprise among the generals that Cyrus had not sent any word; they surmised that he must have gone in pursuit of one of the satraps, or had pressed forward to take Babylon.

Half expecting to find their leader, the Greeks returned that night to their camp. Their disappointment at not finding him there was compounded by the extent of the pillage: the entire baggage train had been looted and there wasn't a morsel of food to be had.

At dawn the generals convened, and were amazed there was still no word from Cyrus. They were about to go forward in search of him when a messenger arrived from Ariaios to say that the prince was dead. The news stunned the Greeks. As the word passed from solider to soldier, a great despondency came over the Greeks. The realization dawned too that they were now isolated, and a long way from home.

At midday messengers came from the King demanding the surrender of their arms. They refused, and the following day the messengers returned to offer a truce. The Greeks were led to some villages where there were supplies, and after three days here, Tissaphernes came to negotiate. The terms offered were that he would lead them back to Ionia; they would undertake not to damage any of the King's property, and to buy what they needed from markets the Persians would provide.

This was agreed, and Tissaphernes went away to make his preparations. But he did not return that week, or the next, or the one after that, and the Greeks suspected that there was a plot against them.

*

Abdullah was my guide in Baghdad, and when he was unavailable I had Kemal to take me around. Travelling alone wasn't a good idea, as somebody might report a sighting and there would be questions.

I tended to follow where I was led, not knowing much about what there was to see, and enjoying the surprise of new places and unusual histories. Abdullah was well acquainted with the city. He was a natural traveller, a self-acknowledged outsider, a condition he attributed to his African origins and Arab background. 'In Africa they say we in Sudan are Arabs, and here they say we are Africans.'

Kemal was much more rooted, and indeed it often took some inducement just to get him out of the house. He was happiest in his *jalabiyah*, reclined on the couch with the remote, a bowl of dates and plenty of cigarettes at hand. He was short and stocky, and had a face like a bulldog. He habitually spoke in a mournful tone, although countering this he had a disarming laugh, a shy chuckle which he tried to hide with his hand. One morning, with the promise of lunch, he dressed up and we called a taxi.

Although we weren't going far, the driver had some difficulty in finding our destination. After he had finally dropped us off, he crept back toward the main street, turning his head periodically to peer curiously at the pair of us.

The place seemed deserted. We walked around the building looking for the entrance, but only came across a steep ramp disappearing into a basement. Urchins kicking a ball in an adjacent patch of scrub pointed us to a prefab on the western side of the block; peering through the window, we could see an elderly security guard asleep on a chair. Persistent tapping roused him. He spluttered into life, blinking as the sun hit him at the doorway. We were, as it happened, just opposite the entrance, although it wasn't very well marked.

Inside it was dark. At the end of a narrow corridor a dim lamp hung over a sign which said to wait and be silent. Kemal coughed and blew his nose. 'Ooh, cold Mr Shane.' Kemal lived by the view that the more inconvenience or hardship he suffered on a task, the greater the reward that was due for his efforts.

Presently a woman in dark clothing and wearing a headscarf appeared in front of us. She asked Kemal to introduce me. As he did so she carefully parted a curtain.

'You are welcome,' she said to me in English. 'Even if you do not believe, I ask you to pray for the souls of the dead.'

We stretched out our hands, palms faced to heaven.

She and Kemal recited the opening verse of the Koran. Her voice was strong and clear, his faint and uncertain. Looking around I could see that we were in a large open space, parts of which were lit by spotlights shining onto partitions, as in an exhibition hall. She gave a brief description of the site before leading us the short distance to its core. We could see the sunlight shining through a hole in the roof. There was a tangle of steel grids and shattered concrete.

This had been a bomb shelter and was in use in 1991 when it was targeted by military planners in America. On the night in February when they struck, the shelter had been half full, mostly with families from the surrounding neighbourhoods. They came here, the woman said, not because they feared that their homes would be hit but to avoid the noises of war. The children were frightened when they heard the anti-aircraft guns and the sound of explosions in the distance. Besides, here there was electricity and running water. The shelters were modern, built by a Finnish consortium in the 1980s for use by civilians in case of chemical attack during the Gulf War. There were over forty of them in the capital, each capable of accommodating 1,000 people, with supplies to last several weeks.

Most of the people present that night would have been sleeping when the missile struck, punching a large hole through the 1.5-metre-thick reinforced concrete roof. In fact few are believed to have died in this initial attack. Its purpose, like a high-tech battering ram, was to open a way for a clean strike by a second missile. The fatal effect of the first one was to cut the electricity, an event which, in the system's design, automatically locked the doors. Nobody could now get in or out. The searing heat from the destruction would have forced those inside against the walls of the shelter.

From the moment of the first missile strike to the second, six minutes passed. The guide repeated this fact twice. It entered through the gaping hole and incinerated the occupants. A final estimate by the authorities put the number dead at over 400, the majority of them women and children. Sixteen people survived.

We moved on to pictures of the aftermath, and of the victims as they were before. Identification of many of the bodies had not been possible. Eerie shadows on the walls and lumps of burnt flesh smouldering on the floor were all that remained of them. The guide stopped in front of random photographs to give us some detail about the faces staring out. She seemed to have got to know all of them in her time working here, and I was struck by how undiminished her passion for representing the dead was. Now and then her voice became unsteady with anger, as in front of a small black and white photo of a boy called Marwan Nader. 'What crime did this child commit?' We looked at the picture, and at the one beside of his sister, Zahra, and said nothing.

Outside, in the soft autumn sun, her intensity subsided. She loosened her headscarf and we strolled together towards the front of the building. I guessed that she was in her late thirties, an attractive woman even when shrouded. I took this to be work garb; certainly, it wasn't common to see educated Baghdadi women attired in this way.

'You have come on a good day. Ramadan begins today. It is the month of fasting and abstention for Muslims,' she said.

We stopped before the perimeter and turned round to look at the two-storey block. Its angled concrete walls and square shape made it a distinctive feature of the urban landscape, but I wouldn't have taken it to be a bomb shelter if I had not been told. When we had arrived I had thought we might well have been at the wrong place; I had expected to find a crater, a 'ground zero' marking the savagery of American aggression. Standing in the silence, I realized that it was its very intactness which made the place so chilling.

The guide looked at me for a thought. I had only one: 'The work of a master butcher.'

We continued across to the road. I called over to Kemal. He had been chatting with the guard at the cabin and had got a cigarette out of him. I said he had probably forgotten it was Ramadan. The woman smiled and we said goodbye.

Abdullah knew the woman. She shopped sometimes in the neighbourhood where he had his workshop. He said her name was Intesar, and that she had lost her husband and children in the attack. Apparently she had gone home for extra clothes, and had returned to find smoke billowing from the roof. Her life since had been dedicated to preserving the memory of those who had perished. 'She is a holy woman,' he commented, whilst inspecting the dinner simmering on a gas stove.

He and Abduljalil must have been starving. They had been fasting all day, and would be for the next thirty or so. Throughout the month of Ramadan, from sunrise to sunset, the devout abstain from all food and drink, smoking, and sexual activity.

The room in which they lived at the rear of the mansion was small and cosy. A weak bulb illuminated the area near the doorway; the TV, enshrined on an upturned crate in the adjacent corner, provided another source of limited light, as did the single-bar electric heater, which I never knew to be switched off. As soon as the *azan* sounded, Abdullah lowered his face into it to light a cigarette. He dragged hard and drew the nicotine deep into his lungs.

Almost at that moment a sharp cry turned our heads to the curtain. Perversely, it echoed in a chain of faint chuckles. Adam, another caretaker, hobbled in after a minute, trailed by four others: Belal, Farraj, a second Adam, and Mohammed. They were all from the same region of Sudan as Abdullah – all from around a town in the south-west called Babanusah. We rose to greet them, an elaborate ritual with them: right hand slapping the other's left shoulder, an embrace, a firm handshake, all in a continuous movement. They took off their shoes and coats and we formed a circle on the floor. '*Allah-bel-kher*,' the blessing passed from one to the other.

There wasn't enough cutlery so only two could eat at a time. I protested when the first bowl went to me. I had eaten substantially with Kemal in a restaurant and wasn't even hungry. I hastened away to let them dine.

In the Ftkhan household there was no such piety. Firas smirked when I asked how he had got on with the fast. He mumbled something in Arabic, which might have been, 'Ramadan, kiss my arse.'

A large plate with fish bones and potato skins lay on the floor in front of Kemal. He had made me promise not to tell anyone we had been to the restaurant: if his mother found out he would be in trouble. As I had seen that day, the fast was taken seriously in the city, and presumably just as much so in the villages. Along the main street in Amiriya we had found most of the restaurants closed, and in the one where we had eaten, a screen had been erected in front of the premises. This was supposed to be to avoid putting temptation in the way of passers-by, but it could as well have been a way of shielding the identity of diners, of whom there were a few.

The doorbell rang shortly after I had sat down. Nobody stirred and it went again, longer this time. Firas roared at Faisal, who was in the middle of his dinner. He hauled himself up and hurried out to the hall. A neighbour, Nassir, entered with a circular tray full of steaming plates. The three of them scanned the fare like alley cats as Nassir placed it on the floor. 'I very hungry Mr Shane,' Kemal sighed aside to me after he had snatched away a greasy leg of chicken.

Nassir was not observing the fast. 'God meant us to eat,' he told me matter-of-factly when I asked why not.

I liked Nassir. He lived in a world of his own, and was wont to break into song anywhere and on any occasion. Tall and wiry like Abdullah, he had the obligatory Arab moustache, and always had a set of beads going in his hand. He took a lot of care over his appearance: his shoes always had a shine, and if you were downwind you could almost smell him coming from the cologne. By training he was an electrician, but he was unemployed, and didn't, I gathered, make great efforts to find work.

It was when he started talking you realized that he was a bit different from other people. When we'd see reports on the TV about the Jewish killers in Palestine, for example, when everybody was saying what the people needed were guns to defend themselves, Nassir always said: 'They need food and water.'

*

Nassir had the occasional use of his cousin's car, and we sometimes took the chance to visit scenic spots around the city; or if it was evening, we would drive up and down the fashionable Mansour district. It was an old 7-series Volvo and not in great condition. One of the headlights was missing, as were all the hubcaps. The exhaust was cracked somewhere down the shaft, and there were a few dents in the bodywork from wear over the years. But by Baghdad standards, we were princes of the road: me in the back with Kemal smoking dozens of cigarettes, Abdullah navigating in front and the sound of Nassir accompanying George Michael on a squeaking tape.

They all considered a car to be the most important thing for courting Baghdad girls. It afforded privacy for conversation, and the means of getting to isolated locations for more intimate contact. The woods at Kadhimiya and Baghdad Island were Nassir's favourite spots. He had a string of *amours* in different districts of al-Karkh, proof that a car was a major advantage in the love game.

When the subject came up they informed me that prostitution was rife in the capital. In the right places girls were available for a minimal cost, and for a bit more they could be brought to your home. 'You in Europe have a different system,' Abdullah explained when I said I hadn't noted any red-light areas. 'Here they don't dress in nice clothes, and stroll along the streets. You must know where, and what to look for.'

Whatever scepticism I had about the supposed level of licentiousness in the city was dispelled after a subsequent episode in the house. Firas mentioned to me one night about midway through Ramadan that there would be someone coming in the morning, and that he had a key. I gave it no further thought. Abdullah had gone to Baygee to look over a consignment of fridges, and I had decided to spend a couple of days reviewing my diaries.

The main living area of the house was divided by a frosted glass partition, and that morning I was in the lesser used part as Kemal was sleeping in the other. We all slept there by the heater except Faisal. I heard the door open and saw the fellow pass along the partition to the rear of the house. The kitchen was located there, and the stairs, and a bedroom which was used by Firas and Kemal's mother and sisters when they came. Some minutes later, I heard the door close, and saw another figure pass along the partition. I knew it wasn't the same person because this one was taller, and took short, distinctive steps, like a woman in heels.

Curious, I put down my map and went out to the landing. There were noises coming from the room, and I was about to open the door when I realized that they were of a sexual nature. The encounter was brief enough. In a matter of minutes the door opened and Abu-Mohammed, a neighbour, strolled out.

'*Shonak?*'

'*Zein. Entay shonak?*'

'*Alhamdulilah.*'

We might have been greeting each other on the street.

He left stroking his moustache. The woman came out of the room shortly afterwards. She was in her late twenties I guessed, and was quite plain. She had lank, medium-length hair, which was tied back with a black bow. Her eyes were small and there were smudges of make-up on her cheeks. We exchanged courteous smiles. On the driveway she pulled a veil from her handbag and covered herself before opening the gate.

Kemal snored through the episode and looked blankly when I asked him later about the visitors. I finished my tea, saying casually that I'd ask Fareed when he came. 'No, no Mr Shane!' He sprang up on the couch. 'Mr Thair and girlfriend, Mr Shane.'

'Girlfriend? Abu-Mohammed's married and has four kids.'

'No girlfriend ... prostitute.'

I was a bit taken aback: Hadji Ftkhan's being used as a brothel. 'Jesus Kemal, what would they say on Jubbah?'

He started to cry. 'No me Mr Shane – Firas, Firas!'

I didn't doubt that Firas was the brains behind the enterprise. He had boasted several times about being able to bring girls to the house:

$10 each or $100 for a virgin. I had taken it as schoolboy fantasy, but after that I began to believe that there was something in it, and that Baghdad, in some respects at least, was not a typical Middle Eastern capital.

*

Shorja, the old Ottoman merchants' quarter of Baghdad, is still today the principal trading district. It occupies a considerable acreage on the Rusafa side of the river, its main thoroughfares being al-Rasheed Street, and to the east of this, al-Jumhuriyah. Everything from books to budgies are sold along these traffic-jammed arteries, while the narrow lanes that meander between reverberate with the sound of weaving machines and printing presses.

Towards the northern end of al-Rasheed Street, two new buildings interpose themselves on the fading architecture of the former empire. On the left, climbing above everything else, is an angular white block, the Central Bank; directly opposite is a vast brick warehouse, the Suq al-Arabi, the market of the Arabs. Businessmen, artisans in overalls, shoppers wearing *burqas* and fashionable dresses, all brush past one another without ceremony on this vital commercial junction.

Before the bank Abdullah and I turned up a straight road running along the side of the *suq*. This linked the parallel arteries of Shorja, an overspill channel that was clogged with mountains of rubbish.

At the top there was a statue of Saddam Hussein standing amidst flower petals, each one inscribed with the name of one of the eighteen provinces of the country. To the right of this, rising above a jumble of buildings, was a large church dome. Abdullah thought it was Latin, and he was certain that the equally imposing structure facing it on the other side of al-Jumhuriyah Street was the Caliph's Mosque. This was not an old building, but its muscular minaret is said to have once been part of an Abbasid structure, contradicting the assertion that nothing from that glorious era survives in the city today.

The area had many other houses of worship, Muslim and Christian, Shia, Sunni, Assyrian and Roman. We could pick out the bell towers and minarets from the vantage point of a pedestrian overpass. We were looking for a Chaldean church, and were eagerly directed to it by a passer-by. In fact it was along the road we had just come up, hidden behind a high wall facing the market.

The Chaldeans are the largest Christian community in Iraq. There are estimated to be upwards of half a million of them, most living in the north of the country and in the capital. The Chaldeans are an ancient branch of Christendom, part of what is known as the Oriental Church. A schism in the sixteenth century saw most of them abandon Nestorianism and become affiliated with Rome, although in recent years a rapprochement with their mother church has begun. The theology and politics of these archaic organizations are devilishly complex. I had been given the name of a priest who I hoped would clarify some of the mysteries.

Over the entrance a discreet sign in English and Arabic read: 'Mother of Sorrows Chaldean Catholic Church'. The gate was slightly ajar and we slipped into an open courtyard. The transition from the bustle of the markets was marked, as though somebody had lowered the volume of the city. We wandered into the centre of the sizeable open space. There was a grotto of Our Lady on the right side, and the church rose up on the other.

A short man with bandy legs and an impressive grey moustache hailed us. Abdullah explained that I had been given the name of a Father Nadheer, the parish priest.

He led us across the courtyard, up a colonnade and into a similar but smaller yard abutting the gable end of the church. There were a few workers trying to repair a broken pipe that was spurting water into the air like a severed artery. They swore at it and the short fellow waded in to try his hand. A youngish man in a tracksuit beckoned us into an office. He spoke some English and explained the problems they were having with the plumbing. 'The building is old. We need repair urgently everywhere.'

The office had a desk at one end, a bookcase behind this, and a computer on a table under the window looking out on the yard. There were pictures of the saints and the clergy on the walls. The Mother of Sorrows hung on her own at the end facing the desk. Set less prominently atop a filing cabinet in the corner was a photograph of the Patriarch with Saddam Hussein.

The man in the tracksuit sat himself in front of the computer. He smiled over at us. He had short curly black hair, a light moustache, and was a little overweight. He spun a silver chain around his neck.

'You like play?'

I looked at Abdullah with an expression of mild disapproval.

'We'll wait for Father Nadheer.'

He started to laugh. 'It's me. Yes.'

I was a bit taken aback. I had expected to meet a frail, elderly man, the last gasp of the Oriental Church.

We all stood up and greeted one another.

Father Nadheer was twenty-eight years of age. He was born and raised in a small village, Bathnai, in the north of the country. The youngest son in a family of eight – three boys and five girls – he entered St Joseph's seminary in Baghdad after finishing school in 1989. Seven years later he was ordained as a Catholic priest.

In the same year he received his appointment here. It was, he stressed, initially only temporary, but the monsignor thought he was doing well, and he was invited to stay on. As we toured the complex, it wasn't hard to see why the boss had been impressed. The young priest had introduced a raft of support programmes, and these no doubt served to enhance the standing of the church in the local community.

On the other side of the inner courtyard there was a clinic, which was staffed every Friday by volunteer doctors. Medicines were donated by friends of the church at home and abroad. On the floor above this there was what he called a factory, though it would be better described as a sewing workshop. Women from hard-up families were trained to use the machines, after which they were supplied with a float of material and allowed to create what they liked. They sold their output in the market and in turn replenished their stocks. At present there were only four machines, not enough to meet the demand, so the priest was planning to expand.

His biggest undertaking was a food programme. A storeroom in the corner of the outer courtyard was ceiling high with tinned tomatoes and large cardboard boxes. On the last Sunday of every month, parcels were distributed to parishioners. The parish was in the heart of the inner city, so the proportion receiving help was high. There was no means test applied: if a family head said he needed assistance, it was given. In all Father Nadheer estimated he had some 750 families in his care.

Our tour culminated in a visit to the church. We entered through the sacristy, emerging into a large cruciform area that reminded me of country churches at home. The walls were painted a light blue, and between the slender stained glass windows, idealist portraits of the apostles and saints stared out. In the bottom corner there was a shrine, fenced by low metal railings. A rack of candles flickered in front of an icon.

I realized after some minutes that Abdullah hadn't followed us. We found him out in the courtyard smoking a cigarette. He pressed his hand to his chest and said he would prefer not to come in.

Father Nadheer regarded him for a moment and they spoke in Arabic. There was a lump in Abdullah's throat. 'Barak Allah fik' ('may God bless you'), he said.

'I tell him,' Father Nadheer explained to me, 'that the Caliph Omar has said the Muslim is allowed to pray in the Christian house.'

Abdullah knew this, and was moved that the priest did so too, and he returned with us to the church.

*

Abdullah had his workshop in Amiriya, a suburb to the west of al-Qudra. It was located in a poor neighbourhood, in a small market area next to the local mosque. Some waste ground with a rusting slide separated the two institutions. There was usually a bunch of pre-schoolers, barefoot and gloriously filthy, flying around this mud patch, and usually when they saw us coming they'd run up. '*Sudani akal al-lahma wa tarakni*' ('the Sudanese ate the meat and left me behind').

Almost every time we passed a group of children this rhyme would be chanted. Abdullah was used to it and just smiled.

The market consisted of two rows of facing retail outlets. They were housed in long, low, brick constructions, rather like suburban lock-up garages with windows. The shops included a barber, two butchers, a sweet shop, a grocer and a seller of pharmaceutical products. There were always people milling about, though business for all the retailers was slow.

Abdullah's premises was stacked with fridges: a narrow passage between them led to a small workbench at the rear. His tools hung on nails above this, and there was a small stove for tea and boiling rice. We went there a few times a week to see if any work was to be done. The cooler months were the lax period, so there was rarely much on. There would be a note slipped under the metal shutter if there was a job, or sometimes a fridge would have been left outside. In that case he would pull on his overalls and see to it while we were there.

People normally paid Abdullah for his work when it was done. Occasionally a family might not be able to pay straight away and he would trust them to do so later – and invariably they did. More often he would be asked to accept a sum less than was agreed, and he usually did. It rarely happened that someone tried to cheat him, although when he had first started out he had been the victim of a brazen dishonesty. He recalled the story for me one morning as we did a bit of tidying.

Not long after he came to Amiriya a man on a bicycle trolley called looking for work. It was summer, and Abdullah had been thinking about employing an assistant, so he gave him a start. The man's job was to pick up and return fridges, and to collect payment when they were returned.

Sometimes, when he came to the shop in the evenings, he'd say to Abdullah that so and so had only 10,000 dinars and had asked to be relieved of the balance, and Abdullah would shrug his shoulders and think nothing more of it.

One day a brother of a customer happened to be chatting outside the shop when the assistant was ticking off accounts. He overheard the man say that his brother had been 3,000 dinars short, and had asked to be excused the debt, 'God have mercy on him.'

When the assistant had gone, this man went to Abdullah and told him that neither he nor anyone else in his family had ever failed to pay an amount they owed. 'By God!' he swore.

'This man who worked for me was Shia,' said Abdullah, continuing the story as we carted the shell of a dead fridge to the dump beside the playground. The Shia, he explained, had an especial devotion to the sons of Ali, Hussein and Abbas, who had been martyred at the battle of Kerbala.

'I say to him the next day, "Abu-Ali, why you didn't give to me all of the money you take yesterday?"'

The man swore that he had. '*Wallah!*'

They were sitting on the floor of the shop drinking tea. Abdullah refilled their glasses. '*Wallah wa Hussein?*'

'By God and by Hussein!' replied the man.

Abdullah looked at him. '*Wallah wa Abbas?*'

This time there was no reply. The man left and came back later that day with the 3,000 dinars he had kept.

'You see,' explained Abdullah, 'the Shia might swear a lie by God – or even Hussein, who may also forgive, but never by Abbas.'

*

Time seemed to fly in Baghdad, and the weeks felt like days. I would have stayed on longer were it not for the news I got from home in late November. The day before my birthday we went to a telex bureau in Bab al-Shargi, run by a friend of Abdullah's. It was actually just a small office on a side street and there was only one telephone. The owner insisted that I come to the head of the queue.

My sister answered, and I told her about the last part of my journey, and then asked to speak to my mother. She wasn't there; she had gone into hospital for an operation on her stomach. It wasn't serious, my sister said, and they expected her home at the weekend. The news none the less came as a shock to me. She had never had health problems before, and was in as good form as she'd ever been when I left in May.

'The mother is the most important,' Abdullah said, as we walked back up to Sadoun Street. We hailed a taxi and drove out to al-Qudra without any further words.

Over the next days I began to think about what I was going to do. I hadn't considered the question for some time, but the news focused my mind. There were two choices: either I go back to Khandari and pick up the trail of the retreating Ten Thousand, or I return home. In the circumstances the latter course seemed the best. Even though the operation was a minor one, my mother was lightly built; even a cold could waylay her for a week. I accordingly made enquires about onward passage but on Abdullah's advice decided to wait until the weekend before finalizing anything.

On the Sunday we returned to Bab al-Shargi. I remember listening to the ring tone, going on and on, and then my mother's voice, a bit frail, but hers. 'Well, how are you? How are the people?'

I replied with my own questions and she said she'd been in hospital for a few days and everything was fine. I was relieved, and soon lost in a summary of everything that had happened since we had last spoken in Aleppo. She was a bit surprised when I ended on the plain, not at Babylon. I explained that the Greeks had never actually got there, and that I was only really using it as a reference point. She said that that cleared it up, but I knew from her tone that she wasn't convinced. My mother always said a person should finish what they started.

On the way back to the house I realized that she was right. Sometimes loved ones can see better than we do the fate that stalks us.

If nothing else, in taking those final steps to Babylon, I would dispel the spectre of Sisyphos.

I said to Abdullah in the taxi that I might go as far as Babylon, which he agreed would be a good thing to do before considering more ambitious plans.

24

Babylon

Endings

How many miles to Babylon?
Three score miles and ten.
Can I get there by candle-light?
Yes, and back again.

Nursery rhyme

That evening we went to see Nassir and asked if he'd take us to the area south of Khandari, so that I could have a look at possible sites for the battle, and start off on the last leg of my walk to Babylon. He arrived early the next morning with the car gleaming, and the three of us set off.

We were cruising along the airport road when the engine stalled. It backfired a couple of times and we coasted to a halt on the hard shoulder. Nassir thought it was the electrics but half an hour splicing wires failed to restart her and we had to hail a taxi.

The orange and white Toyota was several steps down from the Volvo. The suspension on the left side was shot, as was fourth gear, and it looked as if the bearings on the steering mechanism hadn't long to go: there was an excessive amount of play in the wheel, and the shaft jerked like a demon if the driver braked hard.

We continued south as far as Yousoufiya, a distance of about 20 kilometres, before turning off the highway to go south-west towards Abu-Hubbah, another 10 kilometres. This was the location of ancient Sippar, an important Babylonian city from very early times. Reviewing the maps and battle diagrams the night before, it had seemed to me that Sippar would likely have been noticed by Xenophon had the army passed the city on their way to battle. It was around 65 kilometres from Babylon, about the same distance he said the site of the battle was from the city; this suggests that the armies may have clashed just before Sippar. However there is a question about whether or not the summary figures in the *Anabasis* are Xenophon's. Those referred to here (II.2.6) are regarded as an interpolation by editors, which is not to say that they are not accurate, although the other available source, Plutarch/Ktesias, has the battlefield 90 kilometres from Babylon.

We went first to the Euphrates, a handful of winding kilometres past the site. The driver waited at the bridge while we made an excursion inland on foot. It had been raining hard the day before so it was heavy going along a waterlogged track. We soon left this and plodded north-west across tilled land.

The weather was now much cooler than it had been even a week before. A month before, when I had stopped at Khandari, the days were still hot, albeit the nights were becoming cool. By then I was already quite sure that Cyrus and his men had not fought in September but in November.

My first doubts about the conventional September battle date came at Balasem, a village beyond Raqqa on the Syrian Euphrates. It was then mid-September, the time when the river was at its lowest, as it must have been when the army crossed the Euphrates further upstream at Thapsakos. In the crossing, Xenophon reported not a man was wetted above the chest, and he added that the people of Thapsakos had never known this to be possible.

On 15 October it had started to rain. On that night, as I had noted in my diary, there had been several showers, but since then the rainfall had been infrequent, and characterized by heavy downpours, such as the one the previous day in Baghdad. During *Anabasis* 22, the long march through the Iraqi desert, Xenophon described an incident involving wagons that had become stuck in a defile.

Cyrus halted with his table-companions and ordered Glous and Pigres to take a detachment of native troops to help in getting the wagons out of the mud; when he thought they were being tardy, he looked angry and ordered the most important Persians in his company to give a hand with the wagons. And then one might have beheld a sample of good discipline. Wherever they happened to be standing, they threw off their purple cloaks, and rushed forward as though in a race, down a very steep hill ... and leaping at once with all their finery into the mud, they lifted the wagons on to dry ground quicker than anyone would have thought possible.

My guess was that the baggage train had become stuck in a wadi which had recently received the spill off from heavy rains; as there is no rain in Mesopotamia in the summer months, never in fact until October, it seems evident that the incident took place during that month at the earliest.

A later passage also invites dating. Encamped on the Babylonian plain after the battle, the men found dates in abundance in the villages. The date harvest begins in October, and it would be entirely consistent with the present hypothesis to find quantities of them at hand the following month. Moreover, it is probable that Cyrus timed his march to coincide with the ripening of the grain harvest in summer; by starting in early March, as in the traditional framework, he would already have been in Mesopotamia when this was only beginning.

Finally, and coming full circle, there is the weather. Xenophon famously describes the awesome appearance of the King's army on the plain: rising dust and bronze flashing in the sun. To those unfamiliar with this region, this must have been confirmation that the clash had occurred late summer, as it does in the 1850 itinerary of Koch and most subsequent commentators. But the heat on the plains here is intense well into autumn. Such days as immortalized by Xenophon are the norm in October, and not unusual in November.

Ending our cross-country jaunt at a disused shed, we climbed up onto the corrugated roof and surveyed the surrounding plain. Ploughed furrows of coarse soil extended away in all directions, an occasional curtain of trees interrupting the flat. Any of these fields, I remarked to Abdullah and Nassir, could have been the location of one or more of the duels that were fought on that long day in autumn 401. Xenophon's account indeed would have skirmishes over an area of up to 25 square kilometres.

Something struck me while we were on the roof. Given that the Mesopotamian plains are practically featureless, might the *lofos*, 'hill', to which Artaxerxes is said to have been taken after he was wounded by Cyrus, have been a *tell* at Sippar? Could this remarkable feature, noted by Xenophon on the Greek and Ktesias on the Persian side, have been a ziggurat from one of its earlier periods?

Xenophon noted as well that there was a settlement beneath it; he called it a village but in the heat of battle he may not have appreciated its dimensions. It would have made sense for the King to be taken to a place where more substantial care was at hand, as it would have been in Sippar, still then an important city.

The battle for the empire seems to have been decided before even the first arrow was shot, the critical moment being the Greek decision to maintain the river as their flank. Cyrus was no doubt correct to assert that the enemy's centre was the key objective, but Klearkhos was also right in seeing that a charge across the field would have been a potentially fatal manoeuvre. Had the enemy got in behind them, they could have made effective use of their superiority in numbers.

There is a compelling argument that Tissaphernes, the most able of the King's men, had in fact planned to take the Greeks out of the equation. He knew better than anyone else that they were Cyrus' most potent weapon – his best, his only chance of victory. The *hoplite* phalanxes were the tanks of the ancient battlefield. They were unstoppable, and flexible, and had an awesome destructive capacity. Had they managed to engage the centre, even covered as it was by the stoutest of the Persian guard, the King would have been in grave peril. However, he was positioned so far away that had the Greeks marched obliquely across their own left, an attack by cavalry could have been mounted in their rear, an action that would have disrupted, if not disabled the fighting machine. This was what Klearkhos had feared. The argument is that Tissaphernes had arranged the King's line to achieve this effect, hoping that instead of targeting Artaxerxes, the Greeks would come on straight against him, and so might be lured out of the theatre.

In support of this view is the fact that given defeating (or neutralizing) the Greeks had to be his key objective, the King did not concentrate his superior forces (Persian infantry; the scythed chariots) against this element.

Again when Tissaphernes confronted the Greeks for the second time (Xenophon's description of this engagement is confused), it is apparent that his men were ordered to withdraw rather than meet the Greek phalanxes. They were going nowhere, and there was no point in sacrificing strength to slow them.

Whatever of the tactics on the King's side, it is clear that Cyrus was let down by his Greek mercenaries, and implicitly by Klearkhos as their commander. Plutarch, who is among the most prescient of the ancient critics, concludes: 'if he [Klearkhos] sought safety above everything else, and made it his chief object to avoid losses, it had been best for him to stay at home … The caution of Klearkhos rather than the temerity of Cyrus must be held responsible for the ruin of the expedition.'

*

Sippar looked distinctly dreary, a warren of mud-brick walls and shallow trenches extending over a wide area. There was no clue that for millennia this had been one of the most important cities in Mesopotamia. Founded nearly 6,000 years ago, at its height it was a pre-eminent centre for the worship of the sun god, and it prospered as a commercial hub right up to the Christian era. The temple of the sun god, Shamash, has been identified by excavators, as have the quarters of virgins who were dedicated to his worship. Among the artefacts unearthed so far are caches of Neo-Babylonian literary texts. These, written in cuneiform on clay tablets, were discovered in a rack of pigeonholes – an ancient library. There are two ziggurats at Sippar, one quite possibly the 'hill' on which Artaxerxes recovered from his wound.

Orientation in the huge site is problematic without a survey map. Probably the area we drove into had been the religious quarter. Narrow passages ran between high walls which defined dozens of compact rooms. Alternatively, it may have been a part of the merchant district, and these may have been secure storage rooms for valuable goods.

We climbed onto one of the walls for a better view. There was no sign of any ziggurats, and I thought they might have been situated away to the north. We were looking in this direction when, without any warning, the wall gave beneath us. I could feel my feet slipping, and there was a sensation of flight before a jarring landing. Everybody got up quickly, though Abdullah had hurt his knee and we had to help him back to the car. It must have been, I thought as we drove off, that the rain had severely weakened the retaining wall.

We stopped at a tea stall outside Yousoufiya and I prepared to leave for Babylon. I left Ainsworth and my notes in the car, filling the space in my daypack with fruit and some biscuits. Abdullah was disappointed that he wasn't able to come; Nassir offered to accompany me in his place, but I was content to be making this leg on my own. We all shook hands. 'I'll see you tomorrow.'

'*Inshallah.*'

*

The highway, which connected the upper and lower parts of the flood plain, was a raging axis of traffic. A pall of low-grade fuel hung over it, and bits of external car parts and the occasional corpse of a dead dog littered the hard shoulders. The road consisted of two broad lanes separated by a strip of waste ground. Wilting trees in this belt acted as crash barriers for the fast lanes. Settlement was almost continuous, be it villages set back from the highway or small towns that were bisected by it. As it was becoming dark I entered the outskirts of one of these. There was a factory on the other side of the highway to which I didn't pay much attention until an approaching truck laden with corn accelerated past its entrance. A mass of young men who had been loitering at the gate raced after it. Sandals dropped off and *shamags* unravelled as the posse gave pursuit. One by one they fell away, leaving just two. Then the truck slowed and these two leaped onto the back. It turned around and came back up to the factory with the two champions triumphant on the mountain of corn. I figured then that they must have won the jobs of unloading the truck, and was in no doubt that I had entered the impoverished Shia belt.

Beyond the town I stopped at a roadside stall. Cartons of juice, local cigarettes, and a solitary box of mini-sized Mars bars were all that was on sale. The stallholder thought it was too late to be out and invited me to stay at his home. We were about to leave when a youth hurried up and extended the same invitation. He had the sort of look on his face that couldn't be refused, and noticing this as well, the man said he didn't mind if I went with him.

We walked a short way along the highway and then turned right onto a path that ran beside a trickling sewer. There was a cluster of mud huts at the end and the inhabitants spilled out as Ahmed shouted the news of a guest. Several followed us into the guest room of his home. Everyone took off their footwear and took a place on one of the reed mats laid out on the lumpy earthen floor. An infant who had been playing in a corner was snatched away by its mother and taken to a room behind. An older child was allowed to stay, and she continued what she had been doing, trying to catch ants with her fingers. Each time she got one she laughed and threw it back onto the ground. Ahmed smiled, and when she caught a big one, I exchanged it for a small Mars bar.

The walls of the room were plastered and appeared to be dark green in the dull light. There were no windows, and no furniture at all. I had the sense of being in a tent made of mud bricks.

Although he was only twenty, Ahmed already had four children, and was the head of an extended family. His father, whose portrait hung on the wall beside one of Imam Ali, had been killed in the Gulf War in 1986. Abdullah had said to me once that Saddam Hussein had packed his front lines with the Shia, seeing it as a useful way to control their numbers.

A yard chicken was killed for dinner. A few of Ahmed's uncles joined us after the meal and we drank tea late into the evening. Before we turned in for sleep, I gave my host a copy of Cyrus' route and, perhaps misunderstanding the journey, he tacked it on the wall beside Imam Ali.

I left before dawn. Ahmed walked with me until the sun peeped above the plain. We waved one another goodbye: '*Ma'a salaama.*'

For the first hours the road was comparatively calm; when it became busier, where I could I diverted onto canal tracks, trading the danger of being run over for the risk of being harassed by a local. However it became apparent that they weren't as security conscious here as in the Anbar. If somebody saw me passing their door they tended to wave instead of running after me.

With my progress south agriculture became more pronounced. Lazy palm groves and ploughed fields stretched away on either side. A remarkable number of *tells* were also visible, a testament to the shifting but constant presence of civilization. Any one of them, I reflected, could have been the hill to which Xenophon referred in his text.

Shortly after midday I left the highway to join a long ceremonial way. Car parks and ample picnic areas dominated the vast hinterland of the site. Saddam greeted arrivals. I was the only one and doffed my sun hat as I passed. His works were already visible on distant hilltops. Babylon itself was rebuilt by him in his own image. Even the bricks in the pala-tial warehouses bear the stamp of his name: the Nebuchadnezzar of Ouja.

A guard at a kiosk on the intersection of the main avenue and a narrower, tree-lined one, read my paper and insisted that I come in for tea. He telephoned the site director who presently arrived in his car. I explained that I had been following the route of Xenophon. He looked vacant for a few moments, and then recovered himself. 'Yes, he is also known as Arrian.'

They escorted me down the Processional Way towards the Ishtar Gate. This had been the main entrance to the palace complex, which included the royal apartments, the Temple of Marduk (Bel) and the Tower of Babel. The Germans uncovered the gate in 1899 – a magnificent 14-metre-high cobalt blue archway, decorated with pictures of dragons and bulls. Brick by brick they dismantled it and loaded the treasure onto railway skips bound for Berlin. A replica has been erected in its place, but belongs to a Disney theme park rather than an archaeological site.

I thanked them for accompanying me and said I would take a minute on my own. The gate dog sauntered over for a pat and I gave him a packet of crushed biscuits. When he had finished, we strolled together through the archway, and beheld the city of Babylon.

Summary of the Retreat

The first concern of the King was to get the Greeks out of Mesopotamia. They were still a formidable fighting force, and any action in the heartland was inherently risky. At the same time he was perturbed that a foreign force had invaded his lands, and was anxious to punish them, also considering that their destruction would be a warning to others not to follow. He left the matter to Tissaphernes.

It was more than twenty days after the truce was agreed that he returned to the Greek encampments north of Kounaxa. In this period they'd had enough time to reflect on the seriousness of their predicament, and on how difficult it would be to return home without the assistance of the Persians. They had also become suspicious of Tissaphernes' true intent, and were constantly on guard against an attack. Keeping a safe distance behind, they followed his army – he was bound for Sardis as the new satrap – up along the Tigris towards the junction of the Royal Road. Here they would cross the river and head west for Asia Minor. But before they came to the junction, at the place where the Tigris and Greater Zab Rivers meet, Tissaphernes struck. Having summoned the Greek generals to a meeting in his tent, ostensibly to discuss ways of easing the mounting tension between the two sides, he had them seized and executed.

At this desperate time for the Greeks, Xenophon emerged from their ranks as a leader. That night, as they huddled with their arms on the plain, he had a dream in which his father's house was struck by lightning. As it blazed, he awoke in a fever and concluded that the dream meant they were all trapped, and had to flee their station if they weren't to be consumed by the wrath of the King. Under his inspired guidance, the army forded the Zab and fended off repeated enemy forays in the fields beyond. The Persians harried them as far as the road junction, forcing them up into the mountains of Kurdistan. Here Tissaphernes broke off his pursuit, his aim achieved and confident that the Greeks would not have an easy passage home this way.

The Greeks were at once set upon by the Kardoukhoi (ancestors of the Kurds), a fearsome tribe armed with lethal 2-metre longbows. This was the first time they had come up against weaponry that could penetrate their armour. A critical move at this point was the decision to streamline the army: the baggage animals and slaves were slowing progress and tying up fighting capacity, and those carrying non-essential equipment were set free.

It still took the army a week to effect an exit from the Kardoukhian mountains. In the fighting many of the bravest soldiers were killed, among them Leonymos of Sparta, Basias the Arcadian, Cephisodoros the Athenian and Archagoras of Argos.

At almost every turn thereafter the Greeks were attacked by native tribes: the Taokhoi, Khalybes, Scytheni, Makrones and Colchians. These had never been subject to any outside power, and were affronted by the appearance of armed foreigners in their territories.

There were other problems too: they lost their way; and there was the weather, the bitter Armenian winter. Hundreds perished in the snow, and as many were blinded and lost fingers and toes to frostbite.

Then one day in spring 400, when the army had become a slow-moving ghost train, something extraordinary happened. A guide had sworn on his life that within five days he would take them to a place from where they would see the Euxine (the Black Sea), which had been their goal since leaving the Kardoukhian mountains four months previously. Xenophon recalled what happened in his account:

On the fifth day they came to the mountain, and the name of it was Thekhes. When the men who were in the front had mounted the height, and looked down upon the sea, a great shout went up. And when Xenophon and the rearguard heard it, they thought that other enemies were attacking in the front, for enemies were also following behind them from the district that was in flames, the rearguard having killed some of them and captured others by setting an ambush, and they had also taken about twenty wicker shields covered with raw ox-hides. But as the noise kept getting louder and nearer, it appeared to Xenophon that it must be something of great moment. So mounting his horse, and taking with him

Lykios and the cavalry, he hastened ahead to give aid; and presently they heard the soldiers shouting, *The Sea! The Sea!*, and cheering one another on. Then all the troops of the rearguard broke into a run, and the pack animals and horses were driven along at full speed. And when they had all reached the top, the men embraced one another, and their captains and generals, with tears in their eyes.

The army spent a month in the Black Sea port of Trapezous, a Greek colony. Having sacrificed to the gods and held athletic games to celebrate their safe passage, they waited for ships to take them home. But even with piracy they could not secure enough vessels to take them all, and the majority had to recommence the journey on foot. Their destination now was Byzantium, the city at the end of the continent.

Without the permanent threat of destruction by either enemies or the elements hanging over them, the character of the army underwent a marked change. The discipline and camaraderie which had seen the men through the trials of the march downcountry were superseded by opportunism and factionalism. As they moved closer to the straits, so their desire for booty increased, for nobody wanted to arrive home empty-handed.

At Herakleia, a colony of the Megarians close to Byzantium, the soldiers argued and divided into three groups. The Arcadians and Akhaians, 4,500 *hoplites* in all, proceeded by sea to Kalpe, the next station. A second group under Xeirosophos, numbering 2,100 men, marched along the coast, while a third contingent, 2,000 strong, went across country with Xenophon. They were reunited in Kalpe, but again fell to arguing. Finally, having been promised a hero's reception at their journey's end by the Spartans, in the late summer of 400 they set off together on the last stage.

William Ainsworth wrote:

After a long stay and several disasters caused by the restlessness of the Greeks, they started from Kalpe, marching through Bithynia six days to Khrysopolis, the 'golden city' – the modern Uskudar or Scutari, opposite to Constantinople ... The retreat of the Ten Thousand may be said to have ended at this point, for the kind of business which they became engaged in after crossing the Bosphoros, had nothing to do with that in which they were originally taken from their homes by the ambition of Cyrus.

Many of the soldiers, including Xenophon, were subsequently recruited by Sparta to fight against Tissaphernes. Upon his return to Sardis, he had demanded the submission of all the Greek cities on the coast and, fearful of his wrath – for they had supported Cyrus in his rebellion – they had appealed to the Lakedaimonians for protection. Following its victory over Athens in the Peloponnesian War, Sparta was the *de facto* guardian of Greek interests.

Initially the Greeks enjoyed success, and in 395 King Agesilaus surprised Tissaphernes near Sardis and defeated his army. He escaped, but his days were numbered. Parysatis, who blamed him for Cyrus' death, saw her chance for revenge. Her agents found him in a bathtub in Kolossai and cracked open his skull with an axe.

Sparta was not able to build on its victory over the Satrap, and was ultimately ground down by the greater power of the King. Artaxerxes, who was to reign for forty-five years – the longest of any Achaemenid king – began to fund their enemies at home, and eventually they lost their empire.

For the Ten Thousand the new wars were not so unfortunate. They were paid by Sparta at the same rate as Cyrus had started them off on, and the war between the two sides kept them employed for years.

At some time in 399, while he was fighting in Ionia, Xenophon received word that he had been banished from Athens for ever by a decree of the *demos*. The precise reasons are not known, but probably his links with Sparta and his prior friendship with the dead Socrates were the main factors. If anything this act of spite would have confirmed his conviction that his country was in the hands of dilettantes.

He remained in Spartan service for the next ten years, and was rewarded with an estate near Olympia, the site of the Games. He had in the meantime married, and he and his wife raised two sons, Gryllos and Diodoros, in these idyllic surroundings. Xenophon devoted his energies in retirement to writing. Over twenty years he produced works on subjects ranging from hunting to history. He probably wrote the *Anabasis* quite late, in the 370s, perhaps stirred into doing so by his portrayal in the expedition by other writers.

In 371 Sparta was defeated by Thebes in a critical battle at Leuctra, and Xenophon was forced to evacuate his estate. He was now a highly respected figure in Greece, and the Athenians felt obliged to allow him return to his city. Some say he did, others that he refused to go there, and lived out his final years in Corinth.

*

After I had returned from Babylon, I started to follow the army's route up along the Tigris. In late December I entered Iraqi Kurdistan, but was refused exit by the Turks on the other side. The advice given to me by a senior official in Dohuk, a Dr Shawqat, was that I should 'go back to Saddam. He will help.' It was not a course that appealed to me at all, but as his half-hearted attempt to get me into Syria had failed, I had little choice. In the event, he was right, the Ba'athists did help me. A letter from the Governor in Mosul enabled me to leave the country via an official crossing into Syria north-west of the city. From there I made my way around to the Habur gate in Turkey.

Travelling in the south-east of Turkey was different from the way it had been in the west. Early on, a Kurdish man who fed me in his house crossed his wrists when I asked about the life. He meant that it was like being in a prison, and in my experience it did prove to be something like this. There wasn't a day when the Jandarma (paramilitary police) didn't stop and question me about my purpose, and about whom I had spoken to along the road. The most frustrating thing was their attempts to prevent me having any contact with local people. Whenever I came to a village, they would invariably arrive shortly after and insist that I leave.

What they suspected me of varied according to location. Initially, in the Kurdish region, I was taken to be sympathic to their independence cause; crossing into the historic Armenian lands around Muş, they believed that I was rooting for some evidence of the former population; and then finally in the eastern Black Sea region, I was suspected of being a 'Pontic Revivalist' (a person, I believe, who shows more than a passing interest in the ancient cultures of the shore).

After three weeks in the Black Sea port of Trabzon (Trapezous), I continued my journey, walking west along the coast. At Sinope, as the Greeks had done, I took a ship, mine stopping at Zonguldak, an industrial city 40 kilometres before ancient Herakleia. Not far from there I spoke to my mother. It was not a remarkable conversation: we talked about a letter I had sent to a friend, which hadn't yet arrived. She was to get back to me when it came.

I never heard from her again. A week later my father rang and said she was in hospital. It was the same problem she'd had with her stomach he said; it wasn't serious, but he said I should consider coming home when I got to Istanbul. My father was a prudent man, he always did things the right way, and though his report worried me, I did not read anything more into the situation than this.

He rang again two days later and said she was dying. I couldn't believe it. I put down the phone and started to cry.

We spoke again later that night and I told him I had made a decision to finish the journey. I was 110 kilometres from Istanbul, and would be there within two days. At 4 a.m. I set off for my destination.

On the morning of 10 July I came in sight of the Bosphoros, that magical sliver of water dividing the great continents. I met it at Uskudar, and walked along the waterfront to a small Ottoman mosque. There were fishermen standing on the edge of the promenade, and youths flinging themselves into the choppy waters. I took off my pack and sat down. In the circumstances it was hard to appreciate the end, but the Bosphoros is a natural ender of journeys, and the reality that mine was over slowly sank in.

Two days later I was at my mother's side. She had been transferred to the local hospice, and had slipped into unconsciousness. They were no longer giving her liquids, only strong doses of morphine to numb the pain. When the cancer was diagnosed the previous autumn, she had insisted that nobody was to be informed, least of all me. 'It was her way,' my father said.

At 3 p.m. on 15 July she passed away. I was alone with her in the room at the time. The nurse said she was ready to go and had left to advise my sister, who was in the hospice garden. I told them when they came in that like everything else in her life, her leaving of it had been graceful.

Epilogue

Seeing the great destructive force gathering on Iraq's doorstep in January 2003, I felt compelled to return. I wanted to see Abdullah in Baghdad, and to return if I could to Jubbah, the island in the Euphrates where I had stayed on the first part of my trek through the country. I knew that finding a reason to go back that would satisfy the authorities would be difficult, so I told them I wanted to travel through the Anbar with a camera to film the places I had visited on my original journey. They probably should have said it wasn't the right time to do this, but the Ba'ath Party always had a peculiar way of operating. The maintenance of a cool façade in even the most testing of situations was the hallmark of their leadership.

In Baghdad I went straight to al-Qudra. Abdullah knew I was coming, but he hadn't told me he had moved. His former residence on Embassy Street had since been finished, and was scarcely recognizable. A high wall and metal gates guarded an exterior of pretentious columns and stained glass windows.

I was looking at it, bags in hand, when a voice greeted me. In the darkness I couldn't see his face, but I knew from the accent it was Abduljalil. His eyes suddenly appeared in front of me and his giant arms embraced me: 'Ahlan, Ahlan.' He took my bags and I followed him inside. Although the house was finished, the owner had retained him, building a guardhouse in the front yard. This might better be described as a kennel: his bed took up its full length and half the width, and it wasn't tall enough to allow a man to stand up straight. A television and electric heater were his luxuries. The doctor had squeezed in a toilet between the hut and the perimeter wall, and a hose supplied water. Abduljalil's job now was to open the gates for the owner when he blew his horn.

Abdullah's situation could hardly have been more different. He was just around the corner in an elaborate mansion set in spacious grounds. Spotlights lit the façade and the whir of garden sprinklers was audible on the street. The house belonged to a man called Ali Jabir, a metal dealer from Najaf. Ali, I learned, had several similar properties around the city. It seemed that he had planned to live in each one, but his wife was fussy and always complained about something, so he would build another. (Abdullah suspected that she just didn't want to leave their home in Najaf.) Her problem with this one was noise from the school next door, and when the children started singing eulogies to Saddam at 8 a.m., it was hard not to sympathize. Unlike the doctor, Ali treated his guard well. Abdullah had a decent allowance, and if he needed anything, Ali would go out of his way to help.

When we entered the house Abdullah was praying. He heard the heavy wooden door creak and turned on his mat. '*Mashallah!*'

We greeted each other in the Sudanese manner: right hands slap the shoulders, a bear hug, and a jarring handshake.

'*Allah-bel-kher.*'

'*Allah-bel-kher.*'

'*Allah-bel-kher.*'

'I was worried something happened,' Abdullah confided, as he filled glasses with steaming tea. 'We were expecting you before.' I had said on the phone from Amman the previous day that I'd be in Baghdad around nine, but didn't make clear I meant the evening.

The living room was huge, and empty except for a giant air-conditioner fitted into the wall at the school end. Abdullah had made his home in the anteroom adjoining it. There were two reed mats on the floor, a single-bar heater – which was always on and always had a teapot on the metal grid – a telephone and a radio without a casing. A set of open shelves that looked onto the entrance hall contained his possessions, which were few: a small pile of folded clothes, some books, a photo album and a manila folder with documents and letters. He showed me the ones I had written in the time since we had last seen each other. They had been annotated in Arabic and had the stamp of the censor.

Out in the hall he kept his shoes and gardening tools. A large stick bristling with nails at one end stood out among the line of hoes and spades. I pointed at it and Abdullah smiled. 'This is my wheepon of mass destruction.'

There were five other rooms on the ground floor, together with a kitchen and a storage area. A small yard led off the kitchen, and on the wall Abdullah had painted a life-sized mural of a jungle. There were trees and wild plants and a river fading into a distant Sudanese horizon.

Upstairs there were six bedrooms. All the fittings – lights, basins, sockets – were in place: Ali, it seemed, had tried to make it as hard as possible for his wife to find fault.

Above this there was a rooftop balcony that offered fine views of the Karkh skyline. The most prominent features were the needle-shaped Saddam Tower, and to the west of this the skeleton of the Saddam Great Mosque, conceived as the largest in the world. Local landmarks included the flag of the Palestinian Embassy, a Coca-Cola factory, and the minarets of several mosques. The Ftkhans' house was a stone's throw away on the south side, although it was obscured by larger homes in between. It was now empty. Firas was back in Jubbah and Kemal was in the army. Faisal, who had a dispensation from military service because of his asthma, was staying with an uncle in Kadhimiya.

The story was that Firas had rented the house for a month to a group of Jordanian students, who raised hell on the street and were ordered out by the neighbours. Things came to a head when one night they cavorted drunk on the lawn and propositioned two passing girls. A few days later, one of them was killed in a car crash. He had gone for more liquor and smashed into a lamp post near Nafaq-a-Shorta. His head had been crushed to pulp. Abdullah considered this must have been divine punishment.

I was just enquiring after him when Nassir's voice sounded in the hallway. He stuck his head through one of the open shelf compartments and grinned. 'Salaam alaykum.' A song to the moon followed, and then one to Abu-Alwaffa (Saddam), the 'father of brave people'.

In Baghdad I was able to move about fairly freely. Abdullah had informed the local Party secretary that I was staying in the house, that I had numerous papers, and that I was a friend of Farouq Salloum (a junior minister). All of this was somewhat exaggerated, so we thought that before I went to Jubbah, I should go to see Farouq.

We had met by chance two years before at the beginning of the second part of my journey. I had begun this on a one-step-at-a-time basis, having decided that I would stop if I ran into any major problems. I had left the city boundary, and was heading north along the Mosul highway when he pulled alongside and offered me a lift. It was night and he said there might be a problem up ahead at a secure zone.

I was feeling disorientated, a bit overwhelmed by the length of the road in front of me, and just got into the car. We drove onto a flyover and turned back into the city. At his home we drank beer and his wife cooked a savoury meal. He was taken by my journey, and was sympathetic to the difficulties I had had in the Anbar. He was confident the downward trek would be easier. 'The people along the Tigris are better educated,' he said. He wrote out the name of his brother in Tikrit, and a man there in the Ba'ath Party who would help me. When I enquired what he did, he told me he was a poet, and for a living he worked in the Government, as the Director-General of Cinema and Theatre. I gathered that he was related to Saddam through his first wife; Lillian, a Christian, was his second. His first marriage had been arranged and for this reason had been difficult to end; the President himself had intervened, hoping to find a way to keep them together, but he loved Lillian. She was a former ballerina, 'the finest,' he said, 'and the most beautiful in the Middle East.'

I spoke to him on the phone before I left Ireland this time, and he was keen to be of assistance. However, he was away when I called at his offices at the Ministry of Information in Baghdad, and they were vague about when he would be returning.

I decided instead to try the Protocol Department to see if I could get a paper out of them. They had been responsible for me on my previous visit, and the manager, Mr Daud, had been reasonably helpful. The department was primarily concerned with foreign media, ensuring that they were guided to the right stories and steered away from anything unsuitable. A corps of 'guides' was always on hand to show them around.

Their lair was quieter than I expected. I had forgotten how uncomfortable the place made me feel. Walking into the ministry itself brought back memories of being late for school. You half expected a prefect to step out from among the scowling faces and jot you into a red book.

A short man rose from a desk at the far end of the open plan office. 'Journalist?'

I said I had a camera.

He snatched a folder off the top of another desk. 'You're the American producer, Longley?'

I corrected the name and he ran through a list, going through it again with his finger. I leaned over to look as well.

Actually it wasn't likely my name would appear on this or any other list, as I was unregistered with the Residency Department, and at the time of my entry at least, Baghdad had not approved my visa application. The Consul in Athens had issued me the stamp under his own name.

'Who is your guide? How can you have camera?'

'It's only a small one,' I said, lifting the bag up for him to see. I could see he was getting bothered so I produced the letter given to me by the embassy. He read this quickly. 'Who do you know here?'

I told him I'd come to see Farouq Salloum, and a young woman standing near one of the desks came forward to say she knew of me. She had read a fax I had sent to Farouq, and he had told her about my journey. The official ran a finger round the inside of his shirt collar and paced off to another room.

She took me into the manager's office, a partitioned space by the door. There was no sign of Daud, and I wondered if he was still around. The woman's name was Fener. I told her this meant 'lighthouse' in Turkish and she giggled. The name suited her. She exuded energy and was strikingly pretty. This was her first job after graduating in French from Baghdad University. She explained that she was attached to Farouq's office but had been sent down here to help out in the current busy period. She started to talk about my trip and I got the impression that Farouq had given her an enthusiastic account.

Our conversation was interrupted by the short man's return. He sat himself behind the desk and started to copy out my letter of introduction. 'You have to go to Antiquities,' he muttered, without looking up.

I gave Fener a book of Seamus Heaney's poems for Farouq, half hoping she would keep it for herself. I left her with a wave at the lift, and spent the next few days wondering what would become of her when this rotten edifice came crashing down.

Father Nadheer was with some families when Abdullah and I called to the church in Shorja. It was a holy day in the Chaldean calendar, Jumat al Moata, the day of remembrance for the dead. On this day people visited the graves of their relatives and handed out sweets to friends and strangers. We declined but they insisted and we slipped back into the main courtyard with handfuls of sticky confectionery. As we chewed, Abu-Ziyad, the caretaker, called out to us from behind a curtain that had been draped over an arch next to the grotto of Our Lady. A pool table had been installed in the alcove, and half a dozen players wielding cues and cigarettes circled it. It was another of Father Nadheer's social initiatives. He explained when he joined us that the idea was to give the youth something to do, and to bring them together in the church.

Another new development in the two years since I'd been there were night classes. Twice a week, on Wednesday and Friday evenings, seminaries came to teach Aramaic and theology. The courses were intended for young adults, but anybody with an interest could attend. Aramaic is the ancient language of the Chaldeans, the language of Christ himself.

We went to his office for coffee. It was as I had remembered it. The photograph of the Patriarch and the President still sat, facing slightly inwards, on top of the filing cabinet; Our Lady of the Sorrows wept by the entrance, and the computer, with a screen saver of Mary, rumbled on a desk under the window.

'Everything is going good, to the best.' Father Nadheer twirled his finger in the air and laughed. 'And what about you, and you Abdullah?' As they spoke, a thought came to my mind: I asked the priest if I could film the church and follow him around for a while? He was agreeable and invited us to come with him the next day to a parish football match in Hilla.

Another acquaintance of ours in Shorja was Hassan Daii, a bookseller. The Bookshop of the Arab Revolution was at the southern end of al-Rasheed Street, in the shadow of the tall post office building. It was founded in 1959 during the heady period that followed the overthrow of the British-installed monarchy a year previously. Ideas of socialism, universal justice, and Arab unity – ideas that had begun to spread among educated Iraqis in the post-war years – enjoyed open expression, and there was a big demand for political literature.*

---

* Out of this milieu the Ba'ath Party emerged. In October 1959 militants from the organization attempted to assassinate the leader of the new military regime. One of the assailants was said to be a young Saddam Hussein. In 1963 the Ba'ath Party succeeded in overthrowing the military, although their initial taste of power was tantalizingly brief. Internal disagreements over policy and grass-roots ill-discipline left them open to a counter-coup by the army. Saddam Hussein recognized these failings, and set about reorganizing the apparat in such a way that it would be ready to hold onto power when the time came. At the core of his design was an armed security body that was able to enforce the will of the Party leadership. He called this *Jihaz al-Haneen*, the Instrument of Yearning.

Adapting to the reality of one-party rule, in the 1970s the shop broadened its lines to include books on culture and the arts. At this time, on any given day of the week, the modest floor space would be busy with browsers. 'In the Arab world there is a saying,' Hassan told me on the first occasion we met: '"Cairo for writers, Beirut for publishers and Baghdad for readers."'

Tastes in the 1980s became by stages more introspective. Poetry and the philosophers began to take up a greater share of shelf space as the reality of the horrific war with Iran hit home. This wasn't a conflict on a distant front: missiles struck the heart of the city every day. Nobody had any idea where or who would be next.

Then in the 1990s, discernible with each passing year, the numbers visiting the shop fell away. Although some of Hassan's regular customers had by now left the country, or had disappeared in the turmoil of war and repression, most simply could not afford to buy books any more. Indeed, to make ends meet, readers began to hawk their collections on street corners and on the fringes of markets, just as people everywhere in the country were forced at this time to pawn other private treasures.

To try to keep afloat himself, Hassan branched into religious books, then stationery, and finally postcards. We used to go there to buy post-cards. One day Hassan appeared at my shoulder at the back of the shop. I had picked up a book on Gertrude Bell, and was looking through the illustrations when he introduced himself and asked if I had read her works. I said I had read one and found it engaging. He was delighted and began to talk about her, and to explain that once the shop had been full of books on people and topics such as this. 'Now this is all there is,' he concluded with a sigh, ranging his hand over the score of literary titles looking out on the rest of the shop.

On the day in February when we dropped by, Hassan was out, and the shop had no customers in it. We bought some postcards and asked the assistant to pass on our regards.

I rang Farouq Salloum's office several times but he was never in. On Abdullah's advice I decided to follow the course originally recommended by the Protocol Department and visit the Antiquities Office. He reckoned that all I had to say was that Protocol had sent me, and they'd give me a paper. What I had from the embassy in Athens was useful, but it would be better, he thought, if I had a document from one of the government departments before going to the Anbar.

The Antiquities Office was in the same complex as the National Museum. I had been there on my last visit, to see the Director, though in the event we had not met. It turned out that Dr Rabiyah was no longer in the post.

I told the secretary I needed a *kitab* and he asked me to write a summary of my itinerary. He pinned this to photocopies of my documents and asked me to wait.

This time the waiting room was empty, but it was still almost an hour before I was summoned for an audience. The secretary led me solemnly across the hall.

The Director's office was vast, adorned with a selection of the finest treasures of Mesopotamia. He was seated behind a desk at the top of the room, a small, grey-haired man with a pockmarked face and a large, hooked nose. I recognized him at once. We had met at the university on my first visit. I didn't know whether this was a good or a bad thing, so I said nothing for the moment and took the seat offered. He proceeded straight to business.

'You want to visit Rawa and Haditha? Where is Jubbah?'

I informed him it was an island in the Euphrates.

He flipped over the pages before him one by one and then looked up at me. 'You can go there.'

I explained that the Information Ministry had sent me here to get a paper to say so.

He scanned his desk. 'I've received no notice from them.'

The last time I had seen Khalil, his desk was one of four in a draughty second-floor office at the university. I noticed then that he was of a nervous disposition, though competent, and not unhelpful. His area of expertise was the ancient culture of Hatra, a well-preserved city of Roman-era buildings in the desert west of Assur. He had written several papers on this subject, and a book on the pre-Islamic sites of the Jezirah. His rise to power seemed to have effected a considerable boost to his self-confidence.

'Do you know who I am?' he asked.

I took a chance. I spoke glowingly about his Jezirah tome, adding that it was a much-prized volume in the archaeology departments of Western universities. He leaned back in his leather chair and peered out through glass doors that led onto a private garden. 'We've met before.'

I said I didn't recall having this honour, and then, after a pause, wondered if he hadn't at one time taught at the university.

'We met two years ago at the faculty. I believe it was in connection with the same subject.' He sat up again and fixed a slanted stare on me. 'Why have you come back now?'

That was that, I thought to myself. He wasn't going to put his name on anything. I replied curtly that what I was doing was written down in front of him.

He repeated his opinion that I could go to Rawa and Haditha, and to Jubbah.

Abdullah took me to the taxi rank at Hilla and gave instructions to the driver. The trip took about three hours. We crossed the Euphrates at Fallujah and continued up the right bank through Ramadi and Heit. I felt a certain nervousness as the car left the main road to coast down the final kilometres to the river. Jubbah had been something special for me. Perhaps I feared now that somehow it had not really been as I remembered.

We slipped through the small mainland settlement and stopped at the bridge. This had suffered some damage over the winter and was uninviting for vehicles. As the driver surveyed the pontoon, I looked toward Jubbah and could see figures hunkered on the bank. They rose and made for the rickety crossing. Halfway across their features came into focus: Aiham, Wasfi, Kareem. I waved at them and they waved back and we started to laugh.

Sheik Thabet had suffered a stroke. He was sitting on a plastic chair in his room. His *shamag* had been hastily arranged, and his walking stick placed in his hands. His eyes stared ahead at the wall; only at a prompting from his wife did he understand that I was beside him. He muttered and she helped him to his feet. I took his hand and embraced him.

He had good and bad days. Sometimes they said his speech was clear and his thoughts lucid; on others, he was unintelligible. Today he was in between. We sat alongside each other on the floor and greeted the visitors who soon began to arrive. Bahar served tea and took constant instructions from his mother. He pretended that he wasn't listening to her but did what she said all the same. It was the first time I had met her. On my first visit she had been working on the date harvest in another village with her daughter. She was a short woman, slight but strong. She wore a black robe, and a matching veil covered her head.

Her face was attractive, if worn, and marked by tattoos that had long ago lost their vitality.

It was apparent that she liked to be at the centre of whatever was happening. This was unusual for an Arab woman; and more unusual again was her active participation in discussions. I had the sense that on these occasions her sons were a bit embarrassed, but they loved her and were tolerant of her eccentricity.

Arab social gatherings have their own protocol. So long as there is room, any male can take part. The children have to stay out of the way and not be heard, although nobody says anything when they laugh or climb onto a lap. Teenagers likewise are not expected to speak. Young men, at a suitable time, can make a comment, usually praising a speaker, or affirming a point by giving an example of something he has seen or heard recently. As age and experience rise, so does the latitude for expressing opinions. The belief seems to be that no wisdom can ever come from young lips, or from those of a woman. Thabet's wife in this broad scheme had acquired something like the status of a young man, even though her contributions, in as much as I could understand, were in the form of opinions rather than passive comments. Nobody looked at her when she spoke, and there were audible grumblings if she went on for too long. I noted that she had the habit of persistently tugging at her veil, like someone pulling the cords on a hood, and I couldn't help thinking that this was a manifestation of some deep-seated desire to tear it off in public.

Sheik Thabet's quarters were full by early evening, and straining with a raw desire for freedom. 'Come America, come Bush!'

'Saddam Hussein – dog!'

'Away with the Ba'ath!'

These exhortations came from the young men, Raed, Kareem, Bahar and Orhan. The older ones were more restrained, but no less clear in their wishes. Bassim, a school teacher in his early thirties, nodded at his peers as he spoke. 'We want to be free. All of us we want to be free. We don't care who frees us.'

I realized as I listened to them that this was what had brought me back to the island. Here on Jubbah they had told me the truth. On my long journey the worst thing that I had witnessed was ordinary men reduced to lying. Men telling me they had no water in their homes, or that the next village was 10 kilometres away when I could see its outline behind them. Only on Jubbah, the small island anchored like a ship in the Middle Euphrates, did they tell me the truth. There was something so powerful in this, indeed, that it pulled me across the continents.

I admit, however, I was taken aback by the enthusiasm of the Jubbans for their liberty. It hadn't been as fervent as this first time round. 'Come America, come Sharon!' a young, angry voice shouted. I looked up. It was Raed, a shaven-headed nephew of Sheik Thabet's. He was a conscript newly deserted from his unit and was being sheltered on the island. His face contorted in hatred every time somebody said the President's name.

In Iraq, under his rule, the name of Saddam Hussein was rarely mentioned. Even in private, as, for example when I discussed politics alone with Abdullah late at night in the folds of the mansion, the closest we came to a direct reference to the leader was 'the Government'. The walls might have ears.

The Jubbans, perhaps with a false sense of security imbued in them by the island, and certainly with a deep sense of their own traditions, and a humanity typified by Thabet's atheism and his lifelong commitment to Communism, had disregarded this wariness and spoken their hearts. I loved them for this, but I was concerned they were going blindly into the night.

Fareed translated for me. I said I knew how much they wanted their freedom, and that I believed in a short time they would be free of Saddam Hussein. They had to be aware none the less that the Americans were not acting out of concern for them. They had many reasons for removing the dictator, but the welfare of the Iraqi people was not one of them.

I reached into my bag to get a book. Carolyn Whitaker, who had made this trip possible, had given me a travelogue on Yemen by one of her authors, Tim Mackintosh-Smith. I thought Fareed, an Arab scholar himself, would like it. I asked him to translate the following passage:

Round the tortuous Musandam Peninsula and into the inner Gulf, all the emirates and shaykhdoms that cling to the shore are the recent and monstrous spawn of Western politicking and the Western thirst for oil. It is only at the head of the Gulf that, with al-Basrah and Baghdad, you come again to an ancient urban society.

I picked up where Tim had left off. It wasn't any more a question of the oil: they had as much of that as they wanted. What they didn't have was control of the Arab spirit. The American Project was to undermine their ancient culture, and to attempt a form of Westernization, such as they had done with those oil enclaves on the Gulf who didn't even deserve a name. Iraq, established as the frontline in their war against the Arabs, was intended to become the base from which they would export this revolution to the neighbouring lands.

I don't know how accurately Fareed translated that, but the response was disappointingly muted. Saffah, who was seated opposite me, put his amber prayer beads on the floor and waited for the chatter to die. He had a black fur *shapka* on his head instead of the *shamags* worn against the cold by the rest.

'Mr Shane,' he said, 'I have not left Jubbah for fifteen years. Fifteen years. We live in prison.' He paused for a moment, looking at me. 'Only the people in Iraq know Saddam Hussein. *Only* the people in Iraq. If the American get rid of him, they are our friends. If they try to take our country, they are our enemy. America come, America go, Iraq free.' He slapped his hands in a finishing gesture and picked up the beads again.

The next morning we sat out on the track. In the absence of proper medication, the doctors had recommended *heliotherapeia* for Mr Thabet. Plastic chairs were lined against a wall which shielded from the cold wind whirling off the river. There was a carpet in front of the chairs and most visitors sat on this to enjoy the sun.

There were a few I hadn't seen before. Kareem's father was one. In appearance he wasn't at all like his Herculean son, but had the same mischievous smile and good-natured manner. On my last visit he had been in prison in Ramadi along with ten other residents of Jubbah. In June 2000 they had been arrested on a charge of conspiracy arising from their formation of a Dervish lodge. For six months they were locked up together in a sweltering cell measuring 2 × 3 metres. Abu-Kareem didn't seem to have been entirely put off by this ordeal, for while he had given up the Dervishes, he was now a student of the Internet. He had managed to get a book on the subject, and was learning English so that he would be able to participate when the time came.

Another of the 'Jubbah 11' was a Colonel Mumtaz. He approached late that morning from the top of the track, a lonely figure dressed in a shabby wool overcoat and grey, wedge-shaped Cossack *shapka*. He was tall and thin and had a dark grey beard. The conversation paused to allow greetings to be made. Bahar got up and the colonel sat down beside me and introduced himself. His face was drawn and he had sad eyes. I asked where he had learned his English. 'In the military school,' he replied. In his own time, he told me he had spent fourteen years in the army, being discharged after the first American attack in 1991. Then he had been in command of a SAM-2 air-defence battery south of Basra. He recalled as though it were yesterday that they were hit twice, once at 2.30 a.m., and again at 11 a.m. One gunner was killed in the first strike but by the second there were only himself and a radio operator *in situ*. He hadn't tried to prevent anyone leaving.

By midday the temperature in the sun trap was high enough to make me uncomfortable. I took off my sweater and wondered how long it would be before beads of sweat rolled down the colonel's face. His heavy hat remained tight on his head, but he showed no sign of discomfort. He kept looking ahead, and he rolled one cigarette after the other. I could see that there was something he wanted to say to me. I had sensed it for a while from his demeanour. Then, after extinguishing a butt between his fingers, he wiped his hands and put both of them around mine. He looked intently into my eyes. 'Saddam Hussein. Saddam Hussein: we want this away from us.' He moved his face closer to mine. 'Take half my family – take this thing away from us.'

I was invited to lunch at Hadji Ftkhan's. Fareed took me across the river to his father's house. The old man was seated on a stool outside his gate, wrapped up in overcoat and *shamag*. He seemed miles away when I greeted him. A smile came briefly over his face and he led us slowly into the yard.

He said little during the meal and retired soon after. I didn't remember him as being much of a one for conversation, but neither had he been so melancholic. It could have been that his thoughts were with his son in the army. He had already lost two in recent years.

His wife, Um-Fareed, brought the tea and sat behind her stepson as it was being served. She was beside herself with worry for Kemal, who was based in Nasiriyah, a town in the south that would be in the line of any American land attack. They were hoping he'd desert, as apparently great numbers were preparing to do, but as I knew myself, Kemal wasn't much of a one for daring enterprise. I pictured him on his own beneath a table holding his head while explosions sounded around him.

'God bless him,' I said to her, 'he'll be all right.'

She was keen to know about Abdullah. Um-Fareed was like a second mother to him. When she went to Baghdad with food for her sons, and to wash and mend their clothes and clean the house, she always invited Abdullah over; and if he wouldn't come (custom requires multiple refusals), she'd send Kemal across with dishes. I gave her an account of his daily routine – morning prayer, work at Amiriya, midday prayer, the market, afternoon prayer, travels in the city, evening prayer, night-time prayers, and visitors: Abduljalil, Nassir, Kadir, Ibrahim, Adam, Hajar, Selima, Mohammed, Belal – and then at her request I described his appearance, and finally offered an opinion on his well being. 'He is in good spirits,' I said.

'God bless him,' said she.

We were headed for Abu-Kareem's, where I had promised to say something about the Internet, when Bahar came running up to us on the pontoon to say that there was a *Ba'athi* at the house waiting to see me.

He was outside on the mat with Aiham. Furat, the Down's syndrome boy, was in the back of his pick-up jumping up and down. The man was from the nearby town of al-Baghdadi and had come, he said, to wish me a pleasant stay. We drank tea and smiled as Furat performed antics in the cab. The official laughed awkwardly, and I got the distinct impression that had he been on his own he'd have been quick to send Furat on his way. When the tea was finished we shook hands and he went away.

At 3.30 in the afternoon, shortly after Jubbah had gone to sleep, I was woken by Bahar. He said the Amn (security) were outside and wanted to see me. I waited for Aiham to be woken and we went out together. In light of his father's incapacity, and his eldest brother's shyness, Aiham had taken up the role of family head. He didn't have the intellect of Saffah, or the practicality of Wasfi, but he was genial and exuded an air of harmlessness. The security officers listened to him explain our relationship, and then drank their tea and took copies of my documents away.

The next morning there was another visit. It wasn't long after breakfast and a group had already gathered in Thabet's room. Someone was trying to pick up the news on the radio; Bahar was pouring a second round of tea. It was me who saw them first (I was standing by the window, checking to see how long was left on a video tape). There were four of them: two in suits, a casually dressed youth who turned out to be a translator and an armed man in uniform. I told the others. They got off the floor and looked out: there was a momentary pause followed by confusion. People fell over one another as outlaws scrambled for the door; of these only Kareem remained behind, and a clip across the ear from Thabet's wife sent him laughing on his way.

The suited men were from military intelligence in Ramadi. Aiham, who was summoned from his bed by Bahar, made the formal introductions. They asked for my route to Iraq.

'Dublin, London, Athens, Amman, Baghdad.'

'*London-mu?*'

Pencils scribbled. Their translator asked how long I had spent there. I lied that it was only a transit stop: I had flown in and out of Heathrow.

'Did you register the camera at the border?' I did. They checked the paper against the machine.

'Do you have a satellite phone?'

'No.'

After some discussion, like a quiz panel divided on an answer, their translator asked if I would show them my bags. I didn't hesitate and emptied the contents on the floor. They glanced at the bits and pieces and returned to their places.

Bahar, shadowed by his mother, came in with a tray of tea and they relaxed further. Bahar crept out like a mouse but his mother sat into a corner and tugged away at her veil as we spoke.

'Are you registered in Baghdad?'

I wasn't, because my visa wasn't fully official, and even if it had passed, I would have been processed into the system and would have had to leave after ten days. The stamp was now weeks expired, and I knew that it was only a matter of time before they pulled me up.

I answered casually as we sipped our tea that I was dealing with Farouq Salloum at the Information Ministry, and wasn't sure of the details of registration. There was more scribbling and the matter was left at that. Aiham escorted the men off the island. A pack of dogs, mortified by their earlier lapse, was waiting at the gate, and he had to stop frequently to ward them off. The room filled again. Bahar shook his fist at the window. Behind him, Saffah shook his head. 'You see we are in prison. No freedom.'

Early on that third afternoon I met Tahreer. He was supervising work on a new house for his son. We had picked up Orhan on his side of the island and were on our way to football when he hailed us from the roof. 'Why haven't you called? I've been waiting.'

He emerged presently onto the lane and greeted me with a handshake and a wide grin. 'Don't worry. I heard you have been busy with visitors. Well, we are happy you have remembered us. Come on. Let's take luncheon.'

The lads looked disappointed, and I was going to ask Tahreer if we could meet later instead, when he invited them along too. We unlaced our boots in his yard and followed him into the room with the chandelier. The only change I noticed after a quick look around was that the portrait of Saddam smoking a cigar in the desert had been taken down, and was resting sideways on the floor. I remembered once Wasfi taking me to their tribe's meeting room on the Shamia. Inside the door a picture of Saddam lay similarly propped against the wall. 'Just in case,' he smiled as we passed by it. Tahreer's image was on death row, an apt metaphor for the leader's impending fate.

He insisted that I return again in the evening for dinner. As soon as I arrived at six he set about starting the fire (I had enquired after it over lunch out of curiosity). Branches were piled into the hearth and then he lit a crumpled newspaper and stuffed it underneath. 'One minute.' He called out to his son. 'Safe!'

He popped his head round the door, and returned presently with what looked liked a bottle of washing-up liquid. Tahreer took it and pointed the nozzle into the hole. An orange flame rose and a sound not unlike a jet filled the room. I stepped back amazed. As it died down he squeezed the bottle again and tongues of fire darted out into the living room.

Tahreer turned to me. 'Well?'

I said it was very impressive.

We went to the dining table and took seats at either end. I had written to him after my journey following the Greeks had finished, and he now sought more detail. I briefed him on work I was doing on the march chronology, and on distances between settlements in the Pontus.

'And what of Charmande? Have you learned anything more?'

I was surprised he had remembered the minor historical mystery after all this time.

'I'm afraid not, but there are lots of places Xenophon mentions which haven't been identified.'

I could see he wasn't displeased. 'I'm quite sure, Mr Shane, that Charmande will not be found opposite Jubbah. Colonel Chesney, I suspect, was misinformed by his guides.'

Our starter had just been taken away when his brother knocked on the window saying I was wanted at the Party office in al-Baghdadi. My host was surprisingly unconcerned. 'Let them wait, we must eat our meal.'

Half an hour later word came that the chief would come himself in the morning before I left for Baghdad. I hadn't planned to leave just yet, but it seemed that the decision had already been taken for me.

In the morning we sat out in the sun and waited for the Ba'athists.

Before they came I had a visitor from Qsariyat, the village upstream on the Jezirah where I had stayed before Jubbah. It was Nasser, the school teacher. He had shaved his beard and looked younger than I remembered. He brought greetings from his brothers, and from Mr Maiad, and the blind fishmonger, Wazir. They were all fine, he reported, although recently Sadoun had run over a child who had crawled under his truck and fallen asleep. He had been badly shaken by the accident.

Nasser wanted me to return with him, and I had hoped to be able to visit, but we explained what was happening.

This time we had plenty of notice of their arrival. The loose planks on the pontoon rattled loudly as their vehicle stumbled across. The gathering began to break up, and I said my goodbyes to those who were leaving.

Saffah came the other way. He looked tired, as he always did, but I noticed a brightness in his eyes. There had been confirmation on the satellite, he told me, that the regime had begun destroying its Samoud missiles. 'Saddam Hussein is finished.' According to Saffah, at the moment he began to destroy this arsenal, it was the beginning of the end. Even if the Americans relented, without these medium-range missiles, he was incapable of defending himself against regional enemies.

He handed me his *tisbah*, a string of thirty-three amber beads. 'For freedom in Iraq.'

Wasfi helped his father to his feet. 'He is sad because he thinks he won't see you again.' I said to tell him that his health was grand, and we'd meet again in a better time.

When I got back to Baghdad that evening there was a small group of people gathered in Abdullah's living room. He looked up at me and I knew there was something wrong. A friend, Adam, was shouting down the telephone. 'Babanusah! Babanusah!'

The others stood up and we greeted one another, without the normal vigour, in the Sudanese manner. Abdullah took my hand and spoke in a low voice. 'My mother is dead.'

We sat down and observed a long silence.

It seems she had died some months before, but his family in Sudan had been afraid to tell him, and that very afternoon he had found out. Another man from Babanusah had been visiting Amiriya, and called at Abdullah's workshop to offer his condolences.

It took hours to get through to the small town in south-western Sudan. Late at night his sister's voice, a continent away, pierced the empty space with grief.

His friends organized a funeral rite the following week. Mourners read verses from the Koran in the guest room of the house. There were several copies, and they each read a particular section, so that the entire holy book was recited in memory of the deceased. So many people came in fact that it was read through twice; and a second sheep had to be killed to feed the latecomers. Sudanese women cooked it in the traditional way, and boys kept the gathering going on sweets and cups of bitter Arabian coffee.

I felt his loss keenly. It wasn't only that he was my friend, he had been with me when I first learned that my mother was ill in November 2000.

Right up to the end the atmosphere in Baghdad was surreally calm. We would see pictures on the TV of demonstrations abroad and half wonder whether it was here they were talking about. There were no apparent preparations being made to defend the capital, and no outward change in the everyday life of her citizens. The latter at least could be explained by the near total repression under which the people lived: any show of concern would have been construed as mistrust of the party, a questioning of their ability to handle the crisis. It was also true that the people of Iraq had become used to war. They were tired, *taban*, and felt they had nothing left to lose.

Shortly after I had returned from Jubbah in early March, a party official came to the house and asked when I expected to conclude my historical filming. I said there were just a few more things to shoot.

'What is your emergency plan?' he asked, turning to Abdullah. He didn't have one but wasn't caught on the hop. 'I am ready to defend my home and country.'

On the weekend of 16 March 2003 the security services in the cities began rounding up potential opposition. The regime believed they could ride out the American barrage and claw their way back to power, as they had done in 1991, when America had abandoned the people of Iraq.

On the Sunday the official returned and told Abdullah that it was not a suitable time for me to be there. I was at the Mother of Sorrows in Shorja all that day. I had spent much of the week with Father Nadheer and had gone to film the last mass before the war. The service was full. An hour before the start worshippers were arriving in the compound. There was a surge around 5 p.m. when Abu-Ziyad climbed into the tower and the bells of the Mother of Sorrows rang out across Shorja. Father Nadheer held open confessions at the back of the church, while groups of women with white, handkerchief-sized veils on their heads knelt at icons and lit candles for peace.

The sermon, Father Nadheer informed me in the sacristy while he pulled on his vestments, was to be about peace. 'We must pray for peace. We must keep our faith.'

He had given me permission to film wherever I wanted. I trailed him out to the altar like in a real documentary, and then crouched down along the aisle and got up onto the edge of different pews looking for angles like Martin Scorsese or Sean McAllister.

The full house was also in part due to the fact that there were double food parcels to be handed out. Family names were called over a loud-speaker in the courtyard after the mass and the women came forward to accept the charity. I left before the end of these proceedings as the tape had run out earlier and I was afraid Father Nadheer was going to ask to see his sermon played back on the LCD screen. He liked to examine himself after any bout of filming.

Abdullah was sewing buttons when I got back to the house. He told me of the Ba'ath visit and we decided it would be best for me to go to stay in the church the next day.

We were afraid somebody might come that night and moved upstairs to a room looking out on the driveway. I didn't ask him what we'd do if they did. We lay for the whole night on our mats staring up at the ceiling. The security might only get to one home in a hundred, but this must have been what it was like for the other ninety-nine.

Saddam's control over the people by terror went beyond even the end. 'Give me ten days and keep 10 per cent of your weapons and I will respond.' The grip of Saddam Hussein.

In the morning the homeowner came with a workman to remove the air-conditioners. Like Abdullah, he was principally concerned about what was going to happen after the war. They expected that people would come out of Thawrah (a sprawling Shia slum) in their droves, and descend like locusts on the city. I asked Ali if he thought the Shia would rise up in Najaf and strike out for a theocracy. He shook his head. 'We just want to be free.'

After he had left, I packed my things and sat down on the floor beside Abdullah. A cold draught swept into the living room from the gaping hole where the air-conditioner had been. We moved closer to the heater and drank tea and smoked a last cigarette.

Before leaving al-Qudra we called to say goodbye to Abduljalil. The doctor, his wife, and their obese kids, had fled the city for Kirkuk. Abduljalil opened the grand front door with a shy grin on his face. I filmed him standing like royalty on the staircase, a huge chandelier suspended like a UFO above him. Abdullah was worried for him. 'He will defend this house against thieves with his life.'

Next door, Nassir was out. We left word with his mother to say I was going back to Ireland. Abdullah advised me to say this, as one of his brothers, who had a cigarette stall on the main road, was an informant. As we left, I looked across the road at the Ftkhans' house and thought of Kemal.

The church was a hive of activity. In the courtyard a group led by Abu-Ziyad was trying to set up a giant tent. Parishioners were constantly telephoning Father Nadheer to know if they could come to shelter in the church. Some had already arrived and had taken over classrooms in the inner courtyard. Many others had chosen to leave the city to go to relatives in the north. Father Nadheer's brother and sister were taking this course. That afternoon word came through that a bus taking families from another parish to Mosul had been involved in an accident on the highway. Several had been killed. In a separate incident on the same road a car carrying one of his own families had crashed. A pregnant woman was killed and her son blinded. Father Nadheer was visibly down.

A second major operation begun that day was the filling of thousands of plastic bags with water. 'This is the most economic way,' the priest told me, his tracksuit bottoms rolled up to his knees in the waterlogged yard. Two huge exercise-beds were also filled as a reserve for the reserves. Other preparations included taping the windows, and ensuring that there were enough food supplies. Upstairs, Abu-Ziyad's wife and daughter, Martine, were making piles of *khubz*, the traditional Arab bread. They had a machine that worked exactly like the village ovens: the dough was pasted onto the inside of a gas-heated barrel and then peeled off when baked.

I went to the market to get provisions with two of a score of young men who had volunteered to help in the church. I'd never seen the *suq* so crowded. It was like the rush before a holiday, but without the festive mood. It was common to see people arguing with vendors, and occasional skirmishes broke out in the scrum.

The next night, the eve of Bush's deadline for Saddam to leave, the monsignor came on a rallying visit. The gates were opened and his white sedan slipped into the courtyard. A bodyguard got out to open the door and he emerged dressed in the red regalia of Rome. An aide led him to Father Nadheer's office. Their conversation was brief. He came out again and offered his hand to the faithful. They knelt and kissed his ring. I kept filming him and he went back in to the office for a moment. I followed the entourage to the yard and recorded his departure.

Father Nadheer came up beside me as the gates were being closed. 'He asked if you had permission to film.'

I looked at him, and the priest shrugged his shoulders. 'He will forget.'

That night Abu-Ziyad and I started into a supply of *arak* I had bought for him. In spite of the claims on the label, it wasn't the best quality, and we numbed the bite with mouthfuls of appetizers prepared by his wife. She and her daughter and Father Nadheer and a number of the youths who were assisting in the church watched as we matched one another glass for glass.

Abu-Ziyad and his wife, Warina, came from the very far north of the country. Their village, Bersevai, was situated on a plain in the Tigris valley. Pictures of it adorned a bookcase by the door. I remembered it as a stunningly beautiful region of rolling green hills and low-flying clouds. The small populations who lived in this remote border area were evacuated by the Government in the late 1980s and told to live elsewhere. As part of what was known as the Anfal campaign, their homes were razed to the ground. For this, if nothing else, I thought it odd that Abu-Ziyad was an admirer of Saddam Hussein. Whenever he appeared on the TV, he would turn up the volume and stare intently at the screen. It was possible, I thought, remembering how Sadoun in Qsariyat used to do just the opposite, that this might be a form of defiance. On the other hand, because of its secular character, it was the case that the Ba'ath Party enjoyed some grudging support from the small Christian minority. In an Islamic state, for example, the Chaldeans expected that they would suffer official discrimination. The worst-case scenario for them, Father Nadheer told me once, was a Shia theocracy.

I asked Abu-Ziyad now what he really thought of Saddam. He shifted on his chair: I could see he was going to tell me the truth.

'Saddam Hussein – good!' He raised his glass and finished it in one. 'Uday, Qusay, Abid Hamid, Ali Hassan – no good! Saddam strong. Iraq need Saddam.'

That was the other reason for which I suspected he could have supported him. Some Iraqis believed that their country was ungovernable other than by a strong hand. In this view, Saddam Hussein could rule in no other way than by repressive means.

Our dialogue became more disjointed as the night wore on. Father Nadheer, who had been acting as our translator, excused himself. The young men got bored and left, probably vowing never to take up the drink. It was late when we stopped. Martine, the caretaker's teenage daughter, took a bottle off the table and someone led me along the corridor to where I was sleeping.

It happened that at some time during that night, just at the end of the street, Qusay Saddam and his guards visited the vaults of the Central Bank. Two trucks and two hours were needed to cart away the cash reserves: $900 million in $100 bills, and €100 million. This was the al-Tikriti insurance, the money the clan would need to buy its protection, and to fund whatever resistance might emerge after the American takeover.

The following afternoon Father Nadheer took me aside and asked if I could go back to Abdullah's. The monsignor hadn't forgotten me, and had made enquiries.

There was no question of going back to Abdullah. The Party had spoken. Jubbah crossed my mind, but they had marked my card there as well. I was suddenly confronted with the fact that I had become a liability to the people I had come to support. My visa was long expired, I had no proper documentation, and my contact in the Government had gone out of his way to avoid me. If I was detained when the war began, the people sheltering me could be in trouble. I decided that I was going to have to leave.

I phoned Abdullah and told him the news. He said it was too late and I was to come to him. I could lie low upstairs or hide with Abduljalil in the doctor's until the thing had blown over. It was tempting to do so – leaving now was not what I wanted to do, but I knew it was the right thing to do.

At that stage there were about twelve hours to go to the deadline, and it was uncertain what routes out of the country were still open. Abu-Ziyad wobbled off on his motorcycle to see if he could find out. I stood at the gate and watched until he had turned down al-Rasheed Street. The Suq al-Arabi was deserted and all the streets around had fallen quiet. I remember thinking it was strangely peaceable, and wishing I wasn't so hung over.

I was on my way upstairs to get my things when Father Nadheer called me from his office. He was by the door and closed it after I had entered.

'You asked me before about my ordination – what I chose to read at the ceremony.'

I was thinking that this wasn't the time for reminiscences, but I sat down on the couch. He was wearing his priest's garb: black jacket and trousers, black shirt and white collar. He handed me an English-language bible and went to his desk. It was bookmarked at Corinthians I, a letter of St Paul about love. Father Nadheer read it in Aramaic, and I followed his voice in the Good News text.

Love is always patient and kind; it is never jealous; love is never boastful or conceited; it is never rude or selfish; it does not take offence, and is not resentful. Love takes no pleasure in other people's sins but delights in the truth; it is always ready to excuse, to trust, to hope, and to endure whatever comes.

Love does not come to an end. But if there are gifts of prophecy, the time will come when they must fail; or the gift of languages, it will not continue forever; and knowledge – for this, too, the time will come when it must fail. For our knowledge is imperfect and our prophesising is imperfect; but once perfection comes, all imperfect things will disappear. When I was a child, I used to talk like a child, and think like a child, and argue like a child, but now I am a man, all childish ways are put behind me. Now we are seeing a dim reflection in a mirror; but then we shall be seeing face to face. The knowledge that I have now is imperfect; but then I shall know as fully as I am known.

In short, there are three things that last: faith, hope, and love; and the greatest of these is love.

He closed the book and we went out to the courtyard.

Abu-Ziyad came with news that the Syrian border was closed, but there were taxis still going to Jordan with non-nationals. We took the lanes behind the church to a nearby depot. A young parishioner opened up his barber's salon and we waited there in a side street while they searched for a seat.

About 9 p.m. the barber and Abu-Ziyad came in with a tall man in a *shamag*. He looked at my passport and said he'd take me. There were six other passengers, a Jordanian family and a Palestinian man.

Father Nadheer and myself said goodbye. 'I will pray for your journey.'

'*Push Beshlama*.' ('God bless you.')

The taxi driver, even for one plying the Baghdad–Amman route, was unpleasant. He insisted on being paid before we left the city ($75 each) and took us round half Baghdad looking for extra fuel. Appropriately enough, we finally found an open depot beside the Transport Ministry, a tall, freestanding block. All the lights in this building had been left on, and a string of blinking fairy lights had been tied about the exterior like a Christmas tree: two fingers to the Americans and their satellites.

The driver decided he wanted dinner so we stopped at a roadside eatery on the outskirts of the city. The Jordanians stayed in the car and the Palestinian man and I went for a stroll, one eye on the driver lest he try to leave without us. Ahmed was from Hebron in the West Bank. He was completing a doctorate in Arabic language at Baghdad University, and was an advisor to a member of the Palestinian Legislative Council. He was a short, handsome man, polite and inquisitive. His wife had recently given birth to their first child, a girl, and he explained that it was because of them he was leaving. 'God keep Saddam Hussein,' he exclaimed aloud.

It struck me as we walked back to the jeep that a great paradox of the Arab world was the reverence in which most of its citizens held the Iraqi leader, despite the fact that he was widely feared and despised in his own country. Saffah's words on Jubbah came to my mind: 'Only the people in Iraq know Saddam Hussein.'

The highway thinned out quickly and after Ramadi, on our side there was nothing. On the other, a steady line of civilian trucks moved soldiers and equipment towards Baghdad, but after a while this traffic ceased too.

As we crossed the desert, leaving the Euphrates behind, I thought of the Ten Thousand Greeks, Westerners who had come here 2,500 years ago to overthrow a king. I didn't doubt that Bush, with his much larger force, would be more successful, though I wondered if his army wouldn't have the same problems as the Greeks in getting home. The natives had a long history of hostility toward invaders, and history has a tendency to repeat itself.

I was sitting in the front of the car, and had noticed for some time that we were not always on a steady course. The vehicle would fade from one lane to the other before straightening for a spell in the middle. The driver stared out and kept tugging at his *shamag*. I was looking at him when his head suddenly dropped onto the steering wheel. I pushed him aside and took the wheel, alerting Ahmed in the back. We kept him awake until we came to a deserted filling station, where we shoved him, semi-conscious, into the back. He must have been driving back and forth for days, cashing in on the bonus of war.

There was one other car in the forecourt. A woman clad in black hurried over to us crying. They had tried to enter Syria and were refused and now had insufficient fuel to get back to Baghdad. Ahmed and I looked at one another, and then went to the rear of the vehicle and untied several of the containers the driver had paid blood for in Baghdad.

None of the others could drive so I volunteered to take the wheel. Ahmed took my place in the front to be navigator. The vehicle, a heavy American jeep, was an automatic. At first I had a little difficulty with the gearing, but soon we were cruising up the highway and everyone behind was asleep.

At 4 a.m. I stopped and Ahmed and I stepped outside. A freezing wind cut across the moonlit desert. We shivered as we scanned the sky above. Ahmed gripped my hand and said in a low voice that a terrible crime was about to be committed. It might have been. I said nothing. I took Saffah's amber *tisbah* from my shirt pocket, and rolled the beads through my fingers.

*

I was in contact with Abdullah by phone until early April, and everything was fine. The electricity and water were on, and he was even going out to repair fridges in Amiriya. At about that time, suspecting that Saddam was communicating by telephone, US intelligence had every exchange in the city pummelled.

One evening in November I was in my aunt's house, and as I had done hopefully on so many occasions, I dialled Abdullah's number. It rang, and after a moment his voice crackled over the line. A barrage of blessings and greetings to family and friends raced back and forth. Everyone in al-Qudra was fine, Father Nadheer was still in Shorja, and as far as he knew, they were all safe on Jubbah.

The Americans were making life very difficult, he said. They were concerned only about their own safety, and were doing little to get life in order. 'You won't believe some of the things that have happened here.' Abdullah had been through three wars prior to this one. His eyebrows weren't easily raised.

On 14 December 2003 I rang him. It was a Sunday. I remember turning on the news that morning and seeing something I had never expected to: Lucifer dragged from the pit by the American Cerberus. In his black robe and unruly black hair and black beard, Saddam was the very embodiment of evil. It was a haunting, unforgettable sight.

I tried to be upbeat on the phone. 'Now maybe things will start to improve.'

Even 7,000 kilometres away, I could feel the numbness: to have lived for so long in the shadow of a tyrant, to have had your consciousness shaped by his omnipresence, and suddenly to find he's gone.

'*Inshallah*,' said Abdullah, after a short pause, 'things will get better.'

In the spring of 2004 Sheikh Thabet passed away. He had lived to see the overthrow and capture of Saddam Hussein, but not the violent disorder into which his country was then beginning to descend.

At one time he had been the chief of the Communist Party in the Anbar. His dream was for an equal society, where there was education for all, and everyone had the chance to earn a living. Today in the towns and cities of the province, there is little economic activity, and there are 'bad men and killers on the streets'.

Though there is time, it is hard not to conclude that America and her allies have failed the people of Iraq, the great majority of whom welcomed them as liberators. Perhaps only when the American Project is shelved and the Iraqis are left to themselves to try to rebuild their country, will there be an end to the nightmare. They say hope dies last, and on Jubbah at least, they still dream of peace, prosperity and freedom.

Appendix I

Chronology (BC)

559	Cyrus the Great conquers the Medes. Achaemenid Empire founded.
547	Cyrus conquers Lydia and takes control of Asia Minor.
525	Persia conquers Egypt.
522–486	Reign of Darius I (the Great).
499	Greeks in Ionia revolt against Persian rule.
490	Darius invades Greece.
486–465	Reign of Xerxes I.
480	Xerxes invades Greece, burns Athens to the ground.
465–425	Reign of Artaxerxes I.
431–404	The Peloponnesian War.
424–404	Reign of Darius II.
424*	Cyrus the Younger is born.
416*	Tissaphernes is sent to Asia Minor by the King to deal with a rebellion by the Satrap of Lydia. Becomes governor.
407*	Cyrus replaces Tissaphernes as Satrap. Lysander appointed commander of Spartan fleet.
406	Alkibiades made commander of the Athenian fleet.
404	Athens surrenders to Lysander, end of the Peloponnesian War. King Darius dies and is succeeded by his eldest son, Artaxerxes II. Cyrus is accused of plotting a coup, and narrowly escapes with his life. His mother succeeds in having him returned to Asia Minor.
404–401	Cyrus raises his army.
401	The expedition sets out from Sardis. Battle of Kounaxa. Retreat downcountry of the Greeks.

400	The Ten Thousand reach the Black Sea and continue by land and ship to Byzantium. The remnants are enrolled by Sparta to fight Tissaphernes in Ionia.
399	Trial and death of Socrates.
	Xenophon exiled from Athens.
395	Agesilaus defeats Tissaphernes at Sardis.
387	King's Peace signed by Artaxerxes II with Sparta.
370*	Xenophon writes the *Kyrou Anabasis*.
359	Artaxerxes II dies. Succeeded by his son, Artaxerxes III.
333	Alexander of Macedon defeats Darius III at Issos.
330	Alexander burns Persepolis; Darius III is murdered, end of the Achaemenids.

* Date approximate.

Appendix II

The Route of the March Upcountry

STAGE NO.	ROUTE	DISTANCE Parasangs	DAYS	XENOPHON	CHAPTER/ MAP
1	Sardis to the Maeander River [Büyükmenderes Nehir]	22	3	I.2.5	2 / p.12
2	To Kolossai [Honaz north]	8	1	I.2.6	3 / p.12
3	To Kelainai [Dinar]	20	3	I.2.7	3 / p.12
4	To Peltai	10	2	I.2.10	4 / p.12
5	To Keramon Agora [Banaz?]	12	2	I.2.10	4 / p.12
6	To the Kaÿstrou Pedion	30	3	I.2.11	4 / p.12
7	To Thymbrion	10	2	I.2.13	4 / p.56
8	To Tyriaion	10	2	I.2.14	4 / p.56
9	To Ikonion [Konya]	20	3	I.2.19	6 / p.56
10	Through Lykaonia	30	5	I.2.19	8 / p.56
11	Across the Taurus Mountains* [Ayrancı to Tarsus]	30	6	I.2.20	9 / p.56
12	Tarsus to Psaros River [Seyhan Nehir]	10	2	I.4.1	11 / p.108
13	To the Pyramos River [Ceyhan Nehir]	5	1	I.4.1	11 / p.108
14	To Issos	15	2	I.4.1	11 / p.108
15	To the Gates of Syria [Pillars of Jonah]	5	1	I.4.4	11 / p.108
16	To Myriandros	5	1	I.4.6	11 / p.108
17	To the Chalos River [Afrin Nahr?]	20	4	I.4.9	11 / p.108
18	The sources of the Dardas River [Balis?]	30	5	I.4.10	13 / p.108

STAGE NO.	ROUTE	DISTANCE Parasangs	DAYS	XENOPHON	CHAPTER/ MAP
19	To Thapsakos	15	3	I.4.11	14 / p.108
20	To the Araxes River [Khabur Nahr?]	50	9	I.4.19	15 / p.152
21	To Korsote [al-Qaim?]	35	5	I.5.4	16 / p.152
22	To the Gates [Sin al-Deban?]	90	13	I.5.5	17 / p.174
23	Through Babylonia	15	5	I.7.1	21 / p.174
24	Kounaxa [Plain of Sippar?]		1	I.8	24 / p.174
	Total	497	84		

[ ] Modern name
*   Route of Menon. Figures from author's journey.

The conventional start date for the expedition is 6 March 401 BC. By this reckoning the battle of Kounaxa was fought in early September of that year.

Appendix III

The Ten Thousand

Though known by history as the Ten Thousand, Cyrus' Greek auxiliaries actually numbered around 14,000 men.

COMMANDER	SOLDIERS
Klearkhos. Sparta	
Instructed by his country to assist Cyrus. Raised	1,000 *hoplites*
and maintained a force in the Chersonese. Joined	800 *peltasts*
Cyrus at Kelainai in Phrygia	200 archers
Seized on the Greater Zab River and executed by	
Tissaphernes	
Xenias. Arcadia	
Head of Cyrus' garrison troops	4,000 *hoplites*
Deserted the army at Myriandros	
Proxenos. Boiotia	
Guest-friend of Cyrus. Joined at Sardis	1,500 *hoplites*
Executed by Tissaphernes	500 light infantry
Sophainetos. Stymphalos	
Guest-friend of Cyrus. Joined at Sardis	1,000 *hoplites*
Returned to Greece and wrote an account of the	
expedition (lost)	

COMMANDER	SOLDIERS
Socrates. Akhaia Guest-friend of Cyrus. Joined at Sardis Executed by Tissaphernes	500 *hoplites*
Pasion. Megara Joined at Sardis Deserted at Myriandros with Xenias	300 *hoplites* 300 *peltasts*
Menon. Thessaly Joined at Kolossai in place of Aristippos Executed by Tissaphernes	1,000 *hoplites* 500 *peltasts*
Sophainetos. Arcadia Joined Cyrus at Kelainai	1,000 *hoplites*
Sosis. Syracuse Joined Cyrus at Kelainai	300 *hoplites*
Xeirosophos. Sparta Landed by Spartan ships at Issos Died at Kalpe after contracting an illness	700 *hoplites*

An additional 400 *hoplites* deserted to Cyrus from Abrocomas at Issos.

At Kalpe, prior to the last stage to Byzantium, there were 8,600 men.

Xenophon joined Cyrus 'neither as a general, nor a captain, nor a common soldier' (III.2.4). In his account he and Xeirosophos led the Greeks after their commanders had been seized on the Greater Zab River.

Bibliography

Ainsworth, William Francis, *Travels in the Tracks of the Ten Thousand Greeks* (J.W. Parker, London, 1844)

Akurgal, Ekrem, *Ancient Civilisations and Ruins of Turkey*, 3rd edn (Türk Tarih Kurumu Basımevi, Ankara, 1973)

Arundel, Reverend Francis, *A Visit to the Seven Churches of Asia* (Rodwell, London, 1828)

Barnett, Richard, 'Xenophon and the Wall of Media' (*Journal of Hellenic Studies*, 83, 1963)

Başgelen, Nezih, *Anabasis'te Yer Adları* (Arkeoloji ve Sanat Yayınları, Istanbul, 1987)

Boardman, John, *The Greeks Overseas* (Penguin Books, Harmondsworth, 1964)

Briant, Pierre (ed.), *Dans les pas des Dix-Mille* (Presses Universitares Mirail, Toulouse, 1995)

Bunbury, E.H., *A History of Ancient Geography*, 2nd edn (Dover, New York, 1959)

Burn, Andrew, *Persia and the Greeks*, 2nd edn (Duckworth, London, 1984)

Burns, Ross, *Monuments of Syria*, revised edn (Tauris, London, 1999)

Cawkwell, George, Introduction to *The Persian Expedition* (Penguin Books, Harmondsworth, 1972)

Cook, John, *The Persian Empire* (Dent, London, 1983)

Dillery, John, *Xenophon and the History of His Times* (Routledge, London, 1995)

Diodoros of Sicily, *Library of History* (Harvard University Press, Cambridge, Mass.: vols 4–6, translated by C.H. Oldfather 1946–1954; vol. 7, translated by C.L. Sherman 1952; vol. 12, translated by Francis Walton, 1967)

Diogenes Laertius, *Lives of the Eminent Philosophers* (translated by R.D. Hicks, Harvard University Press, Cambridge, Mass., 1925)

Drews, Robert, *The Greek Accounts of Eastern History* (Publications of the Center for Hellenic Studies, Washington D.C., 1973)

Farrell, W.J., 'A Revised Itinerary of the Route followed by Cyrus the Younger through Syria in 401 BC' (*Journal of Hellenic Studies*, 81, 1961)

Freely, John, *Classical Turkey* (Chronicle Books, San Francisco, 1990)

French, David, *Roman Roads and Milestones of Asia Minor* (British Archaeological Reports, Oxford, 1981)

Frye, Richard, *The Heritage of Persia* (Weidenfeld and Nicolson, London, 1962)

Glombiowski, Krzysztof, 'The Campaign of Cyrus the Younger and the Retreat of the Ten Thousand: Chronology' (*Pomoerium*,1, 1994)

Hamilton, William, *Researches in Asia Minor, Pontus, and Armenia* (John Murray, London, 1842)

Hanson, Victor (ed.), *Hoplites: The Classical Greek Battle Experience* (Routledge, New York, 1993)

Herodotus, *The Histories* (translated by Robin Waterfield, Oxford University Press, Oxford, 1998)

Hornblower, Simon, *Mausolus* (Clarendon Press, Oxford, 1982)

Hutchinson, Godfrey, *Xenophon and the Art of Command* (Greenhill Books, London, 2000)

Leake, Colonel W.M., *Journal of a Tour in Asia Minor* (John Murray, London, 1824)

Lendle, Otto, *Kommentar zu Xenophon's Anabasis* (Wissenschaftliche Buchgesellschaft, Darmstadt, 1995)

Lendle, Otto, 'Xenophon in Babylonien. Die Märsche der Kyreer von Pylai bis Opis' (*Rheinisches Museum*, 129, 1986)

Lewis, David, *Sparta and Persia* (E.J. Brill, Leiden, 1977)

Lloyd, Seton, *Ancient Turkey: A Traveller's History of Anatolia* (British Museum Publication, London, 1989)

Manfredi, Valerio, *La Strada dei Diecimila* (Jaca Book, Milan, 1986)

Mellaart, James, *Çatal Hüyük* (Thames and Hudson, London, 1967)

Nussbaum, G.B., *The Ten Thousand* (E.J. Brill, Leiden, 1967)

Özalp, Mehmet, *Marsyas'in İlinden* (Denizli Yayınevi, Denizli, 1997)

Parke, H.W., *Greek Mercenary Soldiers* (Clarendon Press, Oxford, 1933)

Plutarch, *Life of Artaxerxes* (translated by Bernadotte Perrin, Harvard University Press, Cambridge, Mass., 1926)

Ramsay, William, *The Historical Geography of Asia Minor* (John Murray, London, 1890)

Schoff, Wilfred, *Commentary on the Parthian Stations* (Commercial Museum, Philadelphia, 1914)

Snodgrass, Anthony, *Arms and Armour of the Greeks* (Thames and Hudson, London, 1967)

Strabo, *Geography*, translated by Horace Leonard Jones (Harvard University Press, Cambridge, Mass., 1917–1932)

Tuplin, Christopher, 'Modern and Ancient Travellers in the Achaemenid Empire' (*Achaemenid History*, 7, 1991)

Williams, F., 'Xenophon's Dana and the Passage of Cyrus' Army over the Taurus' (*Historia*, 45, 1996)

Xenophon, *Anabasis Kyrou* (translated by J.S. Watson, Harper, New York, 1891)

—— (translated by Carleton Brownson and revised by John Dillery, Harvard University Press, Cambridge, Mass., 1922)

—— (translated by Rex Warner, Penguin Books, Harmondsworth, 1949)

Index